Resolving Conflicts in Grammars: Optimality Theory in Syntax, Morphology, and Phonology

Linguistische Berichte
Sonderheft 11

Edited by
Gisbert Fanselow and
Caroline Féry

BUSKE

Im Digitaldruck »on demand« hergestelltes, inhaltlich mit der 1. Auflage von 2002 identisches Exemplar. Wir bitten um Verständnis für unvermeidliche Abweichungen in der Ausstattung, die der Einzelfertigung geschuldet sind.

Weitere Informationen unter: www.buske.de/bod.

Bibliografische Information der Deutschen Nationalbibliothek

Die Deutsche Nationalbibliothek verzeichnet diese Publikation in der Deutschen Nationalbibliografie; detaillierte bibliografische Daten sind im Internet über ‹http://portal.dnb.de› abrufbar.

ISBN 978-3-87548-314-7

eBook ISBN 978-3-87548-951-4

LB-Sonderheft ISSN 0935-9249

Contents

Editors' Introduction[1]

The history of this collection of articles on Optimality Theory (OT) goes back to a workshop on Conflicting Rules in Phonology, Morphology and Syntax, organized in Potsdam by the editors. Most of the contributors to the volume also participated in the workshop, Vieri Samek-Lodovici and Jochen Trommer being the only exceptions. The editors gave separate talks at the workshop, but included a joint paper to the volume rather than their original contributions.

The common denominator of the papers gathered here is the question of how Optimality Theory accounts for grammatical problems lying beyond the typical set of questions for which the theory was conceived in the first place. The OT model developed by Prince & Smolensky (1993) was originally conceived for phonology, and is an excellent alternative to rule-based frameworks. In the meantime, because of its flexibility, OT has been applied to nearly all domains of linguistics, though only tentatively in some of them. It has a simple and illuminating architecture, consisting of only a few steps and decisions. One of the recurrent questions addressed in the papers is whether maintaining this simplicity could turn out to be too costly in view of the complexity of the linguistic data.

In a nutshell, OT generates a certain number of candidates for each linguistic input. The candidates are evaluated on the basis of a universal set of constraints, ranked in a language-specific way. The pool of constraints is shared by all languages (it constitutes Universal Grammar), but the differences among languages result from distinctive rankings of these constraints. Since the evaluation proceeds in a deterministic way, and the highest ranking constraint on which two candidates differ determines which one of them is "better," each input is predicted to yield an optimal candidate. If the ranking is total, the optimal candidate is unique. Constraints are violable, and they conflict with each other. A constraint can be violated by an optimal candidate if there is one (or more) higher constraints that this candidate fulfills better than the competing candidates.

The phonological background of OT is apparent in several respects. First, the input can be understood as the underlying representation of older generative approaches. The status of inputs is controversial in OT, most of all in OT syntax. Second, violability of the constraints leads to a falsification problem that

[1] The workshop was financed by the German Science Foundation DFG. It marks both the end of the Innovationskolleg *Formal Model of Cognitive Complexity*, and the beginning of the DFG Research Group *Conflicting Rules*, in which different disciplines of cognitive science interact pursuing the goal of identifying the properties of different conflict resolution strategies in different cognitive modules – among which OT figures prominently. We would like to express our gratitude to Kathleen Kalz, Daniela Lentge and Anja Mietz who devoted much of their time formatting and proof-reading the papers.

Linguistische Berichte Sonderheft 11 · © Helmut Buske Verlag 2002 · ISSN 0935-9249

can be resolved in the phonology but not in the syntax: phonological constraints have an acoustic or articulatory base, but this is not true of the other components of linguistics. It is not always clear what kind of nonlinguistic background is needed to establish a syntactic or morphological constraint, and it is not even clear whether such a background exists at all. Nonphonological constraints are thus jeopardized by circularity. Furthermore, constraints can be classified into two big groups, markedness – expressing universal tendencies toward un-markedness – and faithfulness – requiring similarity between input and output. This dichotomy assumes not only that universal tendencies can be recognized and expressed in terms of simple constraints, but also that there is an input to which outputs tend be faithful. Both of these requirements are more or less fulfilled in phonology, but less so in the other linguistic disciplines. The third aspect of OT in which the influence of phonology is strongly felt is the direc-tionality of the grammar. In going from an input to an output, the grammar is production-driven.

In this volume, syntacticians, morphologists and also phonologists discuss new data, new collections of data, or new perspectives on the data, and propose ways of accounting for them by using optimality-theoretic tools. Phonologists tend to focus on problems having to do with the organization of grammar, such as classifying data in categories, prosodic layers, or lexical and postlexical levels. Since OT is usually conceived of as a single grammar evaluating data in parallel, it is not perfectly equipped to account for such hierarchical orderings, and some of the papers propose methods to come to grip with these orderings. Syntacticians are mostly focusing on other problems, having to do with the new perspective from which OT allows linguists to examine well-known data and problems.

Three papers examine aspects of the syntax-morphology interactions, poin-ting to a direct influence of syntax on morphology, and addressing strengths and weaknesses of OT. In "Free Word Order, Morphological Case, and Sympathy Theory," Gereon Müller gives an original answer to the question of how to account for the relationship between scrambling and morphological Case. Starting from the often observed correlation between these two parameters, Müller formulates the hypothesis that Case is a consequence of scrambling, rather than the other way round. The fact that Case also appears on nonscram-bled NPs is explained by Sympathy Theory, a rather powerful extension of Optimality Theory, which has been originally proposed by McCarthy (1999) to account for opacity in phonology. In Müller's model, Case on a nonscrambled candidate is sympathetic to a competitor involving scrambling, and thus forced to bear Case. Müller's insight consists in using Sympathy for a morpho-syntactic phenomenon not necessarily opaque, but which certainly involves existing related outputs.

In the next paper examining morphological facts correlating with syntax, "Agreement Impoverishment under Subject Inversion – A Crosslinguistic Analysis," Vieri Samek-Lodovici looks at the realization of agreement in the domain of phrasal and extended projections. The presence of overt morphological agreement in the extended domain entails realization of overt morphological agreement in the phrasal domain, the concrete domains being spec-head configurations and c-commanded inverted subject. The conclusion of a typological survey is that agreement within local projections is never poorer than agreement within their extended projections. Samek-Lodovici shows that the factorial typology he describes is the result of reranking a small number of well-motivated constraints.

The third paper on the syntax-morphology interface is Jochen Trommer's "Modularity in OT-Morphosyntax," an answer to the debate about the modularity of morphology and syntax. Whereas Bresnan (1999) proposes a model of OT in which syntax and morphology are influencing each other, Trommer prefers a framework in which they are part of two different components, and in which morphology interprets the outputs of syntax. Trommer's approach integrates the insights of Distributed Morphology into OT, and needs a rather abstract kind of morphological component in which phonological instantiation happens late.

Ralf Vogel's "Free Relative Constructions in OT-Syntax," though primarily anchored in the syntax, also examines interactions between syntax and morphology. It addresses the realization of Case in free relative constructions, when the pronoun has to bear two Cases at once. Vogel's observation is that for a Case conflict to be resolvable at all, the realized Case must be higher on the Case hierarchy than the nonrealized one, but the tolerated situations vary from language to language. His solution to the problem needs a revision of the notion of input, which is now a completely specified syntactic object, but which has no phonological instantiation.

The problems addressed in the three papers dedicated to the interface between phonology and morphology are less homogenous. First, Luigi Burzio's "Segmental Contrast meets Output-to-Output Faithfulness" is interested in analogical relationships between related words, and extends the notion of output-output faithfulness from allomorphic variation to segmental variation, arguing that there are parallel neutralization processes in both domains. Burzio shows that allomorphy tends to fail when the allomorphs have not independently been made different, just as segmental contrasts tend to be neutralized in positions (e.g. coda) where extrinsic conditions weaken them, indicating that it is a general property of representations to attract one-another under conditions of close proximity.

The second paper on phonology-morphology interactions is Junko Ito and Armin Mester's "Lexical and Postlexical Phonology in Optimality Theory: Evidence from Japanese," in which the alternation between [g] and [ŋ] in Tokyo Japanese and the rule of Rendaku which voices the initial obstruent in the second part of a compound, are examined. These two processes are in an opaque (counterfeeding) relationship. It is shown that a parallel OT runs into problems, also if set in the framework of Sympathy Theory, since Sympathy requires faithfulness to a specific input, whereas the data involved in the alternations require Richness of the Base. The authors claim that a restricted kind of cyclicity is needed and propose that the grammar has a lexical and a postlexical component in which constraints can be ranked differently.

In "The Phonological and Morphological Status of the Prosodic Word Adjunct," Marc von Oostendorp proposes an original solution to an old problem, namely the asymmetry between the phonological behavior of different kinds of suffixes: some are stressed and some others are not. It is proposed that the morphological and phonological structures of derived and inflected words in Dutch tend to mirror each other, or more specifically, that the prosodic structure of a complex word reflects its morphological structure. Since there are two kinds of mirroring effects, constituent bracketing and heads, which conflict with each other, there are also different ways to resolve the conflict: bracketing wins, or headedness wins, leading to different stress patterns.

Draga Zec's paper "Constraints on Multiple Feature Occurrence" examines different resolutions of multiple feature occurrences in different prosodic domains of Bulgarian. More specifically, it is shown that multiple feature occurrence, a violation of the OCP, is resolved differently in the domain of the syllable and of the foot: feature deletion in the syllable, leading to a reduction of markedness, and assimilation in the foot, resulting in a reduction of syntagmatic contrast.

Finally, in their paper "Ineffability in Grammar," Fanselow and Féry examine one aspect of grammar, ineffability, which is generally considered to be a problem for OT. They discuss examples of ineffable cases from syntax, phonology and morphology and elaborate a typology on the basis of their collection. The upshot is that ineffability arises as a result of gaps in the lexicon, or of the absence of phonetic patterns for some expected lexemes or morphological structures. A different class of ineffabilities comes from unallowed scopal or semantic constellations (as for instance those coming from island restrictions), which can be subject to language-universal or specific restrictions. They sketch a proposal of how the lexically triggered kind of cases could be accounted in OT, making use of the Control component of Orgun & Sprouse (1999).

Ten years after the emergence of OT, linguists working in this framework have proven to be extremely creative in inventing new fields of application of the theory and developing extensions to account for new data. OT remains prolific in all domains of linguistics, as testified by this volume.

Potsdam, August 2002   Gisbert Fanselow and Caroline Féry

Free Word Order, Morphological Case, and Sympathy Theory*

Gereon Müller

Abstract

In this paper, I address the relation between scrambling and morphological Case from an optimality-theoretic perspective. Based on empirical evidence from German, Russian, and Bulgarian, and conceptual evidence involving issues of parametrization, I give arguments against the traditional view that scrambling presupposes morphological Case. The remaining two options are (a) and (b). (a) There is no synchronically relevant relation between scrambling and morphological Case. (b) Morphological Case does in fact presuppose scrambling. I pursue the latter, more radical approach, which implies that morphological Case is not given pre-syntactically (i.e. is not part of the syntactic input), but arises in the syntax. The presence of morphological Case is forced by a constraint that requires a Case marker on scrambled items (i.e. items at the left edge of vP); but morphological Case violates a DEP constraint. The main problem with such an approach turns out to be that morphological Case in languages like German and Russian may show up on an NP even if this NP has not undergone scrambling; in other words: the local property of a given sentence to exhibit morphological Case on its NPs is tied not to the local property of actual scrambling in that sentence, but rather to the global property that the language permits scrambling in minimally different sentences. In order to solve this problem, I develop an approach in terms of sympathy theory (McCarthy (1999)) according to which morphological Case can arise on an NP in situ without actual scrambling, because of a ❀-constraint that demands faithfulness to a competitor that does involve scrambling (and, hence, bear morphological Case).

1   Introduction

This paper addresses the question of whether there is a correlation between free word order and morphological Case, and what such a correlation might look like. I will consider three hypotheses.

(1)   a. If a language has free word order, it also has morphological Case.
       b. If a language has morphological Case, it also has free word order.

* This research was supported by DFG grants MU 1444/1-2,2-2. For comments and discussion, I would like to thank Silke Fischer, Lutz Gunkel, Fabian Heck, Uwe Junghanns, Shin-Sook Kim, Jaklin Kornfilt, Jonas Kuhn, Tanja Schmid, Sten Vikner, Ralf Vogel, an anonymous reviewer, audiences at Universität Leipzig (March 2001, DGfS workshop "Clause Structure and Models of Grammar") and at Universität Bochum (June 2001, GGS meeting), and especially Gisbert Fanselow and Caroline Féry.

Linguistische Berichte Sonderheft 11 · © Helmut Buske Verlag 2002 · ISSN 0935-9249

   c. Free word order and morphological Case are unrelated.

According to (1a), the existence of morphological Case is a prerequisite for free word order in a given language.[1] This hypothesis can arguably be viewed as the standard assumption. It lends itself to a simple functional explanation (see., e.g. Comrie (1981) and Haspelmath (2000)) that can be summarized as follows: A proper interpretation of sentences requires an unambiguous identification of the grammatical function of an argument NP. The grammatical function of an NP can be encoded by morphological Case or by assigning it an invariant structural position. If the first option is available, an argument NP does not have to occupy a fixed position in order for its grammatical function to be identified; however, if there is no morphological Case, a language must resort to an invariant position to ensure that an identification of the grammatical function of an NP is possible. This functional explanation has often been implemented in analyses in the principles and parameters approach. It is compatible both with analyses in which free word order results from the option of variable base generation, and with analyses that account for free word order in terms of scrambling; see, e.g. Haider (1988) for a base generation account that relies on (1a) and Fanselow (1992), Roberts (1997), and Weerman (1997) for scrambling accounts that incorporate (1a).

In contrast, (1b) states that free word order is a prerequisite for morphological Case. This hypothesis has received considerably less attention. Evidently, the two hypotheses make different predictions. (1a) predicts that there is no language that has free word order, but no morphological Case; (1b) predicts that there is no language that has morphological Case but no free word order. Finally, (1c) states that (at least synchronically) there is no linguistically significant correlation between free word order and morphological Case; consequently, no prediction is made that could be empirically falsified.[2]

In what follows, I would like to argue that (1a) should be rejected. As for the remaining two hypotheses, (1c) may eventually prove to be the correct one. Still, what I want to do here is pursue (1b), a more radical hypothesis that strikes me as worth investigating, even though it will turn out not to be entirely unproblematic. Throughout, I will adopt an optimality-theoretic approach. I will do so for two reasons: First, an optimality-theoretic approach will be shown to be hard to reconcile with (1a); arguably, this can be taken to show that (1a) reflects some deeper conceptual problems. And second, optimality theory turns out to offer a solution to what I take to be the most pressing problem that arises under (1b);

---

[1] Here and in what follows, I abstract away from the possibility that NP-V agreement may serve a similar function as morphological Case; see Baker (1996). However, most of what is said below would probably be compatible with replacing the notion of "morphological Case" with the more general concept of "morphological Case or agreement".

[2] A fourth possibility would be a bi-conditional: A language has free word order iff it has morphological Case. I will ignore this in what follows because everything that will be said against (1a) automatically carries over to this option.

this solution will crucially rely on the notion of sympathy (see McCarthy (1999)).

Before I turn to these two issues, a few remarks are in order concerning the derivation of free word order structures. I assume that free word order is derived by a syntactic scrambling operation, not by base generation (be it accompanied by LF lowering, as in Bošković & Takahashi (1998), by LF raising, as in Fanselow (2001), or by no LF movement at all, as in Haider (1988)). Furthermore, I assume that scrambling is typically movement to an outer specifier of vP, in the sense of Chomsky (2000, 2001). Scrambling of an accusative NP to an outer Specv position in front of a nominative NP (that is base-generated in the inner Specv position) is shown for German in (2b) vs. (2a), and for Russian in (3b) vs. (3a).

(2)   a. dass [$_{vP}$ der   Astronaut$_1$ den   Planeten$_2$ entdeckt]   hat
          that   the$_{nom}$ astronaut   the$_{acc}$ planet$_{acc}$ discovered   has

       b. dass [$_{vP}$ den   Planeten$_2$ [$_{v'}$ der   Astronaut$_1$ t$_2$ entdeckt]]   hat
          that   the$_{acc}$ planet$_{acc}$ the$_{nom}$ astronaut   discovered has

(3)   a. čto   [$_{vP}$ brigada$_1$ sostavljaet   programmu$_2$]
          that   brigade$_{nom}$ sets up   programme$_{acc}$

       b. čto   [$_{vP}$ programmu$_2$ [$_{v'}$ brigada$_1$ sostavljaet   t$_2$]]
          that   programme$_{acc}$ brigade$_{nom}$ sets up

Both German and Russian have morphological Case, in the sense that the abstract Case of an NP can be morphologically marked on the noun and on a preceding determiner (or adjective) that agrees with it. The fact that scrambling to Specv is permitted is therefore compatible with (1a) (as well as with (1b) and (1c)).[3]

---

[3] Unlike German, colloquial Russian also permits scrambling to an outer specifier of CP, as in (iab), and long-distance scrambling into a Specv position of a matrix clause, as in (ic) (see Zemskaja (1973) and Yadroff (1991)).

(i)   a. Jy   byl   [$_{CP}$ novuju   školu$_2$ [$_{C'}$ gde   strojat t$_2$]]
           I   was   new   school   where   they build

       b. Ty   znaeš [$_{CP}$ Petr   Ivanyč$_1$ [$_{C'}$ čto   t$_1$ uže   priexal]]?
           you   know   Petr   Ivanych   that   already   came

       c. čto   ty$_1$ menja$_2$ vižu   [$_{CP}$ čto   t$_1$ ljubiš t$_2$]
           that you$_{nom}$ me$_{acc}$ I see   that   love

These constructions may have important consequences for the theory of movement (in particular in view of the fact that wh-movement appears to be much more restricted in Russian, thereby creating a picture that is diametrically opposed to what we see in German; see Müller (1995)). Nevertheless, I will abstract away from scrambling to CP and to the matrix vP in what follows, and leave open the question of whether scrambling in examples like those in (i) is a movement operation of the same type as the relatively local "standard" scrambling operations that I am interested in here.

The non-existence of scrambling in English is shown by (4bcd) vs. (4a). In accordance with (1a) (as well as with (1b), (1c)), English does not exhibit morphological Case.[4]

(4)   a. that John$_1$ [$_{vP}$ t$_1$ gave Mary$_2$ a book$_3$]

         b. *that John$_1$ [$_{vP}$ Mary$_2$ [$_{v'}$ t$_1$ gave t$_2$ a book$_3$]]

         c. *that John$_1$ [$_{vP}$ a book$_3$ [$_{v'}$ t$_1$ gave Mary$_2$ t$_3$]]

         d. *that John$_1$ [$_{vP}$ t$_1$ gave a book$_3$ Mary$_2$ t$_3$]

On the basis of these assumptions, let me now turn to the issue of scrambling in optimality-theoretic syntax.

2   Scrambling in Optimality-Theoretic Syntax

2.1 Premises

It has often been observed that scrambling in languages like German and Russian has information-structural effects (concerning notions like focus, topic, definiteness, etc.). These effects can be viewed as resulting from linearization constraints that refer to these information-structural notions, usually in interaction with other, purely grammar-internal, constraints that determine the base order of arguments.[5] It turns out that nearly all of the existing approaches to scrambling (or, more generally, free word order) that have been developed in optimality-theoretic syntax crucially rely on linearization constraints of this type; see Choi (1996, 1999), Büring (1997, 2001), Legendre (1998), Müller (1999), Heck (2000), Costa (2001), Gouskova (2001), and, for an overview, Müller (2000 chap. 6). In all these approaches, whether or not scrambling applies (i.e. free word order is possible) depends on the relative ranking of constraints that favour rigid (or base) order on the one hand (e.g. the constraint STAY (*t) from Grimshaw (1997) Legendre, Smolensky & Wilson (1998)), and linearization (or alignment) constraints that favour displacement on the other.[6]

A common property of all these approaches is that the availability of scrambling in a given language is exhaustively determined by the relative ranking of these kinds of constraints; as it stands, there is no room for correlating scrambling (free word order) with morphological Case (or any other morphological property of a language). This is in line with a general assumption in optimality-

---

[4] Personal pronouns like she vs. her are an exception that I consider synchronically irrelevant.

[5] See, e.g. Lenerz (1977), Hoberg (1981; 1997), Uszkoreit (1984), Reis (1986), Jacobs (1988), and Primus (1994) on German; and Krylova & Chavronina (1976), King (1995), and Junghanns & Zybatow (1997) on Russian.

[6] The approach developed in Heck & Müller (2000) is an exception. Here, scrambling is triggered either by a constraint that requires certain formal features to be checked by movement, or, exceptionally, by other structural, non-linearization-based constraints that require certain (parasitic) traces to be bound, certain pronouns to have a c-commanding antecedent, etc.

theoretic syntax: Cross-linguistic variation results from a re-ranking of syntactic constraints; ideally, this should be all that has to be said. Accordingly, the optimality-theoretic approach to the Pro-drop parameter developed in Grimshaw & Samek-Lodovici (1998) dispenses with the traditional idea that Pro-drop is related to rich agreement morphology on V; and the optimality-theoretic approach to the V-to-I movement parameter in Vikner (2001a) does not predict a correlation with rich verbal morphology, as it is often assumed. Thus, the fact that the exs-ting optimality-theoretic approaches to scrambling do not envisage a correlation with morphological Case fits into this general picture.

To illustrate what has just been said, I will now sketch a (simplified) optimality-theoretic approach to scrambling in German that is based on work by Choi (1996, 1999) and Büring (1997, 2001). These two approaches (or, to be more precise, these two kinds of approaches – both Choi and Büring have significantly revised their earlier analyses in the published versions) are similar in some respects, and different in others. Consequently, the amalgamation that I will present will probably do neither approach justice; however, it may serve to illustrate the general point about scrambling and morphological Case.

2.2   Scrambling in German: Büring/Choi-Type Approaches

Let us assume that (5) is the base order of NP arguments in German.[7]

(5)   Base order in German:
         $[_{VP} NP_{nom} [_{VP} NP_{dat} NP_{acc} V] v]$

Scrambling, i.e. movement of an NP to an outer specifier of v, invariably incurs a violation of STAY; see (6):

(6)   STAY:
         Movement is not allowed.

Consequently, scrambling must be triggered by constraints that outrank STAY. Among these we can take to be the linearization constraints in (7).

---

[7] This assumption is by no means uncontroversial. Müller & Sternefeld (1994) and Müller (1999) argue that NPacc $\succ$ NPdat is the base order; Haider (2000) argues that the base order of argument NPs is variable in that it depends on the type of V that is involved; and Heck (2000) argues that the base order of argument NPs is even more variable in the sense that factors like animacy play a crucial role (on which see also Fanselow (1995), Vogel & Steinbach (1998), and Müller (1999)). Still, for present purposes, (5) may suffice; alternative assumptions about base order in German would not affect the main line of argumentation below.

(7)   a. TOPIC:
        [+topic] precedes [–topic].

        b. AGENT(IVITY):
        [+agent] precedes [–agent].

        c. DEF(INITENESS):
        [+def] precedes [–def].

        d. FOC(US):
        [–focus] precedes [+focus].

Here and henceforth, I will assume that the constraints in (7) are active only within vP. There are various ways to ensure this. One option would be to explicitly restrict the constraints to the vP domain; e.g. TOPIC could be reformulated as: "Within vP, [+topic] precedes [–topic]". Another option would be to assume that the constraints in (7) hold in all syntactic domains, but that there are higher-ranked constraints against (movement to) outer specifiers of TP, CP, etc.; at least in languages like German. I will leave this issue open.

As an illustration of how scrambling can be effected under these assumptions, consider instances of topic-driven scrambling in German and Russian, as in (8ab).

(8)   a. dass [$_{vP}$ den   Planeten$_2$ [$_{v'}$der   Astronaut$_1$ t_2 entdeckt]] hat
        that   the$_{acc}$ planet$_{acc}$ the$_{nom}$ astronaut   discovered has

    b. čto   [$_{vP}$ rasskazov$_2$ [$_{v'}$ja$_1$ pročital [mnogo t_2]]]
        that   stories$_{gen}$ I   read   many

Assuming that the object is topic-marked and the subject is not, the ranking TOPIC >> AGENT, STAY predicts that the object moves across the subject to satisfy TOPIC, in violation of the lower-ranked constraints AGENT (which favours a subject-first order with verbs like *discover* and *read*) and STAY (which favours objects in situ).[8] The competition is shown in tableau 1. O_2 is the optimal output that involves scrambling to vP.[9]

---

[8] Also see Gouskova (2001) for an optimality-theoretic approach to topic-driven scrambling (and focus-driven scrambling; see below) in Russian that proceeds along these lines. Gouskova also investigates the apparent capability of Russian scrambling to escape from what is otherwise known as a barrier, as in (8b), and suggests treating the prohibition against crossing a barrier in the course of movement as a violable constraint. These issues are orthogonal to my present concerns, though.

[9] Throughout this paper, I confine myself to competitions involving vP since this is the part of a sentence that is important for (the core cases of) scrambling. Additional structure on top of vP (viz., TP, CP, one or more matrix clause(s)) may be assumed to be present but irrelevant; alternatively, under a local optimization approach as in Heck & Müller (2000), Fanselow & Ćavar (2001), such structure may in fact still be absent at the stage of the derivation where vP optimization takes place.

Tableau 1: Topic-driven scrambling in front of the subject

Input: $NP_{nom,-top}$, $NP_{acc,+top}$	TOPIC	AGENT	DEF	FOC	STAY
O_1: [$_{vP}NP_{nom,-top}$ $NP_{acc,+top}$…]	*!				
☞ O_2: [$_{vP}NP_{acc,+top}$ $NP_{nom,-top}$ t_{acc}…]		*			*

Other things being equal, if the object is not topic-marked in the input, the optimal candidate has the object remaining in situ. In this case, O_2's violations of AGENT and STAY are fatal, and O_1 is correctly predicted to be optimal; see tableau 2.

Tableau 2: Blocked scrambling in front of the subject

Input: $NP_{nom,-top}$, $NP_{acc,-top}$	TOPIC	AGENT	DEF	FOC	STAY
☞ O_1: [$_{vP}NP_{nom,-top}$ $NP_{acc,-top}$…]					
O_2: [$_{vP}NP_{acc,-top}$ $NP_{nom,-top}$ t_{acc}…]		*!			*

Similarly, cases of focus-driven scrambling can be derived, the main difference being that here, it is a negatively specified item that scrambles: Focus-driven scrambling involves movement of non-focus-marked material so as to let a focus-marked item end up in a right-peripheral position. Some well-known sentences from German that illustrate the effect are given in (9) (see Lenerz (1977); focus is indicated by small capitals). Note in particular that scrambling of the direct object across the indirect object in (9b) can be considered focus-driven in this sense; (9a) shows that such scrambling does not appear to be obligatory in German; and (9cd) show that scrambling of the focussed NP itself leads to deviance.

(9) a. dass der   Fritz der   MARIA$_1$ das   Buch$_2$ gegeben hat
        that the$_{nom}$ Fritz the$_{dat}$ Maria   the$_{acc}$ book   given   has

     b. dass der   Fritz das   Buch$_2$ der   MARIA$_1$ t$_2$ gegeben hat
        that the$_{nom}$ Fritz the$_{acc}$ book   the$_{dat}$ Maria   given   has

     c. dass der   Fritz der   Maria$_1$ das   BUCH$_2$ gegeben hat
        that the$_{nom}$ Fritz the$_{dat}$ Maria   the$_{acc}$ book   given   has

     d. ?*dass der   Fritz das   BUCH$_2$ der   Maria$_1$ t$_2$ gegeben hat
        that   the$_{nom}$ Fritz the$_{acc}$ book   the$_{dat}$ Maria   given   has

The examples in (9) can be taken to indicate that the constraints FOCUS and STAY are tied, i.e. equally ranked.[10] If so, optionality can be derived for (9ab). This is shown in tableau 3.

Tableau 3: Focus-driven optional scrambling in front of the indirect object

Input: $NP_{nom,-foc}$, $NP_{dat,+foc}$, $NP_{acc,-foc}$	TOPIC	AGENT	DEF	FOC	STAY
☞ O_1: $[_{vP}\ NP_{nom,-foc}\ NP_{dat,+foc}\ NP_{acc,-foc}\cdots]$				*	
☞ O_2: $[_{vP}\ NP_{nom,-foc}\ NP_{acc,-foc}\ NP_{dat,+foc}\ t_{acc}\cdots]$					*

In contrast, the competition underlying (9 c,d) is given in tableau 4. Here, scrambling of the direct object in O_2 violates both FOCUS and STAY, either violation of which would suffice to render O_2 suboptimal. Hence, O_1 without scrambling is the sole optimal candidate.

Tableau 4: Blocked scrambling in front of the indirect object

Input: $NP_{nom,-foc}$, $NP_{dat,-foc}$, $NP_{acc,+foc}$	TOPIC	AGENT	DEF	FOC	STAY
☞ O_1: $[_{vP}\ NP_{nom,-foc}\ NP_{dat,-foc}\ NP_{acc,+foc}\cdots]$					
O_2: $[_{vP}\ NP_{nom,-foc}\ NP_{acc,+foc}\ NP_{dat,-foc}\ t_{acc}\cdots]$				*(!)	*(!)

Focus-driven scrambling in Russian can be exemplified by data such as (10ab) (see Krylova & Chavronina (1976) and King (1995), among others).[11]

(10) a. Etu   knigu₂   PUŠKIN   napisal t₂
         this$_{acc}$ book$_{acc}$ Pushkin$_{nom}$ wrote

      b. $[_{VP3}$ Čitaet   knigu] $[_{vP}$ OTEC t₃]
          reads   book   father

These examples may suffice to illustrate optimality-theoretic approaches to scrambling of the Büring/Choi type. A general property of this kind of analysis is that ideally (i.e. except for the effects of ties), every well-formed output with variable word order in a scrambling language is the sole optimal realization of a given input specification. Needless to say, the preceding discussion has left out many aspects of the Büring/Choi approach to scrambling; and arguably, this approach may eventually prove to be somewhat too strict and suffer from the

---

[10] There are various different concepts of constraint ties in the literature. For present purposes, we can assume a global notion according to which a constraint tie is an abbreviation for the simultaneous presence of two (or more) constraint rankings in a language. A candidate is grammatical if it is optimal under at least one ranking that results from a resolution of the tie.

[11] (10a) presupposes that Focus can outrank Agent in Russian. (10b) looks like a case of VP scrambling. VP scrambling also seems to be involved in some cases of long-distance scrambling in Russian; see the references in footnote 3. This difference between German and Russian will not be addressed in the present paper.

problem of undergeneration (e.g. whereas sentences like (9d) do seem to be highly marked, it is not clear that they should be considered as fully ungrammatical), which may necessitate additional assumptions.[12] But that aside, I contend that the approach just sketched is both linguistically plausible and representative in its essentials of optimality-theoretic approaches to scrambling.

Still, it is evident that there is no room in this analysis for the idea that scrambling is possible only if rich Case morphology is present in a language, i.e. that hypothesis (1a) is correct. Under the present view, scrambling and Case morphology are independent properties of a language; scrambling does not rely on morphology, but on rankings like TOPIC >> STAY or FOCUS >> STAY (in one resolution of the tie). In line with this, the only reason why English does not have scrambling is that STAY is ranked higher than constraints like TOPIC and FOCUS that may force movement to an outer specifier of vP.[13] What can be done in view of this situation?

2.3   Integrating Morphological Case – Two Failed Attempts

Suppose first that we were to adopt a meta-constraint on ranking, as in (11).

(11)   Meta-constraint on ranking:
       vP-linearization constraints can outrank STAY in language L only if L has morphological Case.

This would impose a fixed ranking among certain constraints in languages that do not have morphological Case and thereby correctly predict that, e.g. English cannot have scrambling. However, it is clear that a meta-constraint like (11) is ad hoc; it is basically a statement of the problem, not its solution.

Suppose next that the vP-linearization constraints in (7) are reformulated in such a way that they trigger scrambling only if an NP bears morphological Case. This can be done as in (12).

---

[12] See, e.g. the proposal in Müller (1999), which can be viewed as a slightly more elaborate (and slightly more complicated) version of the Büring/Choi approach.

[13] Depending on whether or not all vP linearization constraints must be grouped together or can freely be distributed over rankings, this approach may open up the possibility that some language has scrambling to satisfy some vP linearization constraints (e.g. Topic, under a ranking Topic >> Stay), and has no scrambling in violation of others (e.g. Focus, under a simultaneous ranking Stay >> Focus). I assume that a language has scrambling if it has at least one kind of linearization-driven movement to an outer specifier of vP, in violation of Stay.

(12)   a. TOPIC′:
          A [+topic] NP with morphological Case precedes [−topic] material.

       b. AGENT(IVITY)′:
          A [+agent] NP with morphological Case precedes [−agent] material.

       c. DEF(INITENESS)′:
          A [+def] NP with morphological Case precedes [-def] material.

       d. FOC(US)′:
          A [−focus] NP with morphological Case precedes [+focus] material.

This, too, would imply that scrambling can only occur in languages with morpholocial Case: In languages without morphological Case, constraints like TOPIC′ simply do not require NP displacement within vP, and any such displacement will therefore fatally violate STAY. However, such a move is also conceptually unattractive for at least two reasons. First, the revised vP linearization constraints are not as simple and general anymore as they arguably should be in an optimality-theoretic approach (see Grimshaw (1999)). Second, the difference between scrambling languages with morphological Case and non-scrambling languages without morphological Case is not due to constraint ranking anymore: A ranking like TOPIC′, ... >> STAY will trigger scrambling in the former, but not in the latter. Thus, the scrambling languages German and Russian on the one hand, and the non-scrambling language English on the other, could have the same ranking of STAY and vP linearization constraints. (However, a ranking STAY >> TOPIC′, ... would block scrambling even in languages with rich Case morphology.) Essentially, then, important aspects of cross-linguistic variation with respect to scrambling would be handled in a non-optimality-theoretic way, even though the general approach remains optimality-theoretic.[14]

In addition to these conceptual considerations, there are severe empirical problems with the view that scrambling depends on the presence of morphological Case: It turns out that scrambling is in fact possible in the absence of morphological Case. This will be shown on the basis of two phenomena: First, scrambling of items without morphological Case in languages that have morphological Case; and second, scrambling in languages that have no morphological Case to begin with. Let me begin with the former issue.

Note that whereas morphological Case is often marked on NPs in scrambling languages like German and Russian, not all NPs do in fact exhibit morphological

---

[14] Note incidentally that the step taken in (12) closely resembles the revised approach to the V-to-I movement parameter in Vikner (2001b). Recall that Vikner (2001a) develops an analysis that does not envisage a relation between V-to-I movement and rich morphology. In Vikner (2001b), this view is abandoned, and replaced by an analysis in which the constraint that forces V-to-I movement applies only if inflectional morphology is sufficiently rich in a given language. Hence, nothing forces V-to-I movement in languages with poor inflectional morphology on verbs, and therefore, such movement is blocked here. On the other hand, V-to-I movement may be blocked despite rich inflectional morphology under a certain ranking of constraints. This parallels the approach to scrambling just sketched in the main text.

Case. For instance, German proper names typically do not bear any Case morphology whatsoever; still, they can undergo scrambling, as shown in (13a).[15]

Similarly, the reflexive pronoun *sich* not only lacks morphological Case; arguably, it may even lack abstract Case in certain constructions.[16] However, it can undergo scrambling; see (13b). Finally, the R-pronoun *da* ('there') can be scrambled out of a PP; see (13c). Whereas the categorial status of R-pronouns (as NPs, PPs, or perhaps underspecified [–V]Ps) is not unanimously agreed on, it is clear that R-pronouns do not bear morphological Case.

(13) a. dass Martin$_1$ keiner   t$_1$ gesehen hat
        that   Martin   no-one$_{nom}$ seen   has

     b. dass sich$_1$ diese Leute t$_1$ nicht leiden können
        that   REFL   these people   not   stand   can

     c. dass da$_1$ der Fritz [$_{NP}$ ein Buch t$_1$ über] gelesen hat
        that   there the Fritz   a   book   about] read   has

Likewise, Russian has more than 350 nouns that cannot bear Case morphology, e.g. *kofe* 'coffee', *pal'to* 'coat', *interv'ju* 'interview' (see Isačenko (1975)); however, NPs that contain only these nouns can scramble.[17]

In addition to NPs without morphological Case, other categories that cannot bear Case for principled reasons (e.g. PPs and CPs) can also undergo scrambling in German; see (14ab).

---

[15] Two remarks. First, proper names in German do bear overt genitive Case morphology. Genitive Case is extremely marginal in the verbal domain, though. Second, proper names are optionally preceded by a definite article in German (as in den Martin 'the Martin'), in which case they also have morphological Case. See section 3.2.4 below.

[16] See Müller & Sternefeld (1994). The basic observation is that German reflexive (and reciprocal) pronouns are immune to Case absorption in the passive; see (ia) vs. (ib).

(i) a. dass sich   hier   nicht gewaschen wird
        that   REFL here   not   washed   is

     b. *dass den   Martin hier nicht gewaschen wird
         that   the$_{acc}$ Martin here not   washed   is

The wellformedness of (ia) implies that sich can remain without (abstract and morphological) Case in German, whereas other NPs must at least bear abstract Case. Of course, this does not mean that sich never bears abstract Case. In constructions involving Case agreement like (ii), e.g. it seems clear that sich must bear an abstract accusative Case because this is the only source that the NP den größten Helden can derive its accusative Case from.

(ii) dass er   sich als den   größten   Helden   sieht
       that   he$_{nom}$ REFL as   the$_{acc}$ biggest$_{acc}$ hero$_{acc}$ views

[17] In both German and Russian, scrambling of an NP without morphological Case across another NP without morphological Case may induce a decrease in acceptability, especially if ambiguity may arise and contextual information is insufficient. However, unlike Lee (1999) and Vogel (2001b) (both based on an insight that goes back to Roman Jakobson), I do not take this to be grammatically significant; rather, I would like to contend that parsing difficulties are involved in these cases.

(14)   a. dass [$_{PP1}$ darüber]   der   Fritz [$_{NP}$ ein   Buch t_1] gelesen   hat
       that   there about the   Fritz   a   book   read   has

       b. dass [$_{CP1}$ das Buch zu   lesen] keiner t_1 versucht   hat
       that   the book   to   read   no-one   tried   has

The same goes for Russian, which also permits VP scrambling (see (10b) and
the examples in Müller & Sternefeld (1993)). Again, these facts are entirely
unexpected if scrambling of some item α depends on the presence of morphological Case on α. (And, of course, PPs and CPs cannot be scrambled in non-
scrambling languages like English.)

Finally, consider the situation in Bulgarian. Bulgarian has a Case system that
closely resembles that of English in that morphological Case does not generally
exist anymore: Subjects and direct objects cannot be distinguished morphologically; and indirect objects and objects that would be expected to bear abstract
genitive Case are preceded by a preposition *na* (corresponding to English 'to'
and 'of', respectively). However, Bulgarian has scrambling of the Ger-
man/Russian type, with roughly the same information-structural effects.[18]
Scrambling in Bulgarian is shown in (15).[19]

(15)   a. Ivan$_1$ otvori   vratata$_2$
          Ivan   opened   door the

       b. Ivan$_1$ vratata$_2$ otvori t_2
          Ivan   door the   opened

       c. Vratata$_2$ Ivan$_1$ otvori t_2
          door the   Ivan   opened

To sum up: On the conceptual side, we have seen that the hypothesis that morphological Case is a prerequisite for scrambling (see (1a)) is difficult to reconcile
with optimality-theoretic approaches to scrambling in a straightforward way. On
the empirical side, it has turned out that the assumption that morphological Case

---

[18] See Molxova (1970), Georgieva (1974), and Rudin (1985), among others.

[19] Note that Bulgarian has clitic pronoun doubling, and the pronouns do indeed bear morphological Case. At first sight one might think that Bulgarian is like German and Russian after all, in
having NP scrambling only in the presence of morphological Case on the doubled pronouns. But
closer inspection reveals that this cannot be the case: Pronoun doubling is optional throughout in
Bulgarian (e.g. there are no doubled pronouns in (15)). Furthermore, it turns out that even pronoun
doubling does not necessarily disambiguate a sentence (see Rudin (1985, 17)): (ia) with a feminine
object clitic has a (preferred) reading in which Marija is the subject, and another (possible, albeit
slightly more marked) reading in which Tanja is the subject.
       (i)   a. Tanja   ja   vidja   Marija
                Tanja   her   saw   Marija
             b. Reading (i): Marija saw Tanja
             c. Reading (ii): Tanja saw Marija
Thus, the existence of pronoun doubling in Bulgarian does not affect the claim that scrambling does
not depend on morphological Case in this language.

is a prerequisite for scrambling is falsified by evidence from German, Russian, and, especially, Bulgarian. That leaves hypotheses (1c) and (1b) as the only remaining options: Either scrambling and morphological Case are unrelated, or morphological Case is not a prerequisite for scrambling, but a reflex of scrambling. As noted above, it may eventually turn out that hypothesis (1c) is the correct one.[20] Still, hypothesis (1b) is arguably more interesting, and for that reason I would like to pursue it in what follows.

The first thing to note is that the more radical hypothesis (1b) directly adheres to a bold assumption that has sometimes been made in optimality-theoretic syntax concerning the relation between syntax and morphology: In contrast to what is often assumed, morphological properties, on this view, do not determine parameter setting; rather, parameter setting (= constraint ranking) can determine morphological properties. This program is pursued, e.g. in Grimshaw's (1997) analysis of *do*-support, and in Legendre, Smolensky & Wilson's (1998) analysis of resumptive pronouns in Chinese. In this context, Legendre, Smolensky & Wilson introduce the slogan "The functional lexicon is slave to the syntax." If we view morphological Case as part of the functional lexicon, the hypothesis presently under investigation lends itself to exactly this interpretation. Thus, the proposal that I would like to advance is the following: The existence of Case morphology in a given language can ultimately be traced back to a constraint ranking that triggers scrambling.[21] I will first outline the approach, and then discuss various pieces of (apparent and real) counter-evidence.

3   The Proposal

3.1   Morphological Case as a Reflex of Scrambling

Throughout, I presuppose that there is a distinction between abstract Case and morphological Case. Abstract Case is a general property of NPs. The choice of the correct abstract Case for a given argument (lexical vs. structural, unmarked structural vs. marked structural) is argued to be determined by optimization procedures in much recent literature; see, e.g. Fanselow (1999), Kiparsky (1999), Stiebels (2000), Wunderlich (2000), Vogel (2001a), Woolford (2001), and Müller (2000 chap. 7) for an overview. Alternatively, the abstract Case of an NP may directly be determined by the GEN component of an optimality-theoretic grammar, without recourse to optimization. In what follows, I will have nothing

---

[20] This would correspond to the view taken in Alexiadou & Fanselow (2001) with respect to the V-to-I movement parameter.

[21] Also see Samek-Lodovici (2001) on the syntactic determination of agreement in optimality theory, and Aissen (2000) on Case. Note that whereas I am concerned with word order as a possible trigger for morphological Case, Aissen identifies inherent properties of a given NP (e.g. its animacy status) as the trigger for morphological Case. The two approaches are not necessarily incompatible. Adopting them simultaneously would demand a weakening of (1b), to the effect that a language has morphological Case only if either scrambling or one of the triggers envisaged by Aissen is present.

new to say on this issue; I will simply assume that each NP bears abstract Case
in the languages currently under consideration, and ignore the issue in what follows (accordingly, specifications like "nom" and "acc" on NPs will
unambiguously signal the presence of morphological Case, never the presence of
abstract Case).[22] However, morphological Case is not a general property of NPs.
By hypothesis, it arises as a reflex of a certain constraint ranking, viz., one in
which vP linearization constraints like TOPIC and FOCUS outrank STAY, and
CASE outranks DEPFUNC. CASE can be defined as follows.

(16)   CASE:
       An NP at the edge of vP has morphological Case.

The notion of edge here is adapted from Chomsky (2000, 2001). Deviating
slightly from Chomsky, I assume that a category is at the edge of an XP if it is in
an outer specifier of XP.[23] CASE then implies that an NP that has undergone
scrambling must be morphologically Case-marked. The radical assumption now
is that morphological Case (in the vP domain) exists only because it is required
by CASE. There is no morphological Case in the lexicon. Therefore, syntactic
inputs (numerations) do not contain morphological Case markers either – morphological Case is not given; it arises as a result of optimization in syntactic
derivations. As a result, the presence of morphological Case invariably incurs a
violation of DEPFUNC, a dependency faithfulness constraint that prohibits the
insertion of functional material in the output that is not present in the input.

(17)   DEPFUNC:
       Functional material of the output must be part of the input.

To see how morphological Case can arise as a reflex of scrambling, consider
first cases of multiple scrambling of all NP arguments across an adverb in German. It is well known that adverbs of place and negation typically show up in a
position close to the verb in German. I will take this to mean that these adverbs
are base-generated in an outer specifier of vP, where they minimally c-command
the base position of subject NPs (i.e. the inner specifier of vP). In the unmarked
case, all NP arguments scramble in front of such an adverbial; see (18ab).

---

[22] This leaves open many important questions concerning, e.g. the number and types of abstract Cases in languages without morphological Case like English and Bulgarian, and the question
of how distinct abstract Cases can be identified in such languages in the first place; see Zifonun et al.
(1997) for a proposal that relies on equivalence class formation.

[23] The main difference to Chomsky (2000; 2001) is that the inner specifier of an XP also
counts as an edge position in his account. If XP adjuncts exist, they may also be at the edge of XP,
but given that scrambling is movement to an outer specifier, not adjunction, this is irrelevant for
what follows (and the differences between the two options are in any case fairly subtle). Note,
however, that the notion of "edge" employed here is not to be confused with the notion of "edge" as
it is widely used in optimality-theoretic phonology; on this, see Chomsky's notion of "phonological
border".

(18)   a. dass [$_{vP}$ der   Fritz$_1$ [$_{v'}$den   Karl$_2$ [$_{v'}$ in der Kneipe [$_{v'}$t$_1$ t$_2$
        that   the$_{nom}$ Fritz   the$_{acc}$ Karl   in the pub
        getroffen]]]] hat
        met   has

     b. dass [$_{vP}$ der   Fritz$_1$ [$_{v'}$ den   Karl$_2$ [$_{v'}$ nicht [$_{v'}$ t$_1$ t$_2$ getroffen]]]] hat
        that   the$_{nom}$ Fritz   the$_{acc}$ Karl   not   met   has

Multiple NP scrambling of this type can be assumed to be triggered by a specific linearization constraint that forces NPs to show up in front of adverbials of this type (see Müller (1999) for a proposal, and for an account of the optionality involved). To simplify the discussion from now on, I will indicate the activity of a linearization constraint that triggers scrambling to an outer specifier of vP by a [scr] specification in the input; SCRCON stands for the ranked set of vP linearization constraints that trigger scrambling.[24] The competition underlying examples like those in (18) in scrambling languages like German and Russian is then shown in tableau 5.[25]

Tableau 5: Morphological Case because of scrambling (German, Russian)

Input: $NP_{1,[scr]}$ $NP_{2[scr]}$,…	SCR CON	STAY	CASE	DEP FUNC
O_1: [$_{vP}$ NP$_1$ v [$_{VP}$ V NP$_2$]]	*!*			
O_2: [$_{vP}$ NP$_{1,nom}$ v [$_{VP}$V NP$_2$]]	*!*			*
O_3: [$_{vP}$ NP$_1$ v [$_{VP}$ V NP$_{2,acc}$]]	*!*			*
O_4: [$_{vP}$ NP$_{1,nom}$ v [$_{VP}$ V NP$_{2,acc}$]]	*!*			**
O_5: [$_{vP}$ NP$_2$ NP$_1$ v [$_{VP}$ V t$_2$]]	*!	*	*	
O_6: [$_{vP}$ NP$_2$ NP$_{1,nom}$ v [$_{VP}$ V t$_2$]]	*!	*	*	*
O_7: [$_{vP}$ NP$_{2,acc}$ NP$_1$ v [$_{VP}$ V t$_2$]]	*!	*		*
O_8: [$_{vP}$ NP$_{2,acc}$ NP$_{1,nom}$ v [$_{VP}$ V t$_2$]]	*!	*		**
O_9: [$_{vP}$ NP$_1$ NP$_2$ t$_1$ v [$_{VP}$ V t$_2$]]		**	*!*	
O_{10}: [$_{vP}$ NP$_{1,nom}$ NP$_2$ t$_1$ v [$_{VP}$ V t$_2$]]		**	*!	*
O_{11}: [$_{vP}$ NP$_1$ NP$_{2,acc}$ t$_1$ v [$_{VP}$ V t$_2$]]		**	*!	*
☞ O_{12}: [$_{vP}$ NP$_{1,nom}$ NP$_{2,acc}$ t$_1$ v [$_{VP}$ V t$_2$]]		**		**

[24] Note that [scr] does not necessarily stand for a specific feature like [±top] or [±foc] that triggers scrambling by constraints like Topic and Focus, and that may or may not be present on an NP in the input. In (18), it is simply the feature [+N] that forces scrambling accross adverbials.

[25] Here and in what follows, I focus on one ranking that produces the intended result. Often, other rankings would also be compatible with the empirical evidence (e.g. re-ranking Stay and Case has no effect in tableau 5). Note also that the linear order of v, V and their complements given here is a simplification that may be correct for Russian, but not for German (see (5)).

First, O_1–O_4 in tableau 5 are outputs in which scrambling does not apply even though there is, by assumption, an input specification on both NPs that forces them to scramble, given SCRCON. Hence, the two NPs in situ incur two SCRCON violations, the first of which is already fatal, independently of the question of whether they exhibit morphological Case or not. Next, O_5–O_8 involve scrambling of the object NP, but the subject NP stays in situ. Again, this incurs a fatal SCRCON violation, irrespective of the issue of morphological Case. Finally, O_9–O_{12} have scrambling of both NPs, which respects SCRCON and violates the lower-ranked STAY non-fatally. Here, the ranking of CASE and DEPFUNC becomes relevant. O_9 does not have any morphological Case on the scrambled NPs, and O_{10} and O_{11} have morphological Case on only one of the two NPs in Specv. All three candidates therefore incur fatal violations of CASE. O_{12} has morphological Case on both NPs, violating DEPFUNC twice but respecting CASE. Therefore, this output is the sole optimal candidate.

If a language maintains the ranking SCRCON >> STAY but reverses the ranking of CASE and DEPFUNC, it will exhibit scrambling, but no morphological Case, as in Bulgarian. This is illustrated in tableau 6.

Tableau 6: Absence of morphological Case despite scrambling (Bulgarian)

Input: $NP_{1\,[scr]}$ $NP_{2\,[scr]}$, ⋯	SCR CON	STAY	DEP FUNC	CASE
O_1: [$_{vP}$ NP_1 v [$_{VP}$ V NP_2]]	*!*			
O_2: [$_{vP}$ $NP_{1,nom}$ v [$_{VP}$ V NP_2]]	*!*		*	
O_3: [$_{vP}$ NP_1 v [$_{VP}$ V $NP_{2,acc}$]]	*!*		*	
O_4: [$_{vP}$ $NP_{1,nom}$ v [$_{VP}$ V $NP_{2,acc}$]]	*!*		**	
O_5: [$_{vP}$ NP_2 NP_1 v [$_{VP}$ V t_2]]	*!	*		*
O_6: [$_{vP}$ NP_2 $NP_{1,nom}$ v [$_{VP}$ V t_2]]	*!	*	*	*
O_7: [$_{vP}$ $NP_{2,acc}$ NP_1 v [$_{VP}$ V t_2]]	*!	*	*	
O_8: [$_{vP}$ $NP_{2,acc}$ $NP_{1,nom}$ v [$_{VP}$ V t_2]]	*!	*	**	
☞ O_9: [$_{vP}$ NP_1 NP_2 t_1 v [$_{VP}$ V t_2]]		**		**
O_{10}: [$_{vP}$ $NP_{1,nom}$ NP_2 t_1 v [$_{VP}$ V t_2]]		**	*!	*
O_{11}: [$_{vP}$ NP_1 $NP_{2,acc}$ t_1 v [$_{VP}$ V t_2]]		**	*!	*
O_{12}: [$_{vP}$ $NP_{1,nom}$ $NP_{2,acc}$ t_1 v [$_{VP}$ V t_2]]		**	*!*	

O_1–O_8 emerge as suboptimal in tableau 6 for the same reason that their counterparts in tableau 5 are excluded: They fatally violate SCRCON. However, given the ranking DEPFUNC >> CASE, O_9 is optimal in Bulgarian instead of O_{12}.

Finally, let us turn to languages like English that do not exhibit scrambling. These languages have a ranking STAY >> SCRCON (i.e. all vP linearization constraints are ranked below STAY). It follows from this ranking that candidates with morphological Case will invariably be suboptimal, independently of how CASE and DEPFUNC are ranked with respect to another; see tableau 7.

O_5–O_{12} are suboptimal outputs in tableau 7 because of fatal STAY violations. Of the candidates that respect STAY by not applying scrambling (and that therefore violate SCRCON twice), none can violate CASE. This is so because no NP is in an outer specifier of vP in any of the candidates (the subject NP being in an inner specifier throughout); hence, CASE is vacuously fulfilled in all four outputs O_1–O_4. That being so, the decision falls to DEPFUNC, which picks out O_1 even if it is lowest-ranked. This way, it follows that morphological Case can only become optimal as a reflex of scrambling.

Tableau 7: Absence of morphological Case without scrambling (English)

Input: $NP_{1,[scr]}\, NP_{2,[scr]},\cdots$	STAY	SCR CON	CASE	DEP FUNC
O_1: $[_{vP}\ NP_1\ v\ [_{VP}\ V\ NP_2]]$		**		
O_2: $[_{vP}\ NP_{1,nom}\ v\ [_{VP}\ V\ NP_2]]$		**		*!
O_3: $[_{vP}\ NP_1\ v\ [_{VP}\ V\ NP_{2,acc}]]$		**		*!
O_4: $[_{vP}\ NP_{1,nom}\ v\ [_{VP}\ V\ NP_{2,acc}]]$		**		*!*
O_5: $[_{vP}\ NP_2\ NP_1\ v\ [_{VP}\ V\ t_2]]$	*!	*	*	
O_6: $[_{vP}\ NP_2\ NP_{1,nom}\ v\ [_{VP}\ V\ t_2]]$	*!	*	*	*
O_7: $[_{vP}\ NP_{2,acc}\ NP_1\ v\ [_{VP}\ V\ t_2]]$	*!	*		*
O_8: $[_{vP}\ NP_{2,acc}\ NP_{1,nom}\ v\ [_{VP}\ V\ t_2]]$	*!	*		**
O_9: $[_{vP}\ NP_1\ NP_2\ t_1\ v\ [_{VP}\ V\ t_2]]$	*!*		**	
O_{10}: $[_{vP}\ NP_{1,nom}\ NP_2\ t_1\ v\ [_{VP}\ V\ t_2]]$	*!*		*	*
O_{11}: $[_{vP}\ NP_1\ NP_{2,acc}\ t_1\ v\ [_{VP}\ V\ t_2]]$	*!*		*	*
O_{12}: $[_{vP}\ NP_{1,nom}\ NP_{2,acc}\ t_1\ v\ [_{VP}\ V\ t_2]]$	*!*			**

3.2 Problems

As mentioned above, the present approach raises a number of questions. I would like to address what I take to be the most conspicuous problems in this section.

3.2.1 Case Paradigms

A first question concerns the nature of Case paradigms, more specifically, the role that morphology plays in the system just outlined. As it stands, it can be ensured that an NP must have some kind of morphological Case (under certain conditions; see below). However, the present approach, as such, does not yet say

anything about the actual form of morphological Case on an NP. Even if we are
prepared to assume (at least for the purposes of this discussion, and for the
languages under consideration) that morphological Case marking is accomplished by specific suffixes, many questions arise: Why do Case markers look
the way they do in a given language? How can the distribution of what (at least
at first sight) looks like zero (phonetically empty) morphological Case markers
be accounted for, and how can such zero Case markers in a language like German be systematically distinguished from the absence of morphological Case in
a language like English? On which items of an NP does a language with morphological Case actually realize the Case marker?[26]

Questions like these belong to the realm of morphology, and the information
needed here is usually assumed to be encoded in Case paradigms. These are
often assumed to be part of the lexicon, or, at least, pre-syntactic, hence, already
available in the syntactic input. However, under the present approach, paradigmatic information of this type cannot yet be available in the input: By
assumption, morphological Case violates DEPFUNC exactly because it is *not* part
of the input. This apparent dilemma would dissolve if we were to adopt a late
insertion approach, at least for inflectional morphology.[27] An alternative solution
would be to assume that morphological properties of Case paradigms can be
derived in the syntax directly. Under this view, the rankings SCRCON >> STAY,
CASE >> DEPFUNC require the presence of a Case marker, and the exact shape
of this marker is determined by violable and ranked morpho-phonological constraints. The interaction of these constraints then predicts Case paradigms, which
therefore emerge as mere epiphenomena. Such a view presupposes that Case
paradigms are highly regular and can be determined in a systematic way. This,
indeed, seems to be the case. Bierwisch (1967), Blevins (1995), Wunderlich
(1997), and Wiese (1999) show that Case paradigms are largely predictable in
German. Building on this research, I develop an optimality-theoretic approach to
morphological Case in Müller (2001b), a paper that complements the present
one. In this approach, the shape and the distribution of Case markers in German
are both determined syntax-internally, without reference to either a non-syntactic
(lexical or morphological) component or the notion of paradigm, by relying on
the sonority hierarchy and a small set of higher-ranked feature co-occurrence
restrictions that block the simultaneous presence of certain morpho-syntactic
specifications and certain phonological features on determiners, nouns, and

---

[26] Thus, German typically expresses morphological Case on a determiner or adjective, much
more than on the noun itself; see the next subsection. In contrast, Russian has morphological Case on
both nouns and prenominal determiners and adjectives.

[27] This might be implemented in a version of distributed morphology (see Harley & Noyer
(1999) for an overview). However, in standard distributed morphology, all lexical items are inserted
after syntax has applied. Additional assumptions would then be necessary to ensure that there is a
difference between (low-ranked) Dep violations incurred by the insertion of content words, and
(higher-ranked) Dep violations incurred by the insertion of function words and inflectional morphology.

adjectives.[28] Given that such an approach can be viewed as empirically successful (in deriving all existing Case markers) and independently motivated (e.g. in contrast to what is the case in other approaches, all instances of syncretism can be shown to be non-accidental), and assuming that it can be generalized to other languages (like Russian), we can minimally conclude that the present analysis – according to which paradigmatic information about the shape of Case markers is not available pre-syntactically – is unproblematic in that respect.

3.2.2 Phonology and Diachrony: Old English and Middle English

According to the linguistic folklore, the primary reason for the loss of morphological Case is ultimately phonological in nature. Evidently, this view is incompatible with the present approach, which implies that morphological Case gets lost because vP linearization constraints are demoted below STAY. Let me illustrate the two approaches on the basis of a well-known phenomenon: the loss of morphological Case in the history of English.

Old English has both rich Case morphology and scrambling. Both properties are lost in the Middle English period (see van Kemenade (1987), and Roberts (1997), among others). The scenario standardly devised for this change looks as follows. First, the variable word stress of Indo-European becomes fixed as initial stress in Germanic. Second, as a consequence of this, phonological reduction affecting final syllables takes place between Old English and Early Middle English. Specifically, unstressed vowels are reduced to schwa, and final nasals are lost. Third, for reasons of paradigm uniformity, morphological levelling takes place. Fourth, as a result of phonological reduction and morphological levelling, morphological Case is lost in Middle English. Fifth and finally, under hypothesis (1a) according to which morphological Case is a prerequisite for scrambling, it follows that scrambling is lost in Middle English.

In contrast, the present approach relies on hypothesis (1b) and takes scrambling to be a prerequisite for morphological Case. Therefore, it suggests a different scenario: First, scrambling is lost in Middle English, due to a demotion of SCRCON below STAY. Second (and finally), as a consequence of the new ranking, morphological Case is lost. Of course, the question now is how the phonological (and morphological) diachronic evidence fits into this picture. Clearly, the new approach leads us to the assumption that phonological developments can in fact not be responsible for the loss of scrambling. As noted, this view is forced by the fact that Bulgarian still has ample scrambling despite a lack of morphological Case on anything but pronouns. (In contrast, Old Bulgarian has seven different morphological Cases.) Moreover, it is instructive to note that a phonological reduction of final syllables also took place in the history of German (between Old High German and Middle High German), without a simultaneous loss of scrambling or morphological Case. There is hardly any

---

[28] Note incidentally that the approach in Müller (2001b) abandons zero Case markers in favour of the assumption that Case can selectively be violated to fufill higher-ranked constraints.

morphological Case marking on nouns anymore in Modern German (recall footnote 26): Feminine nouns have no morphological Case whatsoever in the
singular; there is little more than a genitive *-(e)s* with masculine and neuter
nouns of the most common ("strong") paradigm, and with proper names; and
there is a dative *-n* for plural nouns (at least for those that do not already employ
-n or *s* as a plural marker). All other Case suffixes show up in minor paradigms,
most notably in the "weak" paradigm for masculine nouns. Thus, morphological
Case in German is typically marked on determiners and prenominal adjectives.
At least in the case of determiners, this is perfectly compatible with a monosyllabic word; see, e.g. *der Mann* ('the$_{nom}$ man'); *des Mann-(e)s* ('the$_{gen}$ man$_{gen}$');
dem Mann ('the$_{dat}$ man'); *den Mann* ('the$_{acc}$ man').

I would like to conclude from this that it is by no means a priori implausible
to assume that there is no direct connection between phonological reduction of
unstressed syllables and the presence of morphological Case (such that the former makes the latter impossible). Rather, it seems that if there is a syntactically
determined need for morphological Case in a given language, the language will
find a means to realize it in a way that is compatible with its phonological system. Phonological reduction of final syllables and loss of morphological Case
happened to co-occur in the history of English at roughly the same time; but they
did not co-occur in the history of German.

3.2.3 Morphological Case in Icelandic

Since the present approach views morphological Case in the verbal domain as a
reflex of scrambling, the prediction is that morphological Case should not occur
in a language that does not exhibit scrambling (unless, that is, another trigger can
be found). At first sight, it looks as though this prediction is falsified by evidence from Icelandic. Icelandic has morphological Case on NPs but does not
seem to permit scrambling because the clause-internal relative order of argument
NPs is basically fixed.

However, whereas Icelandic does not exhibit scrambling of the German, Russian, and Bulgarian type, there is good reason to believe that it has scrambling
nevertheless. The relevant phenomena are usually identified as instances of non-
pronominal object shift, i.e. operations that move NPs across an adverbial. Thus,
I would like to contend that non-pronominal object shift in Icelandic is to be
viewed as a scrambling operation that moves an NP to an outer specifier of vP,
just like scrambling in German, Russian, and Bulgarian does (thereby, adverbials
in vP specifiers are crossed). Under this assumption, a fundamental difference
between Icelandic and the other scrambling languages considered thus far must
be accounted for: Scrambling strictly preserves the pre-movement order in Icelandic, and freely changes the pre-movement order in, e.g. German. Strict order

preservation with scrambling in Icelandic is shown by the following data; see Collins & Thráinsson (1996).[29]

(19) a. Ég   lána   [$_{vP}$ ekki   [$_{v'}$ Maríu$_1$ [$_{v'}$ bækurnar$_2$]]]
          I   lend   not   Maria$_{dat}$ the books$_{acc}$

      b. Ég   lána   [$_{vP}$ Maríu$_1$ [$_{v'}$ ekki [$_{v'}$t$_1$ [$_{v'}$ bækurnar$_2$]]]]
          I   lend   Maria$_{dat}$ not   the books$_{acc}$

      c. Ég   lána   [$_{vP}$ Maríu$_1$ [$_{v'}$ bækurnar$_2$ [$_{v'}$ ekki [$_{v'}$t$_1$ [$_{v'}$ t$_2$]]]]]
          I   lend   Maria$_{dat}$ the books$_{acc}$ not

      d. *Ég   lána   [$_{vP}$ bækurnar$_2$ [$_{v'}$ ekki   [$_{v'}$ Maríu$_1$ [$_{v'}$t$_2$]]]]
          I   lend   the books$_{acc}$ not   Maria$_{dat}$

      e. *Ég   lána   [$_{vP}$ bækurnar$_2$ [$_{v'}$ Maríu$_1$ [$_{v'}$ ekki [$_{v'}$ t$_1$ [$_{v'}$ t$_2$]]]]]
          I   lend   the books$_{acc}$ Maria$_{dat}$ not

(19abc) preserve order (by moving either no object at all, only the higher one, or both objects in their pre-movement order), which (19de) do not (only the lower object moves in (19d), and the two moved objects reverse their pre-movement order in (19e)). In Müller (2001a), I propose to account for the data in (19) by invoking a general constraint that requires order preservation (and that is independently motivated on the basis of displacement operations like *wh*-movement, pronoun fronting, and quantifier raising in many languages):

(20)   PARMOVE (Parallel Movement):

       If α c-commands β at level L$_n$, then α c-commands β at level L$_{n+1}$
       (where α, β are argument NPs).

PARMOVE must be ranked below SCRCON in German and Russian, but above SCRCON in Icelandic. Hence, it is predicted that scrambling that is demanded by SCRCON in Icelandic can take place only if the resulting NP order does not violate the higher-ranked PARMOVE; this is exactly what the data in (19) suggest. This way, the main difference between scrambling in German and Russian, and non-pronominal object shift in Icelandic is accounted for, and we can maintain the generalization that morphological Case arises as a reflex of scrambling throughout.[30]

The analysis just given for Icelandic can possibly be extended to Dutch. Except for a construction that looks like (a certain type of) topic-driven scrambling

---

[29] Like scrambling in German, non-pronominal object shift in Icelandic superficially gives the impression of being optional.

[30] There are other differences between scrambling in German and Russian on the one hand, and non-pronominal object shift in Icelandic on the other. One is that scrambling seems to depend on raising of the main verb in the latter, but not in the former languages; another one might pertain to the A- vs. A-bar status of the operation. I assume that these differences, to the extent that they can be proved real, can be traced back to independently established properties of the languages involved.

(but that is called "focus-scrambling" in Neeleman (1994)), scrambling in Dutch normally does not change the pre-movement order of NPs. Arguably, Dutch is like Icelandic in this respect. However, Dutch is like English or Bulgarian in that it has lost morphological Case. This may well follow from a ranking in which SCRCON dominates STAY, as in all scrambling languages, DEPFUNC dominates CASE, as in Bulgarian, and PARMOVE dominates SCRCON, as in Icelandic (with the possible qualification that TOPIC is the sole vP linearization constraint that dominates PARMOVE). To sum up, rankings like those in (21) may account for the variation observed among the languages that have been discussed so far. (These rankings are not necessarily the only ones that are possible.)

(21)   a. PARMOVE >> SCRCON >> STAY >> CASE >> DEPFUNC   Icelandic
       b. PARMOVE >> SCRCON >> STAY >> DEPFUNC >> CASE   Dutch
       c. SCRCON >> STAY >> PARMOVE >> CASE >> DEPFUNC   German,
                                                              Russian
       d. SCRCON >> STAY >> PARMOVE >> DEPFUNC >> CASE   Bulgarian
       e. STAY >> SCRCON >> PARMOVE >> CASE >> DEPFUNC   English

3.2.4 Proper Names in German

Recall that items can be scrambled in German that do not bear morphological Case. As far as scrambled PPs and CPs are concerned, this is unproblematic: No constraint demands morphological Case here; hence, it is correctly predicted that these items can scramble without receiving morphological Case (presence of morphological Case involves an unmotivated, therefore fatal violation of DEPFUNC). However, as noted above, proper names can also be scrambled even though they typically do not seem to be morphologically Case-marked. In (22ab), a proper name object without morphological Case is scrambled – in (22a), in front of a subject NP with morphological Case, and in (22b), in front of a subject NP that is also a proper name without morphological Case.

(22)   a. dass [$_{vP}$ Martin$_1$ keiner$_2$ t$_1$ gesehen] hat
          that   Martin no-one$_{nom}$ seen   has

       b. dass [$_{vP}$ Martin$_1$ Peter$_2$ t$_1$ gesehen] hat
          that   Martin Peter   seen   has

There is one instance where German proper names do bear morphological Case: The genitive singular form of, e.g. *Martin* is *Martin-s*. The question is whether we can plausibly assume that this implies that proper names can bear morphological Case in the vP domain in German. There is reason to doubt this. Abstract genitive Case is fairly marginal in the vP domain in modern German. An older structural genitive of negation has disappeared completely; a lexical genitive is selected only by very few verbs (like *gedenken* ('rembember')), and will probably also vanish in the not too distant future. Interestingly, it turns out that bare proper names are extremely marginal as objects of verbs that require abstract genitive Case; see (23ab).

(23) a. dass wir dies-es Mann-es gedachten
          that we this$_{gen}$ man$_{gen}$ remembered

      b. ?*dass wir Martin-s gedachten
          that we Martin$_{gen}$ remembered

Whatever the reason for the marginality of (23b), it seems plausible to conclude that the proper names in (22) do in fact not bear morphological Case anymore. This would seem to imply that morphological genitive of proper names in German is confined to non-vP domains. The logic of the approach developed here leads us to conclude that there is a high-ranked constraint (one that outranks CASE) that prohibits morphological Case on proper names in the vP domain in German.[31] Such an approach may eventually shed new light on the emergence and increasing use of semantically empty definite determiners with proper names in German, as in (24) (compare (22b)).

(24) dass [$_{vP}$den Martin$_1$ der Peter$_2$ t$_1$ gesehen] hat
      that   the$_{acc}$ Martin the$_{nom}$ Peter   seen   has

Here, the determiner can reasonably be assumed not to be part of the input; hence, its insertion violates a DEPD constraint while at the same time satisfying CASE (and the above-mentioned constraint against morphological Case on the proper names themselves). At present, there is some (speaker-dependent and context-dependent) variability as to whether (22b) or (24) is preferred. For the time being, we may assume DEPD and CASE to be tied (with strict resolutions of the tie into only one of the two rankings taking place in several varieties), and move on to the next problem – the problem that I take to be the most severe one.

3.2.5 Morphological Case in Situ

Thus far, it follows that under a ranking CASE >> DEPFUNC in a given language, an NP has morphological Case if it scrambles. However, it does not yet follow

---

[31] In fact, the prohibition might be more general. In contrast to other NPs, proper names cannot bear morphological genitive Case that is governed by P; compare ?*wegen Martin-s ('because-of Martingen') with wegen dies-es Mann-es ('because-of thisgen mangen'). Furthermore, it turns out that proper names, unlike other NPs, can hardly show up in a postnominal position either (see Demske (2001)): ?*das Buch Martin-s ('the book Martingen') contrasts with das Buch dies-es Mann-es ('the book thisgen mangen'). Thus, the only remaining option for a proper name bearing morphological genitive that is uncontroversial appears to be the prenominal position, as in Martin-s Buch ('Martingen book'). If this proves tenable, we might in fact conclude that morphological Case is always suppressed with proper names in German, and that the prenominal -s of proper names is actually a different phenomenon with a different source, on a par with the similar construction in English.

that an NP also has morphological Case in this language even if it does not scramble, but stays in situ. The problem is that scrambling is optional in the sense that there may or may not be an input specification for which a SCRCON constraint that outranks STAY then obligatorily induces scrambling. If an NP can fulfill all SCRCON constraints in situ, scrambling is blocked by STAY. CASE is then vacuously satisfied, and the presence of morphological Case is wrongly predicted to fatally violate the lowest DEPFUNC constraint. This disastrous consequence is shown in tableau 8: Output O_1, which does not have any morphological Case, should block output O_4, which has morphological Case on all NPs in situ.

A simple way of reconciling the analysis with the existence of morphological Case in situ would be to assume that scrambling is in fact an obligatory operation, such that *all* NPs must show up in an outer specifier of vP in free word order languages. This kind of approach would be similar to what has been suggested by Frey & Tappe (1991) for German (where all NP arguments are base-generated in VP-adjoined positions). However, there is ample evidence from extraction, binding, and many other phenomena that NPs can show up in situ in scrambling languages (see Müller (1995)). Hence, this solution does not appear to be tenable.

Tableau 8: Morphological Case without scrambling (German, Russian): a wrong
　　　　　 prediction

Input: $NP_{1,[-]}\ NP_{2,[-]},\ ...$	SCR CON	STAY	CASE	DEP FUNC
☞ O_1: $[_{vP}\ NP_1\ v\ [_{VP}\ V\ NP_2]]$				
O_2: $[_{vP}\ NP_{1,nom}\ v\ [_{VP}\ V\ NP_2]]$				*!
O_3: $[_{vP}\ NP_1\ v\ [_{VP}\ V\ NP_{2,acc}]]$				*!
O_4: $[_{vP}\ NP_{1,nom}\ v\ [_{VP}\ V\ NP_{2,acc}]]$				*!*
O_5: $[_{vP}\ NP_2\ NP_1\ v\ [_{VP}\ V\ t_2]]$		*!	*	
O_6: $[_{vP}\ NP_2\ NP_{1,nom}\ v\ [_{VP}\ V\ t_2]]$		*!	*	*
O_7: $[_{vP}\ NP_{2,acc}\ NP_1\ v\ [_{VP}\ V\ t_2]]$		*!		*
O_8: $[_{vP}\ NP_{2,acc}\ NP_{1,nom}\ v\ [_{VP}\ V\ t_2]]$		*!		**
O_9: $[_{vP}\ NP_1\ NP_2\ t_1\ v\ [_{VP}\ V\ t_2]]$		*!*	**	
O_{10}: $[_{vP}\ NP_{1,nom}\ NP_2\ t_1\ v\ [_{VP}\ V\ t_2]]$		*!*	*	*
O_{11}: $[_{vP}\ NP_1\ NP_{2,acc}\ t_1\ v\ [_{VP}\ V\ t_2]]$		*!*	*	*
O_{12}: $[_{vP}\ NP_{1,nom}\ NP_{2,acc}\ t_1\ v\ [_{VP}\ V\ t_2]]$		*!*		**

In view of tableau 8, I would like to suggest that what is needed is a way to impose morphological Case on candidates where the context that forces its presence does not exist, on the basis of the fact that there are minimally different contexts where morphological Case is required. In other words: What is needed is a means to integrate a concept of analogy into optimality-theoretic syntax. As it turns out, optimality theory envisages such a concept in the guise of output/output faithfulness. A particularly restrictive version of output/output faithfulness is sympathy theory, and it is this approach that I want to turn to next.

4. Sympathy Theory

4.1 Sympathy and Phonological Opacity

Sympathy theory is developed in McCarthy (1999) for problems posed by instances of phonological opacity for standard versions of optimality theory that are inherently non-derivational ("harmonic parallelism"). In classical derivational, rule-based phonology, two kinds of rule interactions can be called opaque, viz., counter-bleeding and counter-feeding. Consider counter-bleeding first. Suppose that there are two phonological rules R_α and R_β (both independently motivated). R_α would destroy the context that R_β needs to apply; i.e. R_α would bleed R_β. However, the empirical evidence in a given language L shows that R_α does in fact not bleed R_β, i.e. R_α counter-bleeds R_β. In the derivational approach, this implies that R_β must apply in L before R_α has a chance to apply and remove the former rule's context of application. In contrast, in a counter-feeding relation, R_α creates a context that R_β needs to apply; i.e. R_α would feed R_β. However, the empirical evidence in language L shows that R_α does in fact not feed R_β; i.e. R_α counter-feeds R_β. Again, in the derivational approach, this can be handled by rule ordering: R_β must be ordered before R_α in L so as to ensure that the former rule does not find its context of application. The two instances of opaque rule interaction have in common that it does not seem to suffice to exclusively consider the input and the ultimate output, as one is forced to do in non-derivational approaches. Rather, reference to an intermediate derivational stage seems to be indispensable. This problem can be illustrated on the basis of an instance of counter-bleeding in Tiberian Hebrew (see McCarthy (1999); for other relevant cases, see, e.g. Kenstowicz & Kisseberth (1979)).

Tiberian Hebrew has a rule of epenthesis into final consonant clusters, and a rule of glottal stop (ʔ)-deletion outside onsets. An effect of the first rule is shown in (25a), and an effect of the second rule in (25b). The question of rule interaction arises in contexts where a glottal stop is part of a coda in the underlying representation (i.e. the input). If ʔ-deletion applies first, it bleeds epenthesis. However, as illustrated in (25c), this is not the case in Tiberian Hebrew. Rather, ʔ-deletion and epenthesis are in a counter-bleeding relation. In derivational systems, this implies that epenthesis obligatorily applies before ʔ-deletion.

(25)   a. Epenthesis:
           /melk/ → melex   "king"

        b. ʔ -Deletion:
           /qaraʔ/ → qārā_   "he called"

        c. Interaction – Epenthesis → ʔ-Deletion:
           /dešʔ/ → dešeʔ → deše_   "tender grass"

The problem in non-derivational, parallel optimality theory now is that the counter-bleeding effect cannot easily be simulated. Simplifying a bit, the epenthesis rule can be decomposed into a constraint ranking *COMPLEX >> DEP-V; the ʔ-deletion rule translates into a ranking CODACOND >> MAX-C. Given an input like */dešʔ/*, optimization will not determine *deše* as the grammatical output, but the ill-formed **deš* that deletes ʔ (in violation of MAX-C) but fails to insert *e* (because *COMPLEX can be satisfied without violating DEP-V, given ʔ-deletion). Essentially, the result of optimization is identical to the result one would get under a transparent, non-opaque rule interaction (i.e. bleeding).

McCarthy's (1999) solution to this problem is based on the insight that even though there is no intermediate stage between an input and an (optimal) output in standard optimality theory, all relevant properties of an intermediate stage are represented in a suboptimal output that is part of the same candidate set as the optimal output. Assuming that this failed candidate (called the ✿-candidate) can be determined in a principled way, it can fulfill the same function as an intermediate representation in derivational approaches. By invoking a certain type of output/output faithfulness constraint, its properties can crucially determine properties of the actual (optimal) output; output/output faithfulness of this type is called "sympathy". In the case at hand, the intermediate stage of the derivation in (25c), viz., *dešeʔ* , corresponds to a candidate that competes with (and loses against) the optimal form *deše*, but that is more faithful to the input /dešʔ/ in one respect – it maintains the glottal stop. *deše* blocks *deš* because it is more faithful to the candidate that corresponds to the intermediate step in a derivational approach. In what follows, I give a more detailed illustration of this sympathy account.

Consider first the basic tenets of sympathy theory.

(26)   Sympathy theory:

        a. Some (input/output faithfulness) constraint F_i divides the candidate set
           C into two non-overlapping subsets: C_{+Fi} is the class of candidates that
           respect F_i, and C_{-Fi} is the class of candidates that violate F_i. F_i is called
           a "selector".

        b. The optimal member of C_{+Fi} is called ●$_{Fi}$ This is the ✿-candidate se-
           lected by F_i. ●$_{Fi}$ does not have to be optimal in C.

    c. There are ❀-faithfulness constraints that demand faithfulness (sympathy) to a •Fi candidate, rather than to the input itself. If high-ranked, these ❀-faithfulness constraints can render non-transparent candidates optimal and thereby account for opacity effects.

In the case of counter-bleeding that is currently under discussion, the selector (input/output) faithfulness constraint is MAX-C. Given an input /deš?/, the optimal output among the candidates that satisfy MAX-C is *deše?* (which corresponds to the intermediate stage in a derivational approach). Hence, *deše?* is •Max-C, the ❀-candidate. The relevant sympathy (output/output faithfulness) constraint is MAX-V$_{\text{Max-C}}$: This constraint prohibits the deletion of a vowel of the ❀-candidate determined by MAX-C, viz., *deše?*. Due to the high ranking of MAX-V$_{\text{Max-C}}$, the optimal output in the whole candidate set must preserve the vowels of the ❀-candidate. This excludes the "transparent" output *deš* which, as we have seen, is wrongly classified as optimal in standard optimality-theoretic approaches, and correctly predicts the "opaque" output *deše* to be optimal: *deše* has a better constraint profile than the ❀-candidate *deše?* itself since it avoids the latter's CODA-COND violation (it violates the lower-ranked MAX-C constraint, though). The competition just sketched is illustrated in tableau 9, where O_4 is the ❀-candidate, O_2 is the wrong winner under an approach that does without sympathy (which I indicate here by ☞), O_1 is optimal under the sympathy approach, and O_3 and O_5 are other ill-formed candidates that are classified as suboptimal under both approaches.[32]

On a more general note, sympathy theory provides a means to impose properties of a suboptimal output O_i on the optimal output O_j. As noted above, this is exactly what is needed to solve the problem in tableau 8. On this basis, let us return the question of how morphological Case can be brought about without actual scrambling in scrambling languages.

Tableau 9: Counter-bleeding and sympathy in Tiberian Hebrew in McCarthy (1999)

Input: /deš?/	❀MAX-V$_{\text{MAX-C}}$	*COMPLEX	ANCHOR	CODACOND	MAX-C	DEP-V
☞ O_1: deš<u>e</u>					*	*
☞ O_2: deš	*!				*	
O_3: deš?<u>e</u>			*!			*
❀ O_4: deš<u>e</u>?				*!		*
O_5: deš?	*!	*		*		

[32] Note that ❀O4 would more adequately be represented as ❀Max-CO4; there may be other sympathy constraints which require faithfulness to other ❀-candidates. The simplification here is unproblematic as long as we are only concerned with one sympathy constraint. Also note that there are several other rankings that would yield the desired outcome; the ranking in tableau 9 is just one possibility.

4.2 Sympathy, Scrambling, and Morphological Case

Vowel epenthesis in Tiberian Hebrew and morphological Case in German and Russian are similar in that both phenomena are "opaque": Faithfulness to the input does not seem to suffice, and faithfulness to a failed competitor, the sympathy candidate, is called for. However, there is also a basic conceptual difference between the two cases: In the syntactic case, the sympathy candidate does not encode an *earlier* stage in a derivation of an optimal candidate, but a *later* stage that is in fact never reached by the optimal candidate: Morphological Case is triggered in a candidate that has scrambling, and this property is carried over via sympathy to an optimal candidate which has no scrambling. This main difference is also responsible for another difference, one that concerns the selector: Given that the optimal candidate is in fact "closer" to the input than the sympathy candidate (because scrambling does not take place in the former), it is clear that the selector cannot be an input/output faithfulness constraint in the case at hand; rather, it must be a markedness constraint that favours the candidate with scrambling. It is not clear whether these differences should be viewed as problematic. Whereas McCarthy's (1999) original motivation is to account for counter-bleeding and counter-feeding in phonology, and ✿-candidates therefore typically encode intermediate stages of derivations, the sympathy approach as such is completely neutral as to the nature of ✿-candidates. Indeed, sympathy analyses have been developed for other kinds of phonological phenomena, unrelated to opacity, and in line with this, it has been argued that markedness constraints can also act as selectors, for both conceptual and empirical reasons (see Ito & Mester (1997)). Thus, I take the hypothesis that markedness constraints can be selectors to be tenable.[33]

Then, it must be clarified what the sympathy and selector constraints are in the case at hand. I would like to suggest that (27a) is the relevant sympathy constraint, and, consequently, that (27b) acts as the selector.

(27)   a. ✿MAXCASE$_{EP}$:
            Morphological Case of • $_{EdgePhase}$ must be preserved.

        b. EDGEPHASE:
            An NP must be at the edge of a phase.

---

[33] Note also that syntax differs from phonology in being an information-preserving system; devices like traces, selectional features and so forth ensure that virtually no input information gets lost in syntactic outputs. Consequently, it is extremely difficult to come up with convincing instances of syntactic counter-bleeding or counter-feeding that are not straightforwardly accountable for in non-derivational approaches, without resort to a concept like sympathy. Therefore, if sympathy is to play a role at all in syntax (as, arguably, it should do, for reasons of symmetry alone), it seems that it must involve faithfulness to suboptimal outputs that do not correspond to intermediate derivational stages, and that are not selected on the basis of their greater similarity to the input.

Chomsky (2000, 2001) observes that vP and CP are the two "propositional" constituents of clauses; he calls these special derivational units "phases".[34] The edges of phases are the prominent positions for NPs in a clause.[35] Of course, this constraint is often violated in well-formed outputs. From this we can conclude that EDGEPHASE is typically low-ranked (a ranking below SCRCON would be predicted if the latter is derived from the former by local conjunction, as speculated in the last footnote).

EDGEPHASE divides the candidate set into two classes: In one are the candidates that have all NPs in an edge position; in the other one are the candidates that have at least one NP in situ. Among the vP candidates that have all NPs at the edge of vP, the optimal one will have morphological Case if the ranking is CASE >> DEPFUNC. The sympathy constraint ❀MAXCASE$_{EP}$'s task now is to require faithfulness of candidates with NPs in situ to the morphological Case specification of this ❀-candidate with all NPs at the edge of vP. This follows if ❀MAXCASE$_{EP}$ is ranked higher than DEPFUNC. As shown in tableau 10, the problem encountered in tableau 8 is now solved: O_4 (with morphological Case on all NPs even though they are in situ) now blocks O_1 (without morphological Case on the NPs in situ) because the former candidate's DEPFUNC violations are required to avoid the latter candidate's fatal ❀MAXCASE$_{EP}$ violation. O_{12} is the ❀-candidate that imposes morphological Case on the optimal candidate. O_{12} itself is optimal within the subset of candidates that satisfy EDGEPHASE, but suboptimal in the whole candidate set (due to the fact that, by assumption, there is no trigger for scrambling, and a STAY violation is therefore fatal).

[34] Chomsky also assumes that the edge of vP qualifies as an obligatory intermediate landing site for further movement, like A-bar movement into the next phase and pronominal object shift in the Scandinavian languages. If we want to make this assumption in the present approach, it seems that we have to ensure that Case only applies to those NPs at the edge of vP that stay in this position throughout the derivation. Otherwise, Mainland Scandinavian pronominal object shift and English wh-movement could also trigger morphological Case marking. Morphological Case on a topicalized object NP in German would then arise in the same way as on an NP in situ. Restricting Case to surface positions of NPs would be directly compatible with a global approach to optimization, but would demand certain additional assumptions under a local approach (see footnote 9): At the vP optimization stage, one has to know whether an NP in vP will move further in the derivation or stay in this position. That said, it seems to me that assuming the edge of vP to be an obligatory escape hatch for further movement is by no means unproblematic (in contrast to what holds for CPs); see Heck & Müller (2000) for an argument against this view.

[35] Arguably, the ScrCon constraints can be derived from EdgePhase on the basis of local constraint conjunction (see Legendre, Smolensky & Wilson (1998)). The success of such an enterprise depends on a number of assumptions concerning, i.a. the precise nature of ScrCon constraints like those in (7), and the issue of local vs. global optimization – assumptions that I wish to leave open here (see section 2.2 above).

Tableau 10: Morphological Case without scrambling (German, Russian): sympathy

Input: $NP_{1[-]}$ $NP_{2[-]}$, ...	SCR CON	STAY	CASE	⊛MAX CASE$_{EP}$	DEP FUNC	EP
☞ O_1: $[_{vP}$ NP_1 v $[_{vP}$ V $NP_2]]$				*!*		**
O_2: $[_{vP}$ $NP_{1,nom}$ v $[_{vP}$ V $NP_2]]$				*!	*	**
O_3: $[_{vP}$ NP_1 v $[_{vP}$ V $NP_{2,acc}]]$				*!	*	**
☞ O_4: $[_{vP}$ $NP_{1,nom}$ v $[_{vP}$ V $NP_{2,acc}]]$					**	**
O_5: $[_{vP}$ NP_2 NP_1 v $[_{vP}$ V $t_2]]$		*!	*	**		*
O_6: $[_{vP}$ NP_2 $NP_{1,nom}$ v $[_{vP}$ V $t_2]]$		*!	*	*	*	*
O_7: $[_{vP}$ $NP_{2,acc}$ NP_1 v $[_{vP}$ V $t_2]]$		*!		*	*	*
O_8: $[_{vP}$ $NP_{2,acc}$ $NP_{1,nom}$ v $[_{vP}$ V $t_2]]$		*!			**	*
O_9: $[_{vP}$ NP_1 NP_2 t_1 v $[_{vP}$ V $t_2]]$		*!*	**	**		
O_{10}: $[_{vP}$ $NP_{1,nom}$ NP_2 t_1 v $[_{vP}$ V $t_2]]$		*!*	*	*	*	
O_{11}: $[_{vP}$ NP_1 $NP_{2,acc}$ t_1 v $[_{vP}$ V $t_2]]$		*!*	*	*	*	
⊛ O_{12}: $[_{vP}$ $NP_{1,nom}$ $NP_{2,acc}$ t_1 v $[_{vP}$ V $t_2]]$		*!*			**	

This analysis correctly predicts that all NPs bear morphological Case in scrambling languages like German, Russian, and Icelandic.[36] It also accounts for the fact that no NP bears morphological Case in scrambling languages like Bulgarian and Dutch: A ranking DEPFUNC >> CASE invariably leads to ⊛-candidates without morphological Case in these languages, and even with a high ranking of ⊛MAXCASE$_{EP}$, faithfulness to the morphological Case specification of these candidates then requires the absence of morphological Case on optimal candidates with NPs in situ.[37] However, a problem arises with non-scrambling languages like English. Assuming hypothesis (1b), we want to derive that a non-

[36] Unless, that is, independent morpho-phonological constraints force the absence of a Case marker for all NP-internal items, as in German constructions involving bare proper names, or bare (non-dative) plurals; see Müller (2001b). In those contexts, Case must be violated with an NP in Specv; consequently, an NP in situ will show no Case marker either.

[37] As noted by Gisbert Fanselow (p.c.), if we were to assume in addition that a sympathy constraint ⊛MaxCaseStay exists, where Stay acts as a selector, languages of the Bulgarian or Dutch type could also be accounted for in terms of sympathy: Given a high ranking of ⊛MaxCaseStay, a candidate with NP scrambling will not exhibit morphological Case because it must be faithful to the candidate with NP-in situ, which lacks a Case marker under any ranking of Case and DepFunc. Obviously, though, postulating such an additional ⊛-constraint is not necessary in the present approach, the ranking DepFunc >> Case being sufficient to account for languages that have scrambling but no morphological Case. More generally, I take it that a proliferation of sympathy constraints should be avoided if possible – ideally, the postulation of a ⊛-constraint should be motivated in some way. In line with this, I have argued above that Edge Phase is special in so far as it forces an NP into a prominent NP position in a clause, viz., the edge of a phase, a position whose relevance for NPs is independently established.

scrambling language can never have morphological Case on NPs, irrespective of the ranking of CASE and DEPFUNC. But this does not follow anymore. Suppose that an English-type language (without scrambling, due to STAY >> SCRCON) has a ranking CASE >> ⊛MAXCASE$_{EP}$ >>DEPFUNC. As shown in tableau 11, this would wrongly predict Case morphology on NPs, despite the ranking STAY >> SCRCON. The reason is that even though a scrambling output like O_{12} has no chance to be optimal in such a language, it is clearly the most harmonic one among the candidates that satisfy EP; hence, it is the ⊛-candidate. Sympathy will then classify O_4 instead of O_1 as the optimal candidate. Thus, we would end up with an English-type language where morphological Case shows up on NPs in situ despite a lack of scrambling.[38]

As a key to a solution of this problem, note that there is an important difference between O_{12} in tableau 10 and O_{12} in tableau 11: In a language with a ranking SCRCON >> STAY, O_{12} can itself be an output that is optimal (grammatical); in a language with a ranking STAY >> SCRCON, it cannot be. Thus, we are led to the conclusion that ⊛-candidates must themselves be optimal outputs in syntax.[39] This would contrast with the situation in phonology, where ⊛-candidates do not have to be optimal candidates.[40]

As it stands, the status of O_{12} as an optimal output in a scrambling language cannot be determined on the basis of tableau 10, where O_{12} is suboptimal, but only on the basis of another competition with appropriate input specifications that trigger scrambling (see tableau 5); thus, the procedure is translocal (or transderivational) in a way that assimilates the analysis to other, non-sympathetic instances of output/output faithfulness (see Benua (1997)). This consequence results from the fact that I have so far presupposed a Büring/Choi type approach to scrambling according to which distinct semantic specifications concerning features like [±top] and [±foc] give rise to different inputs, and to different candidate sets. This view is abandoned in Müller (1999). In this latter approach, a liberal (disjunctive) notion of tie is adopted (for unrelated reasons having to do with certain undergeneration problems alluded to above) that ensures that O_4, O_8, and O_{12} can all be optimal within one and the same candidate set. In such an approach, the ⊛-candidate O_{12} can be optimal within the same candidate set in which O_4 and O_8 are optimal, and the latter two outputs derive their morphological Case from O_{12} via the sympathy constraint ⊛MAXCASE$_{EP}$.

---

[38] Whether or not there is a [scr] specification in the input is irrelevant, given Stay >> ScrCon. Tableau 11 presupposes that there is no trigger for scrambling in the input, but given Stay >> ScrCon, the outcome would be identical if there were an input specification that demands scrambling (see tableau 7): O_4 rather than O_1 would be predicted to be·optimal.

[39] This is vaguely reminiscent of a mechanism in Wilson's (2001) system of bidirectional optimization, where only those outputs are subjected to a given expressive optimization procedure that are optimal with respect to some interpretive optimization procedure (not necessarily the one that leads to the expressive optimization procedure at hand).

[40] Indeed, ⊛-candidates are usually suboptimal in the phonological applications that McCarthy (1999) discusses. However, it is worth noting that there is nothing that would preclude optimality of ⊛-candidates; and McCarthy explicitly argues for this in the case of nasal harmony in Sea Dayak (based on Kenstowicz & Kisseberth (1979)).

Consequently, translocality can be avoided in the determination of ✿-candidates.[41]

Tableau 11: Morphological Case without scrambling options: a wrong prediction

Input: $NP_{1\,[-]}\ NP_{2\,[-]},\ \ldots$	STAY	SCR CON	CASE	✿ MAX CASE$_{EP}$	DEP FUNC	EP
☞ O_1: $[_{vP}\ NP_1\ v\ [_{VP}\ V\ NP_2]]$				*!*		**
O_2: $[_{vP}\ NP_{1,nom}\ v\ [_{VP}\ V\ NP_2]]$				*!	*	**
O_3: $[_{vP}\ NP_1\ v\ [_{VP}\ V\ NP_{2,acc}]]$				*!	*	**
☞ O_4: $[_{vP}\ NP_{1,nom}\ v\ [_{VP}\ V\ NP_{2,acc}]]$					**	**
O_5: $[_{vP}\ NP_2\ NP_1\ v\ [_{VP}\ V\ t_2]]$	*!		*	**		*
O_6: $[_{vP}\ NP_2\ NP_{1,nom}\ v\ [_{VP}\ V\ t_2]]$	*!		*	*	*	*
O_7: $[_{vP}\ NP_{2,acc}\ NP_1\ v\ [_{VP}\ V\ t_2]]$	*!			*	*	*
O_8: $[_{vP}\ NP_{2,acc}\ NP_{1,nom}\ v\ [_{VP}\ V\ t_2]]$	*!				**	*
O_9: $[_{vP}\ NP_1\ NP_2\ t_1\ v\ [_{VP}\ V\ t_2]]$	*!*		**	**		
O_{10}: $[_{vP}\ NP_{1,nom}\ NP_2\ t_1\ v\ [_{VP}\ V\ t_2]]$	*!*		*	*	*	
O_{11}: $[_{vP}\ NP_1\ NP_{2,acc}\ t_1\ v\ [_{VP}\ V\ t_2]]$	*!*		*	*	*	
✿ O_{12}: $[_{vP}\ NP_{1,nom}\ NP_{2,acc}\ t_1\ v\ [_{VP}\ V\ t_2]]$	*!*				**	

A further potential problem involves cases where it looks as though scrambling is illegitimate in a language like German or Russian. Suppose that we have evidence that NP α cannot scramble in the syntactic context β. Then, an output with α-scrambling can never be optimal in β, and α in situ should not bear morphological Case, as argued for a non-scrambling language like English. In such a situation, additional assumptions would be called for that impose further restrictions on what is a suitable ✿-candidate. However, it seems to me that evidence that unambiguously exemplifies this situation is not as straightforwardly available as one might think. For instance, many of the apparent restrictions on NP

[41] Still, one may ask whether the present approach in terms of sympathy could not be replaced by some other output/output faithfulness approach that does without this concept. It is clear what an alternative output/output faithfulness approach would have to ensure: An optimal output candidate Oi has to be identified that an in-situ candidate Oj (like O₄ in tableau 10) must be faithful to with respect to morphological Case. However, standard identification procedures as they are known from non-sympathetic output/output faithfulness approaches cannot successfully pick out Oi: Oi is not inherently privileged vis-à-vis Oj (as in base/reduplicant and base/truncation relations), and notions like paradigm uniformity do not help either because there are no paradigms in syntax (indeed, given the analysis in Müller (2001b), paradigms as independent objects do not even exist in the domain of Case morphology). The problem is that it is not an intrinsic property of Oi that turns it into a candidate that Oj must be faithful to; rather, it is the property of being optimal among the candidates that have all NPs in scrambling positions. Thus, the identification procedure for Oi is best done by a constraint that forces NPs to be in scrambling positions, and this is exactly what the sympathy approach does.

scrambling in German can be shown to be either spurious, or intimately related to the idea that scrambling must permute the basic order of NPs – an idea that I do not adopt here on independent grounds, see above. Thus, all the ✿-candidates discussed here have all NPs in scrambling positions, which re-establishes (or, at least, may re-establish) the base order.

Consider, as an example, the interaction of weak crossover and scrambling in German. As noted by, e.g. Lee & Santorini (1994), scrambling of a direct object NP across an indirect object NP as in (28b) is ill formed, due to the WEAK CROSSOVER CONSTRAINT (WCC) that requires a syntactic A-binder for a pronoun that is interpreted as a variable; compare (28a). Hence, if (28b) is the ✿-candidate, its suboptimality will pose a problem because it is unclear how (28a) can then derive morphological Case from it (given that this is what makes morphological Case impossible in English). However, (28b) cannot be the ✿-candidate in the first place, because it still violates EDGEPHASE. Rather, the ✿-candidate is (28c), where all NPs have undergone scrambling, and reassembled in an order that respects the WCC.

(28) a. dass jede   Professorin$_1$ [$_{NP}$jedem   Studenten]$_2$ [$_{NP}$ seine$_2$
         that every$_{nom}$ professor   every$_{dat}$ student$_{dat}$ his$_{acc}$
         Dissertation]$_3$ gegeben hat
         dissertation   given   has

      b. ?*dass jede   Professorin$_1$ [$_{NP}$seine$_2$ Dissertation]$_3$ [$_{NP}$ jedem
         that   every$_{nom}$ professor   his$_{acc}$ dissertation   every$_{dat}$
         Studenten] t_3 gegeben hat
         student$_{dat}$ given   has

      c. dass jede   Professorin$_1$ [$_{NP}$jedem Studenten]$_2$ [$_{NP}$ seine$_2$
         that every$_{nom}$ professor   every$_{dat}$student$_{dat}$ his$_{acc}$
         Dissertation]$_3$ t_1 t_2 t_3 gegeben   hat
         dissertation   given   has

Assuming that most of the apparent counter-evidence can be accounted for in this way, at least as long as we restrict ourselves to NP arguments of V, we may tentatively conclude that ✿-candidates must be optimal in syntax (perhaps, more generally, in domains where opacity is not involved), with no further qualification involved.

4.3 Supporting Evidence

There is no inherent reason why a sympathy constraint like ✿MAXCASE$_{EP}$ should be ranked high, as it must be in German and Russian. In principle, it can also be ranked below DEPFUNC. Other things being equal, this would result in a language that has morphological Case only if scrambling takes place, as predicted under the simpler approach without sympathy developed in section 3.

Pieces of empirical evidence that are intriguing in this context are instances of what is sometimes analyzed as Case marker drop in languages like Japanese, Korean, and Turkish. Interestingly, Case marker drop usually takes place in positions close to (usually, adjacent to) V. This might suggest a reanalysis along the lines of the present approach.

Consider Japanese first. Here, structural Case markers are often left out in casual speech, but only in positions close to the verb; see e.g. the examples involving a *wh*-object with and without morphological Case in (29ab), which are taken from Hoshi (1999).

(29)   a. John-ga   nani(-o)$_1$ tabeta   no?
           John$_{nom}$ what$_{(acc)}$ ate   Q

        b. Nani*(-o)$_1$ John-ga t$_1$ tabeta   no?
           what$_{(acc)}$ John$_{nom}$ ate   Q

In the present approach, these data can be analyzed as follows. Suppose that Japanese has the rankings SCRCON >> STAY and CASE >> DEPFUNC, just like German and Russian, but that ⊛MAXCASE$_{EP}$ and DEPFUNC are tied; i.e. the rankings ⊛MAXCASE$_{EP}$ >> DEPFUNC and DEPFUNC >> ⊛MAXCASE$_{EP}$ are both possible. Then, it is predicted that scrambling will always give rise to morphological Case, whereas an NP in situ must bear morphological Case under the ranking ⊛MAXCASE$_{EP}$ >> DEPFUNC, and remains without morphological Case (i.e. exhibits "Case marker drop") under the reverse ranking DEPFUNC >> ⊛MAXCASE$_{EP}$. This correctly accounts for the effect with direct object *wh*-phrases in (29). The effect here can thus be viewed as independent support for the analysis, even though eventually, more needs to be said about other cases – e.g. subject NPs; NPs with oblique Case, which must always be morphologically visible in Japanese; and non-*wh*-phrases.[42]

As noted by Shin-Sook Kim (p.c.), a similar effect shows up in Korean. Data that are similar to those in (29) in Japanese are given in (30). A direct *wh*-object may or may not bear morphological Case in situ; but it must bear morphological Case under scrambling.

(30)   a. Suna-ka   nuku(-lûl)$_1$ manna-ss-ni?
           Suna$_{nom}$ who$_{(acc)}$ meet-Past-Q

        b. Nuku?*(-lûl)$_1$ Suna-ka   t$_1$ manna-ss-ni?
           who$_{(acc)}$ Suna$_{nom}$ meet-Past-Q

The examples in (31) illustrate that, in contrast to what seems to be the case in Japanese, the same effect holds for non-*wh*-objects.

---

[42] For non-*wh*-phrases, Hoshi (1999) assumes that they can be fronted without an overt Case marker because they can be reanalyzed as topics, with an empty topic marker. Such an option is not available for *wh*-phrases because *wh*-phrases are incompatible with a topic interpretation in Japanese.

(31) a. Suna-to   kû   chaek(-ûl)₁ ilk-ess-ta
         Suna-also   that   book$_{(acc)}$ read-Past-Dec

      b. Kû   chaek?*(-ûl)₁   Suna-to   t₁   ilk-ess-ta
         that book$_{(acc)}$ Suna-also   read-Past-Dec

(32abc) show that a scrambled direct object obligatorily bears morphological Case, no matter whether the final landing site is clause-internal or clause-initial:

(32) a. Suna-ka   Minsu-eke   kû   chaek(-ûl)₁   chu-ess-ta
         Suna$_{nom}$ Minsu$_{dat}$ that   book$_{(acc)}$ give-Past-Dec

      b. Suna-ka   kû   chaek?*(-ûl)₁   Minsu-eke   t₁   chu-ess-ta
         Suna$_{nom}$ that   book$_{(acc)}$ Minsu$_{dat}$ give-Past-Dec

      c. Kû   chaek?*(-ûl)₁   Suna-ka   Minsu-eke   t₁   chu-ess-ta
         that book$_{(acc)}$ Suna$_{nom}$ Minsu$_{dat}$ give-Past-Dec

The Korean data lend themselves to the same type of analysis as suggested for Japanese, with roughly the same qualifications concerning, in particular, a strict visibility requirement for oblique Case.

As a final piece of evidence that bears on the present approach, I will briefly consider the distribution of non-specific NP arguments in Turkish (see Kornfilt (2000)). In general, non-specific NPs must show up close to the verb, and they cannot bear the morphological Case marker that one would normally expect them to bear, given their abstract Case. Thus, a non-specific direct object cannot be scrambled, and it must remain without morphological Case, as in (33):

(33) Hasan   çocuğ-un-a   her   akşam   bir   hikâye   oku-r
      Hasan   child$_{3.sg-dat}$ each   evening   a   story   read$_{aor}$

What is interesting here is that with non-specific NPs, the absence of morphological Case is not optional, but in fact obligatory. This, and the fact that non-specific NPs are known not to be able to scramble, may plausibly be taken to suggest that scrambling in Turkish is basically amenable to the analysis given for German and Russian, but that in those cases where scrambling of an NP α is impossible (here: due to a high-ranked constraint against a non-specific interpretation at the edge of vP), there is indeed no suitable ⊛-candidate that may impose morphological Case on the optimal output with α in situ, as speculated above. In other words: The view that ⊛-candidates must themselves be optimal in syntax is strengthened.

5   Conclusion

Let me emphasize again that what precedes is the elaboration of one of the two hypotheses ((1b) and (1c)) that look tenable in light of the cross-linguistic evidence involving scrambling and morphological Case that was presented in section 2. My basic assumption was that the more conservative hypothesis (1c) (according to which there is no synchronically relevant correlation between morphological Case and scrambling) may ultimately be more likely to prove correct, but that the more radical hypothesis (1b) (according to which morphological Case presupposes scrambling) is potentially more interesting, and hence worth pursuing. From a more general point of view, this hypothesis is compatible with the general idea that syntax may directly determine morphology, which has already fruitfully been employed in recent work in optimality-theoretic syntax.

I have argued that there is one fundamental problem with an approach that relies on (1b): In free word order languages like German or Russian, a given clause may or may not involve scrambling of its NPs; but all NPs bear morphological Case, even if they show up in situ. It seems to me that this problem would be quite severe in standard approaches to syntax; but it can be solved in an optimality-theoretic approach that is enhanced by sympathy theory. Such an approach raises a number of problems, only some of which I have been able to address here. Whether it can be maintained in the light of further evidence remains to be seen.[43]

---

[43] An obvious problem that I have not said anything about yet concerns morphological Case outside the domain of verbs: in PPs, NPs, and APs. With respect to some cases, it is worth noting that the analysis here leaves open the possibility that morphological Case may also be triggered by other constraints (than Case or ⊛MaxCaseEP), in other domains. This is likely to hold for prenominal genitive Case in German and English, and for prepositive Case in Russian, which cannot plausibly be assumed to be related to scrambling to Specv (prepositive Case occurs only within PPs, and Russian does not generally permit P stranding by which a PP-internal NP argument might show up at the edge of vP). In addition, some other instances of morphological Case in PPs, NPs, and (attributive) APs may be argued to involve other cases of output/output faithfulness, based on the properties of vP.

References

Aissen, Judith (2000): *Differential Object Marking: Iconicity vs. Economy*. Ms, University of California, Santa Cruz.

Alexiadou, Artemis & Fanselow, Gisbert (2001): *On the Correlation between Morphology and Syntax: The Case of V-to-I*. Ms, Universität Potsdam.

Baker, Mark (1996): *The Polysynthesis Parameter*. Oxford: Oxford University Press.

Benua, Laura (1997): *Transderivational Identity: Phonological Relations Between Words*. PhD dissertation, University of Massachusetts, Amherst.

Bierwisch, Manfred (1967): Syntactic Features in Morphology: General Problems of So-Called Pronominal Inflection in German. In: *To Honour Roman Jakobson*. The Hague/Paris: Mouton. 239–270.

Blevins, James (1995): Syncretism and Paradigmatic Opposition. *Linguistics and Philosophy* 18. 113–152.

Bošković, Željko, & Takahashi, Daiko (1998): Scrambling and Last Resort. *Linguistic Inquiry* 29. 347–366.

Büring, Daniel (1997): *Towards an OT Account of German Mittelfeld Word Order*. Ms, Universität Köln.

Büring, Daniel (2001): Let's Phrase It! In: Müller, Gereon & Sternefeld, Wolfgang, eds. (2001): *Competition in Syntax*. Berlin: Mouton de Gruyter. 69–105.

Choi, Hye-Won (1996): *Optimizing Structure in Context: Scrambling and Information Structure*. PhD dissertation, Stanford University.

Choi, Hye-Won (1999): *Optimizing Structure in Context: Scrambling and Information Structure*. Stanford: CSLI Publications.

Chomsky, Noam (2000): Minimalist Inquiries: The Framework. In: Martin, Roger, Michaels, David & Uriagereka, Juan, eds. (2000): *Step by Step*. Cambridge, MA: MIT Press. 89–155.

Chomsky, Noam (2001): Derivation by Phase. In: Kenstowicz, Michael, ed. (2001): *Ken Hale. A Life in Language*. Cambridge, MA: MIT Press. 1–52.

Collins, Chris & Thráinsson, Höskuldur (1996): VP-Internal Structure and Object Shift in Icelandic. *Linguistic Inquiry* 27. 391–444.

Comrie, Bernard (1981): *Language Universals and Linguistic Typology*. Oxford: Blackwell.

Costa, João (2001): The Emergence of Unmarked Word Order. In: Grimshaw, Jane, Legendre, Géraldine & Vikner, Sten, eds. (2001): *Optimality Theoretic Syntax*. Cambridge, MA: MIT Press. 171–203.

Demske, Ulrike (2001): *Merkmale und Relationen: Diachrone Studien zur Nominalphrase des Deutschen*. Berlin: Mouton de Gruyter.

Fanselow, Gisbert (1992): *Deplazierte Argumente*. Ms, Universität Stuttgart.

Fanselow, Gisbert (1995): *A Minimalist Approach to Free Constituent Order*. Ms, Universität Potsdam.

Fanselow, Gisbert (1999): *Optimal Exceptions*. Ms, Universität Potsdam.

Fanselow, Gisbert (2001): Features, Theta-Roles, and Free Constituent Order. *Linguistic Inquiry* 32. 405–436.

Fanselow, Gisbert & Ćavar, Damir (2001): Remarks on the Economy of Pronunciation. In: Müller, Gereon & Sternefeld, Wolfgang, eds. (2001): *Competition in Syntax*. Berlin: Mouton de Gruyter. 107–150.

Frey, Werner & Tappe, Thilo (1991): *Zur Interpretation der X-bar-Theorie und zur Syntax des Mittelfeldes. Grundlagen eines GB-Fragmentes*. Ms, Universität Stuttgart.

Georgieva, Elena (1974): *Slovored na Prostoto Izrečenie v Bylgarskija Knižoven Ezik*. Sofia: BAN.

Gouskova, Maria (2001): *Split Scrambling: Barriers as Violable Constraints*. Ms, University of Massachusetts, Amherst. [To appear in: *Proceedings of WCCFL 20*.] (also at: ROA-478–1101; http://roa.rutgers.edu)

Grimshaw, Jane (1997): Projection, Heads, and Optimality. *Linguistic Inquiry* 28. 373–422.

Grimshaw, Jane (1999): *Heads and Clauses*. Ms, Rutgers University, New Brunswick, New Jersey.

Grimshaw, Jane & Samek-Lodovici, Vieri (1998): Optimal Subjects and Subject Universals. In: Barbosa, Pilar, et al., eds. (1998): *Is the Best Good Enough?* Cambridge, MA: MIT Press & MITWPL. 193–219.

Haider, Hubert (1988): Θ-Tracking Systems – Evidence from German. In: Marácz, Laszlo & Muysken, Pieter, eds. (1988): *Configurationality*. Dordrecht: Foris. 185–206.

Haider, Hubert (2000): Branching and Discharge. In: Coopmans, Peter, Everaert, Martin & Grimshaw, Jane, eds. (2000): *Lexical Specification and Insertion*. Amsterdam: Benjamins.

Harley, Heidi & Noyer, Rolf (1999): Distributed Morphology. *GLOT International* 4:4. 3–9.

Haspelmath, Martin (2000): Optimality and Diachronic Adaptation. *Zeitschrift für Sprachwissenschaft* 18 (1999). 180–205.

Heck, Fabian (2000): Tiefenoptimierung: Deutsche Wortstellung als wettbewerbsgesteuerte Basisgenerierung. *Linguistische Berichte* 184. 441–468.

Heck, Fabian & Müller, Gereon (2000): *Repair-driven Movement and the Local Optimization of Derivations*. Ms, Universität Stuttgart & IDS Mannheim.

Hoberg, Ursula (1981): *Die Wortstellung in der geschriebenen deutschen Gegenwartssprache*. München: Hueber.

Hoberg, Ursula (1997): Die Linearstruktur des Satzes. In: Zifonun, Gisela et al., eds. (1997): *Grammatik der deutschen Sprache*. Berlin: Mouton de Gruyter. 1495–1680.

Hoshi, Hidehito (1999): The Bare NP-Movement Hypothesis and „Scrambling". *UCI Working Papers in Linguistics* 5. 77–101.

Isačenko, Alexander (1975): *Die russische Sprache der Gegenwart. Formenlehre*. München: Hueber.

Ito, Junko & Mester, Armin (1997): Sympathy Theory and German Truncations. *University of Maryland Working Papers in Linguistics* 5.

Jacobs, Joachim (1988): Probleme der freien Wortstellung im Deutschen. *Sprache und Pragmatik* 5. 8–37.

Junghanns, Uwe & Zybatow, Gerhild (1997): Syntax and Information Structure of Russian Clauses. In: Browne, E. W., et al., eds. (1997): *Annual Workshop on Formal Approaches to Slavic Linguistics. The Cornell Meeting 1995*. AnnArbor: Michigan Slavic Publications. 289–319.

Kemenade, Ans van (1987): *Syntactic Case and Morphological Case in the History of English*. Dordrecht: Foris.

Kenstowicz, Michael & Kisseberth, Charles (1979): *Generative Phonology*. San Diego: Academic Press.

King, Tracy (1995): *Configuring Topic and Focus in Russian*. Stanford: CSLI Publications.

Kiparsky, Paul (1999): *Analogy and OT: Morphological Change as Emergence of the Unmarked*. Handout, 21. Jahrestagung der DGfS, Konstanz.

Kornfilt, Jaklin (2000): *Turkish*. Routledge: London & New York.

Krylova, O. A. & Chavronina, S. A. (1976): *Porjadok Slov v Russkom Jazyke*. Moskva: Russkij Jazyk.

Lee, Young-Suk & Beatrice Santorini (1994): Towards Resolving Webelhuth's Paradox: Evidence from German and Korean. In: Norbert Corver & Henk van Riemsdijk, eds. (1994): *Studies on Scrambling*. Berlin: Mouton de Gruyter. 257–300.

Lee, Hanjung (1999): *The Emergence of the Unmarked Order*. Ms, Stanford University. (also at: ROA-323-0699; http://roa.rutgers.edu)

Legendre, Géraldine (1998): *Why French Stylistic Inversion is Optimal*. Ms, Johns Hopkins University.

Legendre, Géraldine, Paul Smolensky & Colin Wilson (1998): When is Less More? Faithfulness and Minimal Links in Wh-Chains. In: Barbosa, Pilar, et al., eds. (1998): *Is the Best Good Enough?* Cambridge, MA: MIT Press & MITWPL. 249–289.

Lenerz, Jürgen (1977): *Zur Abfolge nominaler Satzglieder im Deutschen.* Tübingen: Stauffenburg.

McCarthy, John (1999): Sympathy and Phonological Opacity. *Phonology* 16:3.

Molxova, Zana (1970): *Xarakter i Upotreba na Člena v Bylgarskija i Anglijskija Ezik.* Sofia: NI.

Müller, Gereon (1995): *A-bar Syntax.* Berlin: Mouton/de Gruyter.

Müller, Gereon (1999): Optimality, Markedness, and Word Order in German. *Linguistics* 37. 777–818.

Müller, Gereon (2000): *Elemente der optimalitätstheoretischen Syntax.* Tübingen: Stauffenburg Verlag.

Müller, Gereon (2001a): Order Preservation, Parallel Movement, and the Emergence of the Unmarked. In: Legendre, Géraldine, Grimshaw, Jane & Vikner, Sten, eds. (2001): *Optimality Theoretic Syntax.* Cambridge, MA: MIT Press. 279–313.

Müller, Gereon (2001b): *Remarks on Nominal Inflection in German.* Ms, IDS Mannheim.

Müller, Gereon & Sternefeld, Wolfgang (1993): Improper Movement and Unambiguous Binding. *Linguistic Inquiry* 24. 461–507.

Müller, Gereon & Sternefeld, Wolfgang (1994): Scrambling as A-bar Movement. In: Corver, Norbert & Riemsdijk, Henk van, eds. (1994): *Studies on Scrambling.* Berlin: Mouton de Gruyter. 331–385.

Neeleman, Ad (1994): Scrambling as a D-structure Phenomenon. In: Corver, Norbert & Riemsdijk, Henk van, eds. (1994): *Studies on Scrambling.* Berlin: Mouton de Gruyter. 387–429.

Primus, Beatrice (1994): Grammatik und Performanz: Faktoren der Wortstellungsvariation im Mittelfeld. *Sprache und Pragmatik* 32. 39–86.

Reis, Marga (1986): *Die Stellung der Verbargumente im Deutschen. Stilübungen zum Grammatik/Pragmatik-Verhältnis.* Ms, Universität Tübingen. [Published in: Rosengren, Inger, ed. (1987): Sprache und Pragmatik. Stockholm: Almqvist & Wiksell International. 139–178.]

Roberts, Ian (1997): Directionality and Word Order Change in the History of English. In: Kemenade, Ans van & Vincent, Nigel, eds. (1997): *Parameters of Syntactic Change.* Cambridge: Cambridge University Press. 397–426.

Rudin, Catherine (1985): *Aspects of Bulgarian Syntax: Complementizers and Wh-Constructions.* Columbus, OH: Slavica.

Samek-Lodovici, Vieri (2001): *Agreement Impoverishment under Subject Inversion. A Crosslinguistic Analysis.* (this volume)

Stiebels, Barbara (2000): Linker Inventories, Linking Splits, and Lexical Economy. In: Stiebels, Barbara & Wunderlich, Dieter, eds. (2000): *Lexicon in Focus.* Berlin: Akademie Verlag. 213–247.

Uszkoreit, Hans Jürgen (1984): *Word Order and Constituent Structure in German.* PhD dissertation, University of Austin, Texas.

Vikner, Sten (2001a): V-to-I Movement and 'Do'-Insertion in Optimality Theory. In: Legendre, Géraldine, Grimshaw, Jane & Vikner, Sten, eds. (2001): *Optimality-Theoretic Syntax.* Cambridge, MA: MIT Press. 424–464.

Vikner, Sten (2001b): *Verb Movement Variation in Germanic and Optimality Theory.* Habilitation Thesis, Universität Tübingen.

Vogel, Ralf (2001a): The Typology of Case Conflicts in Free Relative Constructions. In: Müller, Gereon & Sternefeld, Wolfgang, eds. (2001): *Competition in Syntax.* Berlin: Mouton de Gruyter. 341–375.

Vogel, Ralf (2001 b): *Word Order Freezing as MLC Effect in Bidirectional OT*. Ms, Universität Potsdam & Universität Stuttgart.

Vogel, Ralf & Steinbach, Markus (1998): The Dative – an Oblique Case. *Linguistische Berichte* 173. 65–90.

Weerman, Fred (1997): On the Relation between Morphological and Syntactic Case. In: Kemenade, Ans van & Vincent, Nigel, eds. (1997): *Parameters of Syntactic Change*. Cambridge: Cambridge University Press. 427–459.

Wiese, Bernd (1999): Unterspezifizierte Paradigmen. Form und Funktion in der pronominalen Deklination. *Linguistik Online* 4:3.

Wilson, Colin (2001): Bidirectional Optimization and the Theory of Anaphora. In: Legendre, Géraldine, Grimshaw, Jane & Vikner, Sten, eds. (2001): *Optimality Theoretic Syntax*. Cambridge, MA: MIT Press. 465–507.

Woolford, Ellen (2001): Case Patterns. In: Legendre, Géraldine, Grimshaw, Jane & Vikner, Sten, eds. (2001): *Optimality Theoretic Syntax*. Cambridge, MA: MIT Press. 509–543.

Wunderlich, Dieter (1997): A Minimalist Model of Inflectional Morphology. In: Wilder, Chris, Gärtner, Hans-Martin & Bierwisch, Manfred, eds. (1997): *The Role of Economy Principles in Linguistic Theory*. Berlin: Akademie Verlag. 267–298.

Wunderlich, Dieter (2000): The Force of Lexical Case: German and Icelandic Compared. In: Wunderlich, Dieter, ed. (2000): Papers on Argument Linking. *Arbeiten des SFB 282 „Theorie des Lexikons"*, Nr. 112, Düsseldorf. 81–102.

Yadroff, Michael (1991): *The Syntactic Properties of Adjunction in Russian*. Ms, Indiana University, Bloomington, Indiana.

Zemskaja, E. A. (1973): *Russkaja Razgovornaja Reč'*. Moskva: Nauka.

Zifonun, Gisela, Hoffmann, Ludger & Strecker, Bruno, et al, eds. (1997): *Grammatik der deutschen Sprache*. Berlin: Mouton de Gruyter.

Mannheim   Gereon Müller

Institut für Deutsche Sprache, Postfach 101621, 68016 Mannheim
e-mail: gereon.mueller@ids-mannheim.de

Agreement Impoverishment under Subject Inversion – A Crosslinguistic Analysis

Vieri Samek-Lodovici

Abstract[1]

This paper relates agreement to X'-theory, identifying phrasal and extended projections as the natural domains within which agreement should occur. At the same time, agreement is viewed as costly, due to the associated overt realization of agreement features. The optimality theoretic interaction of these simple constraints is claimed to accurately account for a rich typology of agreement patterns involving lack of agreement, agreement in spec-head configurations, and extended agreement with c-commanded inverted subjects. In particular, the analysis entails that the availability of extended agreement necessarily implies the availability of spec-head agreement whereas the opposite implication does not hold, a generalization that holds of all the 12 languages examined here. The analysis also determines the agreement inventory of each language, which coincides with the set of morphologically realized agreement-feature bundles that each grammar lets emerge as optimal in the relevant structural contexts.

1   Introduction

Spec-head agreement within local phrasal projections is never poorer than agreement across a wider distance within the clause. For example, agreement between I° and subjects in specIP is never poorer than agreement between I° and inverted c-commanded subjects. This generalization, argued for in detail in the next section, raises an interesting dilemma. On one hand, its universal nature calls for an analysis based on universal principles, because language specific definitions of what a head can agree with would leave unexplained why no language chooses to make agreement across the boundaries of local projections richer than spec-head agreement. On the other hand, the analysis must allow for crosslinguistic variation, because different languages show different degrees of agreement impoverishment.

Optimality Theory (Prince & Smolensky 1993) can derive universal generalizations and crosslinguistic variation from the same set of universal constraints and thus constitutes the proper framework to address the above dilemma. Using this theory, I will argue that agreement is a property of syntactic projections and hence sensitive to projection domains. In particular, it is governed by two universal constraints: AGR, requiring agreement within local

[1] This research was made possible thanks to a Research Leave grant awarded by the Arts and Humanities Research Board (AHRB, UK).

X-bar projections (i.e. spec-head agreement) and EXTAGR, for *extended agreement*, requiring agreement within the extended projection of the agreement head (on *extended projections* see Grimshaw 1991, 2000). The interaction of these two constraints with the constraint NOFEATS, which militates against the presence of any agreement morphology, is sufficient to entail the above universal generalization as well as the associated crosslinguistic variation.

The same constraint interaction also determines the agreement inventory of a language, i.e. how much agreement is expressed under each structural configuration. The analysis thus joins a host of similar analyses in OT that derive language specific inventories from universal conditions of grammar, such as Prince & Smolensky (1993: 175) on phonological segmental inventories, Bresnan (1998: 14) on agreement, Grimshaw (2001) on clitics, and Grimshaw (1997), Samek-Lodovici (1996: chap. 2.2.4), and Grimshaw & Samek-Lodovici (1998: 203) on expletives. See also the analysis of Icelandic object agreement by Hrafnbjargarson (2001) based on the same kind of agreement constraints proposed in this paper.

An important issue in this regard is to which degree constraint re-ranking is equivalent to lexical specification. As will be shown in section 4.3, the explanatory depth reached by tying language specific inventories to universal constraints of grammar is unavailable under lexical specification approaches.

2   Agreement Impoverishment

Impoverished agreement with postverbal subjects has been noticed for specific languages by Brandi & Cordin (1989), Saccon (1993: 104), Fassi Fehri (1993), and its universal validity is mentioned or entailed in Moravcsik (1978: 365), Corbett (1979: 218), Barlow (1992: 132), and Manzini & Savoia (1998).

I will consider fundamental to the generalization the *domain* in which agreement occurs: agreement within the local phrasal projection HP of a head H – e.g. spec-head agreement – is never poorer than agreement across the boundaries of HP but within the extended projection of H. The generalization is thus defined as follows:

(1) *Agreement Impoverishment*: Agreement within local projections is never poorer than agreement within their extended projections.

Lacking evidence to the contrary[2], I chose to enunciate the generalization in the most general terms, hence holding of any agreement head and agreeing item, including subjects, objects, indirect objects, and items with any grammatical function. In this work, however, I will limit myself to the analysis of subject

---

[2] Heycock & Kroch (1999) discuss interesting data from Icelandic copular sentences of the kind *"the queen of England is you"* and *"the queen of England may be you"*, observing how agreement in person with the inverted subject is possible in the first sentence but not in the second where a modal is involved. These data do not falsify the above generalization, but indicate that intermediate structural domains could be relevant too, since agreement here ceases when the modal extends the structural distance between the agreeing items.

agreement under inversion in non ergative languages. I will however provide some preliminary evidence supporting the generality of (1) in section 2.2.

2.1   Agreement Impoverishment under Subject Inversion

The evidence for agreement impoverishment examined in this work is summarized in table (2) below, based on data from Fassi Fehri (1993), Haiman & Benincá (1992), Saccon (1993), Brandi & Cordin (1989), and Lu (1994). Additional relevant data not reported in the main body of the paper are listed in the final appendix. For each language, the second and third columns list what features, among *person*, *number*, and *gender*, are overtly expressed on I° when the subject occurs in specIP (spec-head agreement), or in a postverbal position c-commanded by I° (extended agreement). The different rows group languages according to the degree of agreement impoverishment suffered by c-commanded subjects. The first row lists languages where all features are preserved. The second, languages where agreement in number is lost. The third, languages experiencing loss of gender agreement, and the fourth loss of both number and gender agreement. Agreement under c-command is never richer than spec-head agreement; even languages lacking spec-head agreement but allowing for subject inversion, such as Chinese, do not show emergence of agreement under the c-command configuration.

Another way to look at the same table is as in (3) below, where loss of agreement is indexed for each agreement feature f. Three major groups emerge: a first one where agreement on f is preserved across spec-head and extended configurations; a second group where agreement occurs under the spec-head configuration but not under c-command; a third group where agreement doesn't occur in either configuration.[3]

The agreement patterns of Italian, Standard Arabic, and Conegliano, are presented below. They involve both agreement preservation as well as agreement loss, and exemplify the kind of linguistic variation that any theory of agreement must deal with. This includes variation in the set of agreement features that are expressed, and, among these, variation in the set of features that are preserved under subject inversion.

---

[3] An interesting observation emerging from the table is the lack of agreement loss for the person feature, also noted in Manzini & Savoia (1998), where it is central to their argument against the non existence of pro_{expl}. Taraldsen (1996: 199), however, observes how Icelandic loses person agreement whenever the preverbal subject carries oblique case and I° agrees in number with the object, to which it also assigns nominative case; the relevant data are examined in section 2.2.

(2) Subject-I° agreement in gender (gen), number (num) and person (ps)

language:	spec-head agreement:	extended agreement:
Moroccan Arabic	ps, num, gen	ps, num, gen
Italian	ps, num	ps, num
Spanish	ps, num	ps, num
Chinese	none	none
Standard Arabic	ps, num, gen	ps, gen
Fassan	ps, num, gen	ps, (num)[4]
Genoese	ps, num, gen	ps, (num)
Ampezzan	ps, num, gen	ps, (num)
Romagnol	ps, num, gen	ps, (num)
Conegliano	ps, num, gen	ps
Trentino	ps, num, gen	ps
Fiorentino	ps, num, gen	ps

(3) Classification according to agreement type

	Group 1 Preserved agreement		Group 2 Agreement impoverishment		Group 3 No agr
Pers.	Italian Spanish Fassan Genoese Ampezzan Romagnol Conegliano Trentino Fiorentino Moroccan Arabic Standard Arabic				Chinese
Num.	Italian Spanish Moroccan Arabic		Fiorentino Trentino Conegliano (Fassan) (Genoese) (Romagnol) (Ampezzan) Standard Arabic		Chinese
Gen.	Moroccan Arabic Standard Arabic		Fassan Genoese Ampezzan Romagnol Conegliano Trentino Fiorentino		Chinese Italian Spanish

2.1.1 Agreement Preservation: Italian

Preserved agreement is exemplified by Italian, where specIP subjects agree with
I° in number and person, and an equally rich pattern holds with postverbal subjects; compare (4a) with (4b). Postverbal subjects have been consistently

---

[4] The parentheses express the observation that loss in number agreement is restricted to
feminine subjects and it is optional (Haiman & Benincá 1992).

claimed by many authors to be c-commanded by I°, whether adjoined to VP or stranded into specVP position (Rizzi 1982, 1990; Brandi & Cordin 1989: footnote 8; Saccon 1993; Belletti & Shlonsky 1994; Samek-Lodovici 1996). In the data below, slashes separate alternative forms of the auxiliary expressing distinct bundles of agreement features; the ungrammatical ones are starred. Any other conceivable bundle is ungrammatical, but for reasons of space only a few alternatives are shown in each case.

(4) a. Io ho   / *ha / *abbiamo camminato
         I   have.1sg / *3sg / *1pl   walked
         'I walked'

     b. Ho   / *ha / *abbiamo   camminato io
         Have.1sg / *3sg / *1pl   walked   I
         'I walked'

2.1.2 Loss of Number Agreement: Standard Arabic

Agreement preservation coexists with agreement loss in Standard Arabic (Fassi Fehri 1993), where topic subjects occur in specIP but non-topic subjects occur c-commanded by I° in specVP. Gender and person agreement is preserved under both configurations, whereas number agreement occurs in the spec-head configuration in (5a) but not in the c-commanded specVP position in (5b), where the verb is singular by default even though the following subject is plural.

(5) a. L-banaat-u   darab-na   / *-at   l-?awlaad-a
         The-girls-Nom   hit-PAST-3Fpl   / *-3Fsg   the-boys-Acc
         'The girls hit the boys'

     b. Darab-at   / *-na   ?al-banaat-u   Zayd-an
         Hit-PAST-3Fsg   / *-3Fpl   the-girls-Nom   Zayd-Acc
         'The girls hit Zayd'

2.1.3 Loss of Number and Gender Agreement: Conegliano

Agreement impoverishment in number and gender is attested in Conegliano, a northern Italian dialect studied by Saccon (1993). Subjects may occur preverbally in specIP, or postverbally, where they are assigned a presentational interpretation. According to Saccon, postverbal subjects lie within the VP projection, and are therefore c-commanded by I°. Agreement in person, number, and gender is expressed through a preverbal clitic[5] here assumed to be base-

---

[5] For the status of subject clitics as agreement markers see Rizzi (1986).

generated on I°, but see also the more detailed analyses given in Manzini and
Savoia (1998) where the clitic heads its own projection.[6]

Under spec-head agreement the clitic is obligatory, compare (6a) with (6b). It
is however obligatorily suppressed in present tense clauses with c-commanded
postverbal subjects, compare (7a) with (7b). (Examples from Saccon 1993: 99,
107.)

(6)   a.   La   Maria la   riva   b. * La   Maria riva
           The Mary 3Fsg   arrive   The Mary arrive
           'Mary arrives'   'Mary arrives'

(7)   a.   * La   riva   la Maria   b. Riva   la Maria
             3Fsg arrive the Mary   arrive the Mary
           'Mary arrives'   'Mary arrives'

As in other Romance languages, it is important to distinguish the distinct postverbal positions available to inverted subjects. Saccon (1993) properly
distinguishes presentational postverbal subjects, which occur within VP and
suppress the agreement-clitic in the way just considered, from right-dislocated
subjects, which preserve the clitic because a trace is left in specIP by the dislocated subject.[7]

Conegliano is representative of a vast number of northern Italian dialects, see
for example the great variety of dialects showing loss of number agreement
under subject inversion reported by Manzini & Savoia (1998). These authors
also report loss of number agreement under inversion in southern dialects lacking subject clitics, where the loss is visible on the main verb as in the Arabic
case. One such dialect is that of Urbino, see (8) below.

(8)   a.   Ki   bur'dɛi   'dɔrm-ne   de 'la
           Those children   sleep-pl   of there
           'Those children sleep there'

---

[6] Theories where subject clitics head their own projections maintain that relevant aspectual
features of the chains of preverbal subjects occupy the specifier of both IP and the clitic projection
(Manzini and Savoia 1992: 25–27). The spec-head agreement configuration thus obtains for both I°
and the subject agreement-clitic.
   [7] It is precisely the absence of this distinction that casts doubts on Suñer's (1992) alleged
evidence against agreement impoverishment in Fiorentino and Trentino. Like Conegliano, these
dialects show agreement clitics with preverbal subjects but not with postverbal ones (see the appendix). Suñer (1992: 655) notes however that the clitic is preserved in interrogative contexts like the
one below.
   (1) Quando é-la revada la Maria?
       When is cl.3Fsg arrived the Mary?
       'When did Mary arrive?'
But these are precisely the contexts where Romance languages like Italian, Catalan, and Conegliano
would place main stress on the past participle and dislocate the final subject (Valduví 1992; Saccon
1993; Samek-Lodovici 1996). Since dislocated subjects may leave a trace in specIP position, the
presence of agreement is expected. Before accepting Suñer's argument, it is thus necessary to check
where the main stress falls in her data, and ensure that they do not involve subject right-dislocation.

b.   De 'la   'dɔrm-e ki   bur'dɛi
     Of there   sleeps-sg those   children
     'Those children sleep there'

The agreement patterns just examined display a significant degree of linguistic variation concerning which agreement features get expressed, and whether they are expressed under the spec-head configuration alone or also across the local IP projection but within the extended projection of I°. The analysis developed in the next sections will explain this variation through the reranking of AGR, EXTAGR and NOFEATS, while simultaneously deriving the generalization on agreement impoverishment.

2.2   Agreement Impoverishment beyond Subject Inversion

Lacking evidence to the contrary, the generalization on agreement impoverishment in (1) above is stated in the most general terms as a property characterizing agreement *per se*, independently of what agrees with what. Further investigation is necessary to determine if this is correct, or whether the generalization holds for subject inversion alone. I here consider preliminary supporting evidence outside subject inversion.

The first case concerns agreement impoverishment in *past participles*, showing how in Romance the generalization need not concern only I°-agreement. In Italian, for example, agreement in gender and number between past participles and the subjects of unaccusatives is preserved even when these subjects remain in situ in object position. In Conegliano the same circumstances show agreement loss (Saccon; 1989). For example, sentence (9a), and the corresponding structure in (9b), show that a past participle agrees in gender and number with the trace left by a raising subject in the past participle specifier.

(9)   a.   Na   tosa   la-e   riv-ád-a
           A.3sg girl.3Fsg   clitic.3Fsg-is.3sg   arrived-Perf-Fsg
           'A girl has arrived'

      b.   Na   tosa   la-e   [$_{PP}$ t$_{NP}$ riv-ád-a   [$_{VP}$ t$_V$ t$_{NP}$]]

However, when the subject remains in the lower object position, as in (10), the past participle no longer agrees.

(10) a.   El-e   riv-á   na   tosa
           clitic.3Msg-is.3sg   arrived-Perf   a.3Fsg girl.3Fsg
           'There arrived a girl'

      b.   El-e   [$_{PP}$ riv-á   [$_{VP}$ t$_V$ [na tosa]]]]

56 Vieri Samek-Lodovici

The second case concerns *object* agreement in Woolford (1995: 662, 2001), who accounts for how specificity affects agreement in five Micronesian and African languages, where [+specific] objects agree with the verb but non-specific ones do not; see the two examples from Palauan here below.

(11) a. Te-'illebed-ii   a bilis   a rengalek
          3pl-Pf-hit-3sg   dog   children
          'The kids hit the dog'

      b. Te-'illebed   a bilis   a rengalek
          3pl-Pf-hit   dog   children
          'The kids hit a dog/the dogs/some dog(s)'

According to Woolford, [+specific] objects raise to spec-Agr_{Obj} – see (12) below – driven by the syntax-LF mapping principle that forces all [+specific] phrases to vacate VP, as proposed by Diesing (1992) and Diesing & Jelinek (1993). In contrast, [-specific] objects remain in situ, as in (13).

(12) [$_{AgrS}$ Te-[V_j-ii]$_k$ [$_{AgrO}$ Object$_i$ t_k [$_{VP}$ t_j t_i]]   Subject]

(13) [$_{AgrS}$ Te-[V_j]$_k$ [$_{AgrO}$ — t_k [$_{VP}$ t_j Object]]   Subject]

The raised objects enter a spec-head relation with Agr_{Obj} and therefore agree with the verb, which then raises further to Agr_S, whereas non-specific objects remain in situ, c-commanded by Agr_{Obj}, and do not agree. We thus have a situation where object-agreement is richer when occurring within the local projection of Agr_{Obj} rather than across it, in accord with generalization (1).

A final case of agreement loss beyond subject inversion occurs in Icelandic, which appears to preserve number but not person agreement when switching from agreement with subjects to agreement with lower DPs in structures involving oblique-case assignment to subjects (Taraldsen 1996; Hrafnbjargarson 2001).

Example (14) shows that verbs assigning nominative case to their subjects agree with them in person and number.

(14) Við   fór-um   / *-Ø / *-u   til Noregs
      We$_{NOM}$ went-1pl   / -1sg / -3pl   to Norway$_{GEN}$
      'We went to Norway'

Verbs assigning quirky case, however, agree with lower c-commanded nominative DPs. The two examples in (15) below show number agreement with a singular and a plural third person object (Hrafnbjargarson 2001, p.c).

(15) a. Okkur   þótt-i   hann   skemmtilegur
          Us_DAT   thought-3sg   he_NOM   amusing
          'We found him amusing'

      b. Þér   þótt-u   þeir   skemmtilegir
          You_DAT.SG   thought-3pl   they_NOM   amusing
          'You found them amusing'

Agreement in person, on the other hand, is lost, with the apparent agreement in
(15) above due to a third person default inflection that happens to coincide with
the person of the object rather than to true agreement. The loss of person agreement is visible in the following pair of sentences, which according to Taraldsen
are similar to (15) above in requiring agreement with a c-commanded DP (1996:
198–199). While the verb may still agree in number with the third person *fleir*
(they) in (16), much like it did in the two previous examples, person agreement
with *flið* (you_pl) in (17) is not possible. (The cross-clausal nature of agreement in
these examples is discussed in § 6.2.)

(16) Mér   þyk-ja   /   *-irþeir   vera   gáfaðir
      I_DAT   think-3pl   /   *-3sg they_NOM   be   gifted_NOM
      'I think they are gifted'

(17) Mér   þyk-$^?$ir   / $^?$*-ja / *-jið þið   vera   gáfaðir
      I_DAT   think-3sg   / $^?$*-3pl / *-2pl you.pl_NOM be   gifted_NOM
      'I think you are gifted'

Using similar examples, Hrafnbjargarson (2001) shows that number agreement
in Icelandic is dependent on person agreement. The impossibility of person
agreement in (17) thus inhibits number agreement as well, favoring a default
third person singular inflection. An analysis of this dependency along the model
proposed in this work is successfully developed in Hrafnbjargarson (2001).
What interests us here is that Icelandic supports generalization (1), as agreement
loss emerges when moving from spec-head agreement to less local agreement
configurations.

2.3 Alternative Interpretations of Agreement Impoverishment

Finally, I need to establish generalization (1) against competing interpretations
of agreement impoverishment such as that of Barlow (1992), where linear-order
is deemed the crucial factor determining agreement patterns. Barlow analyzes
agreement in terms of discourse stream, relating it to D-linking, and proposing
that the DP-H order – with H as the agreeing head – potentially hosts richer
agreement than the H-DP order because the relevant features can be identified
before reaching the head responsible for expressing them (Barlow's theory is

aimed at phenomena other than agreement impoverishment, and should be examined in its full complexity).

A first problematic aspect is that pure linear order is insensitive to syntactic domains, in principle allowing for agreement across clauses. As we will see in section 5, this is correctly excluded under the analysis advocated here.

A distinction between the two approaches when agreement occurs clause-internally is made difficult by the fact that if specifiers are universally leftward, then spec-head agreement always coincides with the DP-H order that Barlow associates with richer agreement. Distinguishing the two approaches hence requires cases where a DP raises from the right of an agreement head H to its left, but beyond the local projection of H and leaving no trace in its specifier. This should determine agreement enrichment under Barlow's analysis, but not under the domain based approach proposed here. The observation that DP fronting in topicalization structures never gives rise to agreement enrichment then appears to support the domain based approach, although the effects of A'-movement on agreement and any related factor should be carefully examined in order to reach a robust conclusion.

Ultimately, the domain based approach is favored by its stronger theoretical architecture, because the relevance of local and extended projections for the proper analysis of syntactic phenomena is more firmly established than that of pure linear order.

3   Universal Constraints on Agreement

Let us proceed with the formal analysis of. agreement impoverishment. The proposed constraints treat the agreement relation as *present* for some feature f only when it is expressed by some visible morphology varying across different values for f. Thus, Italian is maintained to have agreement in person and number because distinct values for these features produce distinct visible forms for I°. In contrast, agreement is deemed to be absent when varying feature values does not produce any visible effect. For example, Chinese is considered as lacking agreement all together, rather than as hosting non-visible agreement. Likewise, so called 'default' agreement, where agreement features are morphologically expressed but remain invariant despite changes in the feature values of the DP they should agree with, is interpreted as lack of agreement.

The agreement relation is assumed to relate together only the two co-varying items. Thus, if I° agrees with a postverbal subject in specVP, agreement occurs between these two positions and there is no null expletive pro_{expl} in specIP acting as intermediary. SpecIP is assumed to be radically empty, as claimed among others by Haider (1987, 1993), Samek-Lodovici (1996), Grimshaw & Samek-Lodovici (1998), and Alexiadou & Anagnostopoulou (1999). See also Heycock & Kroch's study of copular sentences (1999), where direct long-distance agreement between I° and c-commanded DPs is argued to occur in contexts not involving pro_{expl}.

Discussing in full the arguments against *pro_expl* would take us too far afield. They include its inconsistent binding properties (Rizzi 1982, Samek-Lodovici 1996: chap. 5), unexpected gaps in its distribution (Weerman 1989: 212), and unexpected absence of definiteness effects with the associated postverbal subjects (Alexiadou & Anagnostopoulou 1999: 102). For the time being, consider the following data from Icelandic (Taraldsen 1996: 191), where the subject *okkur* (we) is in specIP but cannot agree with I° because it is lexically marked with dative case. As a result I° assigns nominative case and agrees in number with the object *hestarnir* (horses), as we saw earlier. In his extensive study of Icelandic, Sigurðsson (1992: 204–209) cites a great number of properties showing that oblique subjects occur in specIP, including among other their behaving like nominative marked subjects with respect to reflexivization, extraction, cliticization, control, and distribution. But if the subject *okkur* is in specIP then there simply is no available specIP position for *pro_expl*, and therefore agreement must link I° directly to the object in its VP-complement.

(18)   Okkur   lik-a   /   *-um   hestarnir
        We-Dat   like-3pl   /   *-1pl   horses-the-Nom
        'We like the horses'

The agreement impoverishment generalization itself casts doubts over the existence of null expletives: most analyses proposing *pro_expl* require it to transmit case and agreement to postverbal subjects, but we know from generalization (1) that the degree of agreement that gets transmitted varies across languages. Once again we face the choice between maintaining *pro_expl* and consequently derive the relevant differences by stipulating stronger and weaker *pro_expl* in different languages, or avoid positing *pro_expl* and reach the more principled account proposed in the following.

3.1 The Constraints

Lack of agreement is favored by the constraint NOFEATS – for *no features* – which is violated whenever agreement occurs. NOFEATS thus exerts a delimiting influence on morphological structure analogous to that of similar structure-fighting constraints in OT and Minimalism, such as 'Economy of Structure' (Taraldsen 1996: 94), *STRUC (Prince & Smolensky 1993: 25; Aissen 1999; Legendre 1999), and 'Minimize Structure' (Cardinaletti & Starke, 1994: 38). See also Hrafnbjargarson (2001), where a relativization of NOFEATS to specific features like the one proposed here for AGR and EXTAGR is shown necessary to account for agreement in Icelandic.

(19)   NOFEATS: No agreement features.

The other two constraints, AGR and EXTAGR, require agreement to occur and state its legitimate domain. Since languages differ in the set of features that they express, these two constraints are relativized to specific features through the subscript f, which varies over person, number and gender feature-values (on constraint families see also Prince & Smolensky 1993, and McCarthy & Prince 1993).

The first constraint, AGR_f, is present throughout the generative linguistics literature in one form or another and favors structures where agreement on feature f occurs within the smallest available domain, i.e. the local projection of a head. Locality is here intended in the strictest possible sense, with the path that unites the two agreeing items considered legitimate only if it remains internal to the local X'-projection of the agreement head – circled in the figure below –, i.e. only if it never crosses a phrasal boundary.

(20)   Local projection domain of a head $X°$.

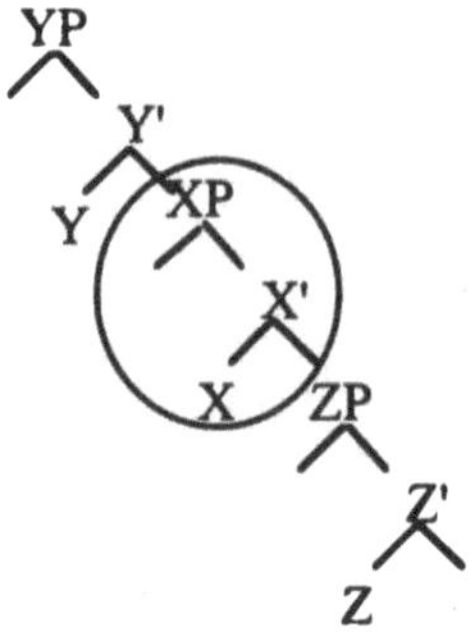

It follows that AGR_f is violated whenever no agreement occurs on f, but also when a head H agrees with a DP contained in its complement, since in this case the agreement relation crosses the complement phrasal boundary. Such a violation, for example, occurs when $I°$ agrees with inverted subjects contained in its VP-complement. The only configuration satisfying AGR_f in the cases examined in this work is spec-head agreement.[8]

(21) AGR_f: An agreement head H and a DP must agree on feature f within the local projection HP.

The constraint $EXTAGR_f$ – for *extended agreement* – imposes a looser condition, only requiring the agreement path to occur within the extended projection of the agreeing head H. When $H=I°$, this domain includes all positions that can be reached via a path never crossing a phrasal node not belonging to the extended projection of $I°$. This includes both in situ subjects in specVP as well as

---

[8] The head-complement relation satisfies AGR_f too, but in the cases considered here the complement is always a VP, hence lacking the relevant features to trigger agreement. I leave open to further investigation whether head-complement agreement indeed occurs, confirming the proposed definition of AGR_f, or whether the constraint must be explicitly restricted to spec-head agreement.

inverted subjects in VP-adjoined position, which thus satisfy $EXTAGR_f$, but not a subject in a complement clause or embedded within some argument of V. Like AGR_f, $EXTAGR_f$ is also violated when agreement is absent.

(22) $EXTAGR_f$:   An agreement head H and a DP must agree on feature f within the extended projection of H.

Note how all structures that satisfy AGR_f necessarily satisfy $EXTAGR_f$ as well, whereas there are structures that satisfy $EXTAGR_f$ but not AGR_f, such as clause-bound agreement between I° and an inverted subject within VP. It is precisely this relation that makes it possible to derive agreement impoverishment while accounting for individual variations across languages.

3.2   The Analysis

The interaction among the above constraints entails the generalization on agreement impoverishment, and governs how much agreement is carried by agreement heads in each specific language.[9]

Determining what may agree with what is an orthogonal problem not analyzed here. We may assume that the input specifies the agreement head H and the DP for which agreement is assessed, here I° and the subject DP assigned nominative case by it. However, nothing principled prevents this relation from being itself concomitantly established via other constraints or already in GEN (see for example chap. 5.2.1 of Samek-Lodovici 1996).

We thus examine in each case a generic agreement feature f, and a potential agreement relation between H and DP on f. We consider two distinct agreement domains: spec-head agreement within the *local* projection of the agreement head H vs. extended agreement within the *extended* projection of H. For each domain we let GEN build two competing candidates, one where H morphologically expresses f and the other where f is left unexpressed. Whether agreement occurs or not in a domain is determined by the interaction of AGR_f, $EXTAGR_f$, and NOFEATS, which partitions the set of possible languages in the three groups shown in table (3) above and repeated below:

Group 1 – Preserved Agreement.

Agreement occurs and is preserved whenever $EXTAGR_f$ dominates NOFEATS. As shown in tableau 1, when H and DP are in a spec-head configuration, the structure with agreement in (a) wins over the one lacking it in (b), because agreement satisfies $EXTAGR_f$ which non-agreement fails. Since $EXTAGR_f$

---

[9] The same interaction could derive which heads may show agreement and which not, through the constraint relativization discussed in section 5. However, it would not explain why some functional heads are more likely to carry agreement then others.

already dominates NOFEATS, the ranking of AGR_f becomes irrelevant, because under this configuration it assesses the same violations as $EXTAGR_f$.

Tableau 1: Preserved agreement

domain = spec-head		EXTAGR$_f$	NOFEATS		AGR$_f$
☞ a.	with agreement		*		
b.	no agreement	*!			*

When the DP occurs elsewhere in the extended projection of H, agreement is preserved. The higher rank of $EXTAGR_f$ in fact ensures that the structure displaying agreement is preferred over the one lacking it. Since no spec-head agreement occurs, AGR_f is violated by both candidates, and can thus once again be ranked anywhere.

Tableau 2: Preserved agreement

domain = extended proj.		EXTAGR$_f$	NOFEATS		AGR$_f$
☞ a.	with agreement		*		*
b.	no agreement	*!			*

Group 2 – Agreement Impoverishment.

Agreement loss arises whenever AGR_f dominates NOFEATS, and this in turn dominates $EXTAGR_f$. Under the spec-head configuration, agreement now wins because it satisfies the highest ranked AGR_f, which the non-agreement structure fails.

Tableau 3: Agreement impoverishment

domain = spec-head		AGR$_f$	NOFEATS	EXTAGR$_f$
☞ a.	with agreement		*	
b.	no agreement	*!		*

When agreement occurs under a non spec-head configuration, however, AGR_f no longer distinguishes among the two competitors, and since NOFEATS dominates $EXTAGR_f$, the winning candidate is the agreementless (b).

Tableau 4: Agreement impoverishment

domain = extended proj.		AGR$_f$	NOFEATS	EXTAGR$_f$
a.	with agreement	*	*!	
☞ b.	no agreement	*		*

Languages with this ranking thus experience agreement loss when the DP shifts from a spec-head configuration with H to another position in the same clause.

Group 3 – Lack of Agreement.

Finally, languages lacking agreement emerge whenever NOFEATS dominates both AGR_f and $EXTAGR_f$. In this case, the no-agreement candidate is optimal in either configuration, because it is the only one satisfying the highest ranked constraint NOFEATS. As the two tableaux below show, this occurs independently of the ranking of AGR_f and $EXTAGR_f$ relative to each other.

Tableau 5: Lack of agreement

domain = spec-head	NOFEATS	AGR_f	$EXTAGR_f$
a. with agreement	*!		
☞ b. no agreement		*	*

Tableau 6: Lack of agreement

domain = extended proj.	NOFEATS	AGR_f	$EXTAGR_f$
a. with agreement	*!	*	
☞ b. no agreement		*	*

A synthesis of the overall interaction is shown in the table below. Remember that the agreement constraints are relativized with respect to agreement features. Therefore, a language may fall into one agreement class relative to one feature but in another with respect to a different one. For example, Italian preserves agreement with respect to person and number, but lacks gender agreement, thus belonging to the no-agreement class gender-wise. A similar picture holds true for Standard Arabic, which preserves agreement in person and gender, but shows agreement loss in number.

All grammars identified by a ranking of these constraints fall into one region of the above partition. Any grammar will in fact either rank $EXTAGR_f$ over NOFEATS, and fall in the first group, or rank them in the reverse order. In this latter case, a grammar will either rank AGR_f over NOFEATS, and fall in the second group, or do the reverse, and fall in the third group. No other agreement pattern is thus possible. What is excluded from this list, and hence predicted impossible, is a language where agreement between a head and a DP outside its local projection is richer than agreement within the same projection. In particular, agreement under c-command cannot be richer than agreement under a spec-head configuration. The generalization of agreement impoverishment thus follows straightforwardly as an entailment of the analysis.

(23)   Agreement Typology via Constraint Reranking.

Agreement-Type	Ranking
Group 1 – Preserved agreement	$EXTAGR_f$ >> NOFEATS (ranking of AGR_f irrelevant)
Group 2 – Agreement impoverishment	AGR_f >> NOFEATS >> $EXTAGR_f$
Group 3 – Lack of agreement	NOFEATS >> {AGR_f, $EXTAGR_f$}

4   Agreement Inventories

The same constraints also determine for any given configuration whether agreement on some feature f may or may not occur. The overall agreement inventory of a language thus follows directly from its grammar, i.e. the constraint ranking that identifies it. There is no need for a separate stipulation of what agreement features a head may express in each configuration.

Agreement inventories are derived by letting alternative morphological realizations for the same head H compete against each other. The competitor set contains any possible combination of agreement features, including the candidate expressing no agreement. The possible combinations of person, gender and number features are listed below. For example, candidate (a) restricts agreement to person alone, candidate (f) restricts it to gender and number, and finally candidate (h) lacks it completely.

(24)   Candidate-set: bundles of agreement features.

a.	ps	c.	num	e.	ps, num	g.	ps, gen, num
b.	gen	d.	ps, gen	f.	gen, num	h.	none

The shown features are those for which agreement *holds*, i.e. those *co-varying* with the person, number, and gender specifications of the subject. Selecting one candidate as optimal determines what *agreeing* features are morphologically expressed by I°, i.e. the agreement inventory for this head in the language at issue. For example, in Standard Arabic, where preverbal subjects agree in person, gender, and number, and postverbal ones only in person and gender, the related constraint ranking will select (g) as optimal in the preverbal case, and (d) in the postverbal one.

Languages, however, may also morphologically express an invariant *default* value for any feature lacking agreement. This default value is not predicted by the current analysis and for the time being is assumed to be lexically specified. To come back to the Arabic example, the lack of number agreement with specVP subjects produces an invariant default *singular* value for the number feature. This value is interpreted as a lexically specified value for the number feature that emerges whenever the head carries no agreement relation. In short, the lack of agreement in number is predicted by the analysis, but its morphological realization as *singular* is stipulated. An OT analysis of agreement avoiding this stipulation turns out to require a finer grained definition of agreement as well as constraints composed out of simpler constraints.

4.1 Italian – Agreement Preservation

In Italian indicative finite-tense clauses, I° shows preserved agreement in person and number, but lacks agreement in gender. This was already shown in section 2.1.1, and is shown again in (25), which presents overt agreement in person and number for both specIP and postverbal subjects within the highest VP-projection node.[10]

(25) a. Le   auto   funzion-ano   / * {o,i,a,iamo,ate}   bene
          The.Fpl   cars.Fpl   work.3pl   / * {1s,2s,3s,1pl,2pl}   well
          'The cars work fine'

      b. Funzion-ano   /   *{o,i,a,iamo,ate}   bene le   auto
          Work.3pl   /   *{1s,2s,3s,1pl,2pl}   well the.Fpl   cars.Fpl
          'The cars work fine'

The overall pattern emerges from the merging of the three rankings characterizing preserved agreement in person, preserved agreement in number, and lack of agreement in gender. As we know from the previous discussion, each of these patterns is characterized by the ranking conditions shown in (26) below. The constraints AGR_{ps} and AGR_{num} are omitted because their ranking is irrelevant for preserved agreement (see section 3.2).

(26) Italian:

    – Preserved number agreement: $EXTAGR_{num}$ >> NOFEATS
    – Preserved person agreement: $EXTAGR_{ps}$ >> NOFEATS
    – No gender agreement: NOFEATS >> {$EXTAGR_{gen}$, AGR_{gen}}

Any total ranking compatible with these ranking conditions will derive the overall agreement pattern of Italian. This is shown for specIP subjects in tableau 7, and for postverbal subjects in tableau 8 below.

In tableau 7, the competition between the optimal person and number agreement in (a), and the agreement in (e) motivates the higher rank of $EXTAGR_{num}$ over NOFEATS, else (a) would lose against (e). Likewise, $EXTAGR_{ps}$ must

---

[10] Italian postverbal subjects have been analyzed as VP-adjoined (Rizzi, 1982), or, more recently, as stranded in rightmost position via leftward movement of anything base-generated to their right (Zubizarreta 1999).

outrank NOFEATS, else (c) would beat (a). These two ranking relations are responsible for the suboptimal status of all other candidates, except for full agreement in (b). This candidate, however, violates NOFEATS one more time than (a) because it expresses gender agreement. The extra violation is fatal, because NOFEATS outranks both $EXTAGR_{gen}$ and AGR_{gen}, leaving (a) optimal.

Tableau 7: Italian: spec-head agreement in person and number

	$E.AGR_{num}$	$E.AGR_{ps}$	NOF	$E.AGR_{gen}$	AGR_{gen}
☞ a. ps, num			* *	*	*
b. ps, gen, num			* * *!		
c. num		*!	*	*	*
d. gen, num		*!	* *		
e. ps	*!		*	*	*
f. gen	*!	*	*		
ps, gen	*!		* *		
h. none	*!	*		*	*

The same ranking hierarchy determines preserved agreement in person and number on inverted subjects, as shown in tableau 8. The only change in the tableau concerns AGR_{gen}, which is now always violated because the subject is never in a spec-head relation with I°. The discussion proposed for the former tableau identically applies to this tableau as well.

Summing up, once AGR_f and $EXTAGR_f$ are relativized to specific features, their interaction with NOFEATS derives at once both which agreement features are expressed by a head (here I°), as well as whether the expressed agreement is preserved or suppressed when moving from spec-head agreement to less local configurations. In the case of Italian, the examined ranking determines both person and number spec-head agreement with I°, as well as its preservation with postverbal c-commanded subjects.

Tableau 8: Italian: extended projection agreement in person and number

	$E.AGR_{num}$	$E.AGR_{ps}$	NOF	$E.AGR_{gen}$	AGR_{gen}
☞ a. ps, num			* *	*	*
b. ps, gen, num			* * *!		*
c. num		*!	*	*	*
d. gen, num		*!	* *		*
e. ps	*!		*	*	*
f. gen	*!	*	*		*
ps, gen	*!		* *		*
h. none	*!	*		*	*

4.2   Standard Arabic – Agreement Impoverishment

Agreement impoverishment is exemplified by Standard Arabic, where I° agrees in person, number and gender with specIP subjects but only in person and gender with specVP subjects (see section 2.1.2). Standard Arabic thus shows preserved agreement with respect to person and gender, but agreement loss with respect to number. Drawing from table (23), we combine together the following ranking conditions:

(27)   Standard Arabic:

– Preserved person agreement: $EXTAGR_{ps}$ >> NOFEATS
– Preserved gender agreement: $EXTAGR_{gen}$ >> NOFEATS
– Agreement loss in number: AGR_{num} >> NOFEATS >> $EXTAGR_{num}$

Any total ranking, consistent with these conditions, yields the desired agreement pattern. This is shown in the two tableaux below. Once again, I omit any irrelevant constraint, here AGR_{gen} and AGR_{ps}.

Consider first agreement in specIP in tableau 9. The higher ranking of $EXTAGR_{ps}$ and $EXTAGR_{gen}$ relative to NOFEATS is sufficient to exclude any candidate that does not express person and gender agreement, leaving only (a) and (b) as potential optima. But (b) lacks agreement in number, and thus fatally violates the next lower ranked constraint AGR_{num}, leaving the full-agreement candidate (a) optimal.

A major change occurs when subjects remain in specVP, and are no longer in a spec-head configuration with I°. The constraint AGR_{num} is now violated by all candidates, and therefore no longer distinguishes between (a) and (b). The next lower constraint, however, is NOFEATS, which prefers (b) to (a) because it expresses one agreement feature less. Candidate (b) thus emerges as optimal under this configuration.

Tableau 9: Standard Arabic: spec-head agreement in person, number and gender

	$E.AGR_{ps}$	$E.AGR_{gen}$	AGR_{num}	NOF	$E.AGR_{num}$
☞ a. ps, gen, num				* * *	
b. ps, gen			*!	* *	*
c. ps		*!	*	*	*
d. ps, num		*!		* *	
e. num	*!	*		*	
f. gen, num	*!			* *	
gen	*!		*	*	*
h. none	*!	*	*		*

Tableau 10: Standard Arabic: extended projection agreement in person and gender

	E.AGR$_{ps}$	E.AGR$_{gen}$	AGR$_{num}$	NOF	E.AGR$_{num}$
a. ps, gen, num			*	* * *!	
☞ b. ps, gen			*	* *	*
c. ps		*!	*	*	*
d. ps, num		*!	*	* *	
e. num	*!	*	*	*	
f. gen, num	*!		*	* *	
gen	*!		*	*	*
h. none	*!	*	*		*

As in the previous case about Italian, the appropriate ranking of the constraints simultaneously determines which features are allowed for spec-head agreement and which are preserved under a c-command configuration.

4.3 Comparison with Parametric Approaches

All agreement patterns listed in table (2) and (3) in section 2 can be derived in the way just outlined for Italian and Standard Arabic, i.e. by merging together the ranking relations required for deriving the expression and preservation of each feature. What features are expressed under each structural configuration, is thus determined by the ranking of the constraints, and need not be stipulated as language specific properties of the agreeing head.

An interesting issue in this regard concerns the difference between deriving inventories via language specific rankings of universal constraints vs. parametric approaches where the inventories are idiosyncratic properties specified language by language, as is for example proposed for agreement by Griffith (1996). At first sight the two approaches might appear equivalent, but they are not. As section 3.2 showed, no ranking of the proposed constraints can make extended agreement richer than the spec-head one. This, however, is possible if heads are allowed to specify what features they can express in each configuration. For example, I° could be specified to agree in number with c-commanded subjects but not with subjects in specIP, against generalization (1).

More sophisticated parametric theories, such as Manzini and Savoia's minimalist account of agreement loss (1998), are able to derive the generalization on impoverishment. In their extensive study of number agreement loss in Italian dialects, Manzini and Savoia maintain that agreement always requires spec-head checking of the relevant features. Checking is always possible with preverbal subjects in virtue of their position, whereas postverbal subjects require covert raising of the relevant features. When a feature fails to raise, agreement on that feature cannot occur. In particular, whether a feature may or may not raise is a parametric and language specific property. The model thus derives generalization (1), because every feature that determines agreement under the spec-head configuration of preverbal subjects may or may not fail to do so with postverbal ones, and hence only agreement impoverishment may ensue.

What this analysis fails to offer is a unified account of agreement impoverishment *and* of agreement inventories, because success/failure of covert raising may at most affect the inventory for extended agreement but cannot determine that for spec-head agreement. The latter must be determined by a separate grammar module, divorcing its explanation from that of agreement impoverishment. The same is not true for the analysis advocated here, where any ranking of the proposed constraints determines at once the agreement inventory under spec-head configurations and its degree of preservation in wider domains.

5   Simultaneous Agreement on Multiple Heads

The analysis proposed here is not specific to I°, and can be extended to other agreement heads. Different heads can involve distinct and even opposite sets of features. For example, in Italian, while I° agrees in person and number but lacks agreement in gender, the past participle of passives and unaccusatives agrees in gender and number but lacks agreement in person, see (29) below.

(28) a. Gianni   é   arrivat-o
          John   is.3sg   arrived-Msg

      b. Maria   é   arrivat-a
          Mary   is.3sg   arrived-Fsg

      c. Le donne   sono   arrivat-e
          The women   are.3pl   arrived-Fpl

      d. Io sono   arrivat-o   / arrivat-a
          I   am.1sg   arrived-Msg   / arrived-Fsg

The proposal explored here is a further relativization of the agreement constraints, which are indexed with respect to functional heads as well. Thus, each constraint in the AGR_f and $EXTAGR_f$ families doubles into a constraint for I° and another for the past-participle head. The group of constraints so generated is listed below, where *P* stands for past participle, and *I* for I°.

(29) Agreement Constraints	$I°$	Past Participle Head
Person	$AGR_{ps.I}$ $EXTAGR_{ps.I}$	$AGR_{ps.P}$ $EXTAGR_{ps.P}$
Number	$AGR_{num.I}$ $EXTAGR_{num.I}$	$AGR_{num.P}$ $EXTAGR_{num.P}$
Gender	$AGR_{gen.I}$ $EXTAGR_{gen.I}$	$AGR_{gen.P}$ $EXTAGR_{gen.P}$

Ranking conditions will now have to be determined for each head. For example, the reader may check as an exercise that the agreement patterns for $I°$ and the past-participle of passives and unaccusatives in Italian is determined by merging together the following ranking conditions:

(30) $I°$ and past-participle agreement in Italian:

   a. $I°$-agreement in person and number:

   $E.AGR_{num.I}, E.AGR_{ps.I} >> NOFEATS >> E.AGR_{gen.I}, AGR_{gen.I}$

   b.   Past participle agreement in number and gender:

   $E.AGR_{num.P}, E.AGR_{gen.P} >> NOFEATS >> E.AGR_{ps.P}, AGR_{ps.P}$

Since the same fundamental interaction underlines agreement on any head, we expect the consequences that we observed for $I°$ to generalize to past participle agreement. In particular, the generalization on agreement impoverishment will now have to hold of agreeing heads other than $I°$. This is indeed the case, as the data discussed in section 2.2 for past participles in Conegliano showed.

   While the number of constraints obtained via feature and head relativization may seem large, the way they are generated is fully systematic. The actual primitives of this analysis of agreement are limited in number and elementary in character, involving only the following elements:

(i)   The set of distinct agreement features.
(ii)   The set of heads that may potentially host agreement; these need not belong to distinct syntactic categories, but should be represented by distinct heads in the phrase-structure representation because the proposed analysis only determines the features for one agreement relation per head.
(iii) A basic fundamental constraint favoring agreement, relativized to the local- and extended-projection domain (i.e. AGR_f and $EXTAGR_f$).
(iv)   The constraint NOFEATS, against any agreement feature.

The relativization of the agreement constraints to features and heads is necessary to account for the distinct patterns of agreement found on different heads.

Hrafnbjargarson (2001) shows that an even higher degree of relativization, with constraints relativized for group of features, is necessary in order to account for the kind of agreement dependencies shown by Icelandic, demonstrating moreover that constraint conjunction of simple constraints is insufficient. The apparent complexity of constraint relativization should however not obscure the overall invariance of the analysis across languages and syntactic structures: whatever head and whatever features it concerns, agreement is always governed by the same fundamental mechanism: the interaction between AGR and EXTAGR with NOFEATS.

6 Additional Issues

This section examines some interesting issues concerning agreement across clauses and with expletives, and the definitions of AGR_f and $EXTAGR_f$.

6.1 Lack of Agreement across Extended Projections

Consider (31) below. When the complement of the raising verb is finite, the matrix verb displays default invariant third person agreement, here interpreted as lack of agreement.

(31) Sembr-a   / *-iamo   che   noi   non   voteremo
      seems-3sg   / *-1.pl   that   we   not vote.FUT.1pl
      'It seems that we will not vote'

Agreement with the lower subject is not possible because the finite subordinate clause forms its own extended projection. Since no constraint favors agreement across extended projections, any structure allowing it always loses against the structure lacking agreement, which performs better relative to NOFEATS.

The relevant tableau is given below, with the ranking found valid for Italian in previous sections. The competition is between the candidate lacking agreement in (a) and candidate (b) with the standard person and number agreement found for c-commanded subjects. The agreement constraints are violated by both candidates, either because agreement is absent, as in (a), or because it does nor occur within the proper domain, as in (b). The only constraint distinguishing the two is thus NOFEATS, which favors the agreementless candidate in (a). Agreement across extended projections is thus predicted impossible.

Tableau 11: Agreement in person and number across extended projections in
Italian

	E.AGR$_{num}$	E.AGR$_{ps}$	NOF	E.AGR$_{gen}$	AGR$_{gen}$
☞ a. none	*	*		*	*
b. ps, num	*	*	*! *	*	*

Note how the violations assessed by each constraint for (b) are never less than
those assessed by (a), and on NOFEATS they are inevitably more. It follows that
(b) is *harmonically bounded* by (a), i.e. no ranking of the above constraints will
ever make (b) better than (a). Therefore, agreement across clauses is predicted
impossible in any language (on 'harmonic bounding', see Prince & Smolensky
1993; Samek-Lodovici & Prince 1999).

The same is true for any candidate c expressing some degree of agreement
with the lower subject. Like (b), in fact, candidate c necessarily violates all the
agreement constraints, either because it lacks agreement on the relevant feature,
or because the agreement relation extends beyond the relevant domain of the
constraint. Moreover, c collects one NOFEATS violation more than the agreementless candidate (a) for every feature it expresses. As a result, (a) harmonically bounds c, and all other things being equal it will always beat it. The
universal generalization that agreement can never occur across extended projections thus follows from the analysis. Note how the same result would not hold if
we based our analysis on linear order as in Barlow (1992), since linear order
cannot distinguish between agreement relation occurring within rather than
across the boundaries of extended projections.

6.2   Agreement in Raising Structures

When the subordinate clause is non finite, as in (32) below, Italian raising verbs
agree with the lower subject across the clause boundary. That the subject occurs
in the lower clause is confirmed by its interpretation, which is under the scope
of the neg-marker of the lower clause whenever stress falls on the auxiliary *aver*
(to have).

(32)   Sembr-ano / *-a   non   AVER   votato   pochi elettori
       seem-3pl / *-3sg not   to-have   voted   few   voters
       'There seem to have been more than a few voters voting'

Under the assumptions made here, which reject the existence of a raising null
expletive *pro*, these structures are problematic, because nothing in the analysis
presented so far triggers agreement across extended projections. They are also
problematic for any other analysis of agreement. For example, choosing
government rather than extended projections as the proper domain of EXTAGR$_f$

would not account for (32) either, because the agreeing subject occurs too low to be governed by the matrix verb.

We already considered an additional case of cross-clausal agreement when examining Icelandic, where an analysis in terms of a raising expletive *pro* is excluded because the specIP position is occupied by a subject assigned quirky case; the relevant data from Taraldsen (1996) showing number agreement with the subject of the lower clause are repeated below.

(33) Mér   þyk -ja   /   *-irþeir   vera   gáfaðir
      I_{DAT} think -3pl   /   *-3sg they$_{NOM}$ be   gifted$_{NOM}$
      'I think they are gifted'

The properties shared by (32) and (33) are the presence of a finite matrix clause whose I° can assign nominative case but lacks an assignee, and a non-finite complement clause with an assignee but no assigner. This appears to trigger cross-clausal case-assignment, and agreement co-occurs with it. On the base of this observation, we may hypothesize a constraint 'CASEAGR$_f$' requiring agreement within the domain of case-assignment. When NOFEATS outranks CASEAGR$_f$ no cross-clausal agreement is possible, whereas the ranking CASEAGR$_f$>> NOFEATS allows for it, but only parasitically to the case-assignment relation.

In these cross-clausal domains, the constraints AGR$_f$ and EXTAGR$_f$ are violated whether agreement is present or not, and their ranking thus cannot affect the outcome of the competition. It does however affect the overall generalization that we expect to emerge from the study of cross-clausal domains. This is predicted to show agreement impoverishment with respect to both spec-head and clause-bound domains for the same reasons that make spec-head agreement potentially richer than extended agreement. For example, for any agreement feature f, the ranking AGR$_f$ >> EXTAGR$_f$ >> NOFEATS >> CASEAGR$_f$ would preserve f-agreement on local and clause bound domains, but not under the cross-clausal domain potentially induced by exceptional nominative case-assignment of the kind shown in (32) and (33). The preservation of number but loss of person agreement described in §2.2 for Icelandic supports this prediction.

This preliminary hypothesis thus appears to derive the correct results. It also identifies an interesting goal for further research: namely the possibility that CASEAGR$_f$ replace EXTAGR$_f$ once its dynamic domain is better understood and defined. All the results discussed in this paper would then follow in the exact same way examined in earlier sections except that they would concern the ranking of CASEAGR$_f$ relative to AGR$_f$ and NOFEATS rather than that of EXTAGR$_f$.

6.3 Agreement with Expletives

In sentences like (34)–(36) below, the main verb appears to agree with an expletive subject. The close parallelism with the Italian subjectless clause in (37), however, suggests that no agreement relation is present, and that the expletive is void of agreement features much like it is void of an interpretation. The verb simply surfaces in its default agreementless form. This view is supported by the German data, where the expletive can be omitted without affecting the agreement morphology on the verb. Equally viable, however, is the hypothesis that in all these cases agreement occurs between the verb and the expletive. Under either hypothesis, these structures are unproblematic for the analysis proposed so far. (The French data show future tense because it does not neutralize agreement in number in the third person. The German data show embedded clauses to ensure that the expletive is not in SpecCP.)

(34)   English: It seems   /   *seem that ...

(35)   French: Il   semblera   /   *sembleront   que ...
               It   seem.FUT.3sg   /   *seem.FUT.3pl   that ...
               'it will seem that' ...

(36)   German: ... dass (es) ihm   scheint   /   *scheinen   dass ...
                ... that it to-him   seems.3sg   /   *seem.3pl   that ...
                ... 'that it seems to him that' ...

(37)   Italian: Sembra   /   *sembrano   che ...
               (It) seem.3sg ...   /   *seem.3pl   that ...
               'it seems that' ...

A more interesting case concerns clauses with an expletive co-occurring with a lower nominal subject, as in (38) below. These structures are salient for the task of determining what agrees with what, since a priori the copula could here agree with either the expletive or the lower thematic subject. As mentioned earlier, I assume that nominative-marked subjects are always targeted for agreement in finite clauses, as is confirmed by (38), which – caveat analyses allowing for agreement transmission via the expletive – should otherwise lack agreement (for a detailed discussion of this assumption, see Samek-Lodovici 1996: chap. 5).

(38)   a.   There is a man in the garden
        b.   There are three men in the garden

Once the agreeing items are known, the agreement patterns they give rise to are subject to the same generalization and analysis proposed in earlier sections. For example, (38) above constitutes an instance of agreement preservation, and should be analyzed as the analogous instances of preserved agreement found in Italian.[11]

If this line of reasoning is correct, we also expect to find instances of agreement loss, where the verb fails to agree with a lower subject. The relevant alternation occurs in some varieties of English reported in Baker (1989: 359) as well as in French, respectively shown in (39) and (49) below.[12]

(39)   a.   Some bats *are* in the bellfry
       b.   There *is* some bats in the bellfry

(40)   a.   Trois hommes arriveront
            Three men arrive.FUT.3pl
            'Three men will arrive'

       b.   Il arrivera trois hommes
            It arrive.FUT.3sg three men
            'There will arrive three men'

While the (b) sentences could be analyzed as involving agreement with the expletive, only an analysis in terms of agreement loss with the inverted subject ensures a structural parallelism between these data and those in (38) above, keeping the agreeing items invariant. It also preserves a structural parallelism between all expletive structures in (38)–(40) above with the non-expletive ones involving inverted subjects examined in earlier sections, with the analysis of agreement preservation and agreement loss kept invariant across both sets of structures.

For example, the analysis of the English pattern in (39) follows that of number agreement loss in Standard Arabic (§4.2): when the spec-head related constraints AGR_{ps} and AGR_{num} outrank NOFEATS, and NOFEATS outranks $EXTAGR_{ps}$ and $EXTAGR_{num}$. As we know, this leads to agreement loss in number and person when the subject is c-commanded by I°. As tableau 12 shows,

---

[11] As noted by an anonymous reviewer, although the corresponding German root clauses resemble those of English, as shown in (1) below, the expletive cannot occur in embedded contexts, as shown in (2). The expletive thus does not occupy specIP, but rather the specCP position typical of German V2-structures. In turn, the thematic subject in (1) either occurs in specIP, or it occurs in specVP in a structure with an empty specIP, with extended agreement subject to the same analysis of postverbal subjects in Italian.

    (1)   Es sind drei Männer im Garten
            It are three men in-the garden
            'There are three men in the garden'

    (2)   ... dass (*es) drei Männer im Garten sind
            ... that (it) three men in-the garden are
            ... 'that there are three men in the garden'

[12] Number loss in French may only occur with third person subjects. Similar inversion structures with 1st and 2nd person subjects are not possible. The analysis presented here does not capture this kind of dependencies between distinct agreement features. The issue is whether these dependencies are inherent to the theory of agreement or follow from independent factors. In the case of French, for example, it could follow from a more general restriction against inverting pronominal subjects, with non pronominal subjects naturally occurring only in the third person.

agreement in (b) wins against lack of agreement in (a) under the spec-head configuration because it satisfies the high-ranked AGR constraints.

Tableau 12: Spec-head agreement

	AGR_{ps}	AGR_{num}	NOF	$E.AGR_{ps}$	$E.AGR_{num}$
a. none	*!	*		*	*
☞ b. ps, num			* *		

When the subject is c-commanded, however, AGR_{num} and AGR_{ps} are violated by both candidates, and NOFEATS breaks the tie in favor of the agreementless (a), which surfaces with a default third person realization.

Tableau 13: Extended projection agreement

	AGR_{ps}	AGR_{num}	NOF	$E.AGR_{ps}$	$E.AGR_{num}$
☞ a. none	*	*		*	*
b. ps,num	*	*	*! *		

6.4　Interaction with Other Constraints

Agreement does not occur in a syntactic vacuum, raising the issue of what patterns arise once the proposed constraints occur as part of a wider grammar.

Let us thus assume that other constraints are present, with the only restriction that they do not govern the expression of agreement features, and, for the sake of simplicity, that NOFEATS, AGR_f, and $EXTAGR_f$ are adjacent to each other in the overall hierarchy.

GEN generates a set of competitors, where the relevant DP and potentially agreeing head H occur in all possible syntactic configurations. Optimization examines the hierarchy according to rank order, eliminating all competitors that are worse than others with respect to the constraint assessed at each step. By the time optimization reaches the agreement constraints only two situations are possible. In the first, all surviving competitors share the same agreement configuration, with some of them expressing agreement and other not doing so. In this case, the agreement constraints apply in the way examined in this paper, further restricting the set of competitors to those structures expressing or not expressing agreement.

Alternatively, the surviving competitors present distinct agreement configurations, which will compete with each other, raising the issue whether the agreement constraints might be able to select among distinct syntactic structures by favoring one configuration over another.[13]

---

[13] My gratitude to an anonymous reviewer for this important observation.

The constraint definitions proposed here welcome this interaction. In particular, whenever a choice is possible AGR_f will favor Spec-Head agreement over other configurations, even if this implies raising the relevant DP to the appropriate specifier. Preliminary evidence in this direction comes from the study of Aux-to-Comp in Italian (Samek-Lodovici 1996), where non finite tenses are unable to host agreement relations and therefore prevent AGR_f from forcing subjects into the same spec-head relation with I° that they enjoy in tensed clauses. The current definitions thus let us reduce this peculiar pattern of Italian infinitivals to their agreement properties.

One could of course investigate a more neutral definition, like the one below proposed by an anonymous reviewer, which penalizes structures lacking agreement in spec-head configurations, but is vacuously satisfied under extended domains independently of whether agreement is present or missing. A similar definition could be proposed for $EXTAGR_f$.

(41) AGR_f: If a DP is in the specifier of an agreement head H, then H and DP must agree on feature f.

The same reviewer properly notes that all the derivations examined in this paper would still follow under the new definition, which only eliminates the carpet-starring of all candidates when considering non spec-head domains, while leaving unscathed the overall neutrality of the constraint in these contexts. Indeed, definitions of this type are used by Hrafnbjargarson (2001) in his analysis of Icelandic, where he also shows how the results concerning agreement impoverishment still apply. Definition (41), however, remains neutral only as long as no higher ranked constraint is sensitive to agreement. If such a constraint is present and happens to eliminate all competitors expressing spec-head agreement, then (41) becomes domain-selective as well, because it favors lack of agreement under a non spec-head configuration (no violation) over lack of agreement under a spec-head one (one violation).

7   Conclusion

The distribution and the inventory of agreement morphology is best accounted for in terms of constraints on the syntactic domain of agreement, supporting a view of grammar where syntax may directly govern morphology, and determine its generalizations.

The analysis supports the relevance of OT for the analysis of morphological and syntactic phenomena, and its potential for deriving universal generalizations, crosslinguistic typologies, and language specific inventories, all from the same fixed set of universal constraints. In this analysis the proposed constraints determine at once (i) language-specific agreement inventories, (ii) the degree of agreement preserved across syntactic domains in different languages, (iii) the universal generalization on agreement impoverishment.

Appendix – Agreement Patterns Crosslinguistically

For the agreement patterns of Italian, Standard Arabic and Conegliano, see sections 2.1 and 2.2.

Moroccan Arabic, (Fassi Fehri 1993).
The following examples show that unlike Standard Arabic, Moroccan Arabic preserves number agreement; compare (42a) with (42b). As (42c) shows, lack of number agreement causes ungrammaticality.

(42) a. L-ulad   ja-w
          The boys came-pl
          'The boys came'

      b. Ja-w   l-ulad
          Came-pl   the boys
          'The boys came'

      c. *Ja   l-ulad
          'Came   the boys'

Fiorentino, Trentino (Brandi & Cordin 1989: 121–122).
Subjects in specIP must occur with an obligatory clitic expressing gender, person and number agreement, see (43) below.

(43) La   Maria   la   parla
      The.3Fsg   Mary.3Fsg   cl.3Fsg   speaks.3sg
      'Mary speaks'

The agreement clitic is obligatorily suppressed whenever the subject occurs in postverbal VP-adjoined position. The position is identified on the basis of scope interactions with sentential negation (Brandi & Cordin 1989: 138, fn 8). The loss in person, number and gender agreement is particularly evident in (44), where the subject is plural and feminine. When the subject is postverbal only a locative clitic precedes the verb (loss of person, number, and gender agreement), and the auxiliary occurs in the singular (loss of number agreement).

(44) a. Gli   é   venuto   delle   ragazze
          Locative-clitic   is.3sg   come.3Msg   some.3Fpl   girls.3Fpl
          'There arrived some girls'

      b. * Le   son   venute   delle   ragazze
            cl.3Fpl   are.3pl   come.3Fpl   some.3Fpl   girls.3Fpl
          'There arrived some girls'

The agreement-pattern of Trentino closely resembles that of Fiorentino, except for the absence of the overt initial clitic *gli* in inversion structures. See Brandi & Cordin (1989).

Conegliano (Saccon 1993).
Loss of gender agreement has already been illustrated in section 2.1. The following example shows loss of number agreement in present perfect clauses.

(45)   El   a   caminá milioni de persone, in te sto' marciapié
         Expl.3Msg has.3sg   walked millions.Mpl of persons, on this sidewalk
         'There walked millions of people, on this sidewalk'

Fassan, Genoese, Ampezzan, Romagnol (Haiman & Benincá 1992).
The following examples from Haiman & Benincá (1992: 193) show loss of gender agreement.

(46)   Fassan: L   e   venu   la vivano
                        He.3Msg is.3sg   come.Msg   the witch.Fs
                        'The witch has arrived'

(47)   Genoese: U   vene   a   Katajning
                        He.3Msg comes.3sg   the.3Fsg   Catherine
                        'Catherine arrives'

(48)   Ampezzan: Agnere   l   e   sta
                        Yesterday he.3Msg is.3sg   been.3Fsg
                        ra sagra inz el nosc paes
                        the.3Fsg feast.Fsg in the our town
                        'Yesterday, there was a party in our town'

(49)   Romagnol: E   chenta   una   turtureina
                        He.3Msg sings.3sg a.3Fsg   turtledove.Fsg
                        'A turtledove is singing'

Chinese (Lu 1994).
Postverbal subjects in Chinese are restricted to a few unaccusative verbs and existential sentences, where they do not display agreement. The following examples are taken from Lu (1994).

(50)   Zhe xueqi   lai   le   sange   xin   laoshi
         This semester come   ASP   three-CL   new   teacher
         'Three new teachers came (to this school) this semester'

(51)   Nabian you sange ren
         There   have three man
         'There are three men'

References

Adger, D., Pintzuk, S., Plunkett, B. & Tsoulas, G., eds. (1999): *Specifiers, Minimalist Approaches.* Oxford: Oxford University Press.

Aissen, J. (1999): Markedness and Subject Choice in Optimality Theory. *Natural Language and Linguistic Theory* 17. 673–711.

Alexiadou, A. & Anagnostopoulou, E. (1999): EPP without Spec, IP. In: Adger, D., Pintzuk, S., Plunkett, B. & Tsoulas, G., eds. (1999): *Specifiers, Minimalist Approaches.* Oxford: Oxford University Press. 93–109.

Baker, C. L. (1989): *English Syntax.* Cambridge: MIT Press.

Barbosa, P., Fox, D., Hagstrom, P., McGinnis, M. & Pesetsky, D., eds. (1998): *Is the Best Good Enough?* Boston: MIT Press.

Barlow, M. (1992): *A Situated Theory of Agreement.* London: Garland.

Batin, A. & Collins, C., eds. (2001): *Handbook of Contemporary Syntactic Theory.* Oxford: Blackwell Publishers.

Beckman, J., Walsh, L. & Urbaczyk, S., eds. (1995): Papers in Optimality Theory. *University of Massachusetts Occasional Papers* 18. GLSA, UMASS, Amherst.

Belletti, A. & Shlonsky, U. (1995): The Order of Verbal Complements: A Comparative Study. *Natural Language and Linguistic Theory* 13:3. 489–526.

Benedicto, E. (2001): Indigeneous Languages. *University of Massachusetts Occasional Papers in Linguistics* 20. GLSA, University of Massachusetts, Amherst.

Black, J. R. & Motapanyane, V., eds. (1996): Microparametric Syntax and Dialect Variation. *Current Issues in Linguistic Theory* 139. Amsterdam: John Benjamin Publishing Company.

Brandi, L. & Cordin, P. (1989): Two Italian Dialects and the Null Subject Parameter. In: Jaeggli, J. & Safir, K., eds. (1989): *The Null Subject Parameter.* Boston: Kluwer.

Bresnan, J. (1998): Explaining Morphosyntactic Competition. Draft of paper later published in: Batin, A. & Collins, C., eds. (2001): *Handbook of Contemporary Syntactic Theory.*

Cardinaletti, A. & Starke, M. (1994): The typology of structural deficiency: A case study of the three classes of pronouns. In: Riemsdijk, H. van, ed. (1999): *Clitics in the Languages of Europe.* (EALT / EUROTYP 20-5.) Berlin/New York: Mouton de Gruyter. 145–233.

Coopman, P., Everaert, M. & Grimshaw, J. (2000): *Lexical Specification and Insertion.* Amsterdam: John Benjamin Publishing Company.

Corbett, G. (1979): The Agreement Hierarchy. *Journal of Linguistics* 15. 203–224.

Diesing, M. (1992): *Indefinites.* (Linguistic Inquiry Monograph.) Cambridge: MIT Press.

Diesing, M. & Jelinek, E. (1993): The Syntax and Semantics of Object Shift. *Working Papers in Scandinavian Syntax* 51.

Fassi Fehri, A. (1993): *Issues in the Structure of Arabic Clauses and Words.* Boston: Kluwer.

Greenberg, J., ed. (1978): *Universal of Human Language.* Vol. 4. Stanford University Press.

Griffith, T. (1996): *Projecting Transitivity and Agreement.* PhD dissertation, University of California, Irvine.

Grimshaw, J. (1991): *Extended Projections.* Ms, Brandeis University.

Grimshaw, J. (1997): Projections, Heads and Optimality. *Linguistic Inquiry* 28. 373–422.

Grimshaw, J. (2000): Locality and Extended Projections. In: Coopman, P., Everaert, M. & Grimshaw, J. (2000): *Lexical Specification and Insertion.* Amsterdam: John Benjamin Publishing Company. 115–133.

Grimshaw, J. (2001): Optimal Clitic Positions and the Lexicon in Romance Clitics. In: Legendre, G., Grimshaw, J. & Vikner, S. (2001): *OT Syntax.* Cambridge: MIT Press. 205–240.

Grimshaw, J. & Samek-Lodovici, V. (1998): Optimal Subjects and Subject Universals. In: Barbosa, P., Fox, D., Hagstrom, P., McGinnis, M. & Pesetsky, D., eds. (1998): *Is the Best Good Enough?* Boston: MIT Press. 193–220.

Haider, H. (1987): *Deutsche Syntax, generativ – Prinzipen und Parameter der Deutschen Syntax.* Habilitation, University of Wien.

Haider, H. (1993): *Deutsche Syntax, generativ.* Tübingen: Gunter Narr Verlag.

Haiman, J. & Benincá, P. (1992): *The Rhaeto-Romance Languages.* London: Routledge.

Heycock, C. & Kroch, A. (1999): *Agreement, Inversion and Interpretation in Copular Sentences.* Ms, University of Edinburgh and University of Pennsylvania. Draft of invited talk at Formal Approaches to Slavic Linguistic 8.

Hrafnbjargarson, G. H. (2001): An Optimality Theory Analysis of Agreement in Icelandic DAT-NOM Constructions. *Working Papers of Scandinavian Syntax* 68, University of Lund, Sweden.

Jaeggli, J. & Safir, K., eds. (1989): *The Null Subject Parameter.* Boston: Kluwer.

Legendre, G. (1999): *Why French Stylistic Inversion is Different.* Ms, Johns Hopkins University.

Legendre, G., Grimshaw, J. & Vikner, S. (2001): *OT Syntax.* Cambridge: MIT Press.

Lu, H. (1994): *Preverbal NPs in Spanish and Chinese.* PhD dissertation, UCLA.

Manzini, R. & Savoia, L. (1998): *Parameters of Subject Inflection in Italian Dialects.* Ms, University of Florence, Italy.

McCarthy, J. & Prince, A. (1993): *Prosodic Morphology I: Constraint Interaction and Satisfaction.* Ms, University of Massachusetts, Amherst, and Rutgers University. (RuCCS-TR-3.)

Moravcsik, E. (1978): Agreement. In: Greenberg, J., ed. (1978): *Universal of Human Language.* Vol. 4. Stanford University Press. 331–374.

Prince, A. & Smolensky, P. (1993): *Optimality Theory: Constraint Interaction in Generative Grammar.* Technical Report TR-2, Rutgers Center for Cognitive Science, Rutgers University.

Riemsdijk, H. van, ed. (1999): The Typology of European Languages. Vol. 8: Clitics in the Languages of Europe. Berlin/New York: Mouton de Gruyter.

Rizzi, L. (1982): *Issues in Italian Syntax.* Dordrecht: Foris.

Rizzi, L. (1986): Null Objects in Italian and the Theory of *pro. Linguistic Inquiry* 17. 501–557.

Rizzi, L. (1990): *Relativized Minimality.* (Linguistic Inquiry Monograph.) Cambridge: MIT Press.

Saccon, G. (1993): Postverbal Subjects. PhD dissertation, Harvard University.

Samek-Lodovici, V. (1996): Constraints on Subjects. An Optimality Theoretic Analysis. PhD dissertation, Rutgers University.

Samek-Lodovici, V. & Prince, A. (1999): *Optima.* Technical Report TR-57, Rutgers Center for Cognitive Science, Rutgers University. (ROA-363-1199; http://roa.rutgers.edu).

Sigurðsson, H. (1992): *Verbal Syntax and Case in Icelandic.* University of Iceland: Institute of Linguistics.

Suñer, M. (1992): Subject Clitics in the Northern Italian Vernaculars. *Natural* Language *and Linguistic Theory* 10. 641–672.

Taraldsen, K. (1996): Reflexives, Pronouns, and Subjects. Agreement in Icelandic and Faroese. In: Black, J. R. & Motapanyane, V., eds. (1996): Microparametric Syntax and Dialect Variation. *Current Issues in Linguistic Theory* 139. Amsterdam: John Benjamins Publishing Company. 189–221.

Vallduví, E. (1992): *The Informational Component.* Garland Publishing.

Weerman, F. (1989): *The V2 Conspiracy.* Dordrecht: Foris.

Wooldford, E. (1995): Object Agreement in Palauan: Specificity, Humanness, Economy and Optimality. In: Beckman, J., Walsh, L. & Urbaczyk, S., eds. (1995): Papers in Optimality Theory. *University of Massachusetts Occasional Papers* 18. GLSA, UMASS, Amherst. 655–702.

Wooldford, E. (2001): Conditions on Object Agreement in Ruwund (Bantu). In: Benedicto, E., ed. (1995): Indigeneous Languages. *University of Massachusetts Occasional Papers in Linguistics.*

Zubizarreta, M. L. (1999): *Prosody, Focus, and Word Order.* (Linguistic Inquiry Monograph.) Cambridge: MIT Press.

London, UK   Vieri Samek-Lodovici

Italian Department, University College London, Gower Street, WC1E 6BT London,
e-mail: v.samek-lodovici@ucl.ac.uk

Modularity in OT-Morphosyntax[1]

Jochen Trommer

Abstract

In Noyer (1993) and Trommer (2001b) models for OT-morphology are proposed, where morphology interprets the output of Syntax along the lines of Distributed Morphology (DM, Halle & Marantz 1993). A major virtue of such a modular architecture is its restrictiveness: Syntactic representations and constraints cannot directly interact with morphological constraints. In contrast, Bresnan (1999a) argues that syntactic constraints *do* directly interact with morphological constraints, and that there is only one morpho-syntactic evaluation procedure. In this paper I develop a modular model of morphosyntax based on Trommer (2001b) and show that the data that Bresnan and others have provided in favor of a global model of OT-morphosyntax can be easily reinterpreted in this model.

1   Introduction

In Noyer (1993) and Trommer (2001b) models for OT-morphology are proposed, where morphology interprets the output of Syntax along the lines of Distributed Morphology (DM, Halle & Marantz, 1993). A major virtue of such a modular architecture is its restrictiveness: Syntactic representations and constraints cannot directly interact with morphological constraints. In contrast, Bresnan (1999a) argues that syntactic constraints *do* directly interact with morphological constraints, and that there is only one morphosyntactic evaluation procedure. In this paper I develop a modular model of morphosyntax based on Trommer (2001b) and show that the data that Bresnan and others have provided in favor of a global model of OT-morphosyntax can be easily reinterpreted in this model.

[1] I thank Alec Marantz and John Frampton for discussions and for making available to me unpublished material. Thanks to Gisbert Fanselow for awakening my interest in Free Relative constructions and for persistent encouragement to write this article. A part of the research reflected in this article has been supported by the DFG graduate programm *Economy and Complexity in Language*.

2 The Framework: Distributed Optimality

In Distributed Morphology (DM, Halle & Marantz 1993), syntax operates on morphosyntactic feature bundles without phonological content. After syntax, these representations are enriched and manipulated by morphological rules. Finally so-called vocabulary items are inserted which interpret morphosyntactic features through phonological material. Thus morphosyntax includes the three levels in (1):[2]

(1)   a. Syntax
        b. Morphological Rules
        c. Vocabulary Insertion

This architecture is illustrated in (2) for the German sentence *wir trinken*, 'we drink'. Syntax yields the representation in (2a). Morphological rules add case and agreement affixes as in (2b). In (2c) vocabulary items are inserted: /wir/ ↔ [+D+1+pl] into [+D+1+pl], /trink/ ↔ [+V] into [+V], and /-en/ ↔ [+Agr+pl] into [+Agr+1+pl]. Note that vocabulary items can be underspecified. Thus, /-en/ ↔ [+Agr+pl] realizes only part of the features of [+Agr+1+pl]. Zero vocabulary items are inserted in [+I] and [+Nom] which are omitted here for legibility.[3]

(2)   a. $[\text{+D+1+pl}]_i$ [+I] $[t_i$ [+V]]$_{VP}$
        b. $[[\text{+D+1+pl}][\text{+Nom}]]_i$ [+I] $[t_i$ [[+V][+Agr+1+pl]]]$_{VP}$
        c. /wir/ ↔ [+D+1+pl] /trink/ ↔ [+V] /-en/ ↔ [+Agr+pl]

The model I propose in this paper is a constraint-based, modular adaptation of DM's architecture. I call this model *Distributed Optimality* (DO, Trommer, 2001b) since it is based on the assumption of different morphosyntactic components, all mapping specific inputs to outputs according to the principles of Optimality Theory (OT, Prince & Smolensky 1993; McCarthy & Prince 1995).

2.1 The Architecture of DO

I assume that morphosyntax involves the following three modules:

(3)   a. Syntax (lexical Items ⇒ syntactic chains)
        b. Chain Interpretation (syntactic chains ⇒ single heads)
        c. Head Interpretation (heads ⇒ vocabulary items)

---

[2] Additionally, Vocabulary Items might be modified by morphophonological readjustment rules. Since processes of this type play no role in the following discussion, I will not discuss readjustment rules here.

[3] [+Nom] tends to be empty crosslinguistically, but is realized by phonological material in some languages such as Latvian (Croft 1990: 104). There might also be the option to leave syntactic heads "unfilled". See Halle & Marantz (1993: 132) for more discussion of null morphemes in DM.

Again, the Syntax component creates abstract syntactic representations which contain neither agreement nor case affixes (while chains might be assigned abstract case). Crucially, Syntax creates chains from lexical items. Chain Interpretation maps chains onto single heads (put another way, traces, i.e. copies produced by movement are eliminated) and adds (abstract) case and agreement heads. This comprises the part of morphology that depends on the structure of chains and non-local parts of phrase structure. As Syntax, this module does not involve phonological features. In Head Interpretation, the abstract heads from Chain Interpretation are mapped to vocabulary items. This step corresponds to Vocabulary Insertion in DM. (4) illustrates the model for our example sentence:

(4)   a.   [+D+1+pl]$_i$ [+I] [[+D+1+pl]$_i$ [+V]]$_{VP}$
        b.   [+D+1+pl][+Nom]] [+I] [~~[+D+1+pl]~~ [[+V][+Agr+1+pl]]]$_{VP}$
        c.   /wir/ ↔ [+D+1+pl] /trink/ ↔ [+V] /en/ ↔ [+Agr+pl]

The syntax generates the representation in (4a). There is a chain comprising the pronoun ([+D+1+pl]) in the specifier of IP and its base position in the VP. Chain Interpretation maps this chain onto (4b), where the chain is reduced to the single head in Spec IP to which the [+Nom] head is added. To V an agreement head is adjoined. Finally, the heads are interpreted by the vocabulary items. Note that not all heads are interpreted by vocabulary items. Thus [+Nom] is simply not realized morphologically. In addition, the vocabulary item for *-en* is not marked for its status as a prefix or a suffix which is determined by the ranking of universal alignment constraints (Trommer 2001).

2.2   Differences between DO and Derivational DM

Consider another example that illustrates further differences between derivational DM and DO: In Turkana (Dimmendaal 1983), finite verbs agree with subjects and objects in person, and the same person markers are used for subject and object agreements. However, each verb bears exactly one person marker. If one of the arguments is 3rd person and the other non-third, agreement is with the latter. Hence, the forms in (5) differ only by the inverse marker *k-* in (5b) which marks the fact that the object is higher in animacy than the subject:

(5)   a.   à- mɪn-à
           D-1-love-ASP
           'I love her' (Dimmendaal 1983: 69).

        b.   k-à-mɪn-à
           D-1-love-ASP
           'she loves me' (Dimmendaal 1983: 123)

Halle & Marantz (1993) assume for a similar case – blocking of person prefixes in the Algonquian language Potawatomi – that it is due to a fusion operation which puts the two relevant nodes (here: AgrS and AgrO) into the same head position while leaving the feature structures themselves intact.[4] By assumption, only one vocabulary item can be inserted into a single head position. Thus a conflict arises whether *à-* is inserted or the 3rd person marker *e-* which appears in intransitive forms or transitive forms without non-third arguments. Halle & Marantz resolve problems of this type by ordering the vocabulary items in a list of the type in (6):

(6)   a.   /à- -/ ↔ [+1]
       b.   /e-/ ↔ [+3]

Vocabulary insertion now inserts the first matching element. Thus for (6b) we get the derivation in (7):

(7)   a.   [+V]   [+AgrS+3]   [+AgrO+1]   Fusion   ⇒

$$\text{b.} \quad [\,+V\,] \quad \begin{bmatrix} [\,+\,AgrS\,+\,3\,] \\ \\ [\,+\,AgrO\,+\,1\,] \end{bmatrix} \quad \text{Vocabulary Insertion} \quad \Rightarrow$$

       c.   /mìn/↔[+V]   /à- -/↔[+1]

While precedence of vocabulary items can be determined in most cases by specificity - a [+1 +pl] item would b e favored over a [+1] or [+pl] item – this is of no use in determining the order of items in (6) which contain each one feature. But since it seems to be a general property of affix blocking cross-linguistically that 1st/2nd person markers "win" over 3rd person markers (cf. Trommer 2001a), the ordering of these items should not be due to arbitrary stipulation. Indeed Halle & Marantz speculate that such an ordering might be determined by reference to a feature hierarchy (1/2 > 3 >...). Compare this to the DO account illustrated in (8). Here the fact that the realization of [+1] is "more important" than the realization of [+3] is captured by a constraint which states that a PERSON feature ([P]) of a [-3] category should be realized if it is adjacent to a [+3] category. Thus, PARSE $[P]^{[-3]/[+3]}$ incurs a constraint violation for each person feature of a [-3] head at the input to Head Interpretation that is not realized in the output. The ban on two agreement affixes is induced by the higher-ranked BLOCK [P] which allows only one simple person affix in a verb form.

The most obvious difference between the accounts is that the morphological rules invoked in DM (here: Fusion) are replaced by constraints (here: the BLOCK constraint). There is however a second, more subtle difference. What the single modules do is to map their input representations into representations of different types (Chains ⇒ heads, heads ⇒ Vocabulary Items). Hence, unlike

---

[4] Alternatively, DM allows rules that delete heads or features or zero affixes. But it is difficult to see how the restriction to one person affix can be achieved without stipulating multiple rules or zero morphemes, which would miss an obvious generalization.

morphological rules, the modules of this model do qualitatively different things
and in different locality domains. Thus, I assume that Head Interpretation operates on small word-like units which I call spell-out domains and which each
comprise a lexical category and all string-adjacent heads from its extended projection (see Trommer 2001 for further discussion), while Chain Interpretation is
defined on chains. Note that the constraints invoked in (8) apply at Head Interpretation. Similar types of constraints seem to play a role for Chain Interpretation, but – due to the more global domain of this module – with somewhat
different consequences. Section 5 gives an example for the application of constraints at Chain Interpretation

(8)   Mixed: $[+\text{Nom} +3]_1[+\text{Acc} +1]_2$

	BLOCK [P]	PARSE $[P]^{[-3]/[+3]}$
☞ $[+1]_2$		
$[+3]_1$		*!
$[+1]_2[+3]_1$	*!	

In Trommer (2001b), I show that the use of violable constraints improves in
many respects on derivational DM. Here, I will just point out some aspects connected with our Turkana example. First, features of the agreement heads occur
also in other affixes coocuring with the person affixes. Thus, subject plural is
standardly marked by a plural suffix:

(9)   ì-los-e-t-è
        2-go-ASP-PL
        'you (pl.) will go' (Dimmendaal 1983:122)

If AgrS and AgrO are fused, in Classical DM a further operation (called
"fission" in Halle & Marantz 1993) has to be assumed that takes the plural
feature from AgrS and transforms it into a separate head (Otherwise *ì-* would
block *-è* or vice versa.)[5]. In DO, the possibility of the plural marker follows
simply from the fact that PARSE [P] is restricted to person features. A further
problem with the derivational analysis becomes obvious if we look at the way
Turkana manages the resolution of Blocking when both arguments are [-3]. In
this case, the person affix corresponding to the [+Nom] head is realized:

(10)   a. k-à-ram-ì
            D-1-beat-ASP
            'I will beat you' (Dimmendaal 1983: 122)

<hr>

[5] That subject person and number agreement correspond to the same syntactic head can be
seen from the fact that 1pl agreement is marked by the single affix *ki-* expressing person and number
(Dimmendaal 1983: 120).

b. k-ì-ràm-e-tè

D-1-beat-ASP-PL

'you (pl.) beat me' (Dimmendaal 1983: 122)

In the DO account, this can be captured by assuming a further PARSE constraint which favors realization for person features of [+Nom] over [+Acc] heads: [6]

(11)   Only SAP Arguments: [+Nom +2] $_1$[+Acc +1] $_2$

	BLOCK [P]	PARSE $[P]^{[-3]/[+3]}$	PARSE $[P]^{[+NOM]/[+AC]}$
☞ [+2]$_1$		*	
[+1]$_2$		*	*!
[+2]$_1$[+1]$_2$	*!		

A fixed ordering of vocabulary items can not account for the data in (1 0). Since this would predict that in (11a) and (11b), the same item would be inserted, i.e. if /à -/ is ranked above /ì-/, /à-/ should appear in both forms, and the same for /ì-/ if the ranking is reversed.

See Trommer (2001b: chap. 2) on more evidence in favor of a constraint-based version of DM which are not relevant for the crucial point I want to make in this paper: that there are no good reasons to assume a global account of OT-morphosyntax. Most of the arguments I use to this aim can also be made – and partially have been made – under the assumptions of derivational DM (see Frampton 2001 and Marantz 2000).

3   The Problem: Global Morphosyntactic Competition

A crucial consequence of the architecture proposed in the last section is that constraints belonging to different modules cannot interact, i.e. be evaluated in the same EVAL procedure. However, there are data that seem to show that the details of morphophonological spell-out can affect syntactic wellformedness. Thus the ungrammaticality of (12b) vs. (12a) seems to be due to a morphophonological constraint against the form *amn't.

(12)   a. Isn't he leaving?
       b. *Amn't I leaving?
       c. Aren't I leaving?
       d. Am I not leaving?

[6] This has to be ranked below PARSE $[P]^{[-3]/[+3]}$. Otherwise the latter would become inactive in (9).

In the literature, there are two main approaches to this problem. Marantz (1999) proposes that conflicting morphophonological constraints can lead to Ineffability. This means that there would be no output for the input that corresponds to (12b). In contrast, Bresnan (1999a) assumes that the sentence is blocked by more optimal sentences such as (12c) or (12d). To make this account work, (12b) and (12c)/(12d) must be evaluated against each other. This evaluation involves syntactic constraints since these are different syntactic constructions, differing in word order. On the other hand, (12d) wins the competition over (12b) under the pressure of a morphophonological constraint (*AMN'T). Hence morphophonological and syntactic constraints must be involved in the same evaluation process. This is impossible under my assumptions.

But also the Ineffability account as proposed by Marantz is not possible in DO: Conflicting constraints in OT cannot lead to ineffability, since it is one of the core assumptions of OT that constraint violation and conflict leads not to ungrammaticality, but to conflict resolution.

What I will propose in this paper is an account in terms of ineffability based on the concept of interpretability (section 4). In sections 5 and 6, it is shown how data that seem to require global evaluation of morphosyntactic constraints can be accounted for by local constraints and ineffability. Section 5 is based on Vogel's (2001) account of Free Relative Constructions and section 6 on Bresnan's (1999a) work on English negation. In section 7, I discuss the problem of modularity under a more general perspective. Section 8 gives a short summary of the paper.

4   Approaches to Ineffability

In this section I discuss different approaches to ineffability[7] and propose a new account which is based on the notion of interpretability. This approach will be used in the following sections to account for apparent cases of global morphosyntactic competition.

4.1   Ineffability as the result of Constraint Conflict (Marantz 1999)

Marantz (1999: 5) interprets morphological ineffability as the situation where "a well-formed syntactic structure fails to yield a pronounceable interpretation because competing morphophonological constraints cannot be reconciled." One case of ineffability Marantz adduces is the matching requirements for free relatives in German:

(13)   a.   Ich zerstöre, was mich ärgert
             I destroy what me upsets
             'I destroy what upsets me'

---

[7] See Müller (2000: 82–88) for a recent overview of approaches to ineffability in OT.

b. *Ich zerstöre wer/wen mich ärgert
    I destroy who:NOM/ACC me upsets
    'I destroy who upsets me'

The idea is that the relative pronoun in these constructions must realize the nominative assigned to the subject position of the embedded relative clause, as well as the accusative assigned from the matrix verb *zerstöre*. This is possible in the neuter gender, where *was* neutralizes the contrast between nominative and accusative, but not in the masculine, where there are two morphologically distinct pronouns.

As Marantz puts it the "vocabulary item for the relative pronoun must be the winning choice both for the case assigned to the free relative and for the case assigned to the trace of the relative pronoun within the free relative. Where the vocabulary items that win the competition for the two sets of case features are different, the structure is ineffable" (Marantz 1999: 5).

This account is problematic in DO since it is not reconcilable with the basic principles of OT, where constraint conflict in principle does not lead to ungrammaticality. In addition, there are empirical and conceptual problems: First, the account is problematic for other cases where two underlying feature structures induce competition for Vocabulary Insertion. Thus, in fusion (see (7) in section 2) two feature bundles are involved that independently would lead to the insertion of different Vocabulary Items: The underlying AgrS head in (7) favors [+3] /e-/, while AgrO favors [+1] /á-/. In contrast to the situation with FRs this does not lead to ineffability, but to conflict resolution. Second, the account predicts that all cases of non-matching FRs should be ungrammatical. But there are languages where such a case conflict does not lead to ungrammaticality (see section 5), and even in German there exist grammatical FRs where the case requirements do not match (Vogel 2001: 2):

(14)   a. weil uns besucht, wen Maria mag
           because us visits who-ACC Maria likes

       b. Ich lade ein wem ich vertraue
           I invite who-DAT I trust

4.2   Ineffability as a Result of the Null Parse

Prince & Smolensky (1993) propose to account for ineffability in phonology by the possibility of the "null parse", i.e. a realization of an input that does not contain any phonological material. If the null parse becomes optimal for a certain input *I*, it blocks all non-null candidates. But since the null parse is unusable for communication, it is nonetheless ill-formed. As a consequence, *I* has no grammatical output at all. This idea which was developed in an early version of OT is somewhat problematic under Correspondence Theory (McCarthy & Prince 1995) which is assumed in DO. Take as an example the ineffable structure in (15a):

(15) a. *Amn't I tall?
      b. Am I tall?

Assume that the null parse is the optimal candidate for the underlying proposition of (15a). Then the null parse should be more harmonic than (15b). But (15b) is better than (15a) for all constraints that require the realization of underlying heads (e.g. PARSE Person, PARSE Number, etc.) and it is difficult to see what type of constraint would favor the null parse over (15b) without also excluding (15b) as the output of the positive question. Hence, the null parse in correspondence-theoretic OT is probably excluded in most cases for principled reasons.[8] Ackema & Neeleman (2000) avoid this consequence by guaranteeing a special status to the null parse. In a model with (apparently) global morphosyntactic evaluation, they assume that all candidates must be semantically equivalent to the input. However, they interpret this "condition such that it removes from the candidate set those candidates that have an interpretation which deviates from that of the other candidates. Since the null parse does not have an interpretation it cannot have a deviating interpretation either. It is therefore never affected by the condition of semantic equivalence. Hence, every candidate set contains the null parse." (Ackema & Neeleman, 2000: 281). The ineffability of *Amn't I tall? can then be accounted for as follows ("0" stands for the null parse):

*AMN'T is ranked above all relevant PARSE constraints, hence the optimal candidate cannot contain *amn't*. However the only candidate which avoids *amn't* is the null parse since all other underparsing candidates (such as *Am I tall?*) are excluded by the principle of semantic equivalence.

(16)

	*AMN'T	PARSE 1sg	PARSE NEG
Amn't I tall?	*!		
☞ 0		*	*

This approach is difficult to include into a modular architecture since it requires that all constraint evaluation presupposes previous semantic evaluation. At a more technical level, Head Interpretation as proposed here would be excluded because the structures resulting at this level do not have a (compositional) se-

---

[8] In Prince & Smolensky (1993) deletion of segments was coded by a diacritic notation in output candidates, not by the relation of input and candidate. This led to the paradox situation that the null parse implied no deletion markers. For the constraints against deletion, deletion of all segments in the null parse meant no deletion at all, which made it a rather harmonic candidate. In correspondence Theory, the null parse implies maximal violation of constraints against deletion. Vogel (this volume: fn.15) also considers the possibility of a null parse account for FRs, and suggests that "there is only one constraint that this candidate violates, namely a constraint 'NoNullParse'". But as already noted the null parse should also violate other constraints, and Vogel himself rejects this approach for independent reasons.

mantics; they are simply strings of vocabulary items, pairing phonological and syntactic features. But the null parse approach also carries with itself inherent problems: The special status of the null parse has to be stipulated. Moreover, it leads to strange effects once other PARSE constraints are taken into account. Assume, for example, a language where all other PARSE constraints are ranked below *AMN'T, but PARSE PREP(OSITION) is ranked above *AMN'T. Since PARSE PREP is irrelevant for (16), *Amn't I tall?* is still ineffable in this language. However, *Amn't I the emperor of Wyoming?* – containing the preposition *of* – is not as shown in (17):

(17)

	PARSE PREP	*AMN'T	PARSE 1SG	PARSE NEG
☞ *Amn' t I the emperor of Wyoming?*		*		
0	*!		*	*

The reason is that any high-ranked Parse constraint can render a structure effable even though the category specified by the constraint is completely un-related to the constraint that would render the structure ineffable. Thus, under the ranking in (17), any preposition at any distance from *am* can "save" the con-struction. Such effects, however seem to be conceptually odd and empirically non-existent. The basic problem with this version of the null parse approach seems to be that it is too non-local.[9] The approach to ineffability that I propose in 4.3 can be seen as a localized version of the null parse approach avoiding this problem.

4.3   An Alternative Approach to Ineffability

As we saw in the preceding sections, existing approaches to Ineffability are not consistent with the architecture of DO and problematic for independent reasons. What I will propose here, is that the crucial notion to account for morpho-syntactic ineffability is *interpretability*. To be grammatical, outputs must be both optimal and interpretable. If a certain input *I* has an optimal output that is not interpretable, *I* is ineffable.

More concretely, I assume that there are exactly two reasons why the output of a morphosyntactic grammar module might be optimal but non-interpretable and hence leads to ungrammaticality:

---

[9] Ackema & Neeleman (2000: 298) propose to circumvent this problem by assuming a special evaluation procedure for PARSE constraints ensuring that these do never interact. However, there are phenomena where PARSE constraints *must* interact (see the discussion of Turkana in section 2.2 and Trommer 2001b). The only further motivation Ackema and Neeleman give for treating PARSE constraints differently from other constraint types is the fact that these allegedly are the only con-straints that have to evaluate output candidates against the input. However, as shown in detail in Trommer (2001b: chap. 4), there is evidence that almost all morphological constraint types exist in versions referring to the input.

Illegibility: The output of a module might not be a suitable input for the subsequent module. This analysis will be applied to free relative constructions in section 4.

Irrecoverability:[10] The suppression of specific morphosyntactic features or categories is excluded because this might make it impossible to recover the semantic content of a syntactic structure.

Irrecoverability partitions morphosyntactic features into two distinct sets: Recoverable features like person and number features can in principle remain unrealized, while irrecoverable features like the lexical features of verbs must surface. This accounts for the fact that there are many cases of zero agreement and pronouns but virtually no instances of lexical verbs that are not overtly realized. This is unexpected if there is any general economy constraint, which could force suppression of all types of features under appropriate constraint rankings.[11] Note that recoverability is not checking syntactic configurations to determine whether features actually can be recovered in a given construction. For example, pro drop is possible even in a language without agreement such as Japanese since person and number are in principle recoverable.

I assume that there are additional violable constraints that require the realization of recoverable *and* irrecoverable features, but – by definition – their effect can be overridden by other constraints. Thus, while a module might have optimal outputs that suppress the lexical verb completely, such a candidate will not be grammatical. An application of the Irrecoverability criterion will be used in section 5 to account for the ineffability of certain English negation constructions.

Irrecoverability is a restricted version of the Null-Parse-Account of Prince & Smolensky (1993)[12] while Illegibility is inspired by the interface conditions of Chomsky (1995).[13] It is crucial that these conditions do not trigger the formation of candidates that conform to them but simply render candidates ungrammatical that do not satisfy them. In the following two sections, I will show that data which seem to require the interaction of constraints from different morphosyntactic modules can be neatly accounted for in terms of ineffability.

---

[10] The idea of invoking irrecoverability is inspired by a related approach in Frampton (2001). See section 6.6 for discussion.

[11] Possible counterexamples to the claim that lexical verbs are never suppressed are sentences such as German *Ich muss nach Hause*, I:NOM must to home, 'I must go home', or *I began the book* implying 'I began to read the book' (thanks to J.D. Bobaljik for these examples). Interestingly, in English, there is independent evidence that *go* is not a lexical verb: It shows suppletion (*went*), which is otherwise only found in functional elements. See the Allomorphy section of the DM website for discussion (http://www.ling.upenn.edu/~rnoyer/dm/).

[12] I.e. here not suppression of all input features leads to unusability, but suppression of specific features.

[13] Müller (1997) uses a similar approach to ineffability invoking uninterpretability at the LF interface.

5   German Free Relatives

Recall from section 4.1 that in German free relative constructions with two non-matching cases are not always excluded, which makes an account in terms of ineffability problematic. In section 5.1, I will outline the approach of Vogel (2001) which relies on global morphosyntactic competition. In 5.2, I sketch my general analysis of FRs and in 5.3 and 5.4, I give an analysis of free relatives in German showing that all the data Vogel provides can be recast in the modular framework given the approach to ineffability from 4.3.

5.1   Vogel (2001)

As Marantz (1999), Vogel (2001) assumes that the grammaticality contrast between (13a) and (13b) is induced by the inventory of FR pronouns, and conflicting constraints. (18) contains a rough paraphrase of the two constraints that are crucial for his analysis.

(18)   a. *REALISE CASE*: For each case feature assigned at LF, there is an element at PF that realizes it. (Vogel 2001: 26)

        b. *INTEGRITY*:   No input element (Free relative pronoun) has more than one output correspondents. (Vogel 2001: 22)

While Vogel does not make it clear what is meant exactly by "realization of a case feature", it seems that *was* is supposed to be able to realize accusative and nominative case at the same time, while *wer* and *wen* realize only nominative or only accusative respectively. To solve the problem that EVAL will always produce an output candidate for a given input – and here the analysis differs crucially from the one by Marantz – Vogel assumes that the input that corresponds to (13b) results in the output in (19):

(19)   Wer mich ärgert, den zerstöre ich.
        who me upsets him destroy I.
        'Who(ever) makes me angry, I destroy him.'

While this output violates INTEGRITY (the free relative pronoun is "split" into a demonstrative and a standard relative pronoun), this is justified by REALISE CASE which is by assumption higher ranked in German, and which would be violated by a free relative which realizes only one case. The tableaux in (20) and (21) show the contrast of *was* and *wer/wen*:[14]

---

[14] While the suboptimal forms in (20) are ungrammatical, the correlative *Was mich ärgert, das zerstöre ich* is grammatical since it is the optimal output for a different (correlative) input LF.

(20)

		REALISE CASE	INTEGRITY
☞	Wer mich ärgert, den zerstöre ich		*
	Ich zerstöre, wer mich ärgert	*!ACC	
	Ich zerstöre, wen mich ärgert	*!NOM	

(21)

		REALISE CASE	INTEGRITY
	Was mich ärgert, das zerstöre ich		*!
☞	Ich zerstöre, was mich ärgert		

It is crucial to note the type of the competitors in Vogel's model. He assumes that inputs are fully specified LF representations while each output candidate is an ordered [LF,PF] pair (Vogel 2001: 15). Thus for the evaluation of morphosyntactic constraints, there exists only one grammar module, and each constraint is ranked with respect to each other constraint.

If something like Vogel's analysis of FRs is correct, DO is untenable, since the spell-out of morphemes (i.e. the choice of *was* vs. *wer/wen*) in a modular model cannot interact with truly syntactic constraints concerning the choice whether a given input results in a syntactic structure like (21) or (20). On the other hand, we cannot say that non-matching structures such as (13b) are uninterpretable in general, since German has non-matching free relatives for other case combinations. In the following sections I propose an analysis of FRs based on constraints at Chain Interpretation, not in Head Interpretation. It will be shown that the contrast between *was* and *wer/wen* in (21) and (20) can also be accounted straightforwardly in this way, without referring to specific vocabulary items.

5.2   FRs, Case Assignment and Interpretability

Recall that the attachment of case features to DPs in DO does not happen in syntax proper, but at Chain Interpretation. It is driven by constraints that require the realization of specific cases on DPs which are assigned to the corresponding chains in Syntax. I will assume that the FR pronoun constitutes a wh-moved DP in the specifier of a CP, but remain agnostic for whether the FR clause contains a D(eterminer) head as in Alexiadou & Varlokosta (1995 22b), or not (Vogel 2001 22a):[15]

(22)   a.   Ich zerstöre $[_{CP}$ $[FR_i$ $[_{C'}$ $\_\_i$ mich ärgert]]]
         b.   Ich zerstöre $\emptyset$ $[_{DP}$ $_D\emptyset$ $[_{CP}$ FR_i $[_{C'}$ $\_\_i$ mich ärgert]]]

[15] There is still a vivid debate on the correct internal structure for FRs and relative clauses in general. See Alexiadou et. al (2000) for a recent overview of possible analyses.

Crucially, Spec(CP) is assigned the case of the matrix verb (m-case), and the base position ($\_{i}$) the case of the verb in the relative clause (r-case). Hence the chain $FR_i \ldots\_{i}$ is assigned two cases, in (22), nominative and accusative. This means that the FR pronoun as the correspondent of $FR_i \ldots\_{i}$ at the output of Chain Interpretation is required to realize two cases.[16]

All accounts of the case conflict in FRs that we have encountered so far are based on the idea that a FR pronoun cannot realize two cases at the same time. I capture this intuition by the assumption that case affixes which contain two instances of case features (e.g. Nom and Acc) are illegible at Head Interpretation. In other words, an input *I* that leads to such a configuration as the output of Chain Interpretation leads to crash, and the grammar as a whole will not generate any output for *I*. On the other hand, Chain Interpretation *can* in principle produce structures with two case specifications in the same affix, and will do so, when the relevant PARSE constraints are ranked higher than all constraints that would disfavor such affixes. This is illustrated schematically in (23):

(23)   Input: $[+Acc]_{m\text{-case}} \rightarrow Chain_i \leftarrow [+Nom]_{r\text{-case}}$

		PARSE Case	...
☞	DP_i [+Nom +Acc] ♱		
	DP_i [+Nom]	*!ACC	
	DP_i [+Acc]	*!NOM	

The chain $Chain_i$ is assigned [+Nom] and [+Acc]. Since PARSE CASE is ranked above all other relevant constraints, both features are realized in the same feature structure, which induces crash at the interface. This is indicated in (23) by the cemetery sign "♱". Under this ranking, we get the distribution of FRs in languages such as Hindi, where no FRs are allowed.[17]

If Chain Interpretation also involves constraints requiring systematic feature neutralization (deletion), we can account for languages where FRs are possible. Thus, we can assume a constraint such as *CaseCase, which disallows two case specifications in a single affix. I suggest further that PARSE Case actually consists of two subconstraints which require the realization of m-case and r-case: If only one of these constraints is ranked higher than *CaseCase, non-matching FRs should become grammatical and the pronoun should consistently show m-case or r-case. Thus for Icelandic, where FRs are possible for all case combinations, and the FR pronoun always bears m-case, we can assume the ranking

---

[16] As an anonymous reviewer points out, the syntactic position of the FR plays a crucial role in determining whether the FR pronoun matches the case of the matrix verb. Thus in Modern Greek, left dislocated FRs do not match the case requirement of the matrix verb (Alexiadou & Varlokosta, 1995: 21). With Alexiadou, I assume that in cases like this the FR is not in (or linked by movement to) an argument position, and the chains of the FR pronoun are only assigned one case. The discussion in the following will be restricted to FRs in (or linked to) argument positions.

[17] Hindi has a correlative construction which is in many respects similar to FRs (Srivastav, 1991). But correlatives also occur in languages with FRs such as German. See Vogel (2001) for more discussion.

in (24). Since *CaseCase is ranked above PARSE r-case, no case affix ever has two cases. Since PARSE m-case is ranked over PARSE r-case, it is always m-case that is realized. (24) illustrates this with the input from (23):

(24)   Input: $[+Acc]_{m\text{-}case} \rightarrow Chain_i \leftarrow [+Nom]_{r\text{-}case}$ (Icelandic Ranking)

	PARSE m-case	*Case Case	PARSE r-case
DP_i[+Acc +Nom]		*!	
☞ DP_i[+Acc]			*
DP_i[+Nom]	*!		

5.3   Accounting for non-matching FRs in German

According to Vogel (this volume), there are (at least) two varieties of German with regard to FRs which he calls German A and German B. In both varieties, sentences with nominative/accusative as the matrix case and an oblique case as r-case are grammatical (14a). The two varieties differ in that sentences such as (14b), where m-case is nominative and r-case is accusative, are ungrammatical in German B, but grammatical in German A. In contrast to Icelandic, the surfacing case is always the r-case, not the m-case, which suggests that the ranking of the corresponding PARSE constraints is reversed. Descriptively, non-matching FRs are grammatical if the FR pronoun has r-case, and this case is higher on the relevant case hierarchy in (25) :

(25)   a. *German A*: nominative < accusative < dative, genitive, PP (oblique)
       b. *German B*: nominative, accusative < dative, genitive, PP (oblique)

I propose to implement these hierarchies by two constraints: PARSE +OBL/-OBL which requires that oblique case of a chain is realized if the chain is also assigned a non-oblique case, and PARSE ACC/NOM which demands realization of accusative for a chain which is assigned accusative and nominative. To derive German B, all that is necessary is to rank these two constraints and PARSE r-case over *CaseCase. For $[+Nom]_{m\text{-}case} \rightarrow Chain \leftarrow [+Acc]_{r\text{-}case,}$ this leads to the situation that PARSE ACC/NOM and PARSE r-case both require the realization of accusative. Since this is the only relevant constraint above *CaseCase, [+Acc] surfaces, and the construction is grammatical:

(26)   Input: $[+\text{Nom}]_{\text{m-case}} \rightarrow \text{Chain}_i \leftarrow [+\text{Acc}]_{\text{r-case}}$ (German B Ranking)

	PARSE r-case	PARSE +OBL/-OBL	PARSE ACC/NOM	*CaseCase
DP_i [+Acc +Nom]				*!
☞ DP_i [+Acc]				
DP_i [+Nom]	*!	*		

If the roles are reversed, i.e. for $[+\text{Acc}]_{\text{m-case}} \rightarrow \text{Chain} \leftarrow [+\text{Nom}]_{\text{r-case}}$, PARSE r-case requires realization of [+Nom], and PARSE ACC/NOM the realization of [+Acc]. Since both are ranked above *CaseCase, both cases are realized, which leads to crash:

(27)   Input: $[+\text{Acc}]_{\text{m-case}} \rightarrow \text{Chain}_i \leftarrow [+\text{Nom}]_{\text{r-case}}$ (German B Ranking)

	PARSE r-case	PARSE +OBL/-OBL	PARSE ACC/NOM	*CaseCase
☞ DP_i [+Acc +Nom] ⚐				*
DP_i [+Acc]	*!			
DP_i [+Nom]			*!	

German A differs from German B only for the fact that the input of (27) leads to a grammatical output. Thus (28) is ungrammatical in German B, but grammatical in German A (Vogel 2001: 8):

(28)   Er zerstörte, wer ihm begegnete
        he destroyed wo him:DAT met

This can be captured by ranking PARSE ACC/NOM below *CaseCase: For $[+\text{Nom}]_{\text{m-case}} \rightarrow \text{Chain} \leftarrow [+\text{Acc}]_{\text{r-case}}$ the only relevant constraint above *CaseCase is PARSE r-case. This leads to (grammatical) realization of r-case, just as in German B.

(29)   Input: $[+\text{Acc}]_{\text{m-case}} \rightarrow \text{Chain}_i \leftarrow [+\text{Nom}]_{\text{r-case}}$ (German A Ranking)

	PARSE r-case	PARSE +OBL/-OBL	*CaseCase	PARSE ACC/NOM
DP_i [+Acc +Nom]			*!	
DP_i [+Acc]	*!			
☞ DP_i [+Nom]				*

5.4 Matching FRs – Vocabulary-driven Ineffability

In the cases discussed so far, there is no interaction between the constraints regulating Head Interpretation and the constraints of other grammar modules. This is no special virtue of my analysis. It is already implicit in Vogel's analysis and ultimately prescribed in the data where the resolution of case conflicts in FRs seems to be completely independent from the choice or inventory of vocabulary items. Given the proposed, modular architecture this strongly suggests that competition of this type happens at Chain Interpretation. This evidence renders the contrast in (13) repeated here as (30) especially problematic, since it seems to be governed by the inventory of vocabulary items.

(30)   a. Ich zerstöre, was mich ärgert
            I destroy what me upsets
            'I destroy what upsets me'

        b. *Ich zerstöre wer/wen mich ärgert.
            I destroy who:NOM/ACC me upsets
            'I destroy who upsets me'

If this would be correct, competition in FRs would be determined by vocabulary items as well as by constraints of Chain Interpretation. This would be impossible under the modularity assumption and hence provide strong evidence against the architecture of DO. The solution to this problem I propose is the following: The contrast in (30) is *not* the result of arbitrary neutralization in the inventory of vocabulary items. Rather the case neutralization in (30b) reflects a constraint against the coocurrence of [-masc] features and structural case features (*[-masc Struc])[18] at Chain Interpretation. If this constraint is ranked above all PARSE constraints for case features, the case features of neuter DP chains will be completely deleted in the course of Chain Interpretation:

(31)   Input: $[+Acc]_{m\text{-case}} \rightarrow Chain_i [+Neut] \leftarrow [+Nom]_{r\text{-case}}$

	*[-masc Struc]	PARSE Gend	PARSE r-case	PARSE ACC/ NOM	*Case Case
DP$_i$[+Neut+Acc+Nom]	*!				*
DP$_i$[+Neut+Acc]	*!		*		
DP$_i$[+Neut+Nom]	*!			*	
DP$_i$[+Acc+Nom]		*!			*
☞ DP$_i$[+Neut]			*		

In contrast, for a [+masc] chain, *[-masc Struc] has no effect and the optimal

---

[18] It might be desirable not to represent the gender features as part of the case affix. This would necessitate a slightly different implementation of this constraint. I leave this question open here.

candidate has two case features leading again to crash:

(32)   Input: $[+Acc]_{m\text{-}case} \rightarrow Chain_i\ [+Masc] \leftarrow [+Nom]_{r\text{-}case}$

	*[-masc Struc]	PARSE Gend	PARSE r-case	PARSE ACC/ NOM	*Case Case
☞ DP_i[+Masc +Acc +Nom]					*
DP_i[+Masc +Acc]			*!		
DP_i[+Masc +Nom]				*!	
DP_i[+Acc +Nom]		*!			*
DP_i[+Masc]			*!	*	

Put another way, the vocabulary item *was* does not cause neutralization. It does only reflect neutralization at a deeper level. Constraints at Chain Interpretation have the effect that nominative and accusative are deleted in neuter categories, and the underspecified item *was* can be inserted that is not specified for case.[19]

There is additional evidence both for the claim that *was* is unspecified for case and for the "deep" character of case neutralization in neuter DPs.

In its interrogative reading, *was* can also be used in contexts in which dative case is assigned.[20] Thus, the preposition *mit* assigns dative case (33b), but can also be used with *was* (33a):

(33)   a.   Mit was hat er sie erschlagen?
              with what has he them killed
              'With what did he kill them?'

        b.   mit dem blutigen Kinnbacken eines Esels
              with the:DAT bloody jaw:bone a-GEN donkey:GEN
              'with a bloody jaw bone of a donkey'

The only case which systematically excludes *was* is the genitive, but there is also no other wh-item that could appear in this context and would imply neuter gender:[21]

(34)   a.   der Titel des Buches
              the title the:GEN book:GEN
              'the title of the book'

---

[19] Note that I do not claim with Bresnan (1999) that the distribution of vocabulary items is completely determined by constraints. See Trommer (2001:chapter 4) for discussion.

[20] This does not mean that *was* is possible in other contexts where dative is assigned. The point here is not to account for these rather complex restrictions, but to show that *was* is in principle compatible with dative case.

[21] *wessen Titel* is grammatical, if *wessen* refers to an animate referent.

    b. *was Titel/*wessen Titel
       'the title of what'

Thus interrogative *was* is possible in all contexts where a neuter wh-word is possible at all. Since there is no reason to assume that interrogative pronouns are expressed by different vocabulary items than FR pronouns, this supports the assumption that *was* has no specification for case.

    There is also evidence that the case neutralization in neuter FRs is not an accidental property of a single vocabulary item. Actually, no neuter DP in German ever shows any differentiation between nominative and accusative. This is illustrated in the following examples for the different case-marking categories of the German DP (relevant items are italic):

(35)   *weak adjectival inflection*: 'a new one'

    a. ein neu-*er* (Nom.)/einen neu-*en* (Acc.)
    b. ein neu-*es* (Nom./Acc.)

(36)   *Determiners*: 'the big one'

    a. *der* gross-e (Nom.)/*den* grossen (Acc.)
    b. *das* gross-e (Nom./Acc.)

(37)   *Nouns*: 'the lion/the heart'

    a. der *Löwe* (Nom.) /den *Löwen* (Acc.)
    b. das *Herz* (Nom./Acc.)

To be sure, there is also accusative/nominative neutralization in masculine nouns. But this is neutralization of a rather different type. Thus, in (38) no case features are realized on the adjective and the noun:

(38)   'the lilac tiger'

    a. der lila Tiger (Nom.)
    b. den lila Tiger (Acc.)

However, in (39), which is syntactically identical to (38) in all crucial respects both categories show an overt case distinctions:

(39)   'the green lion'

    a. der grün-e Löw-e (Nom.)
    b. den grün-en Löw-en (Acc.)

This suggests that the neutralization in (38) is driven by idiosyncratic features of single vocabulary items. In other words, this is the type of neutralization Marantz (1999) and Vogel (2001) claim to hold for the FR pronoun *was* which is argued here to be only a surface reflex of a "deeper" neutralization process.

Of course it is possible to assume that all the neutralizations in (35) to (37) are due to accidental properties, but this seems to miss an important generalization in the morphosyntax of German DPs.[22]

Since the FR data can be accounted for in the global as well as in the modular architecture, the question arises if there are any principled differences between the two approaches. Note that it is no principled problem for the global account to incorporate the insight that neuter DPs neutralize the nominative/accusative distinction. But this would not be connected in any way to the grammaticality contrast in FRs. If the case neutralization in neuter noun phrases was not systematical, i.e. if there were neuter categories in (35) to (37) that would not neutralize, this would falsify the proposed modular architecture, but not the global account. Thus the modular architecture makes much stronger predictions on possible languages.

6   Explaining Morphosyntactic Competition

Joan Bresnan has argued in a number of articles (Bresnan 1996, 1999a, b) for a model of grammar where morphological and syntactic constraints are globally evaluated in the same evaluation procedure.

In contrast to the model of Vogel, her approach is based on Lexical Functional Grammar (LFG, see e.g. Bresnan 2001). In LFG, syntactic objects are represented by pairs of f-structures and c-structures, where f-structures are complex feature structures encoding mostly language-invariant and semantic properties of sentences, while c-structures are phrase structure representations including constituency and linear order. As a consequence, candidates in OT-LFG are f-structure/c-structure pairs and the inputs to morphosyntactic computation are single f-structures. (40) shows the two models in comparison.

(40)   Input   Candidates

    Vogel (2001) LF_0 $\Rightarrow$ $[LF_1,PF_1], [LF_2,PF_2], ...$
    Bresnan (1999a) f-struct$_0$ $\Rightarrow$ [f-struct$_1$,c-struct$_1$],
                                        [f-struct$_2$,c-struct$_2$], ...

While the two models differ in implementation, they are identical in one point: There is only one morphosyntactic evaluation process. A main argument of Bresnan in the cited articles are mainly based on negation data in different dialects of English, which I will discuss in sections 6.2 to 6.6. In 6.1, I discuss the role of phonological spell-out in Bresnan's approach.

[22] The same would have to be said about the same items in feminine DPs which show the same behavior as neuter DPs.

6.1   Phonological Spell-out in Bresnan (1999a)

Corresponding to the vocabulary items of DM, Bresnan assumes that the lexicon
of a language contains pairings of morphosyntactic features and phonological
content. Bresnan simply refers to these items as "pronunciation" and their role
in the grammar is rather different from the one that is played by vocabulary
items. Recall from section 2 that in German verb forms 1 pl agreement is expressed by the [+pl] affix -*n*. The derivation of this fact in DO can be
schematized as in (41):

$$(41) \qquad \begin{bmatrix} +1 \\ -2 \\ +pl \end{bmatrix} \Rightarrow \text{Competition} \Rightarrow \quad [+pl] \leftrightarrow /n/$$

Note that "Competition" in (41) actually comprises a sequential ordering of
competition processes, and vocabulary items are only involved in the last one,
namely Head Interpretation. In Bresnan's approach 'pronunciations' are not
directly involved in any form of morphosyntactic competition. They just interpret the results of competition. This results in something like (42): The output of
the competition process is [+pl]. That the choice of pronunciation is "compe-
tition-free" is symbolized in (42) by the symbol "$\Leftrightarrow$":

$$(42) \qquad \begin{bmatrix} +1 \\ -2 \\ +pl \end{bmatrix} \Rightarrow \text{Competition} \Rightarrow \begin{bmatrix} +pl \end{bmatrix} \Leftrightarrow \begin{bmatrix} +pl \end{bmatrix} \leftrightarrow /n/$$

Actually, (42) gives a wrong picture of Bresnan's representations. Pronunciations refer to parts of c-structure associated with f-structure. It is not clear if
Pronunciations can spell-out single heads or if they always refer to words. The
examples Bresnan gives seem to favor the latter hypothesis. Thus, she gives
something like the following[23]:

$$(43) \quad \text{isn't}: \quad \begin{bmatrix} V \begin{matrix} 0 \\ f \end{matrix} & +ninfl & \begin{bmatrix} BE \\ PRES \\ 3 \\ SG \\ NEG \end{bmatrix} \end{bmatrix} \leftrightarrow /n/$$

[23] This example is reconstructed from the corresponding 1st person form, which according to
Bresnan is zero (**amn't*). See the discussion below. (Bresnan 1999: 35)

6.2 English Negation

Bresnan claims that syntactic constructions sometimes block morphological
ones. She illustrates this with the expression of negation in different dialects of
English. For example, in Hawick Scots, three possible realizations of negation
exist which appear in different (partially overlapping) morphosyntactic contexts:
nae, a clitic usually adjoined to IP, *n't*, a suffix, and *no*, a full form. An adequate
analysis must then fix for every syntactic configuration which markers is possible and which are not.

Bresnan starts from the observation that there are different means to express
negation in different languages and often even in one and the same language.
(affixes, negation verbs, etc.) Bresnan relates the choice of a negation strategy
one by one to different markedness constraints. (Bresnan 1999a: 22)

As long as no other constraints interfere, the choice of negation type simply
depends on the ranking of these constraints: Everything else equal, the strategy
which corresponds to the lowest-ranked markedness constraint is chosen since it
involves the least serious constraint violations.

But, as there are different means and positions to express negation, there are
also different semantic scope positions which are expressed by the position of
negation. The following faithfulness constraint requires that scope is overtly
marked in the output (Bresnan 1999a: 24):

(44)

Negation Strategy	Markedness Constraints
Negation adjoined to C,I,V,VP	*NEG-C, *NEG-I, *NEG-V, *NEG-VP
Negation by an affix on an auxiliary	$*\text{NINFL} - V_f^0$
Negation by an affix on a lexical verb	$*\text{NINFL} - V_{lex}^0$
Negation lexicalized as a verb	*NEG-LEX-V

(45) FAITH^{NEG}: preserve input scope of negation in the output

In Hawick Scots sentence negation, Neg is expressed by *nae*, which is analyzed
by Bresnan as the marker for negation adjoined to INFL. The appearance of *nae*
in sentence negation is then accounted for by the following ranking (46). As
expected, *nae* as the marker corresponding to the lowest-ranked markedness
constraint (*NEG-I) is chosen. The input scope is represented in (46) schematically by bracketing (Bresnan 1999b: 14):

(46)   Input: ¬(POSS(eat(he)))

	*NEG-C	FAITH^{NEG}	*NEG-VP	*NINFL- V_f^0	*NEG-I
he couldn't eat				*!	
☞ he couldnae eat					
he could no eat			*!		

A different result is obtained for questions, where we find the negation markers *n't* and *no* instead. *n't* according to Bresnan is an affix attached to *could* while *no* expresses negation adjoined to VP. By assumption (i.e. by crucially higher ranked constraints), I in Hawick Scots questions must appear in the sentence-initial complementizer position C. For this reason, the constraint *NEG-C, which was irrelevant in (46) becomes decisive, since *nae* (now in C) would violate the highest-ranked markedness constraint. *no* and *n't* avoid this violation, *no* since it is lower than C and *n't* since it is not adjoined to C, but an affix (Bresnan 1999b: 14):

(47)   Input: Q(¬(POSS(eat(he))))

	*NEG-C	FAITH^{NEG}	*NEG-VP	*NINFL- V_f^0	*NEG-I
☞ couldn't he eat				*	
couldnae he eat	*!				
☞ could he no eat			*		

Standard English is analyzed by Bresnan in a similar way, using the same constraints:

(48)   Input: ¬(POSS(eat(he)))

	*NEG-C	FAITH^{NEG}	*NEG-VP	*NINFL- V_f^0	*NEG-I
☞ he can't have been eating					*
☞ he cannot have been eating				*	
he cannot have been eating			*!		

Bresnan uses the orthographically contracted form *cannot* to express Neg adjoined to VP (Scots *nae*), which is not phonologically different from Neg in I in Standard English (*can not*). *NEG-VP is ranked higher here than the tied constraints *NEG-I and *NINFL-V_f^0 which means preference for the two possibilities where Neg is not adjoined to VP. For the same reasons as in Hawick Scots, in interrogatives only "reduced" negation is possible:

106   Jochen Trommer

(49)   Input: Q(¬(POSS(eat(he))))

	*NEG-C	FAITH NEG	*NEG-VP	*NINFL-V_f^0	*NEG-I
☞ can't he have been eating?					*
cannot he have been eating?	*!			*	
can he not have been eating?			*		

What makes these data awkward is the fact that these constraints seem to interact with morphophonological constraints. This seems to be true in the case of the impossible combination *am'nt. In declaratives, where *am'nt would be expected, in analogy to the corresponding contracted 3rd person form (*Isn't he eating*), only *am not* is possible (I omit FAITH[NEG] in the following tableaux where it is never violated):

(50)   Input: declarative

	*AMN'T	*NEG-C	*NEG-VP	FAITH P&N	NINFL-V_f^0	*NEG-I
I amn't eating	*!				*	
I aren't eating			*!	*	*	
☞ I [am not] eating						*
I am [not eating]			*!			

While *am'nt is also impossible in interrogatives, here the conflict is resolved in a different way. The default form *are* is used instead of the 1sg form *am*. This leads to a violation of the constraint FAITH[P&N] which requires the realization of person and number features. This violation is tolerated to avoid the violation of the higher ranked *AMN'T. In contrast to the declarative input, the analytic form *am not* is impossible since this would violate *NEG-C, which is again higher ranked than *NINFL-V_f^0 and *NEG-I (see (51)).

The general point these data provide in favor of an global OT-account is the following: We have one conflict (the otherwise perfect form *amn't* cannot appear), and instead two different strategies are used. In declarative contexts (50), a different syntactic construction is used instead (analytical *am not*). In an interrogative context, *amn't is replaced by a minimally less specified item (*aren't*). To describe the first solution, we need syntactic constraints (e.g. *NEG-VP), for the second one spell-out constraints (*AMN'T and FAITH[P&N]). To describe both scenarios, the two kinds of constraints have to interact. This means globality of constraint evaluation.

(51) Input: interrogative

	*AMN'T	*NEG-C	*NEG-VP	FAITH P&N	*NINL-V_f^0	*NEG-I
Amn't I eating	*!				*	
☞ Aren't I eating				*	*	
Am not I eating		*!				*
Am I [not eating]			*!			

6.3 Why English Negation does not imply global competition

While Bresnan's arguments seem rather compelling, they depend crucially on the model of grammar Bresnan presupposes. In this section I show how the data can be derived in a postsyntactic account. To start with, we have to determine the relevant syntactic structures which form the input at Head Interpretation. Consider the sentences in (52):

(52) a. Isn't she coming?/*Is not she coming.
       b. She isn't coming/ she is not coming.
       c. *Is shen't coming./$^?$Is she not coming?

For all negated sentences, I assume the following basic phrase structure in (53):

(53) $[Tns^0 [Neg^0 [Aux^0 [V^0 ...]]]]$

With Frampton (2001), I assume that in (52b) the auxiliary (Aux) has moved to Tense and attracted the negation head (Neg, 54b).[24] In questions, this complex has moved to the question head Q in the complementizer position to yield (52a, 54a). (54c) corresponds to (52c). This option seems to be only marginally possible in Standard dialects of English. I assume that it results in dialects or registers where there is no obligatory attraction of Neg to Aux. See section 6.6 for more discussion.

(54) a. [[[Aux Tense] Neg] Q]
       b. [[Aux Tense] Neg]
       c. [[Aux Tense] Q] ... [Neg]

Since both, (54a) and (54b), form spell-out domains, the competition between *isn't* and *is not* happens at Head Interpretation inside the predicted locality domain. No matter how this competition is modeled in detail, it can be located in one module of the grammar (Head Interpretation) and no violation of the

---

[24] Wilder (1997: 345) argues that *not* is not "a head governing VP, but a phrasal satellite, like an adverbial." This analysis is in principle also compatible with the account of reduction proposed in the next section as long as the vocabulary item *not* is not related one-by-one to "phrasal" negation.

modularity assumption is necessary. The starting point for my analysis is the
assumption of two vocabulary items for negation:

(55)   a. /not/ ↔ [+Neg]
        b. /n't/ ↔ [+Neg]

There are two options to account for the different distribution of /n't/ and /no/ in
(52): By lexical stipulation or by additional constraints. Frampton (2001)
assumes the first alternative. In the next section, I will explore the second possibility.

6.4   An Alternative Analysis

The idea behind the constraint based analysis I will propose is to formalize the
well-documented observation that elements which are syntactically bound tend
to be phonologically reduced. Clearly, /n't/ is a reduced form of /not/, and Neg
in the head adjunction structures (HAS) of (52) exhibits different degrees of
embeddedness. Thus we have the hierarchies in (56): "Free" refers to (52c)
where Neg is not part of a HAS, "peripheral" to (52b) where it is the outermost
head of a HAS, and "embedded" to a Neg that is deeper embedded in a HAS
(52a). I leave it open here what is the exact phonological correlate of weak and
strong:

(56)   a. *Phonological weight*: Strong form > weak form
        b. *Embeddedness*:   Free > Peripheral > Embedded

Now, interestingly, the two hierarchies correlate: The less embedded a negation
marker is in the terms of (56b), the more likely is it to be weak. This is shown
schematically in (57):

(57)   **Syntactic Structure**   **Description**   **Reduction**
        a. [[[Aux Tense] Neg]Q]   Embedded part of a HAS   Reduction obligatory
        b. [[Aux Tense] Neg]   Peripheral part of a HAS Reduction possible
        c. [Aux Tense] ... [Neg]   Not part of a HAS   Reduction impossible

This observation can be captured by harmonic alignment (Prince & Smolensky
1993; Aissen 1999) of the two hierarchies in (56) into the following fixed constraint hierarchies:[25]

---

[25] In de Lacy (2001) and Trommer (2001) it is argued that harmonic alignment and hence (universally) fixed constraint ranking can be dispensed with. This is also possible for the analysis of
negation presented here. Thus, the constraints in (58) could be replaced by *strong/Adjoined and
*strong/Embedded where Adjoined = {Embedded, Peripheral} under the ranking *strong/Adjoined,
*weak/X » *strong/Embedded. Since the pro and contra of fixed constraint rankings is not crucial in
this paper, I will adopt harmonic alignment here as the more common means to relate markedness
hierarchies to constraints.

(58)   a. *strong/Embedded » *strong/Peripheral » *strong/Free
        b. *weak/Free » *weak/Peripheral » *weak/Embedded

In the following I will show how the distribution of negation markers follows from an interspersing of these constraint hierarchies with other constraints, where the constraints are roughly ranked as follows:

(59)   *weak/Free »...» *strong/Embedded »...» { * strong/Peripheral ; * weak/Peripheral } »...»

{ * strong/Free ; * weak/Embedded }

Crucially *strong/Peripheral and *weak/Peripheral are tied, i.e. not ranked with respect to each other which accounts for the optionality of *not* or *n't* in declaratives. Note that all these constraints are relativized to specific input structures, and are irrelevant for other inputs. For example, if Neg is embedded, all constraints over free and peripheral inputs are vacuously satisfied. In the following I will omit all constraints that are irrelevant in this way from discussion and from the tableaux. (60) to (62) show how the data from (52) can be captured. For comprehensibility, full sentences are given. The items that are actually involved in the evaluations are in boldface:

(60)   Input: [[[Aux Tense] Neg]Q] (embedded Neg)

	*strong/Embedded	*weak/Embedded
☞ **Isn't** she coming?		
Is not she coming?	*!	

(61)   Input: [[Aux Tense] Neg] (Peripheral Neg)

	*strong/Peripheral	*weak/Peripheral
☞ She **isn't** coming		*
☞ She **is not** coming	*	

(62)   Input: ([[Aux Tense]Q] ...) [Neg] (free Neg)

	*weak/Free	*strong/Free
Is she **n't** coming?	*!	
☞ Is she **not** coming?		*

Let us now look at the corresponding sentences in the 1st person:

(63)   a. *Amn't I coming?/*Am not I coming?/Aren't I coming.
       b. *I amn't coming/ I am not coming.
       c. *Am In't coming/?Am I not coming?

The simplest case is (63b). Here I assume that a high-ranked morphophonological constraint against the sequence *amn't* prevents *I amn't coming*. Note that we also have to exclude forms with *are* instead of *am*, which we find in (63a). This is achieved by PARSE PER-NUM which stands here as a shorthand for all relevant PARSE constraints.

(64)   Input: [[Aux Tense] Neg] (Peripheral Neg)

	*AMN'T	PARSE PER- NUM	*strong/ Peripheral	*weak/ Peripheral
I **amn't** coming	*!			*
☞ I **am not** coming			*	
I **aren't** coming		*!		*
I **are not** coming		*!	*	

In interrogative sentences as in (63a), *strong/Embedded and hence the ranking of this constraint with respect to PARSE PER-NUM becomes relevant. Since *strong/Embedded is ranked higher, the form aren't is chosen which does not realize the underlying person and number features, but satisfies *strong/Embedded:

(65)   Input: [[[Aux Tense] Neg] Q] (Embedded Neg)

	*AMN'T	*strong/ Embedded	PARSE PER-NUM	*weak/ Embedded
Amn't I coming?	*!			*
Am not I coming?		*!		
☞ **Aren't** I coming?			*	*
Are not I coming?		*!	*	

Finally, if negation is "stranded" below the subject, Neg forms its own spell-out domain. The only relevant *strong constraint is ranked below *weak/Peripheral. Therefore, the full form is chosen:

(66)   Input: [Neg] (Free Neg)

	*weak/ Free	*AMN'T	PARSE PER-NUM	*strong/ Free
Am I **n't** coming?	*!			
☞ Am I **not** coming?				*
Are I **n't** coming?	*!		*	
Are I **not** I coming?			*!	*

6.5 Hawick Scots

Negation in Hawick Scots differs from Standard English only in small details.
First, there is no ban on *amn't*, hence there is no difference between negation
with 1sg and other forms. Second, as noted before, there are three negation
markers. /no/ and /n't/ which roughly correspond to Standard English /not/ and
/n't/ and the phonological clitic /nae/. (67) shows the distribution of these markers:

(67) a. *Am no I happy?/*Amnae I happy?/Amn't I happy?
      b. I am no happy/I amnae happy/*I amn't happy
      c. Am I no happy?/*Am I nae happy?/*Am I n't happy?

It is natural to extend the phonological weight hierarchy from (56a) to (68):

(68) *Phonological weight hierarchy:* Strong form (no) > clitic > weak form

But, since harmonic alignment is based on binary scales, I assume that this is
decomposed in two binary hierarchies, as in (69):

(69) a. [+dependent] > [-dependent]
      b. [+deficient] > [-deficient]

"deficient" (+def) corresponds to not including a potential syllable nucleus (a
vowel, /n't/). "dependent" (+dep) refers to prosodic dependency i.e. the in-
capacity of an item to form a prosodic word on its own, which seems to be true
of /n't/ and /nae/. (70) shows the assumed feature values for the Hawick Scots
negation markers:

(70)

	+dep	-dep
+def	*n't*	-
-def	*nae*	*no*

Again, phonological weight corresponds closely to syntactic embeddedness:

(71)

	Syntactic Structure	Description	Reduction
a.	[[[Aux Tense] Neg]Q]	Embedded part of a HAS	[+dep +def] (*n't*)
b.	[[Aux Tense] Neg]	Peripheral part of a HAS	[-def] (*nae, not*)
c.	[Aux Tense] ... [Neg]	Not part of a HAS	[-dep -def] (*no*)

Harmonic alignment of the scales in (69) with the embeddedness scale from
(56b) gives the constraint rankings in (72) and (73):

(72)   a. *dep/Free » *dep/Peripheral » *dep/Embedded
        b. *ndep/Embedded » *ndep/Peripheral » *ndep/Free

(73)   a. *def/Free » *def/Peripheral » *def/Embedded
        b. *ndef/Embedded » *ndef/Peripheral » *ndef/Free

To account for the distribution of the single markers, the constraint ranking must include the three subrankings in (74):

(74)   a. *ndep/Embedded,*ndef/Embedded » *dep/Embedded,*def/Embedded
        b. *def/Peripheral » *dep/Peripheral,*ndep/Peripheral » *ndef/Peripheral
        c. *dep/Free, *def/Free » *ndep/Free, *ndef/Free

In (74a), *ndep/Embedded,*ndef/Embedded are ranked highest which ensures that the negation markers in standard questions will be [+dep +def], hence /n't/. In a symmetric fashion the high-ranking of* dep/Free,*def/Free ensures a [-dep -def] element for free negation, which is /not/. The tied ranking of *dep/Peripheral,*ndep/Peripheral has the effect that /no/ and /nae/ are equally harmonic in declaratives. Since *def/Peripheral is ranked higher and *ndef/Peripheral lower than these constraints the [+def] element /n't/ is excluded in this position. Since the options Embedded/Peripheral and Free are mutually exclusive, the constraints from a., b. and c. in (74) do not interact. Thus, all that we need is an overall ranking which obeys the subrankings in (74) and (72):

(75)

$$\left\{ \begin{array}{l} \text{* dep/Free} \\ \text{* def/Free} \end{array} \right\} \gg \text{*def/peripheral} \gg \left\{ \begin{array}{l} \text{*ndep/Embedded} \\ \text{*ndef/Embedded} \end{array} \right\} \gg$$

$$\left\{ \begin{array}{l} \text{*dep/Peripheral} \\ \text{* ndep/Peripheral} \end{array} \right\} \gg \text{*ndef/Peripheral} \gg$$

$$\left\{ \begin{array}{l} \text{* dep/Embedded} \\ \text{* def/ Embedded} \end{array} \right\} \gg \left\{ \begin{array}{l} \text{* ndep/Free} \\ \text{* ndef/Free} \end{array} \right\}$$

6.6   Ineffability Again

Bresnan (1999b: 17) hints at the possibility that there are speakers that spell out sentence negation by *Am I not eating?* instead of **Amn't I eating?* and *Aren't I eating?* i.e. the latter are outranked. If **Amn't I eating?* and *Am I not eating?* are candidates in the same competition involving *AMN'T, this cannot happen at Head Interpretation, since the subject *I* is not part of the same spell-out domain as *am*. Again, this seems to force us to give up modular constraint evaluation.

But, as Marantz (2000: 3) points out, Bresnan's analysis

"makes the prediction that dialects that allow *Am I not leaving?* instead of *Aren't I leaving?* should disallow *Is he not leaving?*. That is, *Am I not leaving?* should be much better as a sentential negation than *Is he not leaving* in such dialects since *amn't drives the grammaticality of *Am I not leaving?* while *isn't* is a fine word. However Bresnan presents no evidence that there is such a [ok]*Am I not leaving?/*Is he not leaving?* dialect, and discussions with native speakers of [??]*Aren't I leaving?* dialects suggests that there is no such dialect. Thus Bresnan's specific proposals are untenable, regardless of the the theoretical assumptions."

This means that in dialects where *Amn't I leaving?* is ungrammatical and cannot be replaced by *Aren't I leaving?*, we have again ineffability.[26] In the modular approach, advocated in this paper, this can be captured by assuming that high-ranked *AMN'T leads to an output for the underlying sentence where Neg is not spelled out at all. (Note that in the preceding tableaus I have assumed silently that PARSE NEG is ranked high enough to prohibit the null parse for Neg.)

(76) Input: [[[Aux Tense] Neg] Q] (Embedded Neg)

	*AMN'T	*strong/ Embedded	PARSE PER-NUM	PARSE NEG
Amn't I coming?	*!			*
Am not I coming?		*!		
Are not I coming?		*!	*	
Aren't I coming?			*!	
☞ **Am** I coming?				*

Following the approach of Frampton (2001) we can make the plausible assumption that [+Neg] is an irrecoverable feature. Hence, the optimal candidate is *Am I leaving?*, which is irrecoverable, and therefore ill-formed. But since it is optimal at Head Interpretation, no other candidate can be used instead.

As is predicted by the modular architecture of DO, morphophonological constraints such as *AMN'T are evaluated locally. Thus, this account is superior conceptually to the one by Bresnan since it is more restricted. But Bresnan's account is also problematic empirically, as we saw in this section, since it predicts competition effects that are not documented. Finally, the account in terms of morphophonological constraints determining the choice of negation markers, predicts the phonological differences between the negation markers in Standard English and Hawick Scots. These are completely accidental in Bresnan's account. Taken together, an approach using local morphological competition seems to give a better account of the data.

---

[26] See Frampton (2001) for more discussion of the empirical evidence that ineffability in this domain exists.

7 Modularity and Restrictiveness

A major appeal of a modular architecture is its restrictiveness. If a module M_1 generates the input of a second module M_2, it is predicted that M_1 influences (via its output) M_2, but that there is no comparable influence in the opposite direction. Thus, much of the work on the morphology/syntax interface in the eighties and in the early versions of the Minimalist Program (Chomsky 1995) followed the idea that morphology consists of an autonomous word-formation module that feeds syntactic computations. In such a "lexicalist" model, morphology drives syntax, but not vice-versa. However, plenty of evidence has been amassed that morphological structure is in many ways sensitive to syntactic structure (see Marantz 2001 and Trommer 2001: chap. 2 for recent discussion), and the English negation data discussed in section 6 constitute a further piece of evidence supporting this conclusion: A lexicalist model has no way to cope with the problem that *am not* competes with *amn't*. The competition which would be necessary to do so cannot be located in Morphology, since *am not* under this approach is not a morphological object. And it cannot be located in syntax because a morphological constraint has to be evaluated (*AMN'T).

Hence, the modularity assumption seems to have failed.[27] However, it has never been convincingly shown that morphology really drives syntax in the sense that syntactic computations are sensitive to morphological details. Symptomatically even work started under the assumption of such an influence comes to the conclusion that the influence is just the other way around (cf. Bobaljik 1995).[28] In the preceding sections, I have argued that two sets of data which seem to show that morphological detail influences syntactic computation can be fruitfully reanalyzed in terms of constraint evaluation restricted to Head Interpretation or Chain Interpretation. Thus, syntactic case neutralization (at Chain Interpretation) in Free Relative construction enforces neutralization at the level of vocabulary items (at Head Interpretation), as we saw for the *was* case in section 5. But idiosyncratic constraints at Head Interpretation cannot influence the evaluation process selecting optimal syntactic structures, as was shown for the ban in *amn't* in section 6. These results strengthen further the hypothesis that syntax triggers morphology, but not vice versa. If this turns out to be correct, it should be reflected in some way in our conception of Universal grammar. The architecture of DO as proposed in this paper is a concrete proposal how this goal can be achieved.

[27] Lexicalist approaches usually assume that the morphology component generates word-internal phrase structures and provides a phonological spell-out for these structures. While spell-out in DO happens at Head Interpretation for all structures, it is in principle possible that there are two structure-building devices, (one for word-internal and one for word-external syntax) interacting in a specific manner. Such a proposal is put forth in Ackema and Neeleman (2000). Since the same authors seem also to assume that spell-out is sensitive to word-external context (Ackema & Neeleman 2001), this seems to open up a further dimension of modularity. Here, I assume with Marantz (2001) that the distinction between word-internal and -external syntax is captured in terms of different syntactic configurations in the same syntactic module.

8   Summary

In this paper I have shown that crucial data which have been used to argue for global competition in OT-morphosyntax can be reanalyzed in a framework with a modular structure, closely related to the assumptions of Distributed Morphology. Moreover, the modularity assumption has led us to the discovery of an important asymmetry in German case neutralization, which has no status in a global approach but is predicted by the modular architecture. A modular analysis of English negation has also be shown to be empirically superior to the global analysis provided by Bresnan (1999a). Finally, it was shown that lexicalist approaches to modularity in fact lead to the problems which seemed to speak against modularity in general.

References

Ackema, P. & Neeleman, A. (2000a): Absolute ungrammaticality. In: Dekkers, J. van der Leeuw, F. & Wijer, J. van de, eds. (2000): *Optimality Theory; Phonology, Syntax, and Acquisition.* Oxford: Oxford University Press. 279–301.

Ackema, P. & Neeleman, A. (2000b): Competition between syntax and morphology. In: Grimshaw, J., Legendre, G. & Vikner, S., eds. (2000): *Optimality-Theoretic Syntax.* Cambridge, MA: MIT Press. 29–60.

Ackema, P. & Neeleman, A. (2001): *Context-sensitive Spell-out and Adjacency.* Handout of a talk given at the Third Mediterranean Morphology Meeting, Barcelona, September 20-23, 2001. (Abstract: http://www.iula.upf.es/mmm3ab17.htm)

Aissen, J. (1999): Markedness and subject choice in Optimality Theory. *Natural Language and Linguistic Theory* 17. 673–711.

Alexiadou, A., Law, P., Meinunger, A. & Wilder, C. (2000): Introduction. In: Alexiadou, A., Law, P., Meinunger, A. & Wilder, C., eds. (2000): *Relative Clauses.* Amsterdam: John Benjamins. 1–51.

Alexiadou, A. & Varlokosta, S. (1995): The syntactic and semantic properties of free relatives in modern greek. *ZAS Working Papers in Linguistics.* Zentrum für Allgemeine Sprachwissenschaft, Berlin. 1–30.

Bobaljik, J. D. (1995): *Morphosyntax: The Syntax of Verbal Inflection.* PhD dissertation, MIT.

Bresnan, J. (1998): Morphology competes with syntax: Explaining typological variation in weak crossover effects. In: Hagstrom, P., McGinnis, M. & Pesetsky, D., eds. (1998): *Is the Best Good Enough?* Cambridge, MA: MIT Press & MIT Working Papers in Linguistic. 59–92.

Bresnan, J. (1999a): Explaining morphosyntactic competition. In: Baltin, M. & Collins, C., eds. (1999): *Handbook of Contemporary Syntactic Theory.* Oxford: Blackwell. 1–44.

Bresnan, J. (1999b): *The Lexicon in Optimality Theory.* Paper presented at the 11th Annual CUNY Conference on Human Sentence Processing, Special Session on the Lexical Basis of Syntactic Processing: Formal and Computational issues. Rutgers University, March 20, 1998.

Bresnan, J. (2001): *Lexical-Functional Grammar.* Oxford: Blackwell.

Chomsky, N. (1995): *The Minimalist Program.* Cambridge, MA: MIT Press.

Croft, W. (1990): *Typology and Universals.* Cambridge University Press.

Dimmendaal, G. J. (1983): *The Turkana Language.* Dordrecht: Foris.

Frampton, J. (2001): The amn't gap, ineffability, and anomlous aren't: Against morphosyntactic competition. *CLS* 37. Papers from the 2001 Chicago Linguistic Society Meeting.

Halle, M. & Marantz, A. (1993): Distributed Morphology and the pieces of inflection. In: Hale, K. & Keyser, S. J., eds. (1993): *The View from Building 20.* Cambridge, MA: MIT Press. 111–176.

Lacy, P. de (2001): Conflation and scales. In: Menendez-Benito, P., ed. (2001): Proceedings of *NELS* 32. Amherst, MA: GLSA Publications.

Marantz, A. (1999): *Morphology as Syntax: Paradigms and the Ineffable (The Incomprehensible and the Unconstructable).* Talk given at the University of Potsdam.

Marantz, A. (2000): *Lecture notes.* Ms, MIT.

Marantz, A. (2001): *Words.* Handout of a talk given at the XX West Coast Conference on Formal Linguistics, University of Southern California. (http://www.usc.edu/dept/LAS/linguistics/wccfl/program1.htm).

McCarthy, J. & Prince, A. (1995): Faithfulness and reduplicative identity. *University of Massachusetts Occasional Papers in Linguistics.* 249–384.

Müller, G. (1997): Partial wh-movement and Optimality Theory. *The Linguistic Review.* 14. 249–306.

Müller, G. (2000): *Elemente der optimalitätstheoretischen Syntax*. Tübingen: Stauffenburg Verlag.

Noyer, R. R. (1993): *Optimal words: towards a declarative theory of word formation*. Ms, Princeton University. (http://www.ling.upenn.edu/126rnoyer/papers.html).

Prince, A. & Smolensky, P. (1993): *Optimality theory: Constraint interaction in generative grammar*. Technical reports of the Rutgers University Center of Cognitive Science.

Srivastav, V. (1991): The syntax and semantics of correlatives. *Natural Language and Linguistic Theory* 9. 637–686.

Trommer, J. (2001a): *Direction marking as agreement*. Ms, University of Osnabrück.

Trommer, J. (2001b): *Distributed Optimality*. PhD dissertation, University of Potsdam.

Trommer, J. (2001c): A hybrid account of affix order. In: Andronis, M., Ball, C., Elston, H. & Neuvel, S., eds. (2001): *CLS 37: The Panels*. Papers from the 37th Meeting of the Chicago Linguistic Society. Chicago: Chicago Linguistic Society.

Wilder, C. (1997): English finite auxiliaries in syntax and phonology. In: Black, J. R. & Motapanyane, V., eds. (1997): *Clitics, Pronouns and Movement*. Amsterdam: John Benjamins. 321–362.

Osnabrück   Jochen Trommer

University of Osnabrück, Institute of Cognitive Science, Katharinenstr. 24, 49078 Osnabrück
e-mail: jtrommer@uos.de

Free Relative Constructions in OT- Syntax*

Ralf Vogel

Abstract

The paper presents an OT account of the typology of free relative (FR) constructions and the resolution strategies for case conflicts in FRs: the FR pronoun has to 'serve' two different case assigners at once. Languages differ as to how big a case conflict must be to cause ungrammaticality. While English requires true categorial matching, German allows the suppression of structural cases, if assigned by the matrix verb. The typology includes 7 different language types. The paper argues that the matching effect is about surface forms. Not abstract features have to match, but their mode of morpho-phonological realisation. A second important fact is that many languages only allow for FRs, if the suppressed case is lower on the (language particular) case hierarchy.

The model of OT-syntax used here has some 'non-standard' features. Both inputs and output candidates are full-fledged syntactic structures - LFs in Chomskyan terms, while PFs are only contained in output candidates. FR constructions as such are marked from a typological perspective, and can only 'survive' via faithfulness. The observed effects of case hierarchies are derived indirectly, by a constraint on case realisation that allows a 'lower marked' case to be 'realisable' by a 'higher marked' one. This requires a 'case module': An actual form given in a candidate is compared with an alternative form, i.e. that of the suppressed case. This alternative form has to be taken from a 'database of case forms'. To account for ineffability, the paper makes use of two different neutralisation strategies, neutralisation to a different form and neutralisation to a FR that has a different meaning and/or might be un-interpretable.

* I would like to thank the following colleagues for helpful comments and fruitful discussions: Artemis Alexiadou, Gisbert Fanselow, Silke Fischer, Hans-Martin Gärtner, Anastasia Giannakidou, Jane Grimshaw, Alex Grosu, Fabian Heck, Gunnar Hrafn Hrafnbjargarson, Shin-Sook Kim, Jaklin Kornfilt, Jonas Kuhn, Geraldine Legendre, Gereon Müller, Stefan Müller, Peter Öhl, Jürgen Pafel, Henk van Riemsdijk, Doug Saddy, Tanja Schmid, Melita Stavrou, Ruth Seibert, Halldor Sigurðsson, Markus Steinbach, Hubert Truckenbrodt, Sten Vikner. I'm further thankful to the audiences of presentations of parts of this paper at the Rutgers University, New Brunswick, Johns-Hopkins-University, Baltimore, the Stuttgart 1999 OT Syntax Workshop, the Workshop on Conflicting Rules in Potsdam and IATL 16, June 2000, Tel Aviv. I also thank two anonymous reviewers. All remaining errors are mine. The work on this paper was fully supported by a grant for the DFG research project "Optimalitätstheoretische Syntax des Deutschen" (MU 1444/2-1), University of Stuttgart.

1 Introduction

This paper is part of a research project on OT-Syntax and the typology of the free relative (FR) construction. It concentrates on the details of an OT analysis and some of its consequences for OT-syntax.[1] I will not present a general discussion of the phenomenon and the many controversial issues it is famous for in generative syntax.[2] An example of an English free relative (FR) clause is the subordinate *wh*-clause in (1), taken from Bresnan & Grimshaw (1978):

(1)   [CP I drank [FR whatever there was]]

The FR clauses that we will be examining here are clauses that stand for a verbal argument. An interesting debate about the correct syntactic analysis of FR clauses took place in the late 1970s and 1980s. The most widely discussed proposals were by Bresnan & Grimshaw (1978) and Groos & van Riemsdijk (1981). The debate concentrated on the question how to represent FRs syntactically, i.e. which node label should replace the 'FR' in (1).

In Vogel (2001) I assume that FR clauses have the structure of other ordinary subordinate clauses and that the label 'FR' is to be replaced by 'CP' in (1). Rooryck (1994) argues for this proposal in detail.[3] Many earlier accounts claim that there must be an NP node heading the FR clause. Bresnan & Grimshaw (1978) assume that this NP node hosts the FR pronoun. Groos & van Riemsdijk (1981), and many others following them, propose that the NP node is occupied by a phonetically empty pronoun, *pro*. However, none of the earlier accounts could convincingly prove the need for the proposed exceptional structure of FR clauses by showing exceptional syntactic behaviour – compared to ordinary subordinate clauses.

The only exceptional property of FRs is the so-called 'matching effect': the FR pronoun seems to be sensitive to the requirements of both the matrix verb and the relative clause internal verb. As an effect of this, English and Dutch, and some other languages, including perhaps variants of German, only have well-formed FRs if the pronoun is able to 'fulfil' both requirements simultaneously. This is the case in (1). But note that the *requirements* of the verbs do *not* match here literally: the matrix verb requires a direct object, while the FR pronoun is the subject of the FR clause. But the *form* of the pronoun is the same for subject and direct object, so its form *matches* both requirements.

---

[1] The analysis to be presented here is a significant revision and extension of the one presented in Vogel (2001).

[2] This is done to some extent in Vogel (2001) and Vogel (to appear).

[3] See also Åfarli (1994) for a similar proposal for Norwegian FRs. In fact, this is a revival of the first generative account of this construction by Kuroda (1968). The latter proposal, to be honest, incorporates both the NP and the CP treatment in a way that was only possible in the pre-X-bar period. The topmost node is an NP node that immediately dominates an S node that hosts all the material inside the FR, including the FR pronoun. With respect to the 'outside world' an FR is an NP, but its internal structure is clausal: [NP [S ... FR ....]].

Rooryck (1994) notes that it is not necessary to assume a more complicated structure in order to allow for such effects. The accessibility of the [Spec,CP] position of the subordinate clause for the matrix verb is also necessary in order to account for complementation in subordinate *wh*-clauses, as in (2):

(2)   [CP Mary asked [CP what Peter said]]

The verb *ask* requires a *wh*-complement, but it is the [Spec,CP] position of the complement clause, and not the CP node itself, where this requirement is fulfilled.[4] Another example in case are so-called ECM-constructions, where the subject of an embedded infinitival clause is 'exceptionally' assigned accusative by the main verb of the superordinate clause, as in (3):

(3)   John expected [IP Mary to leave]

The NP *Mary* occupies the highest specifier of the infinitival complement clause of the verb 'expect', but can nevertheless be assigned case by *expect* into this position.

The situation in the case of FR complements is not very different. In FR constructions, we are dealing with case requirements that have to be fulfilled by the element in the [Spec,CP] position of the subordinate clause.

In languages other than English that have a more elaborated case system, a case conflict can occur on the FR pronoun between the case required by the matrix verb (henceforth m-case) and the case required by the FR-internal verb (henceforth r-case). Consider the following German clauses with the verbs *vertrauen* ('trust'), which requires a dative object, and *einladen* ('invite'), which requires an accusative object:

(4)   a. Ich lade ein *wen/ wem   ich   vertraue
          I   invite   *who-ACC/ who-DAT   I   trust

       b. Ich vertraue *wem/   *wen   ich   einlade
          I   trust   *who-DAT/ *who-ACC I   invite

A case conflict in German FRs need not lead to ill-formedness, as can be seen in (4a). But it can do so sometimes, as (4b) shows. Although the FR pronoun in (4a) has dative case, and although the accusative case is not realised, the clause is well-formed. The same 'violation' leads to ungrammaticality for many German speakers[5], when the FR pronoun has nominative case:

(5)   Ich   lade ein *wen/   *wer   mir   begegnet
       I   invite   *who-ACC/ *who-NOM me-DAT   meets

---

[4] Other crucial data are possible extractions out of a complex *wh*-DP in [Spec,CP]. See (Chomsky 1986) for a discussion of these issues.
[5] Though not for all German speakers, see section 2.4.

The clause in (5) with *wer* has the same 'constraint violations' as (4a) with *wem* – both suppress the accusative case required by the matrix verb and realise r-case on the pronoun. However, (4a) is well-formed, (5) is not.

Standard explanations for data of this kind, which can be found in many languages, rely on the observation that there is a case hierarchy at work. In the German data above, it is not crucial whether accusative is realised or not, but whether of the two conflicting cases that one is realised that is higher on the German case hierarchy. This is the case in (4a) with *wem*, but not in (5) with *wer*. For German, it is quite clear that the case hierarchy must be of the following form (see also Pittner (1991), and Bayer, Bader & Mèng (2000) for additional evidence for this hierarchy from language comprehension):[6]

(6)   nominative < accusative < dative, genitive, PP

The constraints that have to be obeyed in German FRs seem to be the following ones:

[6] One important question that I discuss in detail in (Vogel, to appear) is whether case hierarchies are universal or language particular. First of all, there is no consensus among case theoreticians that there is a universal inventory of cases, let alone what it looks like. Case inventories might well be language particular as such. But even if we take a universal inventory of (abstract) cases for granted, it is not clear that this universal inventory is the crucial factor here. The reason is that it seems to be essential how a certain case is overtly realised in a language. The conflict in German between m-case=accusative and r-case=nominative that yields ungrammatical FRs for many speakers, as we saw above, can be resolved for inanimates, because the inanimate *wh*-pronoun is the same for nominative and accusative. Furthermore, while in German accusative can be suppressed in favor of oblique case, this is impossible in Spanish and Romanian for animate accusatives, presumably because in this case the *wh*-pronoun takes the form of a PP (see Grosu (1994) for further details). If we only used an abstract notion of universal accusative case we would have to determine universally whether accusative can be suppressed in favor of oblique case or not. Depending on which decision one makes, one would fail to predict either German or Spanish/Romanian. One could, however, assume that only the hierarchisation is language particular. As I show in Vogel (to appear), such language particular hierarchisation crucially relies on what surface form a case takes in a language. The assumption that the case hierarchies that take effect in FRs are language particular hierarchies of surface case forms is, as I see it, unavoidable.

This has an important consequence for the grammar model one assumes: How does a grammar, consisting of only universal constraints, determine whether a given FR clause is well-formed, if it has to rely on a language particular hierarchy of forms? The suppressed case could be assumed to be present in the form of an abstract feature that is not spelled out. But this would not be sufficient, we need the surface form that the suppressed case would have had, if it had been spelled out. But this form is not present in the expression to be evaluated. The grammar needs to have access to an (external) 'database' of case forms. This problem, as I see it, calls for modularity of the kind popular in the generative debates of the 1980s in the context of the GB framework. The current minimalist paradigm, avoiding any kind of modular computation or other non-local operations, does not seem to be able to make the generalisations that seem to hold here. One anonymous reviewer tries to reformulate the approach developed here in a derivational way compatible with minimalism. The idea is basically that the FR pronoun leaves the syntax doubly case marked and that a post-syntactic device D that maps chains onto linearized heads which are subject to lexical insertion could work as well as the non-minimalist global account advocated here. This could well be the case, but does not affect the problem just discussed, namely, language particular case form hierarchies. Such a device D would still have to 'know' that hierarchy in order to work correctly. It might contain a universal principle stating that oblique case is more marked than non-oblique case, but what it means to be oblique differs from language to language. So the necessity of a case module will not go away in a derivational model.

(i)   The FR pronoun realises r-case.

(ii)   m-case is not higher than r-case on the case hierarchy.

Other languages have other solutions of the problem. Gothic and Romanian can shift between m-case and r-case on the pronoun. Modern Greek, realising m-case in general, has a resumptive pronoun inside the FR, if the otherwise suppressed case is oblique. More details of the typology will be discussed in section 2. An optimality theoretic treatment appears to be promising for the following reasons:

– FRs seem to be 'imperfect' as such. All possible resolutions of case conflicts in FRs have certain disadvantages. Either one of the two required cases is suppressed, or a resumptive pronoun is inserted to realise both cases, which is 'bad' under considerations of economy.

– We find that different languages use different solutions under different circumstances, which could mean that the different 'imperfections' of the possible solutions mentioned above have different 'weight' in different languages.

– There is a markedness scale of cases at work. OT, in principle, can make use of universal markedness scales in a direct way. However, as the scales at issue might turn out to be language particular scales, it is much less clear how to proceed in our case.

– We have a quite diverse typology. Although other frameworks can also deal well with typology, an OT account might do so in a more transparent and systematic way.

The next section will present some details of the typology to be accounted for. The third section introduces the OT analysis, and section 4 shows how it predicts the given data.

2   The Typology of FRs

With respect to FRs, languages differ in 2 dimensions: first, they differ in whether they have FRs at all, only matching FRs or also some or all non-matching FRs; second, languages differ in the resolution strategies. We observe three different ways of realising FRs: we find FRs with the FR pronoun realising r-case and m-case remaining unrealised, FRs with the FR pronoun realising m-case and r-case remaining unrealised, and we find FRs with the FR pronoun realising m-case and an additional resumptive pronominal element realising r-case. The fourth type of 'resolution' that also has to be considered in an OT account is the shift to another construction like, for instance, a correlative construction, a left dislocated structure or an ordinary headed relative construction. This section will briefly introduce the different language types that have to be considered.

2.1 Languages without FRs

There are languages that do not allow for free relatives. One example in case is Hindi (cf. Dayal 1996). The usual way to translate a clause like 'I didn't like whatever Anu ordered' is by using a correlative construction:[7]

(7) jo   ciizeN anu-ne mangaayi iN **ve** mujh-ko nahiiN pasand aayiiN
     which things Anu-Erg ordered   them I-Dat   not   like   come-P
     'Which things Anu ordered, I didn't like them' (Dayal 1996, 213)

Another language that might belong to this class is Tok Pisin:

(8) Wanem ol   kaikai ol i   givim yu, yu   no   ken kaikai
     what Pl.   food   they give you, you Neg can eat
     'Whatever food they give you you must not eat' (Woolford 1978, 484)

Although Tok Pisin is classified as a language having FRs in the literature (cf. Bresnan & Grimshaw 1978 and Woolford 1978) the data can be interpreted in a different way. The reason is that here the FR looks exactly like a headed relative construction, cf.:

(9) Ol samting mipela salim i go long yu i kamap pinis   long yu
     Pl.thing   we   sent   go to you come Aspect to   you
     'The things that we sent you arrived' (Woolford 1978, 485)

Restrictive relative clauses in Tok Pisin look like ordinary clauses, they are not introduced by a complementiser or a relative pronoun. So we only have to exchange the 'FR' pronoun in (8) with an ordinary NP to yield a headed relative construction as in (9).

Bresnan & Grimshaw argue on the basis of the Tok Pisin data that FRs are structurally different from interrogative *wh*-clauses. Tok Pisin does not have *wh*-movement, i.e. *wh*-pronouns in interrogative clauses remain in situ:

(10) Yutupela sutim husat tru?
     You   shot who   really
     'Who did you really shoot?' (Woolford 1979, 43)

If Tok Pisin has no FRs, then this argument breaks down, and the parallelism of FRs and other subordinate *wh*-clauses is re-established.

---

[7] The example is syntactically parallel to a left dislocated structure. I will treat correlatives and left dislocated FRs on a par.

2.2 Languages with only matching FRs

In languages which only have matching FRs the surface form of the FR pronoun has to 'match' the forms required for the realisation of both m-case and r-case. English is such a language:

(11)   a.   I drank whatever there was
        b.   I'll reread whatever paper John has worked *(on)
        c.   *I'll reread on whatever paper John has worked
        d.   I'll live wherever you live
        e.   I'll live in whatever town you live (in)

(Bresnan & Grimshaw 1978)

If the matrix verb requires an NP, then the FR pronoun has to be of that category, as we see in (11a–c). The same holds for a PP requirement (11e). However, English has preposition stranding. Although there is a conflict in (11b) with respect to the forms required by the verbs – the matrix verb requires a direct object, i.e. an NP, and the embedded verb a PP –, a FR is possible, if the pronoun moves alone and leaves its preposition behind (11b). Pied-piping as in (11c) yields ungrammaticality. This shows again that it is not the requirements of the verbs that have to match, but it is the element in the [Spec,CP] position of the FR that has to match the matrix requirement, and on the other hand fulfil its requirements inside the embedded clause. One might argue that English only has this matching effect, because it has preposition stranding: (11c) is odd because of the possibility of (11b). Groos & van Riemsdijk (1981, 173) show that Dutch is also a matching language, but Dutch does not have English type preposition stranding:[8]

(12)   a. * Ken   jij   met   wie zij   flirt?
             know you   with who she   flirts?
             'Do you know (the person) with who she is flirting?'

        b. Ken   jij   wie   zij   net   kuste?
           know you   who   she   just kissed?
           'Do you know (the person) who she just kissed?'

Norwegian also seems to be a matching language, as reported by Åfarli (1994). German is classified as a matching language by Groos & van Riemsdijk (1981). Pittner (1991) and Vogel (2001) show that many German speakers do accept

---

[8] Dutch only has preposition stranding in a very restricted way:
(i) Waar   heb   je   ob   gerekend?
    where have you on   counted?
    'What have you counted on?'
This is the same in most variants of German, where preposition stranding is also possible only with the r-pronouns *wo* ('where') and *da* ('there'). See Herslund (1984) and Müller (2000) for further discussion.

non-matching FRs. In the latter paper I also show that German speakers vary in which kinds of non-matching FRs they accept. I assume two 'dialectal' variants German A and German B. It cannot be excluded that there are speakers of German who only accept matching FRs, as proposed by Groos & van Riemsdijk (1981). These speakers would then constitute a third variant, German C.

2.3 Icelandic

Icelandic has an interesting and somewhat surprising pattern. The FR pronoun always bears m-case.[9] In addition, there do not seem to be any restrictions on the suppression of cases and Icelandic has preposition stranding. So it is hard to find a configuration that does not yield a well-formed FR.

In the following examples, two headed restrictive relative constructions (13a,c) are paired with two FR constructions (13b,d). The chosen verbs are *hjálpa*, which requires a dative object, and *elska*, which requires an accusative object. In German the same configuration would yield ungrammaticality for (13b). This is not the case here. Icelandic FR pronouns always take m-case and r-case is simply suppressed. This is, however, not very surprising, if we look at restrictive relative clauses. They are uniformly introduced by the complementiser *sem* ('that'), and the relativised argument (which is represented by a relative pronoun in many other languages) remains unrealised, no matter what case it should have:[10]

(13) a. ég hjálpa þeim/   *þann   sem ég   elska
         I   help   those-DAt/ *those-ACC that I   like

     b. ?ég hjálpa hverjum/ *hvern   (sem) ég elska
        I   help   who-DAT/ who-ACC (that) I   like

     c. ég elska *þeim/   þann   sem ég hjálpa
        I   like   those-DAT/those-ACC that I help

     d. ?ég elska *hverjum/ hvern   (sem) ég hjálpa
        I   like *who-dat/ who-acc (that) I   help

The classification of (13b,d) as FRs and (13a,c) as headed relatives is based on two observations: the complementiser can be omitted in the FRs with the *wh*-pronoun, and in (13a,c) the *d*-pronoun can be separated from the relative clause:[11]

---

[9] This phenomenon is called *case attraction* in the literature.

[10] The FRs in (13b,d) are judged as 'archaic' or 'a bit strange' by my informants. But they agree that they are possible. The complementiser *sem* is optional here, contrary to restrictive relative clauses. Many thanks to Halldór Sigurðsson and Gunnar Hrafn Hrafnbjargarson for sharing their expertise with me.

[11] To be honest, (14b) is not just ill-formed because the FR is disrupted. The *wh*-pronoun *hverjum* can be interpreted as interrogative. The variant of the clause with an overt complementiser is then odd because of difficulties to connect the relative clause to its antecedent and make

(14) a. þeim   hjálpa ég sem ég elska
         those-DAT help   I   that I like

      b. *hverjum hjálpa ég (sem) ég   elska
         who-DAT   help   I (that) I   like

2.4 German A

German has matching FRs and, in addition, non-matching FRs, if m-case is
one of the structural cases nominative and accusative. As already noted, we can
identify at least two, if not three different variants of German with respect to
FRs. In Vogel (2001) I discuss two variants I call German A and German B.
These differ only in the treatment of one particular case conflict, namely, if
m-case is accusative and r-case is nominative:[12]

(15) a. *Er   zerstörte, wer   ihm   begegnete
          He   destroyed who-NOM   him-DAT met
          'He destroyed who he met'

      b. Er   zerstörte was   ihm   begegnete
         he   destroyed what-NOM him-DAT met
         'He destroyed what he met'

The given judgement is for German B. German A differs from German B in that
here (15a) is fine. One possible interpretation of these facts could be that in
German B FRs are sensitive to the case hierarchy: only FRs that suppress the
lower marked case are acceptable. German A could then be seen as a kind of
mirror image of Icelandic in that it does not care about the case hierarchy and
always realises the FR pronoun with r-case, suppressing m-case.

The difference to Icelandic is, however, that oblique cases, i.e. dative and
genitive and PPs, cannot be suppressed at all in German. But the fact that in
Icelandic relative clauses any case form can be suppressed is quite exceptional
and surprising anyway.

Further examination suggests an explanation for this phenomenon that sheds
some light on the functioning of case systems as such. Let us compare the
dative in German and Icelandic: German has a phenomenon called 'free dative'.

___

sense of the clause. Interrogative pronouns usually cannot be relativised.

[12] The well-formedness of (15b) is due to the fact that the FR pronoun *was* has the same
form for accusative and nominative – because of this we find a matching configuration here,
although the required/assigned cases are in conflict. Cf. the analogous case in English discussed
above. The examples in (15) are taken from (Pittner 1991). One anonymous reviewer pointed out
that (15a) is odd for the independent reason that *zerstören* is quite unusual with animate direct
objects. This is true. However, on the other hand there is a difference between a judgement of
ungrammaticality and a judgement of being unusual and informants usually are able to keep the
two apart. But the effect, of course, occurs with any German transitive verb. The verb in (15a)
could be replaced by *verletzen* ('hurt') or *töten* ('kill') without a change in the grammaticality
status of the datum.

Dative objects can be added in many clauses, receiving a benefactive, malefactive, 'affected possessor' or similar reading:

(16)   Ich   backte   meiner   Mutter   einen   Kuchen
       I   baked   my   mother-DAT a   cake-ACC
       'I baked my mother a cake'

Contrary to German, Icelandic does not have free datives (cf. Holmberg & Platzack 1995, 202):[13]

(17)   *Èg   bakaði   mömmu   minni   köku
        I   baked   mother   my   (a) cake

This 'gap' might suggest the following conclusion: The case systems of German and Icelandic have different 'places' in their grammars. In German, case is comparatively autonomous. Oblique case plays an independent role in semantic interpretation.[14] Suppression of oblique case thus yields uninterpretability. In Icelandic, case is always lexically licensed,[15] and because of this case suppression is easily recoverable via the lexical entry of the verb. No semantic information is lost by case suppression. This explains why on the one hand in relative clauses all cases can be suppressed, but, on the other hand, case forms do not make an independent contribution to the meaning of the clause and hence cannot occur freely.

With respect to the OT analysis that I will propose below, there is an interesting consequence. We might get winners of OT competitions in German A and in Icelandic that both suppress dative case. While the Icelandic example would be fine, the German A example is odd, although it is the winner: the reason for this lies in the fact described above, namely, that dative case is semantic information in German that gets lost under suppression: The German A winner fails in the semantic component of the grammar.

---

[13] Free dative FRs are o.k. in German, while they seem to be uninterpretable, if not unparsable in Icelandic:
(i) a.   Ich backe einen Kuchen   wem   ich vertraue
          I   bake a   cake-ACC who-DAT I   trust
          'I bake a cake for whom I trust'   (German)

     b.   *Èg bakaði köku   hverjum/hvern   ég elska
           I   bake   a cake   who-DAT/who-ACC I   like
          'I bake a cake for whom I like'   (Icelandic)

[14] For a recent proposal that oblique case has some semantic implications see Wunderlich (2000).

[15] This claim has previously been made, among others, by Holmberg & Platzack (1995).

2.5 German B

As shown above, German B is a language that has matching FRs. It also has non-matching FRs, but only if the suppressed case is hierarchically lower than the case realised on the FR pronoun. In addition, the FR pronoun cannot bear m-case, obviously for a general reason. This means that FRs are impossible in German B, if m-case is higher than r-case, but possible in the opposite situation:[16]

(18)   a. m-case=ACC;r-case=NOM:
          *Er   zerstörte, wer   ihm   begegnete
           He   destroyed who-NOM   him-DAT   met
           'He destroyed who met him'

        b. m-case=NOM;r-case=ACC:
           Ihm   begegnete, wen   er zerstören   wollte
           Him-DAT   met   who-ACC he destroy   wanted
           'Him met who he wanted to destroy'

(19)   a. m-case=DAT;r-case=ACC:
          *Er   begegnete, wen   er zerstören   wollte
           He-NOM   met   who-ACC he destroy   wanted
           'He met who he wanted to destroy'

        b. m-case=ACC;r-case=DAT:
           Er   zerstörte,   wem   er   begegnete
           He-NOM   destroyed   who-DAT   he-NOM   met
           'He destroyed who he met'

2.6 Gothic and Romanian

German and Icelandic are languages that uniformly realise either m-case or r-case on the FR pronoun, but cannot shift between the two. This is possible in Gothic and Romanian. In these languages, it is always the 'higher' case that is realised.

(20)   Romanian, nominative vs. dative

        a. Cui   i   se   dă   de mîncare trebuie să   muncească
           who-DAT him self give of food   must   SUBJ   work
           '(He) who gets food must work'   (Grosu 1994, 116)

---

16 The verbs in the following examples differ in that *zerstören* requires an accusative object, while *begegnen* requires a dative object.

    b. Mă   voi   adresa   cui mă poate întelege
       me   will-I   address   who-DAT
       'I shall turn to who can understand me'   (Grosu 1994, 120)

In (20a) the embedded verb requires dative on the pronoun, while the FR is the subject of the clause. In (20b) the FR pronoun is subject of the FR clause, while the FR itself serves as dative object of the matrix clause. In both instances, the FR pronoun must bear dative case.

The same behaviour can be observed in Gothic, as reported by Harbert (1983):[17]

(21)   Gothic, nominative vs. accusative (Harbert 1983, 248f)

    a. jah   *þo*-ei   ist   us   Laudeikaion jus ussiggwaid
      and Acc-Compl is   from Laodicea   you read
      'and read (the one) which is from Laodicea' (Col 4: 16)

    b. *þan*-ei   frijos   siuks   ist
      Acc-Compl you-love sick   is
      '(The one) whom you love is sick' (Joh. 11: 3)

In (21a) the m-case is accusative and in (21b) it is the r-case. Nevertheless, the FR pronoun bears accusative morphology in both instances. Accusative is, however, always suppressed, if it conflicts with higher marked dative or genitive:

(22)   Gothic, accusative vs. dative/genitive (Harbert 1983, 248f)

    a. hva   nu   wileiþ   ei   taujau *þamm*-ei   qiþiþ   þiudan Iudaie?
      What now you-want that I-do   dat-Compl you-say king   of-Jews
      'What now do you want that I do to him (whom) you call the king of Jews?' (Mk 15: 12)

    b. bugei *þiz*-ei   þaurbeima
      buy   gen-Compl we-might-have-need-of
      'Buy (that) of which we might have need' (Joh 13: 29)

If one tried to reduce the hierarchies at work here to a two-element hierarchy of, say, 'marked' and 'unmarked' (which actually could not really be called a 'hierarchy'), one would have to decide whether accusative counts as marked or as unmarked. Depending on what this decision would be, it would either be predicted that accusative cannot lose against dative or genitive (because it is marked) or that it cannot win against nominative (because it is unmarked). In these two languages, and also in German B, we are really dealing with a scale, not only with, e.g. a distinctive feature.

---

[17] The glosses are as given by Harbert (1983).

2.7 Modern Greek

Modern Greek shares with Icelandic that the FR pronoun always bears m-case:

(23)   a. Agapo opjon/*opjos   me   agapa
           love-1Sg whoever-ACC/*NOM me   loves
           'I love whoever loves me' (Alexiadou & Varlokosta 1995, 12)

The FR pronoun shows obligatory case attraction. If the otherwise suppressed r-case is an oblique dative/genitive, then there has to occur a resumptive clitic realising r-case:

(24)   a. Tha voithiso   opjon   tu   dosis   to onoma mu
           FUT help-1S   whoever-ACC cl-GEN give-2S   the name   my
                            *opjou   'whoever-gen'
                            *s'opjon   'to whoever'
                            *opjou tu   'whoever-gen him-gen'
           'I will help whoever you give him my name'
           (Alexiadou & Varlokosta 1995, 13)

This is another way of resolving the case conflict: both cases are realised without giving up the FR structure. This option is chosen in Modern Greek, when m-case is nominative or accusative and r-case is dative/genitive.

2.8 Summary

Tableau 1 gives a summary of the typology to be accounted for. There are languages without FRs and languages with only matching FRs. And then there is a language with an overall strategy, Icelandic. The other languages are obviously sensitive to the case hierarchy. German A and Modern Greek seem to make use of the case hierarchy in a different way than the others. They only change their strategy, when their standard mode of conflict resolution would yield suppression of oblique case. German A has no FRs in this situation, while Modern Greek uses the resumptive pronoun strategy. Gothic and German A also take care of accusative-nominative conflicts. As shown above, many of these typological patterns are observed in more than one language.

Tableau 1: Typology of case conflict resolution in FRs

Conflict[18]	Hindi	Engl.	Icel.	Ger. A	Ger. B	Gothic	M. Greek
m=NOM;r=ACC	–		M	R	R	R	M
m=NOM;r=OBL	–	–	M	R	R	R	RES
m=ACC;r=OBL	–	–	M	R	R	R	RES
m=ACC;r=NOM	–		M	R	–	M	M
m=OBL;r=NOM	–	–	M	–	–	M	M
m=OBL;r=ACC	–	–	M	–	–	M	M
m=r	–	FR	FR	FR	FR	FR	FR

There is no need to assume that Tableau 1 is complete. On the other hand, the data suggest a certain systematicity. The conflicts are sorted into two groups: in the first three conflict types r-case is higher than m-case, the next three types have the opposite pattern. Only two languages do not seem to have a uniform strategy for the same group of conflict types. But this might be an artefact of the mode of presentation. If German A and Modern Greek only distinguish between structural and oblique case and judge the two structural cases nominative and accusative as equivalent, although they are morphologically distinct, then the pattern is quite uniform again: nominative and accusative would not conflict.

Four of the seven language types are sensitive to the case hierarchy, while they differ in whether they use a two-element hierarchy (structural vs. oblique, as in German A and Modern Greek), or a three-element hierarchy (nominative, accusative, oblique, as in German B and Gothic).

Each possible strategy to resolve case conflicts in FRs has certain problematic aspects. Neither solution is 'perfect'. So there is no a priori universal 'default'. It might not be a surprise that this quite diverse typology occurs in such a situation.

A language's preference for a certain strategy mirrors specific properties of its grammar. The tradition in generative grammar is to conceive these as language particular parametrisation of universal principles. In Optimality Theory, such a parametrisation is expressed through the ranking of constraints. The next section spells out the details of the OT account that I propose and section 4 shows how this account is able to capture the typology described here.

18 Only those forms of nominative and accusative are taken into account that differ, so English has no conflicts between nominative and accusative forms, because these forms match. The abbreviations M, R, and RES stand for the three different types of FRs: those with the pronoun realising r-case (R) and m-case (M), and those that use the resumptive pronoun strategy (RES). These abbreviations will be used throughout the paper.

3 The OT account

The phenomenon provides at least three interesting challenges for OT-syntax:

(a) We need a way to account for the ungrammaticality of FRs in some languages.
(b) As the crucial elements are surface forms, we need a syntax model that integrates surface representations of clauses with more abstract representations.
(c) The case hierarchies that are used here seem to be language particular, because they are hierarchies of forms, not of features. OT is good at integrating universal markedness scales. But here it is less obvious, how we have to proceed.

Problem (a) is solved by a strategy called 'neutralisation': The winner is a candidate that is slightly different from the input, in our case this can be either a correlative/left dislocation construction, or a headed relative construction.

The solution for problem (c) lies in the assumption of modularity. Instead of assuming a whole array of constraints on the realisation of individual cases, I assume three general constraints on case realisation, which are differently liberal. These constraints use a language particular 'database' of case forms to determine whether the given form in an expression meets the requirements defined in the constraint. The most rigid constraint wants for each abstract case feature one surface case morpheme, and vice versa. This is only satisfied by FRs with an additional resumptive pronoun as exemplified by Modern Greek (cf. (24)). If the constraint that punishes resumptive elements is ranked high together with the just described constraint, then a language has no FRs.

A more liberal constraint allows for one case morpheme to serve as realiser of more than one abstract case. This constraint is fulfilled in matching FRs, but not in non-matching ones (except again for those with an additional resumptive pronoun). An even more liberal version of the latter constraint can be satisfied by a different case morpheme if it is higher on the case hierarchy. This constraint is important in languages with alternating strategies like Gothic, German and others. The relative ranking of these three constraints determines whether a language has no FRs, only matching ones or also non-matching ones.

The most difficult task is problem (b), not only for an OT analysis, but for any account of the phenomenon. How can the FR pronoun be sensitive to the requirements of the embedding verb and itself be located in the lower clause? Harbert (1983) already proposed that case attraction, i.e. the situation where the FR pronoun surfaces with m-case, is a PF phenomenon. He assumes case assignment at the level of PF. This sounds a bit strange, because PF is not a syntactic level, but case assignment is presumably a syntactic process. Instead of this, I assume that case attraction is indeed a PF phenomenon, but the case is already assigned at LF – to the whole FR clause. The FR pronoun can surface with m-case, because the C^0 head of a FR is an agreement head.[19] The specifier-head relation between FR pronoun and C^0 can be interpreted in the process of LF-PF mapping such that the FR pronoun surfaces with m-case. I do not assume that this is possible in specifier-head relations in general, only FRs have this property and this is what makes them FRs.

On the other hand, FRs are not the only phenomenon where something like this might happen. A subordinate *wh*-clause is often assumed to be marked as interrogative by the element in its [Spec,CP] position. In the same way one could assume a FR to be marked as dative object by the dative object in its [Spec,CP]. As I said, this must be restricted to FRs, their C^0 head has this specific property, most other heads do not. Another example in case might be exceptional case marking (ECM), where the subject of an embedded infinitival clause is assigned accusative by the verb from the upper clause. Traditional analyses assume that nothing prevents this, because infinitival INFL is no intervening case governor. Alternatively, one could assume that infinitival INFL is a case assigner, and that it only has no case to assign by itself, but inherits accusative case from the upper verb. It can transfer this case to the subject, because it is in a specifier-head relation with it. This way the case assigned to the whole infinitival clause can surface in its highest specifier position.

A couple of case theoretic background assumptions are also needed. I discuss this aspect of the problem in detail in (Vogel, to appear). For the present purposes, it will be sufficient to assume the following:

(a) abstract case is assigned syntactically to maximal projections.

(b) morphological case is also a property of the PF correspondents of maximal projections, but it may surface in several ways: on the heads as inflection, as (affixal or prepositional) case markers, or, as a sort of alternative 'last resort' method, in the specifier of a maximal projection that is headed by a head with agreement functions.

(c) abstract case is assigned by lexical items (oblique case) or functional heads (like INFL for subjects and whatever functional head one assumes for direct objects).

(d) the question why which argument surfaces with which case is not touched upon at all here. See Aissen (to appear), Woolford (to appear), Wunderlich (2000) and Fanselow (2000) for such a discussion within OT, and Vogel (to appear) for a critical review.

The system I am going to propose makes extensive use of the Chomskyan claim that a linguistic expression is an [LF, PF] pair. Pesetsky's (1998) version of OT-syntax uses an LF as input and several possible PFs as candidates. The model used here also assumes that an LF can be paired with different PFs – the different types of FRs differ only in their PFs, not in their LFs. In addition, however, it is also possible to have candidates with different LFs – this is

---

[19] Rooryck (1994) was the first one to assume that the C^0 head of an FR has agreement properties.

necessary to account for ineffability. The question that immediately arises in such an approach is how to restrict the candidate set. I will use a specific version of the candidate generating function *Gen* to reach this aim. The following subsections discuss the details of the just sketched approach.

3.1 On the Architecture of the OT-Syntax Model

The general model of an OT grammar can simply be described as follows: An input representation I is mapped onto a set of output candidates C_O by a generation function *Gen*. The elements of C_O are then evaluated according to a set of constraints *Con*. The evaluation function is called *H-Eval* – for 'harmonic evaluation'. The output O is the most harmonic candidate as determined by *H-Eval*.

We can distinguish two general ways of modelling syntax in OT. They differ in how they conceive the input and *Gen*. Let us call them the 'derivational picture' and the 'representational picture'. In the derivational picture the input is an initial stage in the syntactic derivation of the clause to be processed. Grimshaw (1997*b*) thought of it as the argument structure plus some other semantic specifications. If this is a syntactic representation at all, then it is one at a very early stage. Other derivational models are used by Heck (1998, 1999), Heck & Müller (2000) and in LFG (e.g. Bresnan 2000).

In these approaches *Gen* is a generator in two ways: it literally generates the candidates and that way forms the candidate set. *Gen* can also be defined as generating only the candidate *set*, without generating each candidate each time. This latter task can be performed by another function that is presupposed by the OT-syntax model. Let us assume that an independently existing universal sentence generation function[20] already generated the universe U_S of possible sentence or LF patterns. As U_S is not language particular, there cannot be access to lexical information. The generation of the candidate set performed by *Gen* is now a process of selecting a subset of U_S. Output candidates must pass a certain criterion that defines the competition.

The system proposed by Legendre et al. (1998) can be interpreted in that way. Here, the candidates have to be *similar* to a given *target* LF, but might depart from it minimally in a restricted, pre-determined way. This proposal shares with that of Grimshaw (1997b) and others that the input in syntax is a representation of semantic properties. However, Keer & Baković (2000) show that the input sometimes needs to contain purely formal information in order to account for phenomena like, e.g. the complementiser optionality in the following example:

(25)   John thinks (that) Mary is polite

---

[20] This function can be seen as the 'core' of the Universal Grammar in generative syntax: The X-bar schema plus the universal inventory of syntactic categories (including their general selection restrictions, if there are any) and a combinatorial or merging mechanism.

In their proposal the verb *think* in (25) would exist in two versions, one selecting for a complementiser-introduced complement clause, and the other selecting for a clause without complementiser. That way we get two different inputs, depending on which version of *think* is chosen. Each of the two variants in (25) is more faithful to its corresponding input than the other. That way, both can be winners of their own OT competition, but they both take part in both competitions.

If it is unavoidable to assume functional material as part of the input then the input itself is already a fully elaborated syntactic structure. A representation that contains lexical information, as required by Grimshaw (1997b), scope information, as required by Legendre et al. (1998) and functional information, as required by Keer & Baković (1999), is a complete syntactic structure, e.g. the Logical Form (LF) as defined by Chomsky (1995).

In order to account for ungrammatical FRs it might be necessary to include within the candidate set at least one candidate that is not a FR.[21] This candidate is supposed to win, when a FR is ungrammatical. But it should also be as similar as possible to the structure of a FR. Good and natural candidates are sentences with correlative or left-dislocated FRs, as in (7) or in (26):

(26) German:
      Wer   einmal   lügt,   *(dem)   glaubt man nicht
      who-NOM   once   lies   *(the-DAT) believes one not
      'Whoever lies once, one doesn't believe him anymore'

The minimal difference to FR constructions is the occurrence of a resumptive element (the bracketed pronoun in (26)) picking up the referent introduced by the dislocated FR. But this is only a difference in the *formal or functional* inventory of the clause, not in its meaning or its (non-functional) lexical material.

There is also, on the other hand, *optionality* of this dislocation or correlative structure:

(27) German:
      Wer einmal lügt, (der)   lügt   auch ein zweites Mal
      who-NOM   once (the-NOM) lies   also a   second time
      'Whoever lies once, (he) lies a second time, too'

---

[21] There is another way of accounting for absolute ungrammaticality that I do not want to discuss here because of its minor theoretical appeal: assume that the 'null parse' takes part in every competition and that there is only one constraint that this candidate violates, namely a constraint 'NoNullParse'. The ranking of this constraint with respect to others which are crucial for FRs determines the possibility of FRs. A third way of accounting for ungrammaticality is 'uninterpretability'. A winning candidate might be uninterpretable, e.g. in semantics. This option will be discussed below as a possible account of German A. It cannot, however, derive optionality of FRs and correlatives.

This means in OT terms that a correlative is able to win in situations where it *is* possible to have a FR. The two clause types are not in complementary distribution. For a FR competition, we would want the FR to win against the correlative most times. But the correlative is the more frequent construction: whenever a FR is possible, it has a well-formed corresponding correlative construction, but not vice versa. This case is parallel to the one discussed by Keer & Baković (1999). In order to let the correlative win, we have to distinguish it from the FR in the input and give it some advantage via faithfulness in its own competition. But this can only be done by encoding functional material of the clause already in the input.

For this reason I will explore here a radical version of what I called the 're-presentational picture': the 'input' is itself the LF of an output candidate, the most faithful one. Its competitor LFs are chosen from U_S by *Gen* according to a similarity criterion.

But the LF, as element of U_S, is only one out of *three* constitutive parts of a candidate. Elements of U_S lack everything language particular: They do not contain lexical items, neither syntactic information introduced by these. The LF is paired with a language-particular 'phonetic form' (PF). Candidates are ordered [LF, PF] pairs.[22]

We only want those structures to compete that contain the same (non-functional) lexical material. So an element of U_S, conceived as input, stands for a whole family of competitions that differ in the used lexical items.

The functions of *Gen* and input in the proposed OT-syntax model can be summarised in the following way:

- U_S is the universe of sentence or LF patterns.
- Each of these patterns defines its own family of OT competitions.
- Candidates of the same competition have an LF that is 'similar' in a way to be determined to the LF pattern that defines the competition.
- In addition, candidates of the same competition have identical lexical[23] material in corresponding syntactic positions.
- Candidates are [LF, PF] pairs. PFs are derived from their corresponding LFs.

The set of universal LF patterns U_S is of central methodological importance for the current task. We want to model, how languages express FR constructions. The assumption that the FR pattern is universal guarantees that the FR constructions of different languages can be compared. If there was no U_S, we could not guarantee that the candidate sets of the FR competitions in different languages are alike, and thus would not be able to compare the competitions. In the end, we would not be able to come up with a proposal for the typology of

---

[22] This is the standard assumption in current generative syntax, see, for instance, Chomsky (1995).

[23] The attribute 'lexical' here refers to open class items, lexical categories, not to function words and functional categories. We want to allow for variation in the functional architecture, but keep the lexical material constant within a single competition.

this construction. Something like U_S, as I see it, is a 'conditio sine qua non' for doing typology within OT-syntax.

A competition is defined by a universal LF pattern plus a 'lexical index', i.e. a set of lexical items that occupy the terminal nodes of the LF pattern. FR constructions can be (part of) such universal LF patterns.[24]

We then derive a set of candidate LFs – in our example there are only two such alternative LFs, the FR and the correlative. The candidates are then derived by pairing each LF with possible PFs. We considered three possible PFs for a FR-LF – differing in the overt case morphology of the FR pronoun and in whether an additional resumptive element 'spells out' $r-case$. We only considered one type of correlative, but there may be many of them: with the relative clause preposed, extraposed or intraposed, with or without a resumptive pronoun, with all kinds of distributions of overt case markers etc. The several stages of the *Gen* function are summed up in tableau 2.

Tableau 2: The *Gen* function

1. Select 'input' LF pattern	2. Select 'simlar' LF patterns	3. Add lexical 'index'	4. generate [LF, PF] pairs
FR	FR	FR_{LEX}	$FR_{LEX} - M$ $FR_{LEX} - R$ $FR_{LEX} - RES$
	CORR	$CORR_{LEX}$	$CORR_{LEX} - ...$

A FR competition can be seen as 'inputless' insofar as the information attributed to the input is fully represented in at least one of the candidates, the one that contains the selected 'input LF'.[25] Candidates that contain the 'input LF' will be marked with a '⊙'.[26] The competitions for FR and correlative might have identical candidate sets and differ only in which of the LFs of the candidates is chosen as defining the competition:

---

[24] The term 'index' is used by Legendre et al. (1998) instead of 'input'. In much the same way as described here, the function of the index is only to define what competes. Output candidates compete, if they share a certain property, i.e. 'have the same index'. I therefore often use this notion instead of 'input' below.

[25] For a more extended discussion of why OT syntax needs no input as a genuine level of representation, see Heck et al. (2000).

[26] This is the astronomical symbol for 'sun'. It is open to the reader to find deeper reasons for why this symbol is used here. There is no formal difference between the ⊙-LF and an output-LF. The '⊙' marks those output candidates that contain the LF that is used as input or 'index' in defining the competition. ⊙-LF-to-O(utput)-LF faithfulness is only a special version of input-output faithfulness.

Tableau 3: Candidate sets for FR and CORR competitions

FR competition	CORR competition
⊙FR-M_{LEX}	FR-M_{LEX}
⊙FR-R_{LEX}	FR-R_{LEX}
⊙FR-RES_{LEX}	FR-RES_{LEX}
CORR$_{LEX}$	⊙CORR$_{LEX}$

Instead of input-output faithfulness, we will speak of '⊙-LF faithfulness' below. Candidates are evaluated with respect to their 'similarity' to the candidates
that have the initial LF pattern. As the same LF may be able to be paired with
more than one PF, more than one ⊙-candidate can occur. This does not
matter.[27]

3.2   Ineffability and Optionality

OT offers two strategies to account for ungrammaticality: uninterpretability and
neutralisation. The uninterpretability strategy lets a winner 'crash' at some interface, which could be the 'conceptual-intentional' or the 'articulatory-perceptual'
interface. The neutralisation strategy lets a candidate win that is 'unfaithful' to
the input. This is the strategy described above: in languages without FRs, a FR
is 'neutralised' to a correlative construction. Let us have a closer look at the two
strategies.

3.2.1   Ungrammaticality with Uninterpretability

Consider the following German data again (remember that *folgen* assigns dative
and *bewundern* accusative to its object):

(28) a. *Ich   folge   wen   immer ich   bewundere
          I   follow   who-ACC   ever I   adore

      b. *Ich   folge   wem   immer ich   bewundere
          I   follow   who-DAT   ever I   adore

[27] Evaluation of candidates with respect to their similarity to another candidate has first
been introduced in sympathy theory for OT phonology (see McCarthy 1998). Sympathy was
invented to deal with opacity phenomena. To yield the correct results we sometimes need to refer
to what has been an intermediate stage in derivational phonology. In a strictly output-oriented
theory like OT such intermediate stages are invisible. Sympathy has been designed to 'emulate'
access to such intermediate stages. An intermediate stage is 'represented' by one of the output
candidates, designated through an extra 'sympathy competition'. The present discussion has nothing to do with problems of this kind. It is the character of syntax as such that lets an approach
appear attractive that may be reminiscent of sympathy.

Let us assume that under the German constraint ranking only candidates with
r-case on the FR pronoun win. Then (28b) loses against (28a). But in (28a)
an oblique case is suppressed. This, we further assume, results in an unrecover-
able deletion of semantic information. As a consequence, the FR cannot be
interpreted in the semantics. From this perspective, we could allow (28a) to win
an OT syntax competition without predicting that it is judged as well-formed
by native speakers. But now consider the following example again which is
ungrammatical in German B, but well-formed in German A:

(29)   (*)Er   tötet,   wer   immer   ihm   begegnet
        He   kills   who-NOM   ever   him-DAT   meets

If the ungrammaticality of this clause in German B was also due to uninterpretability, then it should also be blocked in German A. As this is not the case,
the syntax-semantics interface cannot be held responsible for the ill-formedness.
In (28a), we have suppression of a presumably semantically significant oblique
case, while in (29) we have suppression of a semantically relatively empty structural case. (28) can be explained by uninterpretability, but not (29)! Uninterpretability may be taken into account for some instances of ineffability, but not for
all of them.

3.2.2   Ungrammaticality with Neutralisation

Neutralisation requires the inclusion of a candidate in the candidate set that is
not a FR, but only minimally different from it. I showed above that correlatives
or headed relatives are perfect for this task. The only difference to FRs is the
occurrence of a pronoun 'heading' the relative clause that now can be interpreted
as an ordinary restrictive relative clause. The structure for a headed relative
clause would be roughly as in (30):

(30)   [DP PRON+m-case [CP RELPRON+r-case ...]]

The advantage of this candidate is that both cases are realised – m-case on the
'head' pronoun and r-case on the relative pronoun. Its disadvantage is that it
is *unfaithful* to the FR structure. The inclusion of this candidate requires a
'relaxed' definition of *Gen* and faithfulness to functional features which are
specified in the input. The basic idea that I will follow here is that the FR pronoun stands for a bundle of features. In a headed construction as in (39) this
feature bundle is split into two separately projecting functional heads.
   The content of the features that the FR pronoun is composed of is less clear.
My proposal is speculative, though perhaps plausible. I assume that the semantic property that distinguishes an ordinary relative pronoun from a FR pronoun
is referentiality: a simple restrictive relative clause cannot represent or introduce
a discourse referent by itself, it always has to be connected to a 'head'. A free

relative clause is referential.[28] So let us assume two features [±REF] for 'referentiality' and [±REL] for characteristics of the relative operator (these features may be further decomposable into other features, but this is a different issue). This is represented in Tableau 5.

Tableau 5: The composition of FR pronouns

	[REF]	[REL]
pronoun	+	−
relative pronoun	−	+
FR pronoun	+	+

I assume that the feature bundle of a FR is contained in the C^0 head of the FR and that the morphological properties of the FR pronoun are reflections of the SpecHead agreement between FR pronoun and FR head.

In a FR 'input' LF pattern, the feature bundle of the C^0 head contains the 'sub-bundle' [[+REF][+REL]] and maybe more features. The function *Gen* selects all structures that contain the same functional material as the 'input' FR, including those structures where the features are distributed in a different way.[29] The correlative or headed relative candidate results from splitting up the feature (sub-) bundle of the FR pronoun and letting each of the two features project on its own.

(31)   *Input*:   { ... [[+REF][+REL]] ... }

      Output 1:   [FR [c^0 [[+REF][+REL]]] ...]
      Output 2:   [DP [D^0 [+REF]] [CP [c^0 [+REL]] ...]]

The 'feature bundle split' strategy is only one way to 'expand' the structure of a FR without changing its functional/formal inventory. True instances of left dislocation as in the German (26), repeated below, might be different.

(32)   Wer   einmal lügt,   *(dem)   glaubt man nicht
      who-NOM once   lies   *(the-DAT) believes one not
      'Whoever lies once, one doesn't believe him anymore'

---

[28] Wiltschko (1999) presents many pieces of evidence that FR pronouns are semantically indefinites.

[29] Different distribution must be restricted to cases where a feature projects on its own – in a 'stacking' fashion: The projection of one feature must immediately dominate that of the other feature in this case:
    (i) [XP [X^0 F1+F2]]
    (ii) [YP [Y^0 F1] [XP [X^0 F2]]]

Here, the structure of the FR is kept, but it is placed outside of the matrix clause. A resumptive pronoun ('dem') is inserted into the matrix clause representing the FR.

This is another way of deviating from the functional architecture of the 'input LF' without changing its contents. Let us call this strategy the 'placeholder' strategy. The 'feature bundle split' strategy would yield the following structure for the example :

(33) Man   glaubt   einem,   der   einmal lügt,   nicht
      one   believes   (some)one-DAT   the-NOM once   lies   not

(32) has the advantage of keeping the feature bundle of the FR pronoun intact, but it duplicates the FR with a resumptive pronoun. The FR in the 'input LF' has two correspondents in the output LF, and it has the FR moved outside of the matrix clause. (34) splits the feature bundle of the FR pronoun, but leaves the relative clause inside the matrix clause.

Which strategy is more optimal in which language is an interesting issue, but not central for our discussion here. So I will abstract away from the difference between (32) and (33) in this paper. I will use the label 'CORR' for the non-FR candidate and leave open which one of the two options is actually chosen.[30]

3.3   Correspondence

The concept of correspondence as introduced by McCarthy & Prince (1995) is of central importance for the analysis that will be developed here. Candidates are ordered pairs of two representations LF and PF. All sorts of constraints on the correspondence of LF and PF can be imagined, and I will make use of some. The second important correspondence relation holds between the designated

---

[30] It is interesting that one can (marginally) use a *wh*-pronoun as head for the relative clause in (33):
    (i) ?Man   glaubt   wem   nicht, der   einmal lügt
        one   believes   (some)one-DAT   not   the-NOM once   lies
While (i) counts as a structure with a headed relative clause where the relative clause is extraposed – a very frequent pattern in German–, the clause in (32) contains a FR. But the only difference is the distribution of the pronouns. It is interesting that the pattern in (32) is impossible with a right dislocated FR:
    (ii) *Man   glaubt dem   nicht, wer   einmal lügt
         one   believes the-DAT not   (some)one-NOM   once   lies
The distribution of *wh*- and *d*-pronoun seems to be governed by a simple rule that requires the referentially independent *wh*-pronoun to be first, and the anaphoric *d*-pronoun to occur whenever a previously introduced discourse referent is picked up again. If we abstract away from this, the difference between (i) and (32) reduces to whether the relative clause is left or right dislocated. In turn, this interpretation could mean that whether a pronoun is called 'resumptive' or 'head of a relative clause' depends on whether it follows or precedes the relative clause. Be this as it may, what interests us here is that this pronoun is obligatory in these cases, and can be omitted in other cases – the latter cases are called free relative constructions.

'input' or '⊙'-LF and the LFs of output candidates (O-LF). There is, however, no correspondence between the PF of an output candidate and the ⊙-LF.

3.3.1 ⊙-O correspondence

The objects that correspond in the ⊙-LF and an O-LF are syntactic chains. ⊙-O correspondence is crucial for the unfaithful correlative candidate(s). While there is only one chain of the FR (index 'i' in (34)) or the FR pronoun (index 'j' in (34)) in the ⊙-LF, an LF with a correlative FR contains either two chains of the FR itself, or of the ⊙-FR pronoun, depending on which of the strategies described in section 3.2.2 is chosen:

(34) a. $[_{CP} \ldots [_{FR} \text{FR-PRON}_j \ldots]_i \ldots]$ ⊙-LF
      b. $[_{CP} \ldots [_{DP} D_j^0 \ [_{CP} C_j^0 \ldots]]_i]$ O-LF with 'feature bundle split'
      c. $[_{FR} \text{FR-PRON}_j \ldots]_i \ [_{CP} \ldots \text{PRON}_i \ldots]$ O-LF with left dislocated FR

As the indices show, in both (34b) and (34c), there is one chain in the ⊙-LF that corresponds with two chains in these candidates. The type of faithfulness constraints that is sensitive to this kind of deviation is called 'INTEGRITY' in (McCarthy & Prince 1995):

(35) INTEGRITY – 'No Breaking'
      No element of S_1 has multiple correspondents in S_2.
      For $x \in S_1$ and $w, z \in S_2$, if $x\Re w$ and $x\Re z$, then $w = z$.

For the present purpose, S_1 is identified with the ⊙-LF and S_2 with an O-LF. In (34b), there are two correspondents of the FR pronoun, and in (34c), there are two correspondents of the whole FR. The constraint violated here will be called 'INTEGRITY-⊙-LF'.

The opposite pattern must also be considered. (34a) could be a candidate of a different competition with (34b) as ⊙-LF. In this case (34a) violates 'UNIFORMITY' (cf. McCarthy & Prince 1995):

(36) UNIFORMITY – 'No Coalescence'
      No element of S_2 has multiple correspondents in S_1.
      For $x, y \in S_1$ and $z \in S_2$, if $x\Re z$ and $y\Re z$, then $x = y$.

This constraint gives the correlative candidate an advantage in a non-FR competition. High ranking of these two faithfulness constraints leads to optionality of correlative and FR – each of them wins its own competition.

3.3.2 LF-PF correspondence

Output Candidates are ordered pairs of two representations, LF and PF. Elements of these representations stand in correspondence. At LF, the elements in question are again chains. At PF, we are dealing with words and strings of words. It can occur that an LF element has two PF correspondents. This happens, for instance, when resumptive pronouns spell out traces of moved elements in addition to the PF string that spells out the head of the chain of that element, as in example (24) from Modern Greek:

(37)   O-LF: XP_i ... t_i
        O-PF: FR-*pronoun ... resumptive pronoun*

The LF chain $\{XP_i, t_i\}$ counts as one syntactic element. But there are no chains at PF: only one link of the chain should be spelled out, but in (37) we have an additional resumptive pronoun and hence two PF correspondents for a single LF chain. The constraint that is violated by such a candidate is 'INTEGRITY-LF-PF'.[31]

LF-PF correspondence is also crucial for the way case conflicts are resolved in FR constructions. We saw that the form of a FR pronoun, i.e. its PF representation, is the element that fulfills case requirements. The problem is that the FR pronoun is able to fulfil the requirements for a chain that it does not correspond to. It has its own syntactic chain.

The syntactic analysis that I proposed in section 1 relies on specifier-head agreement: The FR pronoun occupies the [Spec,CP] position and agrees with the C^0 head of the FR. This agreement configuration is assumed to be responsible for the FR pronoun's sensitivity to case requirements that are imposed on the CP and should normally be fulfilled by the PF correspondent of C^0.

The problem now is: How can we say that the PF correspondent of the FR pronoun realises the abstract case assigned to the FR, if it does not correspond to it? If m-case is a feature of the FR, then we want the PF-correspondent of the FR to bear the appropriate case morphology. The FR pronoun is *part* of the string that corresponds to the syntactic structure of the FR at LF, it is even the initial element, but it is not the *head* of the FR – the complementiser is the head, which has no PF correspondent at all in the FRs of many languages.

(38)   LF: [$_{CP}$ XP_2 C^0 ... t_2-r-case]$_1$-m-case
        PF: / /FR-pronoun(+m/r-case)/$_2$... /$_1$

The configuration in (38) describes a FR with a matching FR pronoun. This alternative PF realisation of a syntactic feature introduces an asymmetry: although the FR pronoun realises m-case, we cannot say that the PF representation of the FR has the morphology of m-case – the CPs in the languages

---

[31] Note that here the LF in question is the O-LF, and *not* the ⊙-LF.

under discussion have no case morphology. That is to say, the specifier strategy is a way of realising the case feature of a category, but it is *not* a way of case-marking it. On the other hand, at LF the FR has an abstract case feature, and this syntactic case feature has a PF correspondent within the FR. But from the perspective of PF, there is no case morphology on the FR that 'seeks for' a corresponding LF case feature.

This asymmetry is an intrinsic 'structural defect' of FRs. It might be formulated in terms of feature identity, again a family of constraints introduced by McCarthy & Prince (1995):[32]

(39)   IDENT(F)
        Correspondent segments have identical values for the feature F.
        If $x\Re y$ and x is [γF], then y is [γF].

If we replace x with the LF representation of a FR and y with its PF representation, and further assume the feature F to be case, then we get what we want:

(40)   IDENT(CASE)-LF-PF
        Correspondent LF chains and PF strings have identical values for the
        feature case.
        If $x\Re y$ and x is [γcase], then y is [γcase].

This constraint is violated by FRs in general, except that they are CPs that are inflected for case. It is also violated by non-matching FRs with case attraction, i.e. where the FR pronoun surfaces with m-case. In this case, the abstract case feature of the chain of the FR pronoun, i.e. r-case, is different from its overt case morphology, i.e. m-case.

The FR candidates with case attraction violate IDENT(case)-LF-PF twice[33] (see tableau 6).

---

[32] An anonymous reviewer remarks that this constraint should be a MAX constraint rather than an IDENT constraint. I think that this would be misleading. A MAX constraint, as defined by McCarthy & Prince (1995) talks about existing correspondence relations, i.e. MAX is fulfilled for an element of LF iff it has a correspondent at PF. IDENT constraints talk about existing correspondence relations and evaluate whether corresponding elements are identical. What has to be clarified is whether a case feature is an element of LF in this sense or whether it is just a property or feature of an element. The standard assumption would be the latter: elements of syntactic representations are syntactic categories (NP, VP, N^0 etc.), or, as I assume here, *chains* of syntactic categories. Syntactic categories can be composed of features like case features, but these features are not syntactic elements by themselves. However, much of the current work in generative syntax tends to give up this distinction and treats many syntactic features as heads that project on their own. From this perspective, the anonymous reviewer would be right. The 'unanswered question' that lies behind this problem is how to deal with the periphrastic/synthetic distinction: case can be expressed in many ways, by prepositions, as well as by morphological affigation of nominal stems. What should a uniform account look like? In this paper, I take the more conservative point of view. In the resumptive pronoun FRs of Modern Greek a pronoun occurs in the position of the trace of the FR pronoun to spell out the case assigned to it. If only the case needs to be spelled out, why does there not occur a pure case morpheme? Why do we have a pronoun? The answer is: because case does not project by itself, it is a feature of NPs, not their governor, so it takes an NP to 'spell out' a case feature.

Tableau 6: Violations of IDENT (CASE)-LF-PF in non-matching FRs

Candidate	IDENT(CASE)-LF-PF
⊙ FR-R	*
⊙ FR-M	**
⊙ FR-RES	**
CORR	

A language like German seems to make a distinction between single or double violation of this constraint. While it tolerates single violation, allowing for FRs with the FR pronoun realising r-case, it does not allow case attraction, where IDENT(CASE)-LF-PF is violated twice. This difference cannot be captured by simply counting the violations. We will need a second constraint that punishes double violation of IDENT(CASE)-LF-PF. The technique of constraint conjunction has already been used for syntax, e.g. by Legendre et al. (1998). The constraint we assume can be defined as in (41):

(41)   IDENT(CASE)-LF-PF$^2_{CP}$
       No double violation of IDENT(CASE)-LF-PF within the same CP.

Tableau 7 shows the violations of this constraint. It is generally assumed that conjoined constraints must be ranked higher than the constraints they are composed of, but this might be a neglectable convention.[34]

[33] Interestingly, the two ways of violating this constraint differ. The FR pronoun realises the wrong case in case attraction. The FR-CP realises no case at all. An alternative account might use this difference to formulate two different constraints.

[34] This assumption can be seen as a relict of connectionist modelling: if violations of constraints are interpreted as 'weights' in a connectionist model, then it can be assumed that double violation of a constraint results in a heavier weight than a single violation. But this translation into the connectionist perspective might be too literal: If a candidate violates a conjoined constraint A&B, then its overall constraint profile is worse than that of another candidate that does not violate A&B, no matter where A&B is ranked. The 'overall (negative) weight' of the candidate is increased. Assume the following table:

	A	B	C	A&B
cand.1	*	*		*
cand.2	...			

If candidate 1 is still in the competition when the evaluation comes to the constraint 'A&B', then there is no co-competitor that performs better or worse than candidate 1 on the constraints A and B. But this could mean that A&B cannot be decisive either, because the candidates should again have identical numbers of violations here. Note on the other hand that conjoined constraints are always relativised to a domain (in (41) this domain is CP). This need not hold of its constituent parts. We might then have a situation, where two candidates both violate A and B, but one candidate has these violations within the same domain and the other in different domains. In this case, only the first candidate also violates A&B. Thus, A&B would be decisive, although it is ranked below its constituent constraints. I see no reason why this should be ruled out.

Consider another situation: the table above also says that it is worse to violate A twice than to violate A and B only once (within a certain domain). If A&B was ranked higher than A, then we would need another higher ranked constraint A&A to emulate this effect. The convention in question might only produce notational variants. For an interesting exploration of the power of constraint conjunction see Fischer (2001). Note, finally, that connectionist models in principle could allow for inhibitory effects: a violation of A might be less problematic if B is also violated. This

Tableau 7: Violations of $IDENT(CASE)\text{-}LF\text{-}PF^2_{CP}$ in non-matching FRs

Candidate	$IDENT(CASE)\text{-}LF\text{-}PF^2_{CP}$
☉FR-R	
☉FR-M	*
☉FR-RES	*
CORR	

3.3.3 Case

If the constraint IDENT(CASE)-LF-PF was the only constraint affected by case conflicts in FR constructions, then the contrast of 'matching' and 'non-matching' languages would be a surprising fact. Although the FR pronoun cannot 'case-mark' the FR, it is nevertheless a possible 'realiser' for m-case and this has not yet been rewarded. Let us assume a constraint 'REALISE CASE' that is defined in the following way:

(42)   REALISE CASE:
        If γ is the abstract case feature of XP at an LF_i, then its corresponding
        PF_i contains an element x that bears the case morphology of γ. x has to
        be a correspondent of either a., b. or c.:
        a. XP
        b. X^0
        c. YP, the element occupying [Spec,XP] at LF, if X is an AGR-head.

Languages have different strategies of making case features morphologically visible. Some use extra markers that are attached to the phrase they mark, like prepositions or postpositions. In other languages the case feature is 'reflected' by inflection of the words contained in a case marked phrase, in others it is only the determiner that realises the case of an NP. The really exceptional and unusual way of realising case is the specifier strategy that is chosen in FR constructions. But remember that a candidate fulfilling (42c) is only generated if X is an agreement head, as I assume this for the C^0-head of FRs to be the case. One other instance of (42c) might be exceptional case marking as in:

(43)   John expects [$_{IP}$ Mary to win the game]

Under the traditional analysis, the NP *Mary* occupies SpecIP and is assigned case by *expect*, i.e. from outside of its host IP. It might not be unreasonable to subsume ECM under the matching effect in a parallel fashion: *expect* assigns case to IP and the element in [Spec,IP] realises that case feature, another instance of case attraction.

does not seem to be expressible at all in OT, as it stands.

REALISE CASE is obeyed in matching FRs. It rules out non-matching FRs. Thus, it is ranked high in, e.g. English, and low in the non-matching languages.

The next issue is the question of how to implement case hierarchies. We could replace the general constraint in (42) by a series of constraints for each case in a universally fixed ranking:

(44)   REALISE OBLIQUE >> REALISE ACCUSATIVE >> REALISE NOMINATIVE

We can check whether the case hierarchy should be encoded directly in the constraint set of the grammar by the predictions of this method for case conflicts in FRs. For the sake of the example, let us assume the fixed hierarchy in (44) as given.

The system that we explore has two candidates: a free relative structure with the pronoun realising r-case and a correlative structure. Ungrammaticality of a FR in this system means that the correlative wins. In order for the correlative not to always win, there must be a constraint that bans correlatives. We use the constraint 'Integrity-⊙-LF' as introduced in section 3.3.1.

Correlatives have the advantage that all cases can be realised, while in non-matching FRs only one of them is realised. This, together with the constraint hierarchy in (44) should suffice for the data of German B as introduced in section 2.5. Let us assume the following ranking for German B:

(45)   REALdat >> REALacc >> INT-⊙-LF >> REALnom

This ranking makes the correct prediction for non-matching FRs with accusative and nominative, see (46) – (47).

The problem arises with accusative and dative. Because both REALdat and REALacc are higher than INT-⊙-LF, the correlative is always better than the FR. But such a FR is well-formed, if m-case is accusative and r-case is dative. The FR pronoun carries dative morphology here, and this is in accordance with the case hierarchy. So here we get a wrong prediction, see (48).

(46)   The 'index':
        m-case = NOM ; r-case = ACC
        is correctly predicted to yield a well-formed FR:

NOM – ACC	REAL dat	REAL acc	INT-⊙-LF	REAL nom
☞ ⊙FR *wen* ('who-ACC')				*
Correlative			*	

(47)   The 'index':
       m-case = ACC ; r-case = NOM
       is correctly predicted to yield an ill-formed FR:

ACC – NOM	REAL dat	REAL acc	INT-⊙-LF	REAL nom
⊙FR *wen* ('who-ACC')		*		
☞ Correlative			*	

(48)   The 'index':
       m-case = acc ; r-case = dat
       is wrongly predicted to yield an ill-formed FR:

acc – dat	REAL dat	REAL acc	INT-⊙-LF	REAL nom
☹ ⊙FR wen ('who-acc')		*		
☞ Correlative			*	

With a different ranking, we would get the correct result for (48): INT-⊙-LF
should be higher than REALacc. But this would now wrongly predict a well-
formed FR for the pattern in (47). We have a so-called 'ranking paradox', which
is a major way of proving the falsehood of a particular OT analysis. The crucial
problem of the proposed model is that we encoded the case hierarchy directly
into constraints. This set of constraints does not express the relative markedness
of accusative. The constraint INT-⊙-LF constitutes a split within the case hierarchy that in fact divides the case forms into two groups of unmarked and marked cases. The system does not express relative, but absolute markedness. The
solution of this problem that I want to propose consists of two crucial steps:

(a)   Language particular hierarchies of case forms are determined in a separate
       module of the grammar. They are presupposed by the core OT-syntax
       system. This 'case module' might have an OT architecture, but it does
       not need to.[35]
(b)   In addition to 'REALISE CASE' there is a second constraint 'REALISE
       CASE (relativised)' that is sensitive to the case hierarchy. For this con-
       straint, a case x counts as 'realised' not only, when a PF element has the
       case morphology of x, but also, when it bears the morphology of a case
       that is higher than x on the case hierarchy.

(49)   REALISE CASE (relativised):
       If γ is the abstract case feature of XP at an LFi, then the corresponding
       PFi contains an element x that bears the case morphology of γ or the
       case morphology of another case δ for which holds that $\gamma < \delta$ on the

---

[35] For a more detailed discussion of this matter see Vogel (to appear).

language particular hierarchy of case forms. x has to be a correspondent of either a., b. or c.:

a. XP

b. X^0

c. YP, the element occupying [Spec,XP] at LF, if X is an AGR-head.

While REALISE CASE distinguishes between matching and non-matching FRs, REALISE CASE (relativised) distinguishes between non-matching FRs that are in accordance with the case hierarchy and non-matching FRs that are not. To account for the complete typology, we need both constraints:

(50)   a. English FRs violate neither REALISE CASE nor REALISE CASE (relativised)

       b. German B and Gothic FRs can violate REALISE CASE, but not REALISE CASE (relativised)

       c. Icelandic FRs can violate both REALISE CASE and REALISE CASE (relativised)

3.3.4   What we have so far and why Icelandic is missing

Tableau 8 gives an overview of the constraints we introduced up to now and shows for each of them the violations in each of the three FR competition types.

We can see in this tableau whether there are any candidates that are 'harmonically bounded', i.e. candidates that can never win because their constraint violations are supersets of the constraint violations of another candidate. This is indeed the case: candidate M can never win the 'm-case < r-case' competition. It is bounded by candidate R. This is an unwanted result, because in Icelandic (and in Modern Greek, if m-case is nominative and r-case accusative) candidate M wins this competition.

In order to let candidate M win the 'm-case < r-case' competition, we need an additional constraint that favours realising m-case on the FR pronoun as such. If there was no general advantage of doing so, it would be mysterious, why Icelandic chooses this option in all instances.

I cannot come up with a conclusion that I find fully satisfactory. What I propose is a bit speculative, though there are some interesting facts that can be related to the proposal I want to make.

The advantage of realising m-case is that the grammatical function of the FR within the matrix clause is made explicit. Especially non-matching FRs where the FR pronoun realises r-case can pose problems. German native speakers tend to judge (51b) worse than (51a), although they differ only in the order of FR and matrix clause.

Tableau 8: Preliminary Summary of constraints, competitions and violations

	INT⊙-LF	INT-LF-PF	IDC	IDC^2_{CP}	RC	RCr
m-case < r-case						
⊙R			1		1	
⊙M			2	1	1	1
⊙RES		1	2	1		
CORR	1					
m-case > r-case						
⊙R			1		1	1
⊙M			2	1	1	
⊙RES		1	2	1		
CORR	1					
m-case = r-case						
⊙R/M			1			
⊙RES		1	1			
CORR	1					

Abbreviations: INT-⊙-LF: INTEGRITY-⊙-LF; INT-LF-PF: INTEGRITY-LF-PF; IDC: IDENT(CASE)-LF-PF; IDC^2_{CP}: IDENT(CASE)-LF-PF^2_{CP} ; RC: REALISE CASE; RCr: REALISE CASE (relativised)

(51) a. Ich besuche oft, mit wem ich mich gut verstehe
       I   visit   often with who I   myself well understand

  b. ?? Mit wem ich mich gut verstehe, besuche ich oft
       with who I   myself well understand visit   I   often
     'I visit often who I get on well with'

A plausible explanation for this contrast might lie in the fact that nothing in the FR tells us about its grammatical function in the matrix clause. In (51a) the matrix clause is already parsed when the FR occurs and so the parser 'knows' that there is only the direct object 'slot' to fill and the FR can easily be connected to it. (51b), however, starts with the FR, which has a PP in [Spec,CP] and the parser has to hypothesise its grammatical function within the matrix clause. Most likely, it will assume that it is matching or perhaps the subject of the clause. Direct object is certainly not the default. This reasoning predicts a kind of a garden path effect with clauses like (51b). The constraint that I want to assume reflects this disadvantage of non-matching FRs realising r-case:

(52) Matrix Integration (MI):
      This constraint is violated by constituents that contain no indication
      about how they are integrated into their clause.

One might wonder, whether there is an equivalent kind of restriction on sub-ordinate clauses. This may or may not be, but it cannot have the same 'weight' as MI. Omitted arguments and empty operators are very frequent in, e.g. infinitival subordinate clauses and relative clauses of many languages. Dropping of Matrix arguments is comparatively rare. Topic-drop and pro-drop are frequent phenomena. But these are mostly restricted by discourse requirements: a subject or topic can only be dropped, if it is recoverable from the previous discourse. And, of course, these phenomena are optional.

MI is only violated by candidate R under non-matching. Candidate M is no longer harmonically bounded in the 'm-case < r-case' competition, as can be seen in tableau 9. Candidate RES is still harmonically bounded by candidate R/M in a matching competition. As we have no empirical counter-evidence up to now, this may be a wanted result.

Tableau 9: Summary of constraints, competitions and violations

	INT⊙-LF	INT-LF-PF	IDC	IDC^2_{CP}	RC	RCr	MI
m-case < r-case							
⊙R			1		1		1
⊙M			2	1	1	1	
⊙RES		1	2	1			
CORR	1						
m-case > r-case							
⊙R			1		1	1	1
⊙M			2	1	1		
⊙RES		1	2	1			
CORR	1						
m-case = r-case							
R/M			1				
RES		1	1				
CORR	1						

4 Results: The Factorial Typology

We distinguish three competition types, two competitions for non-matching FRs, each with four candidates, and a competition with matching FRs with three candidates. Each of the candidates, except for ⊙RES in the matching competition, is a possible winner. So the total number of logically possible outcomes is 4 × 4 × 2 = 32. The proposed system of constraints shrinks the number of predicted outcomes down to 10. 22 logically possible languages are predicted never to occur.[36] Tableau 10 gives an overview of the seven existing and predicted language types. All the languages contained in the typology discussed in section 2 are predicted (cf. tableau 1).

Tableau 10: Predicted typology of case conflict resolution in FRs

Conflict	Hindi	Engl.	Icel.	Ger. A	Ger. B	Gothic	M. Greek
m-case < r-case	CORR	CORR	M	R	R	R	RES
m-case > r-case	CORR	CORR	M	R	CORR	M	M
m-case = r-case	CORR	R/M	R/M	R/M	R/M	R/M	R/M

These seven attested outcomes are produced by the following (families of) constraint rankings:

(53)   Hindi: IDC (INT-LF-PF) (IDC^2_{CP}) (RC) (RCr) (MI) >> INT-☉-LF
       English: INT-LF-PF RC (IDC^2_{CP}) (RCr) (MI) >> INT-☉-LF >> IDC
       Icelandic: INT-☉-LF INT-LF-PF MI >> IDC^2_{CP} RC RCr IDC
       German A: INT-☉-LF INT-LF-PF IDC^2_{CP} >> IDC RC RCr MI
       German B: INT-LF-PF IDC^2_{CP} RCr >> INT-☉-LF >> RC IDC MI
       Gothic: INT-☉-LF INT-LF-PF RCr >> IDC^2_{CP} RC IDC MI
       Modern Greek: INT-☉-LF RCr MI >> INT-LF-PF (IDC2CP) (IDC)
          >>RC

Only the crucial rankings are indicated. Constraints that occur in brackets are ranked as high as possible, but could also be ranked lower. Three of the four candidates have a constraint that 'switches it off': MI is only violated by the R candidate, INT-LF-PF is only violated by the RES candidate and only the CORR candidate violates INT-☉-LF.

A language like Hindi that has no FRs, has INT-☉-LF ranked low. Because CORR violates no other constraints, it is sufficient to rank INT-☉-LF below a constraint that is violated by all other candidates, like, e.g. IDC. MI is only relevant for Icelandic. It does not seem to play a role in the other languages (but see the discussion above about possible effects of MI with fronted FRs in German).

English has only matching FRs. This results from the sub-ranking 'RC INT-LF-PF >> INT-☉-LF >> IDC». RC is violated by non-matching FRs, except for candidate RES which violates INT-LF-PF. Ranking either RC or INT-LF-PF or both of them lower than INT-☉-LF allows for non-matching FRs.

<hr>

[36] The factorial typology was calculated with the assistance of the constraint ranking software OTSOFT, developed by Bruce Hayes (1998).

Tableau 11: The FR competitions in German B

	INT-LF-PF	IDC$^2_{CP}$	RCr	INT-⊙-LF	RC	IDC	MI
m-case < r-case							
☞ ⊙R					1	1	1
⊙M		1!					
⊙RES	1!						
CORR				1!			
m-case > r-case							
⊙R			1!				
⊙M		1!					
⊙RES	1!						
☞ CORR				1			
m-case = r-case							
☞ ⊙R/M						1	
⊙RES	1!						
CORR				1!			

The constraint IDC$^2_{CP}$ is only relevant for German B. Tableau 11 displays the paradigm for German B. In order to have FRs at all, IDC has to be ranked below INT-⊙-LF. RC also has to be ranked low to allow non-matching FRs. If IDC$^2_{CP}$ was not there, then candidate M would wrongly win the 'm-case > r-case' competition. German A differs from German B in that RCr is also ranked below INT-⊙-LF. This means that in German A candidate R always wins. As already discussed in section 2.4, this wrongly predicts that a clause with suppressed dative case is well-formed:

(54)   *Ich helfe   wen   ich   mag
        I   help   who-ACC   I   like

The verb *helfen* requires a dative object. An explanation in terms of uninterpretability is possible, as indicated in section 3.2.1: the clause in (54) may win the syntax competition, but 'crash' in the semantics component of the grammar.

The difference between German A and German B can also be explained by attributing it to differences in the case hierarchies of these two variants of German, instead of differences in their constraint rankings. Assume that German A has the ranking of German B. Assume further that nominative and accusative, though morphologically distinct, do not count as distinct for the case hierarchy and the constraint RCr in German A. Nominative and accusative can then 'realise' each other alternatively. In this case, there would be no violation of RCr, even when accusative is suppressed in favour of nominative.

Modern Greek poses a similar problem: It is correctly predicted that in Modern Greek a resumptive dative pronoun occurs, if m-case is nominative or accusative, and r-case is dative. But the same thing should also happen, if m-case is nominative and r-case is accusative. But we have no resumptive pronoun in this case. If nominative and accusative are treated as equivalent by the case hierarchy of Modern Greek, then no violation of RCr would occur, and candidate M would correctly be predicted to win.

Three further languages are predicted to exist that have not yet been attested:

Tableau 12:   Predicted, but not attested patterns of case conflict resolution in FRs

Conflict	Unattested #1	Unattested #2	Unattested #3
m-case < r-case	R	RES	CORR
m-case > r-case	RES	RES	M
m-case = r-case	R/M	R/M	R/M

These three unattested outcomes are produced by the following (families of) constraint rankings:

(55)   Unattested #1: INT-⊙-LF RCr >> IDC$^2_{CP}$ (IDC) >> RC (MI) >> INT-LF-PF

Unattested #2: INT-⊙-LF RC (RCr) (MI) >> INT-LF-PF IDC IDC$^2_{CP}$

Unattested #3: INT-LF-PF RCr MI >> INT-⊙-LF >> RC IDC IDC$^2_{CP}$

None of these grammars is unreasonable. The first language is a mirror image of Modern Greek in that its default strategy is realising r-case on the pronoun. It switches to the resumptive pronoun strategy, when m-case is higher than r-case. A mirror image of German B is the third language. Its default is realising the FR pronoun with m-case. If r-case is the higher case, an FR is impossible. The second language uses resumptives for both non-matching FR types. This is also a reasonable strategy. Future research will show, whether these languages exist, and whether there are other languages that are predicted not to exist in this typology.

The format of the constraints used in this paper is very general. It should be possible to verify the proposed rankings by applying them to further phenomena. The OT syntax system developed here might be an alternative model for capturing the relation between LF and PF. The phenomenon of 'case attraction' found in FRs and other relative constructions of many languages was often considered to be a PF phenomenon precisely because it seemed to violate syntactic constraints (cf. Harbert 1983). An account within the classical principles and parameters framework, let alone minimalism, was never really in sight. OT can allow for LF-PF mismatches and at the same time restrict these mismatches to a minimum. Other properties of PF, like linear ordering or the interaction of syntactic movement and intonation patterns, might also be a topic of further research on LF-PF correspondence that can be done in a very systematic and fruitful way in OT correspondence theory.[37] The way in which we integrated markedness scales of case forms presupposes a 'case module'. Thus, this paper argues for a revival of the idea of modularity. Whether the non-derivational 'inventory perspective' proposed in this paper is the optimal choice for OT-syntax is a matter of future research.

5   Epilogue: On Neutralisation

In section 3.2, I showed two possible ways of accounting for ungrammaticality in OT syntax, uninterpretability and neutralisation. The two strategies are kept separate throughout the paper and I made use of both of them in accounting for the typology of FRs. In this section, I will briefly show how the two strategies can be united in a different account that is based on *neutralisation to an un-interpretable candidate*.[38] Consider the following German clause that is usually judged as ungrammatical:

(56)   *Ich   helfe   mit   wem   ich   gut   arbeiten   kann
        I   help   with   whom   I   well   work   can

The explanation for the oddity of (56) that I gave in this paper was that *helfen* requires a dative object and that the FR stands in place of the dative object. The dative case feature, however, is semantic information that is not recoverable, if it does not surface – so the clause is uninterpretable. A conceptual oddity of this reasoning is that in the present account the dative feature is still present at LF, but not at PF. In order for the argument to hold, the PF must be assumed to be interpreted, and the case information of the PF must somehow 'override' the case information of the LF at the syntax-semantics interface.

If this is so, why should we assume that the clause in (56) contains a dative feature at all? Note the following two facts about *helfen* that can be repeated for many other verbs with oblique complements, at least in German. First, it is not impossible to have *helfen* without a dative object (57a), and second, it is possible to have a *mit*-PP on the side of *helfen* (57b):

(57)   a. Ich   half   bei   der   Ernte
          I   helped   at   the   harvesting

       b. Ich   half   mit   Peter   bei   der   Ernte
          I   helped   with   Peter   at   the   harvesting

<hr>

[37] Büring (2001) developed an account of word order in German with an OT-syntax model that integrates syntax and prosodic structure.

[38] Neutralisation to a candidate with a slightly different meaning is the strategy that is also chosen by Legendre et al. (1998).

We are neither forced to assume that *helfen* obligatorily needs a dative object to yield a well-formed clause, nor that it must not be accompanied by a *mit*-PP. We know that matching FRs are well-formed in German. So the clause in (56) should be well-formed syntactically with a matching FR. In fact, it might be possible to get such a reading in a suitable context:

(58)   ?Ich helfe bei der Ernte   nur, mit wem ich gut arbeiten kann
        I   help at the harvesting only with whom I   well work   can
        'I only help at the harvesting together with someone who I can work well with'

This reading might be hard to get, also for pragmatic reasons. But it is possible in principle, and this is what counts here: the oddity of (58) depends on whether we get a reading for the clause. With respect to syntax it is well-formed. If (58), and likewise (56), 'crashes', then it crashes in the semantic component of the grammar.[39]

We can use this insight to change the way we accounted for ungrammaticality in this paper. Instead of assuming that in the case of ungrammatical FRs the competition is neutralised to a formally unfaithful non-FR candidate, we can assume that it is neutralised to a FR with a different intended interpretation. We can then eliminate the CORR candidate from our candidate sets and keep *Gen* more restrictive than we did before: the candidate set only contains candidates with the syntactic structure of FRs.

For instances of ill-formed non-matching FRs, the neutralisation candidate that replaces the CORR candidate is a *matching* FR. Let us discuss the example that makes a difference between German A and German B:

(59)   German B:
        *Ich   lade ein wer   mir   begegnet
         I-NOM   invite   who-NOM   me-DAT   meets
         'In invite whoever meets me'

The FR has the abstract case feature ACC here. It serves as direct object of the matrix verb:

(60)   I-NOM invite [CP who-NOM me-DAT meets]-ACC

In the original analysis with the constraints ranked as in (61), the candidate with the form in (60) loses against the neutralisation candidate, because it violates RCr, which is ranked higher than the highest ranked constraint violated by the CORR candidate, which is INT-⊙-LF.

---

[39] This presupposes that subcategorization information provided by the verb can be erased. See Vogel (2000) for further arguments for why lexeme specific subcategorization should be dispensed with as much as possible on independent grounds.

(61)   German B: INT-LF-PF RCr >> INT-⊙-LF >> RC IDC MI

Assume that instead of CORR we have a FR with different abstract case
features, i.e. *Gen* may not allow for variation in the functional heads or feature
distribution, but it may allow for variation in the values of features. The candidate I have in mind is a matching candidate with exactly the same 'surface
structure' as in (60), but with the abstract case feature nominative on the FR, as
in (62):

(62)   I-NOM invite [CP who-NOM me-DAT meets]-NOM

This candidate does not violate RCr or RC, because it is matching, so there is
no problem with case realisation at all (remember that the constraints on case
realisation are constraints on output candidates without any reference to the
⊙-LF). This clause is odd, because the FR cannot be interpreted now. It cannot
be the subject of the clause, because 'I' is the subject, and it cannot receive
nominative by means of, e.g. a comparative structure, as in (63), because there
is no comparative or other structure that would 'license' a second nominative
case marked constituent besides the subject.

(63)   Die Maria   ist   größer   als   der   Peter
        the Maria-NOM   is   taller   than   the   Peter-NOM

So there is no way to make sense out of (62), it 'crashes' in the semantics. It
probably does not crash at the syntax-semantics interface. The oddity of (62) is
purely semantics-internal. But (62) nevertheless wins the OT syntax competition.
    All we have to do is replace the now useless constraint INT-⊙-LF with
another ⊙-LF faithfulness constraint that is sensitive for the change from (60)
to (62). It is quite obvious that it is IDENT(CASE)-⊙-LF, because it is a case
feature that changes:[40]

(64)   IDENT(CASE)-⊙-LF
        Correspondent ⊙-LF and output LF chains have identical values for the
        feature case.
        If x$\Re$y and x is [γCASE], then y is [γCASE].

---

[40] Note that we now have to assume that the ⊙-representation that a clause is faithful to is
an element of U_s with a specific language particular lexical index, because case has to be
considered as partly language particular, at least with respect to some of the oblique cases and PPs
that also have to be taken into account here. The use of the notion 'index' is now the same as in
(Legendre et al. 1998), where 'index', more or less a 'criterion' defining the (finite) candidate
set, replaces 'input'. If the structural accusative case feature is assumed to be assigned in a specific syntactic position, then the candidate in (62) also departs from the faithful candidates in that
the FR may no longer occupy or be otherwise connected to this position. It has to be represented as
an adjunct syntactically.

The constraint takes the position of INT-⊙-LF in the rankings:

(65)   German B: INT-LF-PF IDC-LF-PF$^2_{CP}$ RCr >> IDC-⊙-LF >> RC IDC-LF-PF MI

This accounts for languages that have some well-formed and some ill-formed FRs. But how can we treat languages without any FRs like Hindi and Tok Pisin? The answer is again 'neutralisation to a candidate with a different meaning'. But now we do not change a feature, as we did above with abstract case, but rather *delete* a feature. The FR may be turned into a subordinate interrogative clause (deletion of the m-case feature and/or the REL feature of the FR) or an ordinary restrictive relative clause (deletion of the 'referentiality feature' of the FR). In either case the result should be uninterpretable. Either a verb selecting for a [–*wh*] complement is accompanied by a [+*wh*] complement clause, or there occurs a restrictive relative clause without a head noun. These candidates again imply no violations of the kind induced by FRs and may win the FR competition if IDC-⊙-LF or another suitable faithfulness constraint is ranked very low.

If the approach sketched in this section is reasonable, then we have two alternative theories. How can we decide between the neutralisation strategy developed in section 3.2.2 and the one developed in this section? There may be no need for such a decision. The two strategies are complementary and answer different questions. When we ask: "How does a language express what is meant by a given FR input?", we optimise the form and may get a correlative construction as output. And when we ask: "How is the structure of a (particular) FR interpreted in a given language?", we might sometimes get no ('crash' in the semantics) or a non-FR interpretation. The two strategies can also be considered as two sides of the same coin, combined in a more complex perspective on OT-syntax known as *bidirectional optimisation*.[41] Whether this is the best path to follow in OT-syntax, or not, is an open issue. As it stands, the optimal architecture of the OT-syntax model is still to be found.

[41] For a serial conception of bidirectional optimisation see Wilson (to appear); for a parallel conception see Blutner (2000). Smolensky & Wilson (2000) sketch a model of 'dual optimisation' that assumes that the selection of the candidate set is itself an OT competition – in some respect an extension of Wilson (to appear).

References

Åfarli, Tor A. (1994): A promotion analysis of restrictive relative clauses. *The Linguistic Review* 11. 81–100.

Aissen, J. (to appear): *Markedness and Subject Choice in Optimality Theory.* In: Grimshaw, J. et al., eds. (2001): *Optimality Theoretic Syntax.* Cambridge, MA: MIT Press. 61–69.

Alexiadou, A. & Varlokosta, S. (1995): The Syntactic and Semantic properties of Free Relatives in Modern Greek. *ZAS Working Papers in Linguistics* 5. 1–30.

Archangeli, D. & Langendoen, D. T., eds. (1997): *Optimality Theory. An Overview.* Malden, MA/Oxford: Blackwell.

Barbosa, P., Fox, D., Hagstrom, P., McGinnis, M. & Pesetsky, D., eds. (1998): *Is the best good enough? Optimality and competition in syntax.* Cambridge, MA: MIT Press.

Bayer, J., Bader, M. & Meng, M. (2001): Morphological Underspecification Meets Oblique Case: Syntactic and Processing Effects in German. *Lingua* 111. 465–514.

Blutner, R. (2000): *Some Aspects of Optimality in Natural Language Interpretation.* Ms, Rutgers Optimality Archive. (ROA-389-0400; http://roa.rutgers.edu).

Bresnan, J. (2001): *Optimal Syntax.* In: Dekkers et al., eds. (2000). 334–385.

Bresnan, J. & Grimshaw, J. (1978): The Syntax of Free Relatives in English. *Linguistic Inquiry* 9. 331–391.

Büring, D. (2001): Lets's Phrase it. Focus, Word Order, and Prosodic Phrasing in German Double Object Construction. In: Müller, G. & Sternefeld, W. (2001): *Competition in Syntax.* Berlin: Mouton de Gruyter. 69–106.

Chomsky, N. (1986): *Barriers.* Cambridge, MA: MIT Press.

Chomsky, N. (1995): *The Minimalist Program.* Cambridge, MA: MIT Press.

Dayal, V. (1996): *Locality in WH Quantification.* Dordrecht: Kluwer.

Dekkers, J., Leeuw, F. van der & Weijer, J. van de, eds. (2000): *Optimality Theory: Phonology, Syntax and Acquisition.* Oxford: Oxford University Press.

Fischer, S. (2001): On the Integration of Cumulative Effects into Optimality Theory. In: Müller, G. & Sternefeld, W. (2001): *Competition in Syntax.* Berlin: Mouton de Gruyter. 151–173.

Grimshaw, J. (1997a): The Best Clitic: Constraint Conflict in Morphosyntax. In: Haegemann, L., ed. (1997): *Elements of Grammar: A Handbook in Contemporary Syntactic Theory.* Dordrecht: Kluwer. 169–196.

Grimshaw, J. (1997b): Projection, Heads and Optimality. *Linguistic Inquiry* 28. 373–422.

Grimshaw, J., Legendre, G. & Vikner, S., eds. (2001): *Optimality Theoretic Syntax.* Cambridge, MA: MIT Press.

Groos, A. & Riemsdijk, H. van (1981): Matching Effects with Free Relatives: A Parameter of Core Grammar. In: Belletti, A., Brandi, L. & Rizzi, L., eds. (1981): *Theories of Markedness in Generative Grammar.* Pisa: Scuola Normale Superiore di Pisa. 171–216.

Grosu, A. (1994): *Three Studies in Locality and Case.* London/New York: Routledge.

Haider, H. (1988): Matching Projections. In: Cardinaletti, A., Cinque, G. & Giusti, G., eds. (1988): *Constituent Structure.* Dordrecht: Foris. 101–123.

Harbert, W. (1983): On the Nature of the Matching Parameter. *The Linguistic Review* 2. 237–284.

Hayes, Bruce, Tesar, Bruce, & Zuraw, Kie (2000): *OTSOFT, software package.* http://www.linguistics.ucla.edu/people/hayes/otsoft/.

Heck, F. (1998): *Relativer Quantorenskopus im Deutschen – Optimalitätstheorie und die Syntax der Logischen Form.* MA thesis, University of Tübingen.

Heck, F. (2001): Quantifier scope in German and cyclic optimisation. In: Müller, G. & Sternefeld, W., eds. (2001): *Competition in Syntax.* Berlin: Mouton de Gruyter. 175–210.

Heck, F. & Müller, G. (2000): Successive Cyclicity, Long-Distance Superiority, and Local Optimization. *Proceedings of WCCFL* 19. 218-231.

Heck, F., Fischer, S., Müller, G., Schmid, T., Vikner, S. & Vogel, R. (2000): *On the Nature of the Input in Optimality Theory.* Ms, Stuttgart University.

Herslund, Michael (1984): Particles, Prefixes, and Preposition Stranding. *Topics in Danish Syntax* 14. 34–71.

Hirschbühler, P. & Rivero, M.-L. (1983): Remarks on Free Relatives and Matching Phenomena. *Linguistic Inquiry* 14. 505–520.

Holmberg, A. & Platzack, C. (1995): *The Role of Inflection in Scandinavian Syntax.* Oxford: Oxford University Press.

Izvorski, R. (1996): (Non-)Matching Effects in Free Relatives and pro-drop. *Proceedings of ESCOL* 12. 89–102.

Jacobson, P. (1995): On the Quantificational Force of English Free Relatives. In: Bach, E., Jelinek, E., Kratzer, A. & Partee, B., eds. (1995): *Quantification in Natural Language.* Dordrecht: Kluwer Publishers. 451–486.

Keer, E. & Baković, E. (to appear): *Optionality and Ineffability.* In: Grimshaw et al., eds. (2001): *Optimality Theoretic Syntax.* Cambridge, MA: MIT Press. 97–112.

Kuroda, S.-Y. (1968): English Relativization and Certain Related Problems. *Language* 44. 244–266.

Legendre, G., Smolensky, P. & Wilson, C. (1998): *When is less more? Faithfulness and Minimal Links in WH-Chains.* In: Barbosa et al. (1998): *Is the best good enough? Optimality and competition in syntax.* Cambridge, MA: MIT Press. 249–289.

Leirbukt, O. (1995): Über Setzung und Nichtsetzung des Korrelats bei Relativsätzen mit *wer* im heutigen Deutsch. In: Popp, H., ed. (1995): *Deutsch als Fremdsprache. An den Quellen eines Faches.* München: Iudicium. 151–163.

McCarthy, J. (1998): Sympathy and Phonological Opacity. *Rutgers Optimality Archive.* (ROA-252-0398; http://roa.rutgers.edu).

McCarthy, J. & Prince, A. (1995): Faithfulness and Reduplicative Identity. In: Beckman, J., Walsh-Dickie, L. & Urbanczyk, S., eds. (1995): *Papers in Optimality Theory.* University of Massachusetts Occasional Papers in Linguistics 18. Amherst, MA. 249–384.

Müller, G. (1999): Optionality in Optimality-Theoretic syntax. *GLOT International* 4:5. 3–8.

Müller, G. (2000): Das Pronominaladverb als Reparaturphänome. *Linguistische Berichte* 182. 139–178.

Müller, G. & Sternefeld, W., eds. (2001): *Competition in Syntax.* Berlin: Mouton de Gruyter.

Pesetsky, D. (1997): Optimality Theory and Syntax: Movement and Pronunciation. In: Archangeli, D. & Langendoen, D. T. (1997): *Optimality Theory. An Overview.* Malden, MA/Oxford: Blackwell. 134-170.

Pesetsky, D. (1998): *Some Optimality Principles of Sentence Pronunciation.* In: Barbosa et al., eds. (1998): *Is the best good enough? Optimality and competition in syntax.* Cambridge, MA: MIT Press. 337–384.

Pittner, K. (1991): Freie Relativsätze und die Kasushierarchie. In: Feldbusch, E., ed. (1991): *Neue Fragen der Linguistik.* Tübingen: Niemeyer. 341–347.

Pittner, K. (1995): Regeln für die Bildung von freien Relativsätzen. Eine Antwort an Oddleif Leirbukt. *Deutsch als Fremdsprache* 32:4. 195–200.

Pittner, K. (1996): Attraktion, Tilgung und Verbposition: Zur diachronen und dialektalen Variation beim Relativpronomen im Deutschen. In: Brandner, E. & Ferraresi, G., eds. (1996): *Language Change and Generative Grammar.* Opladen: Westdeutscher Verlag. 120–153.

Prince, A. & Smolensky, P. (1993): *Optimality Theory. Constraint Interaction in Generative Grammar.* Ms, Rutgers University & University of Colorado, Boulder.

Riemsdijk, H. van (1998): *Treesand Scions – Science and Trees*. (http://mitpress.mit.edu/chomsky-disc/riemsdyk.html).

Rooryck, J. (1994): Generalized Transformations and the WH-Cycle: Free Relatives and bare Wh-CPs. *GAGL* 37. 195–208.

Smits, R. J. C. (1989): *Eurogrammar. The Relative and Cleft Constructions of the Germanic and Romance Languages*. Dordrecht: Foris.

Smolensky, P. & Wilson, C. (2000): *The Architecture of the Grammar: Optimization in phonology, syntax and interpretation*. Handout of a talk presented at the Utrecht conference on the optimization of interpretation in Utrecht, January, 2000. 4–5.

Suñer, M. (1984): Free Relatives and the Matching Parameter. *The Linguistic Review* 3. 363–387.

Vogel, R. (2000): *Polyvalent Verbs*. PhD dissertation, Humboldt-Universität, Berlin. (http://dochost. rz.hu-berlin.de/dissertationen/vogel-ralf-1998-07-13/PDF/Vogel.pdf)

Vogel, R. (2001a): *Case Conflict in German Free Relative Constructions. An Optimality Theoretic Treatment*. In: Müller, G. & Sternefeld, W. (2001): *Competition in Syntax*. Berlin: Mouton de Gruyter. 341–375.

Vogel, R. (2001b): Towards an Optimal Typology of Free Relative Constructions. In: Grosu, Alex, ed. (2001): *IATL8*. Papers from the 16th Annual Conference and from the Research Workshop of the Israel Science Foundation 'The Syntax and Semantics of Relative Clause Constructions', Tel Aviv University 2000, Israel Association For Theoretical Linguistics. 107–119.

Vogel, R. (to appear): Surface Matters. Case Conflict in Free Relative Constructions and Case Theory. In: Brandner, E. & Zinsmeister, H., eds. (to appear): *New Perspectives on Case Theory*. CSLI Publications.

Vogel, R. & Steinbach, M. (1998): The Dative – an Oblique Case. *Linguistische Berichte* 173. 65–90.

Wilson, C. (2001): *BidirectionalOpimization and the Theory of Anaphora*. In: Grimshaw, J. et al., eds. (2001): *Optimality Theoretic Syntax*. Cambridge, MA: MIT Press.

Wiltschko, M. (1999): Free Relatives as Indefinites. In: Shahin, K., Blake, S. &. Kim, E.-S., eds. (1999): *The Proceedings of the Seventeenth West Coast Conference on Formal Linguistics*. CSLI. 700–712.

Woolford, E. B. (1978): Free Relatives and Other Base Generated WH Constructions. *Papers from the Fourteenth Regional Meeting of the Chicago Linguistic Society*, University of Chicago. 482–490.

Woolford, E. B. (1979): Aspects of Tok Pisin Grammar. *Pacific Linguistics, Series B* 66. Department of Linguistics, Research School of Pacific Studies, The Australian National University, Canberra.

Woolford, E. (2001): Case Patterns. In: Legendre, Geraldine, Grimshaw, Jane & Vikner, Sten, eds. (2001): *Optimality-Theoretic Syntax*. Cambridge, MA: MIT Press. 509–544.

Wunderlich, D. (2000): *The Force of lexical case: German and Icelandic compared*. Ms, University of Düsseldorf.

Stuttgart/Potsdam   Ralf Vogel

Universität Potsdam, Institut für Linguistik, Postfach 601533, 14415 Potsdam,
e-mail: rvogel@ling.uni-potsdam.de

Segmental Contrast meets Output-to-Output Faithfulness*

Luigi Burzio

Abstract

Work on segmental contrast and work on allomorphic variation within OT has been converging on the conclusion that outputs are not calculated only from unique 'inputs', but are rather also influenced by other outputs, in a way that seeks to eliminate weak contrasts. I propose a unified approach to this effect and note that it thus unifies solutions to a significant number of empirical problems for OT, that go from 'cyclicity, to 'Non-Derived-Environment Blocking' effects to 'opacity', revealing that this is a crucial development.

1   Introduction

Two major lines of work have been converging on the single conclusion in (1).

(1)   Output representations are not calculable from individual inputs alone, as in (a). Rather, they require simultaneous reference to some 'other' representation(s), as in (b).

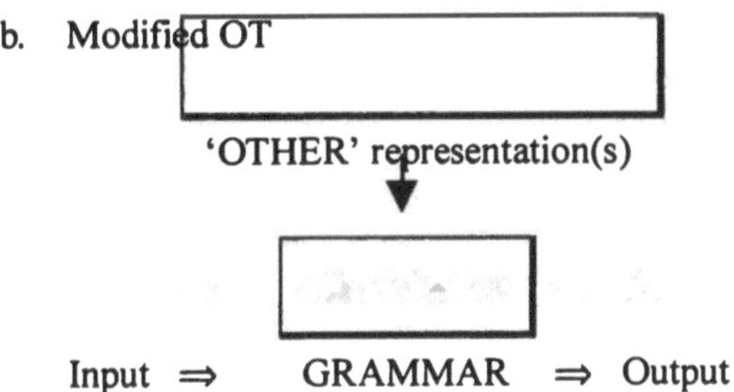

* The present article has also appeared, with minor differences, in *The Linguistic Review* 17, 2–4 (2000), 368–384. Thanks to Laura Benua, Matt Goldrick, Fero Kuminiak, Paul Smolensky, and Colin Wilson for valuable comments and various help.

The first line of work concerns allomorphic variation, and advances the general claim in (2).

(2)   The surface form of a morpheme is conditioned by that of other allomorphs. E.g.: *américanist* (exceptional stress, by influence from *américan*); *leviable* (failed '*CiV*'-lengthening, cf. *alle:viate*, by influence from *levy*.). See Benua (1997); Burzio (1994a, 1996, 2000, in press); Kager (1999b); Kenstowicz (1996, 1997); Steriade (2000); and others.

The references in (2) implement the architecture in (1b) by means of constraints that compare different surface forms --Output-to-Output Faithfulness constraints, in Benua's terminology.

The second line of work to introduce the structure in (1b) concerns segmental inventories and patterns of segmental neutralization, and is aimed at capturing the two related claims in (3a, b) respectively.

(3)   a.   Segmental inventories tend to maximize perceptual distance between members. See Flemming (1995).

        b.   Neutralizations of (laryngeal, place or other) segmental contrasts occur in positions in which perceptual cues to the contrast are weak. See Steriade (1994, 1997).

The claims in both (3a, b) entail the architecture in (1b) by appealing to the notion of contrast, which entails comparison between representations that are not related to the same input.

I have argued in Burzio (in press) for a unification of the two strands in (2) and (3) under a single assumption about the nature of mental representations that makes sense of the modified architecture in (1b). Thanks to significant contributions by Wilson (2000), the resulting unification successfully addresses a number of important empirical problems, ranging at least over the following:

(4)   a.   Problems standardly addressed by OO-FAITH constraints: cyclicity and other effects (references in (2), and general review in Kager 1999a, chapter 6)

        b.   Characterization of the class of OO-FAITH relations and solution to OO-FAITH ranking paradoxes (Burzio, in press).

        c.   Certain cases of 'Non-Derived-Environment Blocking' (Łubowicz 1998, Burzio, in press).

        d.   Positional repairs intractable within original OT (Wilson 2000).

        e.   Opacity (counterfeeding/ counterbleeding) effects (Wilson 2000).

While approaches to individual items in (4) exist outside of the modified architecture in (1b), it seems rather unlikely, at the moment, that any will generalize to the whole set, strongly suggesting that the structure in (1b) (anticipated in some of its elements in Burzio 1994a and earlier[1]) is the correct one.

In section 2 following, I will present the basic idea under which the two strands of (2) and (3) can be unified. In section 3, I will review the form of the solutions to each of (4a–e), and in section 4 conclude.

2   Gradient Attraction

The idea that unifies the two strands in (2) and (3) is that similar representations 'attract' one another, and that they do so 'gradiently': the more similar they are, the greater the attraction. Thus, allomorphs of the same morpheme influence one another as in (2), because being 'allomorphs' defines (in theory-specific terms) some high degree of independent similarity (in sound and meaning). Members of segmental inventories keep at a maximal distance from one another, as in (3a) (resulting in the tendency towards equidistance among members), because maximal distance corresponds to minimal attraction, which would otherwise compel members to merge. Neutralization of certain contrasts occurs under weakness of perceptual cues as in (3b), because weakening the 'cues' that crucially distinguish two representations is tantamount to enhancing their similarity, and hence the attraction, whence the neutralizations. Gradient attraction (GA) can be illustrated with a gravity-based analog, by taking each mental representation --a point in multidimensional space, to be the center of a hole whose walls get steeper and steeper in approaching that center, as in (5).

(5)   Gradient Attraction Effect

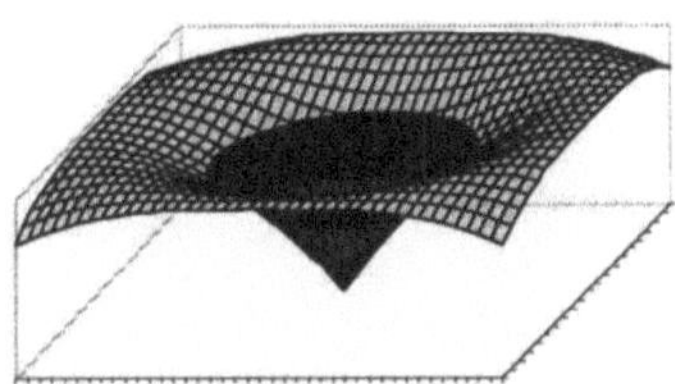

Representations that are proximate to the one in the center can be thought of as masses on the slopes, being pushed into the center by gravity. The closer they are to the center, the steeper the slope and thus the stronger the push. GA is of course not the only component of the grammar --it is simply *the* missing component in the original OT model (1a). The other components are the two

<hr>

[1] See Burzio (1991), DiFabio (1990), and other work related to Burzio (1994a), which utilizes the notion of 'Output-to-Output faithfulness' under the name of 'Consistency'.

original ones: Markedness and Input-to-Output Faithfulness (IO-FAITH). GA can be thought of alternatively either as a second form of markedness or as a second form of faithfulness. The reason is that it expresses on the one hand the notion that there is instability or 'markedness' in being similar but not identical, while on the other hand it also expresses the notion that similarity will compel further similarity, alias faithfulness --indeed the OO-FAITH of recent literature. The other two components: IO-FAITH and standard Markedness will have the ability to oppose GA; hence, accounting for the fact that highly similar representations often do exist, despite the pressure for them to neutralize. There is, however, a fundamental difference between GA and the other two components, related to GA's reliance on the 'other representation(s)' of (1b). Whereas the original two components can be thought of as governing the entire representational space, GA is a 'local' force, effectively giving rise to local 'mini-grammars' around specific points (the 'other' representations). We will see that this 'take over' or 'deflection' effect is what gives rise to opacity, once thought to be due to rule ordering.[2]

The question, of course, is what could be the basis for the GA effect, and an answer comes from the simple assumption in (6), which can in turn be related to principles of neural behavior.

(6)   *Representational Entailments* (RE): Mental representations constitute sets of entailments --a representation AB generating the entailments $A \Rightarrow B$, $B \Rightarrow A$.

The assumption in (6) is a virtual restatement of Hebb's (1949: 62) rule of mental learning, according to which neurons that co-fire develop a synaptic connection that renders their co-firing necessary. How RE (6) yields GA (5) can be seen with the simple example in (7), where a four-component representation ABCD is compared with another four-component representation.

<hr>

[2] A third domain, beside the ones described in (2) and (3) above, in which GA may prove fruitful is that of segmental assimilations, including vowel harmony. Assimilatory pressure can be reduced to GA by taking articulatory adjacency to be a form of similarity (similarity in time). Assimilations will then be expected to be more likely between segments that are relatively more similar to one-another. A number of cases bear this out, including the phenomenon of 'parasitic' vowel harmony (e.g. Yawelmani, where harmony occurs only between vowels of equal height). On the articulatory adjacency of harmonizing vowels, see Gafos (1996). For a discussion of assimilation from this general perspective, see Wilson (2000).

(7)   *Dis-harmony* ⇑

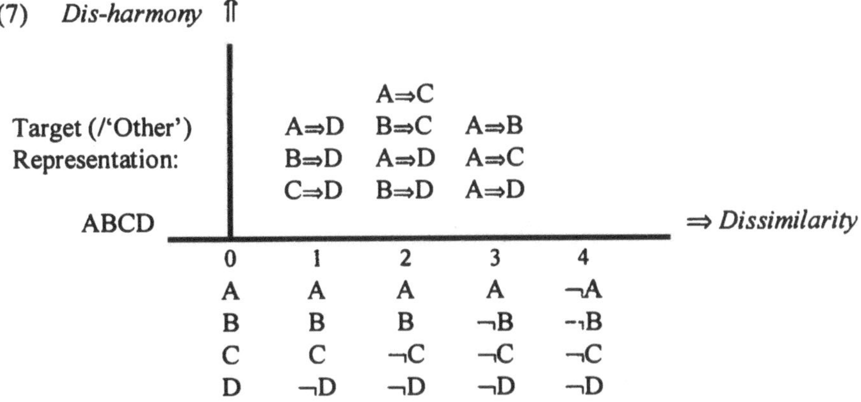

The diagram in (7) plots disharmony for a four-component representation given its similarity to a target representation ABCD. The horizontal axis gives dissimilarity in one-component steps, while the vertical axis gives disharmony in terms of number of entailments violated. Violated entailments are listed in vertical columns, so that disharmony is effectively the height of the column. Full identity (ABCD) gives no violation, but a one-component dissimilarity (ABC¬D) violates three of the entailments generated by the target, namely A⇒D, B⇒D, C⇒D. A two-component difference (AB¬C¬D) yields a four-entailment violation: A⇒C, B⇒C, A⇒D, B⇒D. In general, violated entailments are given by pairing all components that are still identical --the entailers, with all the components that are no longer identical --the entailed. As (7) show, the function from dissimilarity to dis-harmony is a curve that passes through zero both at total identity and at total misidentity, and peaks at 50% identity.[3] The first half of the upside-down 'U' curve detectable in (7) is in fact the slope defining the hole in (5). 'Attraction' is given by the first derivative (i.e. the 'steepness') of the curve in (7) or slope in (5). That derivative is a linearly decreasing function. That is, as can be seen in (7), the increments in disharmony are linearly decreasing, going from 3 to 1, to -1, to -3. Hence attraction is 'gradient' in the sense that it decreases linearly with distance. So, at point 1 in (7), attraction is 3 --the 'incentive' in terms of the entailments that would be satisfied, for the representation at point 1 to move to the next point in space, namely point 0. In contrast, at point 2, attraction is weaker, the 'incentive' to move to the next point, namely point 1, being only one entailment. Note that (7) compounds disharmony over all four dimensions A, B, C, D, the contributions of individual dimension to disharmony for the pattern of change in (7) being as in (8), where totals thus equal the 0, 3, 4, 3, 0 pattern of (7).

---

[3] The mathematical function for the curve in (7) is $y = x(N\text{-}x)$, where y is disharmony, x is dissimilarity in number of components, and N is the total number of components.

(8)

A	0	0	0	0	0
B	0	0	0	1	0
C	0	0	2	1	0
D	0	3	2	1	0
Totals	0	3	4	3	0

In many cases, it is sufficient to consider the effetcs of GA on a single dimension, as in the following illustration, where '*CiV*-LENGTH' refers to the constraint(s) responsible for the regular lengthening of vowels in the context '__Consonant-*i*-Vowel', as in *cana:d-ian*, etc.

(9)   a.

base: *lévy*	OO-F	*CiV*-LENGTH
☞ lévi-able	✓	*

      b.

base: *rémedy*	*CiV*-LENGTH	OO-F
☞ remé:diable	✓	*

Non occurrence of *CiV*-lengthening in *leviable* (9a) is attributable to OO-FAITH to the base *levy*, but regular occurrence in *reme:diable* (9b) will then require the opposite ranking than in (9a) -an apparent paradox. GA resolves this paradox by relying on the independent difference/ unfaithfulness that exists in (9b) but not in (9a): stress. We can relate the two different situations to the charts in (7) and (8) by taking the representations of bases and stems in (9) to have four components in them, representing, respectively: (A) segmental structure; (B) semantics; (C) stress pattern; and (D) the length of the stressed vowel, as in (10).

(10)   a.

	lévi	lévi-(able)
segments	A	A
semantics	B	B
stress	C	C
V-length	D	D

b.

	rémedy	remé:di-(able)
segments	A	A
semantics	B	B
stress	C	¬C
V-length	D	¬D

Such a breakdown of complex representations is of course arbitrary, but will serve to illustrate the point. The crucial difference between the two cases is that the base *rémedy* has antepenultimate stress, which results in considerable pressure for re-stressing when further syllables are added as in *remé:di-able* (Burzio 1994a). This gives rise to ¬C in (10b) despite several violated entailments. Given ¬C, however, the pressure against lengthening (¬D) is – in this simplified discussion – only two entailments, namely A⇒D, B⇒D. In contrast, the pressure against lenghtening in *lévi-able* (10a) is at three entailments, due to the fact that there is no restressing, resulting in C rather than ¬C. In turn, this stress invariance is evidently due to the fact that, in *lévi,* stress is only *pen*ultimate, so that it need not shift in *lévi-able*. The paradox is thus resolved, the reason why OO-FAITH of (9a) is higher-ranked being that it compounds three entailments, while the one of (9b) compounds only two.

The introduction of RE (6) has two major implications for OT. One is the rejection of strict ranking of constraints. While each of the entailments generated under (6) can be understood as a constraint in the system, the GA effect requires summation of the violations, as in the numerically based 'Harmony Theory' (Smolensky 1986). Note that strict ranking is made independently problematic by the proliferation of 'constraint conjunctions' that the OT literature has witnessed, and the variety of conditions under which these seem required (see Kager 1999a, 9.2.6 for a review). Rather than postulating strict ranking of constraints, only to postulate in addition that it can be violated via constraint conjunctions, it seems no less reasonable to take the system to be inherently summatory (as in Burzio 1994a, esp. section 8.2.3), leaving any residual 'strict ranking' tendency or effect to be explained or derived in some fashion (see Burzio, in press). Once the GA effect is thus characterized in terms of contributed (dis-/) harmony, it actually becomes immaterial whether it is classified as a form of markedness or a form of faithfulness.

The second implication of RE is a blurring of the distinction between constraints and representations, with representations now constraining other representations by virtue of the entailments they generate. This allows for the existence of regularities that are 'self generated', and have no basis in independent or universal constraints. 'Morphological' regularities, e.g. the fact that there are 'morphemes' with specific distributions in the lexicon, are from the present perspective regularities of this type (Burzio, in press). The distinction between phonological and morphological regularity is correspondingly blurred. Consider in this regard the unclear status of a process like 'velar softening' in English: *electri[k]/ electri[s]-ity*. Is this regularity dictated by the phonology or is it rather, at least syncronically, just a property of a few affixes? From the present point of view it can easily be both, and in fact cannot fail to be, at least in part, a property of the affix (see Carstairs-McCarthy (1999) for similar conclusions on German umlauting plurals and much discussion of this general issue).

3   The Range of Empirical Problems

In this section I turn to the problems listed in (4), beginning with the motivation for OO-FAITH constraints in accounts of allomorphy (partially reviewed in Kager 1999a, chapter 6).

3.1   OO-Faithfulness versus Cyclicity

The most direct motivation for postulating faithfulness between surface forms is that morphologically related words often share properties which are due to the phonology, in addition to those that can be attributed to a common underlying representation, as in (11).

(11)   a.   phenÓmenon   b.   amÉrican
              phenÒmenó-logy   amÉrican-ìst

Stress in the base forms in (11) is predictable, and thus cannot be underlying. Underlying representation (UR), while sufficient to capture the segmental parallelism within each pair in (11), is thus insufficient to capture the accentual parallelism. The traditional means to deal with such patterns --the cycle, proves ineffective for several reasons. At least for rule-based versions of the cycle, there is an immediate 'duplication problem' (the tell-tale sign that the architecture is parallel rather than serial). Preservation of stresses from 'earlier cycles' mimics closely the conditions under which stresses are assigned in the first place. Specifically, stress is never preserved when it leads to ill-formed feet: *ca(tàs)tróphic*,   or   *(cómpensa)tòry* (Burzio 1994a). Hence, the characterization of possible feet will have to be stated twice: once in the definition of the 'cycle' and once in the formulation of the stress-assignment rule(s). In contrast, in the present -parallel- approach, the range of well-formed feet will be defined only once, as surface constraints (Burzio 1994a). OO-FAITH is evidently dominated by the latter constraints, hence having an effect in (11) but not in *càtastróphic*, etc.

A second problem, not only for rule-based, but also for OT-based versions of the cycle, involving successive layers of optimization (Kiparsky 1998), is that not only stems, but all morphemes tend to prosodic invariance. So, to account for *títanic, which would preserve the stress of titan, one needs to appeal to the metrical invariance of the suffix -ic, which parses in a way that gives stress on the immediately preceding syllable, an effect which evidently prevails over the metrical invariance of the stem (Burzio 1994a, b). So, the -ic of titán-ic is in effect being faithful to that of dynám-ic, barbár-ic, etc. yet surely there is no 'cyclic' relation among these items, only one of surface-to-surface similarity. The Italian cases in (12) make a similar point.

(12)   a.   i.   vádo (*ándo)   'I go'
            ii. andiámo (*vad-iámo)   'we go'

       b.   i.   fin-ísc-o (*fín-o)   'I finish'
            ii. fin-iámo (*fín-isc-iámo)   'we finish'

       c.   i.   vínc-ere   'to win'
            ii. vín-to (*vínc-ito)   'won' (PART)

       d.   i.   fin-íre   'to finish'
            ii. fin-íto (*fín-to)   'finished' (PART)

The alternation in (a) is driven by metrical consistency: the morpheme vád-, in (i) and in various other forms, occurs only if stressed, while its suppletive alternant and- occurs only as unstressed. Similarly, in (b) -isc- occurs only if stressed, and is suppressed otherwise. Still similarly, in (c, d) participial ending -íto occurs only if stressed, its unstressed counterpart being rather the syncopated -to. The difference between (c) and (d) is that in (c), but not in (d), the syncopated participial affix is needed to satisfy the metrical consistency of its stem with the infinitive (stem-stressed in (c) but not in (d)). As argued in Burzio (1998), DiFabio (1990), these patterns of 'metrically conditioned' suppletion reveal a competition between segmental and metrical types of consistency/ OO-FAITH, with the latter winning out: by invoking a different segmental structure when the metrical conditions (stress) change, the association between a given segmental structure and stress is kept invariant, while some other association, say that between meaning and the segmental structure is forced to change ('go'= vad-/ and-). It is easy to see that these facts are not reducible to the 'cycle'.

A third fatal problem for the cycle or any sequential organization is that OO-FAITH can obtain from multiple bases simultaneously, as in the cases in (13).

(13)   a.   vinc-it-ore   'winner'
              base 1: vin-to   'won'
              base 2: vinc-ere   'to win'

       b.   [groz] arbre   'big tree'
              base 1: [gro]   'big-MASC'
              base 2: [grɔs]   'big-FEM'

In the Italian case in (a), the derivative in the top row inherits segmentism from both participle and infinitive (Burzio 1998). Similarly, in the French case in (b), the masculine 'liaison' form *groz* has much segmentism from the masculine citation form including vowel quality, while its final consonant, aside from voicing, is due to the feminine form (Steriade 1999). In the present approach, both 'bases' in (13) generate entailments affecting the form in the top row and are thus potentially relevant. In contrast, any serial organization would have to choose between bases, either way incorrectly.

In sum, OO-FAITH seems indispensable in accounting for allomorphy given several cases in which serial means relying on URs are sharply ineffective.

3.2   Bases of OO-Faith and Ranking Paradoxes

The introduction of OO-FAITH constraints raises problems of its own, however, two in particular, which the present framework can tackle as well.

One general problem is that of determining which representations trigger OO-FAITH / exert attraction in the calculation of any individual item. The influential proposal of Benua (1997) claims that the trigger of OO-FAITH is the 'base' in the traditional morphological sense. While that hypothesis seems relatively simple and workable at first, several considerations militate against it. One is the fact noted in (13) that OO-FAITH effects can arise from multiple bases simultaneously, and also the noted fact that they affect affixes as well as stems. Another is that traditional morphological machinery and surface-to-surface relations are in fact competing conceptions. The function of both is to characterize patterns of similarity among words, the former by postulating abstract URs decomposable into morphemes, the latter by direct comparison. Since traditional morphological means have proved insufficient and surface-to-surface relations necessary, cogency compels us to the hypothesis that what is necessary is also sufficient. As argued in Burzio (2002, in press), the conception based on the RE assumption (6) that establishes a common currency between representations and constraints in fact permits a wholesale reinterpretation of morphology in terms of surface-to-surface relations, thus superseding the traditional machinery. In that conception, 'morphemes' are clusters of interdependent entailments. Allomorphy is the break-up of such clusters under the usual anti-OO-FAITH forces: Markedness, as in *cat-[S]/ dog-[Z]*, and IO-FAITH, as in *compEL/ comPULS-ive* (see Burzio 2000, 2002, in press). Word-formation rules themselves reduce to entailments generated by the various representations. For example, structures like *natur-al* will generate an entailment that *-al* occur attached to a noun, which is then satisfied by *parent-al*, etc., just as if there was an extrinsic word-formation rule. From this point of view, morphemes are not actual objects --the atoms of URs, but are rather abstractions over the lexicon. They are in effect distributional patterns, definable as entailment clusters. The same is true of phonemes. There is no level of representation or compartment in the system where 'phonemes' are defined or listed (like the first page of a dictionary --a point that holds even in original OT). Rather, phonemes are structures that reoccur through the lexicon, like morphemes, except for their different level of granularity. They, too, are entailment clusters which can be broken under compulsion, whence 'allophonic' variation. Concretely, in this view, the [ɔ] of *dog* is being faithful to the [ɔ] of *cost*, because this is what it means to instantiate the same member of the inventory, analogously to what it means to be allomorphs of the same morpheme.

Returning then to the question of the sources of OO-FAITH, a first-pass answer is that it is partial similarity that induces further similarity/ identity --Gradient Attraction. Words seem to be generally influenced by words within the same morphological paradigm because the notion of 'paradigm' is defined by similarity in sound and meaning. There are two further empirical issues, however. One is that bases affect derivatives (the 'base-priority' effect, captured in Benua's system): *phenÓmenon* ⇒ *phenÒmenó-logy*, but not equally vice-versa: *parÉnt-al* ⇒ **parÉnt*. The other is that OO-FAITH effects due to the traditional 'morpho-syntactic base' are more pervasive than effects due to other members of the paradigm. Beginning with this second issue, in the present system there are actually two sources of 'identity' entailments to be reckoned with. For example, in the word *módern-ist*, the stem is conditioned by *módern* by virtue of the independent similarity with that word. In addition, however, it is also conditioned by the effect of the suffix *-ist*. Because the suffix attaches to adjectives, it will entail the existence of an adjective to its left --the present equivalent of a subcategorization frame for the suffix. Since the word *modern* is indeed an adjective, the suffix in *modern-ist* will, in effect, 'promote' the relationship between its stem and that word, essentially enhancing the latter's attraction. This is what gives the 'morpho-syntactic base' a privileged status among the possible attractors, and hence why it is *módern*, rather than *modérn-ity* that determines the stress pattern of *módern-ist* (on the stress-preserving character of *-ist* versus the re-stressing character of *-ity*, see Burzio 1994a). As for the issue of 'base-priority' and the ineffectiveness of *parént-al* in influencing *párent*, this follows from the asymmetry in entailment structure. The word *parent-al* will entail among other things that there be a string *-al* next to the string *parent*. This entailment, namely 'if there is a string *parent*, it must be followed by the string *al*' is obviously violated by the single word *parent*. The latter word will therefore be relatively 'out of range' of the attraction by its derivative *parent-al*. In other words, because *parent* is a substructure of *parent-al*, the set of entailments it generates/ satisfies is only a subset of the set generated by *parent-al*. As in (7) above, violating some of the entailments has the effect of weakening the attraction. In contrast, the stem in *parent-al* has the potential for satisfying all of the entailments generated by the word *parent* (like: 'if there is a *p*, it must be folollowed by and *a*, etc.). Hence, the word *parent* attracts the stem in *parent-al* strongly. In sum, both the priority of the base over derivatives and the priority of what was once the true morphological base over other bases can be understood without categorical exclusion of either other bases or of 'back-copying' (derivative influencing a base), both attested ((13) above and Burzio, in press).

The second problem for the OO-FAITH approach is in certain ranking paradoxes, such as the one involving the pair *lévi-able/ remé:di-able* of (9) above. We have seen that GA and the RE assumption (6) provide a solution to such paradoxes. A wide array of these, all explicable along the same lines, is discussed in Burzio (in press).

3.3   Non-Derived Environment Blocking

Łubowicz (1998) addresses a class of cases like the Polish one in (14).

(14)   a.   Palatalization:
            kro[k]/ kro[č]-ek   'step/ little step'

       b.   Palatalizn. and spirantization:
            dron[g]/ dron[ž]-ek   'pole/ little pole'

       c.   No spirantization:
            bry[ɟ]/ bry[ɟ]-ek (*bry[ž]-ek)   'bridge/ little bridge'

Velar stops turn into palatal affricates before a front vowel: (14a). However, if the velar and hence the resulting affricate is voiced, that affricate further weakens to a fricative: (14b). Yet there is no weakening unless the affricate is 'derived' via palatalization: (14c). Łubowicz provides several other examples of such 'blocking'. It is clear from the present point of view that the effect in question is simply GA. In (14b) palatalization has the effect of distancing the derivative from its base/ attractor. The distance lessens the attraction (OO-FAITH) which enables spirantization to apply. In (14c) there is no independent distancing, so attraction is maximal and spirantization is 'blocked', just as *CiV*-lengthening was in (9a). Łubowicz proposes a solution in terms of constraint conjunction: in (14b) failure to spirantize the palatal would violate the spirantization constraint *conjoined with* the faithfulness constraint already violated by palatalization. While the spirantization constraint is by itself sufficiently low-ranked to be violated as in (14c), the conjunction of the two is high ranked, demanding satisfaction, whence (14b). Such markedness-faithfulness conjunctions in fact directly paraphrase GA. Under GA, when faithfulness is violated on one dimension, markedness constraints on other dimensions appear more successful, as if their rank had been boosted. Conjoining them with the already violated faithfulness constraint is a practical way to boost their rank. While such conjunctions describe GA, they lack in underlying principles, as other conjunctions seem equally conceivable. Note as well that while Łubowicz' analysis uses IO-FAITH, it is indeed OO-FAITH that is relevant. While the 'constraint conjunction' paraphrase of GA is extendable to (9) above, in (9b) it is the *stress* difference from the base *rémedy*, rather than the difference from some input that enables *CiV*-lengthening in *remé:di-able*. Note too that morphologically underived items show regular *CiV*-lengthening: *A:sia*, *So:nia*, etc. This is because the inhibiting factor --OO-FAITH, is absent. If it was because their stress was not in the input and this made them 'derived', then lengthening should occur in *levi-able* as well, whose stress is surely not in the input (since it comes from another output).

In sum, one of the classical cases of 'Non-Derived Environment Blocking' is a GA effect, attributable to the RE assumption in (6) like others. (For other cases of NDEB, see Burzio 2000)

3.4   Positional Repairs

Wilson (2000, 2001) points to the intractability of the following generalization in original OT.

(15)   a.   Simplification of CC clusters systematically eliminates the *first* C, not the second.

     b.   E.g. Diola-Fogny: /let-ku-jaw/ $\Rightarrow$ lekujaw   'they won't go'

The generalization in (15) (not captured by the 'Alignment' analysis of (15b) in Kager 1999a, 3.6.3) may seem innocuous at first: the C affected is in the notoriously weak 'coda' position. The problem, however, is that being a coda is not a property of either the input or the output. Whichever C survives will be an onset in the output, and that should be all that matters. Deletion of the second C should in fact be preferred when the first is intrinsically less marked, e.g. a coronal as in (15b), predicting *letujaw*. The problem persists when one trades in the 'coda condition' for weakness of perceptual cues (Steriade 1994, 1997): whichever C survives will be well-cued (pre-sonorant position) in the output. The problem is that the repair is not determinable on the basis of actual outputs, but only on the basis of what would be an output just short of the repair. As Wilson argues, what is needed is a formal implementation of the notion that weak contrasts are repaired in a specific way: by turning the more marked member of the pair into the less marked member (neutralization), although epenthesis is also a possibility (see below and Wilson 2000). In (15b), the pre-obstruent *t* forms a weak contrast with zero, into which it therefore turns. Since weakness of contrast is another term for similarity, neutralization of segmental contrasts is a GA effect, which thus obtains with segments just as it does with morphemes. Wilson's formal approach is to introduce a new class of markedness constraints, which he refers to as 'targeted', whose property is that they establish harmonic orderings only within weakly contrasting pairs of candidate representations. Calculation of (15b) now proceeds as in (16), where '$\Rightarrow$' identifies the targeted constraint.

It is easy to see from the distribution of asterisks that original OT would incorrectly select candidate (c). What makes the difference in Wilson's system is that the targeted constraint only declares (b) better than (a), saying nothing about (c).

(16)

	let-ku-jaw	⇒*WEAK C	DEP	MAX	*VELAR	*CORONAL
a.	letkujaw	*		a≻b,c	*	*
b. ☞	lekujaw	b≻a		*	*	b≻a,c
c.	letujaw	---		*	c≻b,a	*
Harmonic ordering:		b≻a	---	b≻a≻c	---	---

Its function is to express the neutralization of weak contrast (=GA). In (a), the *t* is perceptually similar to zero, and therefore the representation that contains it is only similar to *lekujaw*, not at all to *letujaw*. The other constraints in (16) work as usual, and the harmonic ordering they establish is recorded. The bottom row tallies harmonic ordering of candidates from left to right, giving priority to higher ranked constraints. Ordering by the two rightmost constraints is either contradicted or already established, and hence inconsequential. Candidate (b) is thus the winner. Wilson's targeted constraints can be seen as an implementation of entailment summation under RE (6). When two representations are identical on a large number of dimensions, there will be a large number of entailments pressuring the remaining differences into identity. A high-ranked targeted constraint expresses that pressure.

Hence it is representations in general that attract one-another gradiently under similarity. It happens to allomorphs because they are highly similar representations by definition. It happens to segments when contextual conditions mask crucial perceptual cues that would keep them distinct. Work on allomorphy has characterized attraction by means of faithfulness constraints --OO-FAITH. Once one realizes that the trigger of OO-FAITH is independent similarity, however, markedness can serve just as well: it is marked to be similar but unfaithful (= *WEAK CONTRAST). One could thus use Wilson's targeted constraints in lieu of OO-FAITH just as well, as in (17).

(17)

	base: *lévy*	⇒*WEAK CONTRAST	*CiV*-LENGTH
a. ☞	lévi-able	a≻b	*
b.	lé:vi-able	*	b≻a
	Harmonic ordering:	a≻b	---

The 'weak contrast' in (17) is given by the stem *lé:vi-* versus the verb *lévy*. There is no comparably weak contrast in *remé:di-(able)/ rémedy* of (9b) because of the contrasting stresses, hence the targeted constraint is (absent or) lower-ranked in that case.

3.5   Opacity

Wilson has shown further that the above account of neutralization simultaneously also provides an insightful account of opacity (counterfeeding/ counterbleeding) effects. The Serbo-Croatian case in (18) (Kenstowicz 1994: 90ff.) illustrates (although Wilson does not provide this particular example).

In the actual output (18b), vocalization of *l* to *o* counterbleeds epenthesis, which is to avoid CC# clusters. What is needed to yield the counterbleeding effect is the natural assumption that *l*-vocalization is neutralization of a weak contrast. In word-final position, the *l* is realized as 'dark', rendering it perceptually similar to another member of the inventory of Serbo-Croatian: *o*. As in the cluster-simplification case, neutralization of contrast is attributed to a targeted constraint. As before, what this means is that the constraint, here *WEAK *l*# compares only '*l*' candidates with otherwise identical '*o*' candidates, thus declaring 'b≻c' and 'd≻a', establishing no other ordering of candidates. The orderings that would be established by the non-targeted version of the constraint are parenthesized in (18), and it is thus crucial that the contents of the parentheses be ignored in the tally. Tallying the overall harmonic ordering left-to-right this way identifies the correct winner (b). It is easy to see that, without the targeted property, namely with the contents of the parentheses *in*cluded, the winner would be the transparent but incorrect candidate (d), which satisfies both DEP and *CC# simultaneously. The overall harmonic ordering in that case would simply be the one already detectable in the distribution of asterisks. Note that the constraint banning final clusters should in fact also be targeted, like the one in (16) above, but that property is inconsequential in this case, since Serbo-Croatian repairs clusters by epenthesis (by virtue of MAX >> DEP. See Wilson 2000). Hence opacity follows from taking *l* to be attracted to *o* --part of the inventory of Serbo-Croatian, and the 'other' representation of the modified architecture (1b). This is a case of GA because the source of the attraction is the independent perceptual similarity that *l* bears to *o* when occurring in final position. When such *l* neutralizes to *o* in a complex representation like *okrugl* or *okrugal*, the rest of the representation will naturally remain unaffected in the present perspective, whence the fact that the targeted constraint in (18) only makes the specific pairwise comparisons noted.

(18)

'round' okrugl	*CC#	⇒* WEAK *l*#	IDENT$_{(+cons)}$	MAX	DEP
a. okrugl	*	*	a≻b,d		a≻b,c
b. ☞ okrugao	b≻a	b≻(a),c	*		*
c. okrugal	c≻a	*	c≻b,d		*
d. okrugo	d≻a	d≻a,(c)	*		d≻b,c
Harmonic ordering:	b≻a, c≻a, d≻a	b≻c≻a, d≻a	b≻c≻d≻a	---	---

Wilson's solution to opacity is formally similar to McCarthy's (1999) Sympathy Theory (reviewed in Kager 1999a, section 9.2.5). What makes the output 'opaque' to the original OT grammar, with standard markedness and faithfulness governing the space at large, is the existence of some overriding factor locally to a specific region. The 'local' factor in Wilson's system is the 'other' member of the weak contrast, while in McCarthy's system it is the 'flower' candidate. Similarity notwithstanding, McCarthy's system does *not* instantiate the modified architecture (1b) above, the reason being that the flower candidate is a function of the same, rather than a different, input. Sympathy Theory thus falls wholly within the architecture (1a), and as such does not relate to the rest of the package: cluster simplification and other segmental neutralizations; structure of segmental inventories; patterns of allomorphy that call for OO-FAITH. Concerning OO-FAITH, note in fact that the proposed unification predicts that, if opacity arises from segmental neutralizations (as per Wilson), it should also arise from neutralization of allomorphs (OO-FAITH). Indeed, this is true, as in the case of 'Canadian raising' in (19) (once part of the Bromberger and Halle 1989 arsenal of defenses for rule-based derivations), which shows voicing/ flapping conterbleeding raising of [ay] to [ʌy] before voiceless stops.

(19)

rʌyt (write)	*V́ {+coron, -voice} V	OO-IDENT		*ʌy
		(voice)	(V-height)	
a. ☞ rʌyDər		*		*
b. rayDər		*	*	

This 'opacity' effect was reanalyzed as OO-FAITH as early as Burzio (1994a; 190f, fn. 16). In the winning candidate (19a), the raised diphthong [ʌy] of *writer* satisfies OO-IDENT (V-height) with the base *write*, where the raising is properly conditioned. At the same time, the top-ranked constraint ensures that *t* is voiced/ flapped to *D*, in violation of OO-IDENT (voice). As in the case of *léviable* in (17) above, we could replace OO-FAITH/ IDENT with its alternative label *WEAK CONTRAST, highlighting the parallelism with Wilson's solution of (18). Since allomorphs constitute weak contrasts by definition, they will tend to neutralize, just like segmental contrasts, whence (19a).

Consider here that McCarthy's motivation for devising Sympathy Theory has been that alternatives, in particular OO-FAITH, seemed insufficient. The reason is that there are cases, just like the Serbo-Croatian case in (18), in which no allomorph exists on which the relevant OO-FAITH could be based. McCarthy's once pointed conclusion is now undercut, however, by the present unification. If OO-FAITH needs to be understood as GA (to solve the ranking paradoxes), and if GA is manifested by segments as well (in inventories and patterns of neutralization), then the extension of what was OO-FAITH to segments predicts a corresponding extension of the class of opacity effects, from mutual attraction of allomorphs to mutual attraction of segments --exactly Wilson's finding.

4   Conclusion

Both the study of segmental inventories and neutralizations, and the study of allomorphic variation, reveal that optimization involves comparison with 'other' existing forms as in (1b). In addition, both reveal that the influence of other forms is one of Gradient Attraction. This convergence indicates that the effect is not dictated by properties of either segments or morphemes, or specifically tied to auditory perception. Rather, it must come from properties of mental representations at large. The Gradient Attraction effect follows, in fact, directly from the assumption that mental representations are sets of entailments, an assumption that echoes known principles of neural behavior. I have argued that a unified approach under (1b) holds the solution to a considerable number of problems in Optimality Theory, including those over which derivational approaches could still have claimed some advantages, like opacity. If the unification is correct, a new benchmark is set: competing approaches will have to solve the whole package of problems, not just one.

References

Benua, Laura (1997): *Transderivational Identity: Phonological Relations between Words.* PhD dissertation, University of Massachusetts, Amherst.

Bromberger, Sylvain & Halle, Morris (1989): Why phonology is different. *Linguistic Inquiry* 20:1. 51–70.

Burzio, Luigi (1991): On the metrical unity of Latinate affixes. In: Westphal, Germán, Ao, Benjamin & Chae, Hee-Rahk, eds. (1991): *Proceeding of the Eighth Eastern States Conference on Linguistics*, Department of Linguistics, Ohio State University. 1–22. [Reprinted In: *Rivista di Grammatica Generativa 16.* 1–27. Revised Version In: Campos, Héctor & Kempchinsky, Paula M., eds. (1995): *Evolution and Revolution in Linguistic Theory: Essays in Honor of Carlos Otero.* Georgetown University Press. 1–24.]

Burzio, Luigi (1994a): *Principles of English Stress.* Cambridge: Cambridge University Press.

Burzio, Luigi (1994b): Metrical consistency. In: Ristad, Eric S., ed. (1994): *Language Computations.* Providence, RI: American Mathematical Society. 93–125.

Burzio, Luigi (1996): Surface constraints versus underlying representation. In: Durand, Jacques & Laks, Bernard, eds. (1996): *Current Trends in Phonology: Models and Methods.* European Studies Research Institute: University of Salford Publications. 123–141.

Burzio, Luigi (1998): Multiple correspondence. *Lingua* 103. 79–109.

Burzio, Luigi (2000): Cycles, Non-Derived-Environment Blocking, and Correspondence. In: Dekkers, Joost, Leeuw, Frank van der & Weijer, Jeroen van de, eds. (2000): *Optimality Theory: Phonology, Syntax, and Acquisition.* Oxford University Press. 47–87.

Burzio, Luigi (2002): Missing Players: Phonology and the Past-tense Debate. *Lingua* 112. 157–199.

Burzio, Luigi (in press): Surface-to-Surface Morphology: When your Representations turn into Constraints. In: Boucher, P. & Plénat, M., eds. (in press): *Many Morphologies.* Cascadilla Press. (Preliminary Version: ROA-341-0999; http://roa.rutgers.edu/)

Carstairs-McCarthy, Andrew (1999): Umlaut as signans and signatum: Synchronic and diachronic aspects. In: Booij, Geert & Marle, Jaap van, eds. (1999): *Yearbook of Morphology 1999.* Dordrecht: Kluwer. 1–23.

DiFabio, Elvira (1990): *The Morphology of the Verbal Infix /-isk-/ in Italian and in Romance.* PhD dissertation, Harvard.

Flemming, Edward (1995): *Auditory Representations in Phonology.* PhD dissertation, UCLA.

Gafos, Adamantios (1996): *The Articulatory Basis of Locality in Phonology.* PhD dissertation, Johns Hopkins University. [Published in: New York: Garland Publishing, 1999]

Hebb, Donald O. (1949): *The Organization of Behavior: A Neuropsychological Theory.* New York: John Wiley & Sons.

Kager, René (1999a): *Optimality Theory.* Cambridge: Cambridge University Press.

Kager, René (1999b): Surface Opacity of metrical structure in Optimality Theory. In: Hermans, Ben & Oostendorp, Martin van, eds. (1999): *The derivational residue in phonological optimality theory.* Philadelphia: J. Benjamins. 207–245.

Kenstowicz, Michael (1994): *Phonology in Generative Grammar.* Cambridge, MA: Blackwell.

Kenstowicz, Michael (1996): Base-identity and uniform exponence: Alternatives to cyclicity. In: Durand, Jacques & Laks, Bernard, eds. (1996): *Current Trends in Phonology: Models and Methods.* European Studies Research Institute, University of Salford Publications. 363–393.

Kenstowicz, Michael (1997): Uniform exponence: Exemplification and extension. In: Miglio, Viola & Morén, Bruce, eds. (1997): *University of Maryland Working Papers in Linguistics 5: Selected Phonology Papers from H-O-T 97.* 139–155.

Kiparsky, Paul (1998): *Paradigm effects and opacity.* Ms, Stanford.

Łubowicz, Anna (1998): *Derived environment effects in OT*. Ms, Rutgers Optimality Archive. (ROA-239-0198; http://roa.rutgers.edu/)

McCarthy, John (1999): Sympathy and phonological opacity. *Phonology* 16. 331–399.

Prince, Alan & Paul Smolensky (1993): *Optimality Theory: Constraint Interaction in Generative Grammar*. Ms, Rutgers University, New Brunswick & University of Colorado, Boulder.

Smolensky, Paul (1986): Information processing in dynamical systems: Foundations of harmony theory. In: Rumelhart, David E. & McClelland, Jay L., eds. (1986): *Parallel Distributed Processing: Exploration in the Microstructure of Cognition*. Vol. I: Psychological and Biological Models. Cambridge, MA: MIT Press. 194–281.

Steriade, Donca (1994): *Positional neutralization and the expression of contrast*. Ms, UCLA.

Steriade, Donca (1997): *Phonetics in Phonology: The case of laryngeal neutralization*. Ms, UCLA.

Steriade, Donca (1999): Lexical conservatism in French adjectival liaison. In: Bullock, B., Authier, M. & Reed, L., eds. (1999): *Formal Perspectives in Romance Linguistics*. John Benjamins. 243–270.

Steriade, Donca (2000): Paradigm uniformity and the phonetics-phonology boundary. In: Broe, Michael & Pierrehumbert, Janet, eds. (2000): *Papers in Laboratory Phonology 6*. Cambridge University Press.

Wilson, Colin (2000): *Targeted Constraints: An Approach to Contextual Neutralization in Optimality Theory*. PhD dissertation, Johns Hopkins University.

Wilson, Colin (2001): Consonant Cluster Neutralization and Targeted Constraints. *Phonology* 18:1. 147–197.

Baltimore, MD   Luigi Burzio

JHU/Cognitive Science, 243 Krieger Hall/ 3400 N. Charles Street, Baltimore MD 21218-2685
e-mail: burzio@jhu.edu

Lexical and Postlexical Phonology in Optimality Theory: Evidence from Japanese[*]

Junko Ito and Armin Mester

Abstract

Using examples from the phonology of Japanese, this paper argues, against the claims of radical parallelism, that lexical and postlexical phonology remain separate and serially related systems in Optimality Theory. Crucial evidence comes from opaque interactions involving allophonic masking processes, which cannot be properly understood in parallelist Sympathy Theory without compromising a basic tenet of OT regarding the unrestrictedness and universality of inputs ("Richness-of-the-Base"). It is suggested that, within a given grammar, ranking differences between the lexical and the postlexical systems are tightly restricted, perhaps limited to lexical demotions of contextual markedness and faithfulness.

Introduction

A characteristic feature of conservative varieties of Tokyo Japanese (Hibiya 1999) is the interaction of a morphophonemic process of compound voicing with a general allophonic process of g-weakening. Given the current interest in parallelist approaches to the masking of certain phonological generalizations on the surface (dubbed "opacity" in Kiparsky 1973), the immediate goal of this paper is to demonstrate that this interaction represents a type of opacity that cannot be described in an adequate way by means of Sympathy (McCarthy 1998), which has been suggested as a general and strictly parallelist tool to deal with all types of opacity in Optimality Theory (henceforth, OT; Prince & Smolensky 1993). Mistakenly put forth as an argument for Sympathy in our own earlier work (Ito & Mester 1997b) the case receives a superior understanding under familiar conservative assumptions, where the opacity arises naturally out of the serial interaction of the lexical and postlexical modules of phonology. Construed more broadly, this result constitutes an additional argument for the

[*] For useful comments and suggestions, we are indebted to two anonymous reviewers, the members of the *Special Research Project for the Typological Investigation of Languages and Cultures of the East and West* at Tsukuba University (7/99), the audience at a *PAIK* meeting at Kobe University (12/99), and the participants at the *Workshop on Conflicting Rules in Phonology and Syntax* at the University of Potsdam (12/99). Special thanks are due to Luigi Burzio, Caroline Féry, Haruka Fukazawa, Shosuke Haraguchi, Bruce Hayes, Takeru Honma, René Kager, Mafuyu Kitahara, Haruo Kubozono, Gereon Müller, Akio Nasu, Sam Rosenthall, Philip Spaelti, Shin-ichi Tanaka, Markus Walter, Richard Wiese, Noriko Yamane, Teruo Yokotani, Yuko Yoshida, Hideki Zamma, and Draga Zec.

weakly parallel architecture of Optimality Theory argued for in Ito & Mester (2001), which maintains lexical and postlexical phonology as different and serially connected systems, without necessarily embracing the entirely separate assumption of serially connected levels within the lexical phonology itself argued for by Kiparsky 1998.

1   The masking interaction: compound voicing and g-weakening

The interaction in question involves two well-known processes. The first is *Rendaku* (1) (literally, *sequential voicing*), a process replacing voiceless obstruents by their voiced counterparts at the juncture of word-word compounds (specifically, at the beginning of second members). A general phonological characteristic of Rendaku is the fact that it is systematically blocked in second members that already contain a voiced obstruent (2).

(1)   Compound Voicing (*Rendaku*):   C → [+voi] /]+[__ X]

        tama 'ball'   teppoo+dama   'bullet'
        sono 'garden'   hana+zono   'flower garden'

(2)   Condition (*"Lyman's Law"*): X does not contain [+voi, -son]
        (OCP on [+voice, -son] or [*VoiObs^2]$_{Stem}$, following Ito & Mester 1998):

        taba 'bundle'   satsu+taba   'wad of bills'   *satsu-daba
        sode 'sleeves'   furi+sode   'long-sleeved kimono'   *furi-zode

As argued in detail in Ito & Mester (1986), compound voicing has all the properties of a lexical process listed in (3).

(3)   a. Essential reference to morphological structure (voicing appears only in a narrowly circumscribed class of compounds, see also Otsu 1980 & Haraguchi 2001)

        b. Existence of numerous exceptions (see Rosen 2001 for the most exhaustive recent study), c.f. the names of the two different versions of the Japanese syllabary: hira+gana (with voicing) vs. kata+kana (without voicing)

        c. Sensitivity to subdivisions of the vocabulary (native Yamato vs. Sino-Japanese/Foreign items, similar in kind to the distinction in the English vocabulary between native Germanic vs. Latinate/Greek items)

        d. Nongradiency and contrastiveness

        e. Cyclicity.

Compound voicing is thus a textbook example of a lexical process (this point apparently also holds for earlier stages of the language, see Unger (2000: 17)). In terms of the points listed in (3), it contrasts sharply with g-weakening (4), an allophonic process replacing non-initial /g/ by [ŋ] (e.g. /gai/→[ŋai] in [koku+ŋai] 'abroad', vs. word-initial [gai] in [gai+dʒiɴ] 'foreigner').[1]

(4)   g -weakening: / g /→ [ŋ] / ₚᵣWd[X ___   (where X =[+seg])

    a. ₚᵣWd[g............]   b. ₚᵣWd[..........ŋ ..]

       gai+dʒiɴ   'foreigner'   koku+ŋai   'abroad'
       guu+zeɴ   'accidental occurrence'   soo+ŋuu   'meet accidentally'
       geta   'clogs'   kaŋi   'key'
       go   '(game of) Go'   tokaŋe   'lizard'

The properties of g-weakening are typical of postlexical processes: phonetic gradiency, non-contrastiveness, and sociolinguistic variation. There is significant gradiency in the degree of nasalization found in the results of g-weakening, depending on factors such as speech rate and speech register. In a number of dialects, the result of g-weakening is not [ŋ], but rather a segment more similar to [ɣ]. The different status of the *contrastive* voicing that marks compounds and the *noncontrastive* nasality caused by weakening is clear to native speakers and finds a tangible expression in the fact that the first one, but not the second one, is marked by a diacritic in the native syllabaries. Hibiya (1999) shows in detail how the process is subject to systematic sociolinguistic variation, governed by regional, social, and generational factors.

It is in this last context that morphological factors start to have an effect on the allophonic weakening process--for example, recent loans are found to resist g-weakening more easily than older loans, etc. In addition, in compound words underlying [g] at the beginning of second members often remains unlenited, echoing the unlenited [g] found at the beginning of the isolation form of the simplex word in question. In Ito & Mester (1997a), this prototypical case of analogy is shown to be better analyzed in terms of parallelist Output-Output correspondence than in a traditional serialist-derivational framework. While the process in question thus provides arguments for some kind of parallelism, it is especially interesting, as we will now show, in that it at the same time does not sit well with a radical form of parallelism that denies the separation and serial interaction of lexical and postlexical phonology.

Turning to the interaction of the processes, it is easy to see that in rule terms, compound voicing feeds g-weakening in the focus of the rule ((5a): k→g→ŋ), and is itself counterfed by it in the environment of the rule, i.e., when the sonorant [ŋ] replacing the obstruent /g/ appears inside the second compound

---

[1] Since the phonotactics of Japanese do not permit word-final [g] or [ŋ], "non-initial" is in effect co-extensive with "word-medial".

member (5b). Note that reversing the order of application would result in the wrong output *[saka+doŋe].

(5)   a. feeding: b. counterfeeding:

                         'folding paper'   'reverse thorn'
                         /ori + kami/   /saka + toge/

compound voicing: ori   gami   – blocked by (2) –
g-weakening: ori   ŋami   saka   toŋe
                   [ori ŋami]   [saka   toŋe]

A preliminary OT-analysis of the two interacting alternations distilled from previous work appears in (6) and (8).[2] The subhierarchy responsible for compound voicing is given in (6), followed by illustrative tableaux in (7).

(6)

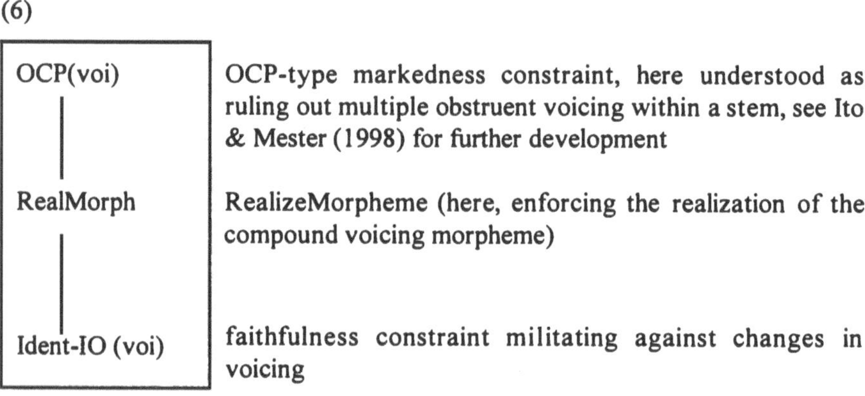

OCP(voi)	OCP-type markedness constraint, here understood as ruling out multiple obstruent voicing within a stem, see Ito & Mester (1998) for further development
RealMorph	RealizeMorpheme (here, enforcing the realization of the compound voicing morpheme)
Ident-IO (voi)	faithfulness constraint militating against changes in voicing

RealizeMorpheme (REALMORPH) is here used as the constraint resulting in the appearance of sequential voicing. We assume (see Ito & Mester 1986 for motivation) that the input for word-word compounds contains a linking morpheme carrying the specification [+voiced], whose realization is regulated by REALMORPH.[3] In order to conserve space, our tableaux here and throughout feature only the most plausible candidates, leaving out potential rivals that violate obvious phonotactic, segmental, or faithfulness constraints.

[2] A detailed treatment of the Rendaku-related phonology of Japanese is given in Ito & Mester (1998). The g-weakening part of the analysis appears first in McCarthy & Prince (1995) and is taken up in Ito & Mester (1997a,b), see below for an alternative and arguably superior approach.

[3] This is somewhat akin to the "Fugen-s" of German in cases such Geburts+tag 'birthday', where the feminine gender of the first member provides no inflectional support for a genitive -s.

(7)   a. OCP(voi) » RealMorph

/satsu-[+v]-taba/	OCP(voi)	RealMorph	IO-Ident(voi)
satsu-daba	*!		*
☞ satsu-taba		*	

     b. RealMorph » IO-Ident(voi)

/hana-[+v]-sono/	OCP(voi)	RealMorph	IO-Ident(voi)
☞ hana-zono			*
hana-sono		*!	

The sub-hierarchy responsible for g-weakening is shown in (8), followed by illustrative tableaux in (9) and (10).

(8)

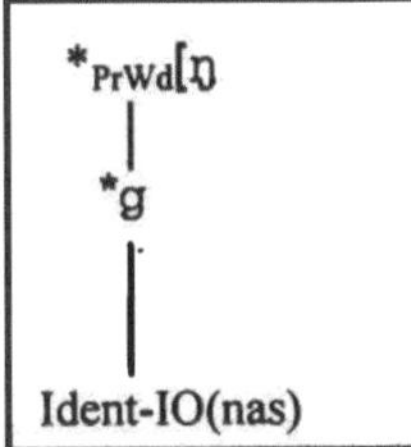

positional markedness constraint against PrWd-initial ŋ

markedness constraint prohibiting voiced dorsal obstruents

faithfulness constraint against changes in nasality

An important background assumption is that Japanese compounds, which as a rule contain at most one accent, consist of single prosodic words, different from English and many other languages (see Kubozono 1993 for justification). What matters here is not so much this specific assumption about prosodic words, but rather the fact that compounds constitute single prosodic domains of type α, and [ŋ] is barred from appearing initially in α. Relevant tableaux are given in (9) and (10), where the only difference between the two different input variants lies in violations of low-ranking IDENT(NAS). This brings out a detail important for the argument to be developed later in this paper: It concerns the freedom of specification of voiced velar segments as either nasal or oral in the input. Since the two segments do not stand in contrast and their distribution is allophonically determined,[4] Richness-of-the-Base (see Prince & Smolensky 1993) dictates that either of them is a viable input.

---

[4] See Ito & Mester (1997a) for further details, with a treatment of the Output-Output-based variability associated with g-weakening in certain derived environments – these complicating factors have no bearing on the core cases under discussion here.

(9)   /g/ as input:

	/ geta/ 'clogs'	*PWd[ŋ	*g	IO-Ident(nas)
☞ a.	geta		*	
b.	ŋeta	*!		*
	/kagi/ 'key'	*PWd[ŋ	*g	IO-Ident(nas)
c.	kagi		*!	
☞ d.	kaŋi			*

(10)   /ŋ/ as input:

	/ŋeta/ 'clogs'	*PWd[ŋ	*g	IO-Ident(nas)
☞ a.	a. geta		*	*
b.	b. ŋeta	*!		
	/kaŋi/ 'key'	*PWd[ŋ	*g	IO-Ident(nas)
c.	c. kagi		*!	*
☞ d.	d. kaŋi			

(11) combines the two subhierarchies in (6) and (8) into a single constraint system.

(11)

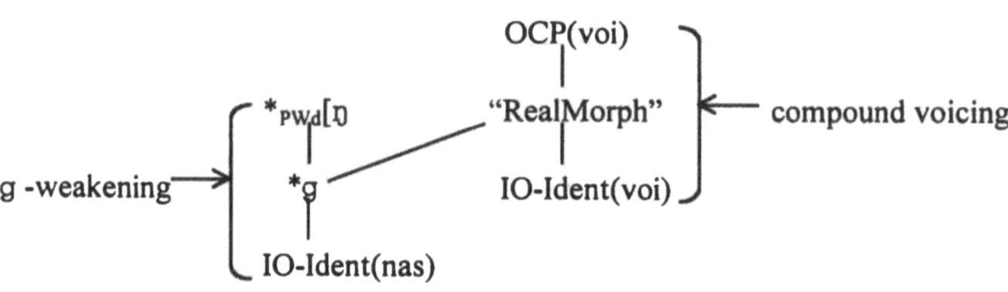

Ito & Mester (1997b) show that this analysis successfully deals with the transparent (feeding) interaction (5a) as in (12a), but predictably fails for the opaque (counterfeeding) interaction (5b), as shown in (12b).

(12)   a. Feeding relationship – correct result

/ori-kami/ 'paper folding'	*pwd[ŋ	OCP (voi)	Real Morph	*g	IO- Id(nas)	IO- Id(voi)
ori-kami			*!			
ori-gami				*!		*
☞ ori-ŋami					*	*

    b. Counterfeeding relationship – wrong result:

/saka-toge/ 'reverse thorn'	*pwd[ŋ	OCP (voi)	Real Morph	*g	IO- Id(nas)	IO- Id(voi)
saka-toge			*!	*		
saka-doge		*!		*		*
☹ saka-toŋe			*!		*	
☞!! saka-doŋe					*	*

2   Sympathy and Richness of the Base

The Sympathy-based alternative to the failed transparent analysis developed in
Ito & Mester (1997b) appears in (13). The gist of the approach is to force the
grammar to select saka-toge (13a) as the sympathy-candidate (marked by "✿"),
in virtue of being the optimal member of the set of *non-nasalizing co-
candidates*. (13a) then serves as a role model for the overall winner, as far as the
non-application of compound voicing is concerned. Technically, this is
implemented by setting the selector constraint as IO-IDENT(NAS)✿, and the
sympathetic faithfulness constraint as ✿O-IDENT(VOI), which, ranked above
REALMORPH, forces the winner to echo the ✿-candidate's voiceless [t].

(13)

		/saka-toge/	*pwd[ŋ	OCP (voi)	✿O- Id(voi)	Real Morph	*g	IO- Id(nas)✿	IO- Id(voi)
✿	a.	saka-toge				*	*!		
	b.	saka-doge		*!	*		*		*
☞	c.	saka-toŋe				*		*	
	d.	saka-doŋe			*!			*	*

The ✾O-IDENT(VOI) constraint column in (13) shows that the winning candidate (13c), with its voiceless [t], is sympathetically faithful to the ✾-candidate, whereas the competing candidate (13d) (the erstwhile problematic winner in (12)) is now excluded because of its unsympathetic [d]. The ✾-candidate itself (13a), while trivially fulfilling ✾O-IDENT(VOI), loses to (13c) on the *g-constraint.

A serious liability of this analysis is already recognized in Ito & Mester 1997b.[5] It tacitly presupposes that the input is in some way or other fixed as /saka-toge/ (as opposed to /saka-toŋe/) – only then can faithfulness to a non-nasal input /g/ trigger the desired chain of Sympathy effects. However, this crucial prerequisite of Sympathy Theory seems difficult to reconcile with core tenets of OT. The segments [g] and [ŋ] do not stand in contrast, and the surface distribution of the two variants is fully predicted by the constraint system. Familiar Richness-of-the-Base considerations require, therefore, as already explained earlier in connection with (9) and (10), that the ranking of output constraints alone be responsible for the derivation of the distribution of the two variants. No specific requirement for inputs to contain /g/ as against /ŋ/ in certain positions should be necessary (or even possible). In other words, the grammar must be able to deal with input variants like /saka-toŋe/[6] – this is what it means in OT for an alternation to be allophonic. Here the Sympathy-based approach to opacity strays off course: in the same way that sympathetic faithfulness to input nasality leads to the right winner in (13), it homes in on the wrong winner (namely *saka-doŋe) in (14).

(14)

	/saka-toŋe/	*pwd[ŋ	OCP (voi)	✾O-Id(voi)	Real Morph	*g	IO-Id(nas)✾	IO-Id(voi)
	saka-toge			*!	*	*	*	
	saka-doge		*!			*	*	*
☹	saka-toŋe			*!	*			
☞!!✾	saka-doŋe							*

Just as with the examples from German phonology discussed in Ito & Mester (to appear b), where this argument is developed in greater detail and in a broader theoretical context, the general result is that Sympathy cannot cope with the rich inputs demanded by Richness of the Base whenever the masking process of an opaque interaction is allophonic.

---

[5] See note 4 in Ito & Mester (1997b), which expands on an observation by Kazutaka Kurisu & Philip Spaelti.

[6] If Lexicon Optimization (Prince & Smolensky 1993; Ito, Mester & Padgett 1995) is accepted as a principle, /toŋe/ is in fact the best input for the output [toŋe].

3   Serial opacity

The strategy advocated here is in some respects the opposite of the Sympathy approach. It begins with the observation that opacity is not necessarily a unified phenomenon produced by a single device that is assigned the task to bring it about.[7] In our view, it arises rather as a by-product of the fact that OT-grammars have a particular kind of internal architecture, which includes both parallel and serial elements of structure. On the one hand, a certain type of constraint conjunction (markedness & faithfulness, see Lubowicz 1998) results in faithfulness-enhanced markedness effects ('parallel opacity', Ito & Mester to appear). On the other hand, the separation of lexical and postlexical phonology as distinct and serially connected systems leads to the partial masking of word-level generalizations by phrase-level effects ('serial opacity'). We focus here on the second type.

The resulting picture of the grammar, worked out in greater detail in Ito & Mester (2001), differs in three ways from the strictly serialist conception of opacity in Kiparsky (1998): (i) We assume that cyclic effects are due to Output-Output constraints. There is thus no cyclic re-application of the constraint system, following the morphological build-up of the word (as in Kiparsky 1998, 42–50; see Ito & Mester 1997a for discussion). (ii) A genuinely parallelist variety of opacity is recognized. (iii) The serial variety of opacity is restricted to the large-scale distinction between lexical and postlexical phonology, maintaining the lexical phonology as a single, parallel, and unitary constraint system.

Lexical phonology and postlexical phonology are characterized by the three essential properties listed in (15).

(15)   a. The lexical and postlexical modules constitute separate constraint systems.

      b. They share many (not necessarily all)[8] constraints, but rankings can differ in limited ways.

      c. The two modules interact serially, with the output of the lexical module serving as the input to the postlexical module.

In broad outlines, the distinction is well-known from the theory of Lexical Phonology (see Kiparsky 1982 and related work), and it is unsurprising that this two-stage structure of the grammar results in opacity. Regarding (15b), we also do not exclude the possibility that the postlexical system might be quite different in character from the lexical one. (echoing an earlier proposal in Liberman & Pierrehumbert 1984). For example, only the latter might turn out to

---

[7] This is in fact implicitly admitted by Sympathy Theory insofar as it excludes the 'chain shift' type of opacity from its own purview, see Ito & Mester (2001) for discussion.

[8] Thus it is at least conceivable that certain types of phonetic constraints, calling for quantitative modes of evaluation, are literally not part of the lexical module.

be a strict OT-system, whereas the former might be a more broadly optimization-based quantitative system. But for present purposes and given the limits of our current understanding, we will continue to assume that both are strict OT-systems. After completing our analytical work, we will return to the question of how the rankings in the two components can differ. It is clear that not all pairings of lexical and postlexical constraint systems will yield viable languages, and we will make some proposals regarding the types of rerankings that are possible within a single grammar.

3.1 Reanalyzing g-weakening

It is useful to start out by scrutinizing the treatment of [g~ŋ] allophony seen so far on its own merits, abstracting away from its involvement in opaque alternations. The basic idea of the analysis has been that no specific constraint against intervocalic [g] is involved. Rather, all effects were due to the general constraint against [g], mitigated by a specific constraint against word-initial [ŋ]. In other words, the word-internal weakening of [g] is not seen as contextual weakening, but rather as a context-free markedness effect. We will now show that a traditional weakening analysis is in fact superior to this view in several respects.

The crucial part of the context-free markedness approach adopted so far appears in (16),[9] now expanded to include the presupposed ranking of basic segmental markedness constraints as *g »*ŋ. Assuming total ranking, this must hold in order for *g to be the operative force resulting in /g/→[ŋ] replacements since the opposite ranking would never permit [ŋ] to appear as a way of resolving a *g violation.

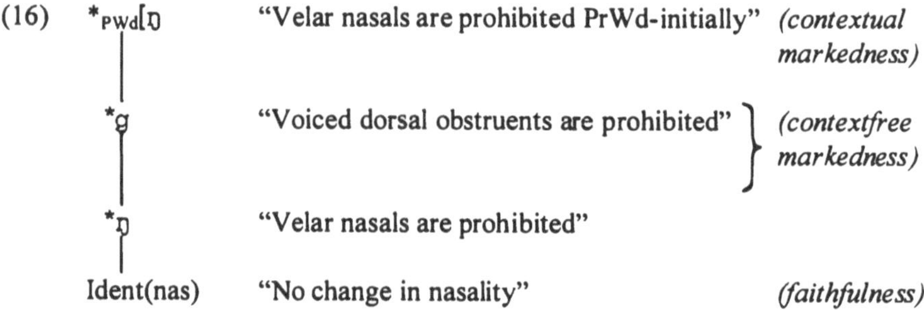

(16)   *PWd[ŋ   "Velar nasals are prohibited PrWd-initially"   *(contextual markedness)*

        *g   "Voiced dorsal obstruents are prohibited"   } *(contextfree markedness)*

        *ŋ   "Velar nasals are prohibited"

        Ident(nas)   "No change in nasality"   *(faithfulness)*

The constraint hierarchy in (16) has three questionable aspects. First, it might be problematic to be committed to the ranking [*g » *ŋ] since, under traditional generative assumptions, the underlying inventories of familiar languages such as English have contrastive /g/ but no contrastive /ŋ/ (i.e. with all surface [ŋ]

---

[9] By a general M»F default ranking in the absence of evidence for F-activity (see Smolensky 1995 and Ito & Mester 1999, to appear for arguments), *ŋ»IDENT(NAS) holds by default.

deriving from nasal+velar clusters: /sɪNg/ → [sɪŋ], etc.).[10] Such considerations are not an infallible guide, however, and Ito & Mester (1997a, 449–451) show, with cross-linguistic occurrence statistics based on Maddieson (1984), that the case under discussion remains somewhat ambiguous. On the one hand, the cross-linguistic frequency of contrastive ŋ increases when one considers surface inventories, where English, for example, has phonemic /ŋ/ in forms like / sɪŋ/. On the other hand, the very fact that inventory statistics such as those of Maddieson (1984) are based on taxonomic-phonemic inventories means that they do not provide a direct window on underlying inventories in the sense of generative phonology.

A second and independent problem for the contextfree makedness analysis (16) concerns the attempt to interpret the intervocalic replacement of [g] by [ŋ] strictly as a direct aerodynamic effect, with *g literally taken as a "phonologization" of Boyle's law (as in McCarthy & Prince 1995 and Ito & Mester 1997a). Given the expandability of the walls of the supraglottal cavity, this is not entirely straightforward in terms of the underlying physics, as Bruce Hayes & Patricia Keating have reminded us (*voce*). It is especially in intervocalic position that the aerodynamic difficulties connected with [g] are negligible – this is where [g] is in fact often found to replace [k], along with the other voiced stops (e.g. in most of the native languages of Australia, which lack an underlying voicing contrast, see Dixon 1980).

Such considerations tend to undermine any attempt to view the word-internal weakening of [g] strictly as a context-free markedness effect against the voiced velar plosive as a segment, and enhances the plausibility of the alternative contextual lenition account. The most plausible general assessment of the situation is found in Vance (1987, 111–112), where the word-internal weakening of [g] is seen as lenition, but with the usual ("natural") spirantized outcome [ɣ] preempted by ("unnatural") nasalization, for reasons internal to Japanese (as pointed out earlier, there are dialects with [ɣ] instead of [ŋ]).

McCarthy & Prince (1995), arguing against a lenition analysis and citing examples like iʃʃuukaN-ŋurai 'one week approximately', point out that the change /g/→[ŋ] here takes place post-consonantally, not intervocalically. At least in derivational terms, however, "post-consonantal" here reduces to "post-N", the nasal glide of Japanese lacking consonantal closure, i.e. a vocalic

---

[10] As is well known, [ŋ] behaves as an NC clusters not only in being absent from onsets, but also in being absent after heavy nuclei in codas – banning [ŋ] from onsets by means of a special *_[ŋ constraint tells only one half of the story. The facile adoption of such positional markedness constraints to cover some distributional facts may result in an overall loss in depth of explanation. Note, incidentally, that in our proposal in earlier work (Ito & Mester 1998) to reduce complex contextual markedness constraints to their simpler ingredients by means of constraint conjunction, e.g. coda conditions as conjunctions of NoCoda and *X (see also Ito & Mester to appear for many examples and discussion), no obvious way of expressing the force of a putative constraint *$_{Pwd}$[ŋ (or *_[ŋ) suggests itself, in the absence of elementary constraints *against* onsets and word-initial positions. Besides the obvious problems besetting constraint conjunction, this underlines the intrinsic restrictiveness of the conjunctive-reductionist approach to contextual markedness (e.g. in comparison to approaches freely fabricating constraints as the analysis develops).

segment. And considering a place-assimilated surface configuration, we find assimilation of g to ŋ ([iʃʃuukaŋ-gurai] → [iʃʃuukaŋ-ŋurai]) in a familiar context, as in the historical sequence [zɪŋgən] > [zɪŋŋən] > [zɪŋən] 'to sing' in German and other postnasal g-deleting languages, where assimilation is followed by degemination (see also Vance (1987, 108–109) and works cited there on the close relation of obstruent voicing to nasality in the history of Japanese). If so, g-weakening in Japanese is another example illustrating non-uniformity of causation in OT.

Another potential problem brought up against a lenition analysis – namely, why weakening should affect velars, but not labials and dorsals – is in fact a point in its favor since it falls under a well-known hierarchy of strength among places of articulation (cf. Foley 1977), with velars being cross-linguistically more prone to lenite than other places of articulation (as an historical example, compare the off-glide [j] in English *nail* to the corresponding [g] of the cognate German *Nagel*). Japanese itself shows intervocalic deletion of velar stops, for example, in the historical development of inflected adjectives (aka-ki > aka-i 'red-Present', cf. aka-ku 'red-Adverb'), and verbs (kak-i-te > ka-i-te 'write-Gerund', cf. kak-u 'write-Present')

A third point providing food for thought is the following. In order to get off the ground, the context-free markedness analysis (16) needs to assume the ranking *g »*ŋ. However, in a sudden reversal, the analysis needs to simultaneously rank the corresponding contextual markedness constraints in the opposite order *ₚwd[ŋ » *ₚwd[g.[11] Unless a good reason can be given for the reversal, this must count as a major liability for the analysis.[12] It remains baffling why [ŋ] should be singled out by a special proscription in word-initial position. Along the lines of Smith 2001, one could perhaps attempt to view *ₚwd[ŋ as a case of initial augmentation, but for the present case it remains unclear whether this is more than another name for the problem.

We could simply marvel at the wonders of the phonetic world and accept the exalted role of *ₚwd[ŋ as a basic fact of life, trusting that accounts in terms of "ease of articulation" or "perceptibility" can perhaps be made precise enough to be compared with a formal analysis. However, it seems reasonable at this point to reconsider the merits and demerits of a traditional lenition analysis as an alternative. Upon reflection, *ₚwd[ŋ looks more and more like an instance of one of the pitfalls of OT-analysis: the quasi-automatic conversion of cross-linguistic generalizations into constraints of Universal Grammar (the same holds, mutatis mutandis, for the syllable-initial version of the constraint, see note). While it is tempting to interpret the *cross-linguistic observation* that many languages lack "as direct evidence for the existence of a *universal constraint* *'", this is not a valid conclusion. Nothing within Optimality Theory guarantees the existence of such a position-specific markedness constraint. In the absence of solid (minimally: non-circular) reasons why word-initial [ŋ] should attract Universal Grammar's special ire, it seems more fruitful to pursue a reductionist strategy, making the absence of initial [ŋ] instead follow from the general prohibition against dorsal nasals, coupled with higher-ranking constraints leading to the appearance of [ŋ] in internal positions. But here we are on familiar territory: [ŋ] arises in certain non-initial environments because the ban against [ŋ] is overridden by well-understood phonology, including the following factors: (i) place assimilation constraints affecting nasals, (ii) lenition constraints affecting intervocalic stops, and (iii) clustering constraints affecting [ŋg], coupled with the necessity to preserve a sufficient number of place contrasts in outputs (implemented either by MaxPlace constraints (Lombardi 1998) or by direct regulation of contrasts, as in the work of Flemming 1995 and Padgett 1997).

We have at this point arrived at an arguably superior conception of [g~ŋ] allophony: The basic segmental markedness ranking is *ŋ »*g, and the contextual effect concerns word-medial [g] rather than word-initial [ŋ].

(17)

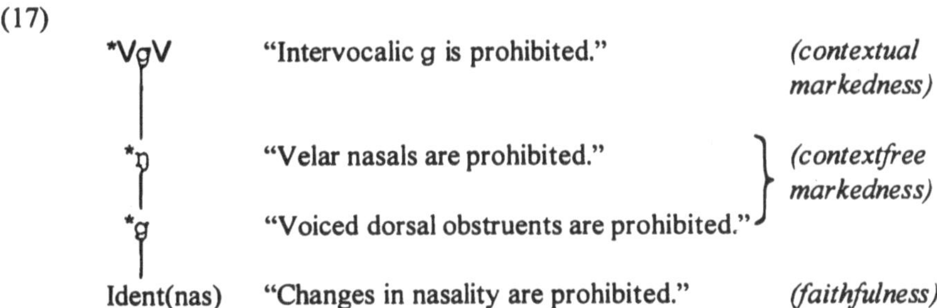

This basic analysis is illustrated in (18) and (19), using examples from the earlier discussion.[13]

A last remaining issue concerns the original motivation for the analysis in McCarthy & Prince (1995), viz., the underapplication of g-weakening in reduplicated mimetics in Japanese, as in [g]ara-[g]ara, *[ŋ]ara-[ŋ]ara, *[g]ara-[ŋ]ara 'rattling'. Their model of over- and underapplication has the property that underapplication only arises under the pressure of a specific structural constraint, otherwise overapplication (or normal application, depending on the

---

[13] A reviewer raises the question of how languages like English or German, similar to Japanese in lacking initial ŋ, but differing in allowing medial VgV, are possible in this approach. In the light of (17), the answer is simple: Such languages differ from Japanese in having *VgV ranked below IDENT(NAS).

ranking of IDENT-BR) is always optimal. In the Japanese case, it is *$_{PrWd}$ [ŋ that plays the role of the specific structural constraint leading to underapplication, as shown in (20).

(18)   input /g/:

/geta/	*VgV	*ŋ	*g	Ident(nas)
☞ geta			*	
ŋeta		*!		*
/kagi/ 'key'	*VgV	*ŋ	*g	Ident(nas)
kagi	*!		*	
☞ kaŋi		*		*

(19)   input /ŋ/

/ŋeta/	*VgV	*ŋ	*g	Ident(nas)
☞ geta			*	*
ŋeta		*!		
/kaŋi/	*VgV	*ŋ	*g	Ident(nas)
kagi	*!		*	*
☞ kaŋi		*		

(20)

/gara–RED/	Ident-BR (nas)	*$_{PrWd}$[ŋ	*g	Ident-IO (nas)
a. [ŋara–ŋara]		*!		*
b. [gara–ŋara]	*!		*	
☞ c. [gara–gara]			**	

With the new ranking in (17), this way of capturing the apparent underapplication of an allophonic process is not available since the crucial dominating constraint *$_{PrWd}$[ŋ is not present (21).

Fortunately, this is not a problem since further investigation has revealed that this putative case of an underapplying allophonic process is instead simply a case of lawful non-application: reduplicated mimetics consist of two separate prosodic words, with two accents: $_{PrWd}$[ga'ra]-- $_{PrWd}$[ga'ra], as in (22).

(21)

	/gara–RED/	Ident-BR (nas)	*VgV	*ŋ	Ident-IO (nas)
☞!!! a.	[ŋara–ŋara]			**	*
b.	[gara–ŋara]	*!		*	
c.	[gara–gara]		*!		

(22)

	/gara–RED/	Ident-BR (nas)	*VgV	*ŋ	Ident-IO (nas)
a.	[ŋara–ŋara]			**	*
b.	[gara–ŋara]	*!		*	
☞ c.	[gara–gara]				

As further support, note that in non-mimetic cases of reduplication in Japanese, where the two parts do not form separate prosodic words, ŋ-weakening applies normally. This is true both for bound reduplicative compounds like ge+ŋe 'lowest' and for free reduplicative compounds like kuni+ŋuni 'various countries' (with Rendaku-induced g further replaced by ŋ).

The upshot is that (20) is a misanalysis, (17) encounters no problem, and Japanese mimetic reduplication presents no obstacle to a theory of reduplication, less powerful than that of McCarthy & Prince (1995), which rules out any underapplication of allophonic processes.

3.2   The lexical and postlexical modules of phonology

We are now ready for the decisive move which resolves the opacity of the interaction of g-weakening with compound voicing. In the conception of an OT-grammar assumed here, the traditional distinction between lexical phonology and postlexical phonology persists as a serial interface between two separate modules of grammar. As an allophonic alternation prone to variation, g-weakening was shown in section 1 to be a prime candidate for the postlexical module. Once this is taken seriously, the ranking seen so far (given in (17)) is the postlexical one, which differs from the lexical ranking in one crucial respect: The fact that weakening is not a lexical phenomenon means that the lenition-forcing constraint *VgV must lexically rank lower than *ŋ. This is shown in (23).

(23)   Lexical ranking: no ŋ anywhere (including intersonorant position)

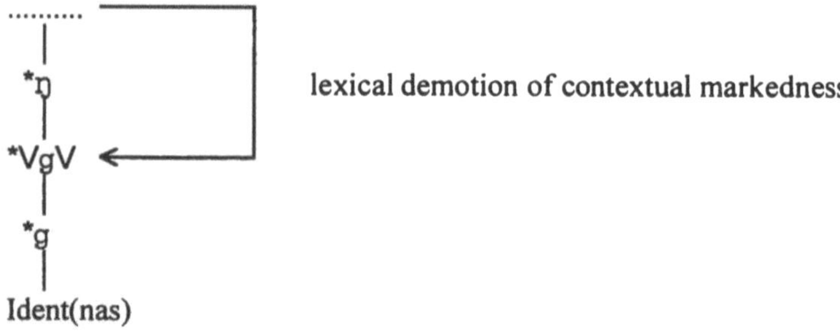

This kind of lexical demotion of contextual markedness results in the familiar restrictiveness of lexical segment inventories, in particular, as far as the admissibility of positional variants of segments (here, [ŋ] as a variant of /g/) is concerned (cf. the lexical-phonological notion of "structure preservation", see Ito & Mester to appear b). Ranked where it is in (23), i.e. immediately above its superconstraint *g, which is violated whenever *VgV is, the latter cannot do independent work at the lexical level. This OT-based notion of lexical structure preservation in no way infringes on the Richness of the Base Hypothesis. Both /ŋ/ and /g/ are viable lexical inputs, but because of high-ranking *ŋ, the candidate with [ŋ] will not be the lexical winner, as shown in (24).[14]

In accordance with the basic premises of OT, the lexical segment inventory, like any phonological inventory, is not defined separately, but derives from the constraints and their ranking in (23). The traditional lexical-phonological principle of structure preservation, built on strictly underspecificationist assumptions (see Kiparsky 1985, 92), has the effect that lexical outputs never contain elements whose specification is not possible in lexical inputs (and vice versa). In OT, the problematic link to underspecification is severed,[15] and structure preservation ceases to be a separate principle of the grammar. Instead, all structure preservation effects flow directly from the lexical constraint hierarchy. Applying Lexicon Optimization to the two tableaux in (24) and constructing a tableau des tableaux (see Ito, Mester & Padgett 1995) in (25), the /ŋ/-input is seen to be occulted by the /g/-input in the familiar way.

---

[14] This is not to say that underspecified inputs are impossible in OT. On the contrary, Richness of the Base demands that in cases like (24) representations such as /kaGi/, unspecified for [nasal], are in principle viable inputs. Because faithfulness is low-ranking, the correct output will be chosen in this case as well (see Ito & Mester 1997a, 425 – 426 for discussion).

[15] This has the independent advantage that prosodic shape and size restrictions, which could never be successfully subsumed under underspecificationist structure preservation (as already recognized in Kenstowicz & Kisseberth 1979, 434), are now dealt with in the same way as segmental restrictions.

(24)

input: /g/	/kagi/	* ŋ	*VgV	*g	Ident(nas)
	☞ kagi		*	*	
	kaŋi	*!			*
input: /ŋ/	/kaŋi/ 'key'	* ŋ	*VgV	*g	Ident(nas)
	☞ kagi		*	*	*
	kaŋi	*!			

(25)

input	output	*ŋ	*VgV	*g	Ident(nas)
☞ /kagi/	☞ kagi		*	*	
/kaŋi/	☞ kagi		*	*	*!

As seen earlier, the postlexical module admits outputs with [ŋ] under the pressure of the contextual markedness constraint *VgV, which now dominates its antagonist *ŋ.

(26)   (=17) Postlexical module: no [g] word-medially (instead: [ŋ])

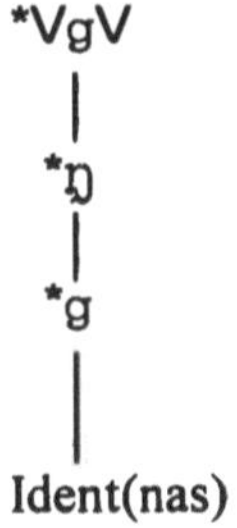

For two modules to interface serially means that the output of the first module is the input to the second module. The result is here that the lexical module has a filtering function in that lexical outputs contain no ŋ. As we have seen, the lexical constraint ranking has the effect that lexical outputs are broadly speaking phonemic. Postlexical inputs are crucially no longer *rich* and *free* , since lexical outputs, in virtue of having already run through the lexical constraint gauntlet, are ŋ-free, whereas postlexical outputs show medial [ŋ], as seen in (27). As we will see, this removes the Richness-of-the-Base problem created by opaque interactions whose masking process is allophonic.

(27)   postlexical input: always /g/

/kagi/	*VgV	*ŋ	*g	Ident(nas)
kagi	*!		*	*
☞ kaŋi		*		

We are now in a position to combine the new analysis of g-weakening with the subpart of grammar responsible for Rendaku voicing. The overall ranking of the lexical module combining all the relevant constraints is given in (28).

(28)

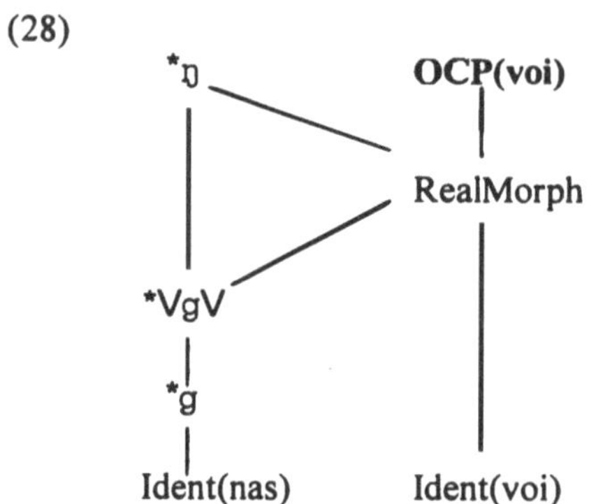

As shown in section 1, Compound Voicing has all the properties of a lexical phenomenon, being morphologically conditioned, having phonologically arbitrary exceptions, and not being subject to significant dialectal variation (i.e. no dialect has ori-kami or ike-hana), whereas velar nasalization is not only allophonic, but also subject to significant dialectal variation (many dialects have [kagi], etc. with [g], and some have [kaɣi]).

Tableau (29) shows how the structure-preserving lexical module selects outputs with Rendaku voicing realized as [g] while eschewing [ŋ]. (29) motivates the ranking REALMORPH » *VgV.

(29)   Lexical:

/ori-kami/	*ŋ	OCP (voi)	Real Morph	*VgV	*g	Id (nas)	Id (voi)
ori-kami			*!				
☞ ori-gami				*	*		*
ori-ŋami	*!					*	*

The other diagonal domination line in (28), *ŋ » REALMORPH, is motivated in (30).

(30)

/saka-toge/	*ŋ	OCP (voi)	Real Morph	*VgV	*g	Id (nas)	Id (voi)
☞ saka-toge			*	*	*		
saka-doge		*!		*	*		*
saka-toŋe	*!		*!			*	
saka-doŋe	*!						*

Since it is independently clear that REALMORPH » IDENT(VOI) (see (b) in section 1), we have *ŋ » IDENT(VOI) by transitivity. This contains an important clue for the proper understanding of the relations between the lexical and the postlexical systems.

Given what has been said so far, the overall ranking of the postlexical module appears to be the one in (31), with high-ranking *VgV triggering g-weakening.

(31) *Postlexical ranking (preliminary--to be changed)*

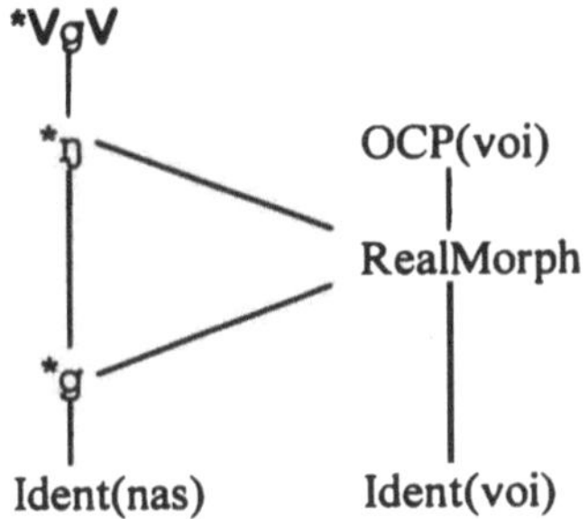

It turns out, however, that this does not yet fully capture the relation between the lexical and the postlexical phonology of voicing. The low ranking of IDENT(VOI) in (31) is an inheritance from the lexical situation, where it is demanded by the fact that Compound Voicing takes place at all. It leads to the selection of the wrong postlexical winner, as shown in (32). (32) demonstrates that the ranking *ŋ » IDENT(VOI) is only a lexical phenomenon, postlexically IDENT(VOI) ranks higher, forstalling devoicing as a repair strategy. The correct postlexical ranking is the one in (33), and (34) shows how the correct candidate [ori-ŋami] is selected.[16]

---

[16] If, adopting a richer theory of faithfulness, IDENT(+VOI) and IDENT(-VOI) are separated as distinct constraints, their ranking can be fixed as IDENT(+VOI) » REALMORPH » IDENT(-VOI) in both the lexical and the postlexical modules. This would also account for the fact that saka-toge wins over *saka-doke, see Ito & Mester (1998) for further discussion.

(32)   Postlexical:

/ori-gami/	*VgV	*ŋ	OCP (voi)	Real Morph	*g	Id (nas)	**Id (voi)**
☞!! ori-kami				*			*
ori-gami	*!			·	*		
ori-ŋami		*!				*	

(33)   Postlexical ranking (final version)

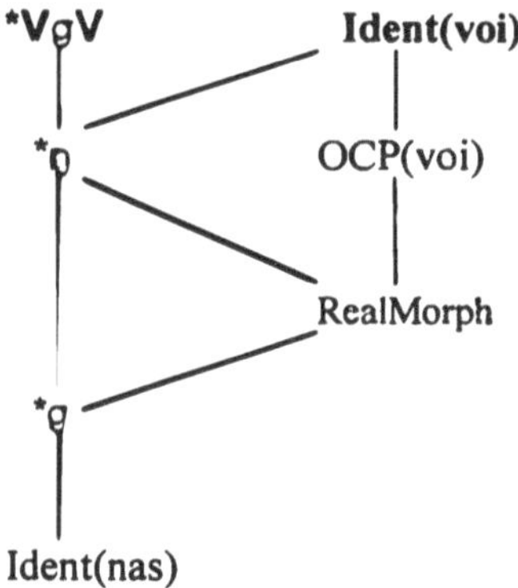

(34)   Postlexical:

/ori-gami/	*VgV	Id (voi)	*ŋ	OCP (voi)	Real Morph	*g	Id (nas)
ori-kami		*!			*		
ori-gami	*!					*!	
☞ ori-ŋami			*				*

It is now time to return to the opaque interaction that was problematic for Sympathy. Combining the separate lexical and postlexical tableaux seen earlier, (35) shows that this case of opacity resolves itself in a straightforward way--as a partial masking of a lexical pattern by a superimposed postlexical pattern. For this type of opacity, serialism remains the simplest and most explanatory account. (35a) illustrates how ŋ-less lexical outputs have no problem with overapplication of Rendaku: Since they contain medial g, voicing is blocked in the familiar way. Postlexically (35b), nasalization is enforced through high-ranking *VgV, and at the same time the lexical voicing pattern is frozen in place by high-ranking IDENT(VOI): Hence no postlexical reshuffling of Rendaku voicing patterns is possible, and sake-toŋe emerges as the ultimate winner.

(35)   a. Lexical:

/saka-toge/	*ŋ	OCP (voi)	Real Morph	*VgV	*g	Id (nas)	**Id (voi)**
☞ saka-toge			*	*	*		
saka-doge		*!		*	*		*
saka-toŋe	*!		*!			*	
saka-doŋe	*!						*

   b. Postlexical:

/saka-toge/	***VgV**	**Id (voi)**	*ŋ	OCP (voi)	Real Morph	*g	Id (nas)
saka-toge	*!				*!	*	
saka-doge	*!	*				*	
☞ saka-toŋe			*		*		*
saka-doŋe		*!	*				*

4   Conclusion

We have seen that a weakly parallel model of OT not only recaptures the central insights behind the traditional lexical/postlexical distinction, but also avoids the difficulties that Sympathy Theory faces: The Richness of the Base hypothesis is maintained, and the problem posed by opaque interactions whose masking process is allophonic disappears. A crucial role is played by the lexical module, which exerts a filtering function by restricting lexical outputs to a limited inventory ('structure preservation').

Finally, we turn to what is perhaps the most important open question: What are the limits on constraint reranking/demotion? Restricting reranking to demotion in the lexical system is a first step towards imposing limitations (in line with a suggestion by Tesar & Smolensky 1998). Note that the proposal in Ito & Mester (1999) dealing with the stratification of the lexicon is stated in terms of promotion of faithfulness in more peripheral areas, but can equivalently be characterized as demotion of faithfulness in more core areas and thus falls within the present perspective. But restricting reranking to demotion is clearly not sufficient. If nothing else is said, a promotion of a with respect to b, c and d can in general be mimicked by a demotion of b, c, and d with respect to a. Furthermore, unlimited freedom of demotion is clearly too powerful since there is nothing to prevent unwanted combinations, such as the lexical phonology of Dutch paired with the postlexical phonology of Indonesian, or the lexical phonology of Hindi with the postlexical phonology of English, etc.

While it is easy to identify the problem, it is much harder to come up with a solution. One way of restating the findings of this paper in a more general way is as follows: The monostratalism of strict parallel versions of OT undeniably has restrictiveness in its favor, as far as weak generative power is concerned. But the simultaneous loss of descriptive and explanatory adequacy is too high. We anticipate that the correct theory will impose tight limits on possible demotions. Besides the distinction between faithfulness and markedness constraints (see Ito & Mester 1999), substantive factors are likely to play a major role in defining what kinds of demotions are possible in a lexical system based on a given postlexical system. For the time being, let us take note of what the case under discussion has taught us. Taking the postlexical ranking as a baseline, perhaps acquired first (e.g. before any morpheme-specific facts are learned), we hypothesize that the more abstract lexical phonology is then acquired by the learner on its basis, by a few strategic steps of constraint demotion. For the case at hand, this is most easily seen by placing the two systems side-by-side.

(36)

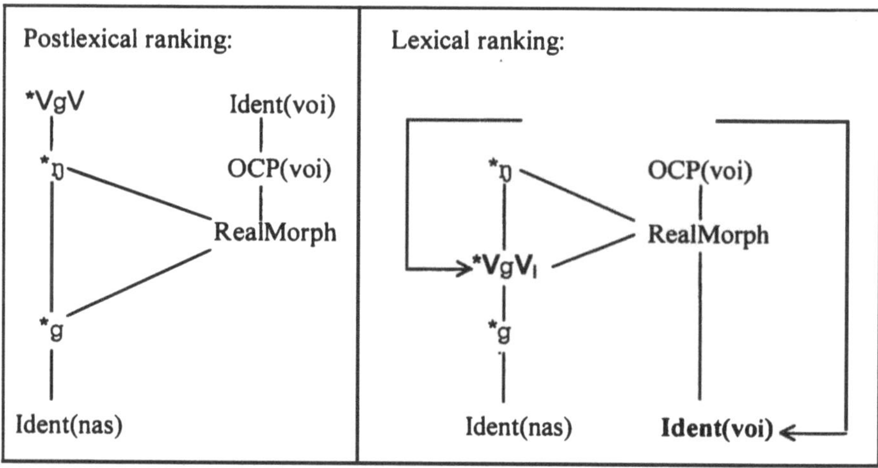

We find lexical demotions of two kinds: (i) Contextual markedness (here, *VgV) is downgraded, making the weakening of [g] a strictly postlexical affair. (ii) Faithfulness (here, IDENT(VOI)) is downgraded, enabling compound voicing as a strictly lexical process. We tentatively suggest that these two kinds of constraint demotions exhaust the range of possibilities, pending the results of further studies. The resulting picture is summarized in (37), in juxtaposition with the concepts familiar form Lexical Phonology.

(37)

constraint-based Optimality Theory:	rule-based Lexical Phonology:
faithfulness is lexically demoted	rule applies only lexically (is "turned off")
contextual markedness is lexically demoted	structure preservation holds only lexically

Finally, note that we have not seen a case of a lexical demotion of contextfree markedness below an antagonistic faithfulness constraint. This is not surprising since it would mean that the lexical system has a richer inventory than the postlexical one, with some lexical contrasts postlexically obliterated in all contexts. We speculate that abstract systems of this kind cannot arise simply because they are not learnable, i.e. the corresponding restriction need not be a formal one.

References

Barković, Eric (2000): *Harmony, Dominance, and Control*. PhD dissertation, Rutgers University, New Brunswick.

Beckman, Jill N. (1997): Positional faithfulness, positional neutralization and Shona vowel harmony. *Phonology* 14. 1–46.

Dixon, Robert M. W. (1980): *The Languages of Australia*. Cambridge: Cambridge University Press.

Flemming, Edward S. (1995): *Auditory Representations in Phonology*. PhD dissertation, UCLA, Los Angeles.

Foley, James (1977): *Foundations of Theoretical Phonology*. Cambridge: Cambridge University Press.

Haraguchi, Shosuke (2001): On Rendaku. *Phonological Studies*. Tokyo: Kaitakusha. 9–32.

Hibiya, Junko (1999): Variationist Sociolinguistics. In: Tsujimura, N., ed. (1999): *A Handbook of Japanese Linguistics*. Oxford: Blackwell. 101–120.

Ito, Junko, Mester, Armin & Padgett, Jaye (1995): Licensing and underspecification in Optimality Theory. *Linguistic Inquiry* 26:4. 571–614.

Ito, Junko & Mester, Armin (1997a): Correspondence and compositionality: The ga-gyo variation in Japanese phonology. In: Roca, I., ed. (1997): *Derivations and Constraints in Phonology*. Oxford: Oxford University Press. 419–462.

Ito, Junko & Mester, Armin (1997b): Featural Sympathy. In: Karvonen, D., Katayama, M. & Walker, R., eds. (1997): *Phonology at Santa Cruz (PASC)* 5, Santa Cruz, CA. 29–36.

Ito, Junko & Mester, Armin (1998): *Markedness and word structure: OCP effects in Japanese*. Ms, University of California, Santa Cruz. (ROA-255-0498; http://roa.rutgers.edu/)

Ito, Junko & Mester, Armin (1999): The phonological lexicon. In: Tsujimura, N., ed. (1999): *A Handbook of Japanese Linguistics*. Oxford: Blackwell. 62–100.

Ito, Junko & Mester, Armin (to appear): On the sources of opacity in OT: Coda processes in German. In: Féry, C. & Vijver, R. van de, eds. (to appear): *Structure and Typology of the Syllable*. Cambridge, UK: Cambridge University Press.

Ito, Junko & Mester, Armin (2001): Structure preservation and stratal opacity in German. In: Lombardi, Linda, ed. (2001): *Segmental Phonology in Optimality Theory*. Cambridge: Cambridge University Press. 261–295.

Kenstowicz, Michael & Kisseberth, Charles (1979): *Generative Phonology: Description and Theory*. New York: Academic Press.

Kiparsky, Paul (1973): Abstractness, opacity and global rules. In: Fujimura, O., ed. (1973): *Three Dimensions of Linguistic Theory*. Tokyo: TEC. 57–86.

Kiparsky, Paul (1982): Lexical phonology and morphology. In: Yang, I. S., ed. (1982): *Linguistics in the Morning Calm*. Seoul: Hanshin. 3–91.

Kiparsky, Paul (1985): Some consequences of Lexical Phonology. *Phonology* 2. 85–138.

Kiparsky, Paul (1998): *Paradigm effects and opacity*. Ms, Stanford University.

Kurisu, Kazutaka (2001): The Phonology of Morpheme Realization. PhD dissertation, Department of Linguistics, University of California, Santa Cruz.

Liberman, Mark & Pierrehumbert, Janet (1984): Intonational invariance under changes of pitch range and length. In: Aronoff, M. & Oehrle, R., eds. (1984): *Language, Sound, Structure*. Cambridge, MA: MIT Press. 157–233.

Lombardi, Linda (1998): *Evidence for MaxFeature constraints from Japanese*. Ms, University of Maryland.

Lubowicz, Anna (1998): *Derived environment effects in OT*. Ms, University of Massachusetts, Amherst. (ROA-239-0198; http://roa.rutgers.edu/)

Maddieson, Ian (1984): *Patterns of Sounds*. Cambridge: Cambridge University Press.

McCarthy, John J. (1998): *Sympathy and phonological opacity*. Ms, University of Massachusetts, Amherst. (ROA-252-0398; http://roa.rutgers.edu/)

McCarthy, John J. & Prince, Alan S. (1995): Faithfulness and Reduplicative Identity. In: Beckman, J., Urbanczyk, S. & Walsh, L., eds. (1995): *University of Massachusetts Occasional Papers in Linguistics UMOP* 18. Amherst, MA: GLSA. 249–384.

Otsu, Yukio (1980): Some aspects of Rendaku in Japanese and related problems. In: Farmer, A. & Otsu, Y., eds. (1980): *MIT Working Papers in Linguistics*. Cambridge, MA: Department of Linguistics and Philosophy, MIT.

Padgett, Jaye (1997): Perceptual distance of contrast: Vowel height and nasality. In: Karvonen, D., Katayama, M. & Walker, R., eds. (1997): *Phonology at Santa Cruz (PASC)* 5, Santa Cruz, CA. 63–78.

Prince, Alan & Smolensky, Paul (1993): *Optimality theory: Constraint interaction in generative grammar*. Ms, Rutgers University and University of Colorado, Boulder.

Rosen, Eric Robert (2001): *Phonological processes interacting with the lexicon: Variable and non-regular effects in Japanese phonology*. PhD dissertation, University of British Columbia.

Smolensky, Paul (1996): *The initial state and 'Richness of the Base' in Optimality Theory*. Ms, Johns Hopkins University. (ROA-154-1196; http://roa.rutgers.edu/)

Tesar, Bruce & Smolensky, Paul (1998): Learnability in Optimality Theory. *Linguistic Inquiry* 29. 229–268.

Unger, J. Marshall (2000): Rendaku and proto-Japanese accent classes. In: Nakayama, M. & Quinn, J. C. J., eds. (2000): *Japanese Korean Linguistics* 9. Stanford, CA: CSLI. 9–30.

Santa Cruz   Junko Ito and Armin Mester

University of California, Santa Cruz, Department of Linguistics, Santa Cruz, CA 95064, U.S.A. e-mail: *ito@ling.ucsc.edu, mester@ling.ucsc.edu*

The Phonological and Morphological Status of the Prosodic Word Adjunct

Marc van Oostendorp

Abstract

This paper claims that the morphological and phonological structures of derived and inflected words in Dutch tend to mirror each other. There are two types of mirroring: the constituent structures (brackets) of the morphological and the phonological structure can be aligned, or the morphosyntactic headedness can be reflected in phonological headedness, i.e. stress. In the case of derivational morphology, it is impossible that the two notions of mirroring converge: the suffix is the morphological head, so it needs to be stressed, but if the bracketing is faithfully mirrored, the suffix ends up in a phonologically adjoined position, in which it cannot receive stress. This tension causes there to be three different types of suffix: one in which the bracketing is mirrored faithfully, one in which headedness is mirrored faithfully, and one in which a compromise between the two demands is struck.

Introduction

Early versions of Prosodic Phonology, as proposed by Nespor and Vogel (1986), Selkirk (1986), Hayes (1989) and others, were based on a small set of strict, inviolable principles, such as NONRECURSIVITY, disallowing, for instance, recursive Prosodic Words (PWs), or in more general terms, tree structures such as the one in (1b):[1]

(1)   a.   NONRECURSIVITY (Selkirk 1986)
           A node at level n should not dominate another node at level n.

      b.

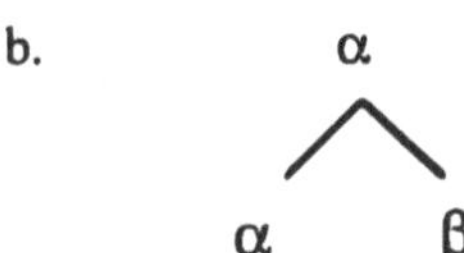

During the past years, this strict approach has been abandoned. Former 'principles' such as NONRECURSIVITY are now seen as violable constraints in an

---

[1] Thanks are due to Birgit Alber, Geert Booij, Ben Hermans, Anthi Revithiadou, Francine Swets and two anonymous reviewers for *Linguistische Berichte* for comments on a previous version.

Optimality Theoretic system (Prince and Smolensky 1993), and recursive PW structures are allowed by many scholars (cf. Selkirk 1996).

This new freedom, of course, should not go unconstrained. Even within an Optimality Theoretic analysis, NONRECURSIVITY is still a grammatical constraint, only to be violated if there is a higher-ranking constraint forcing such a violation. What are these higher-ranking constraints? Which morphological or phonological material is allowed to occur in the adjoined position to a PW (i.e. a structures of type (1b) in which α is a PW)? Concentrating on recursive PWs in Dutch these are the questions I will explore in this article.

The idea is that there are phonological restrictions and morphological requirements on position β. Phonologically, the adjoined position can only support elements that do not need a lot of licensing, hence that are (almost) empty as far as phonological features are concerned. For this reason, only schwa and coronal consonants turn up in this position. From the point of view of the interface, phonological recursive structures are used to express similar structures in the morphology. Morphological structures are of course abundant with trees of the type in (1b): in an inflected noun, for instance, α is the category N, and β the inflectional material. I will argue below that it is desirable to mirror morphological recursivity in the phonological structure. This gives us a violation of NONRECURSIVITY, provided the phonological constraints just discussed are met.

This line of reasoning then gives us some insight into two aspects of inflectional affixes. In the first place, the fact that they only consist of coronal consonants and schwa; and in the second place that they are invisible for stress. Both aspects follow from the fact that the inflectional elements end up in position β and the assumption that stress is assigned on the basis of the structure in α.

As for derivational suffixes, the issue is further complicated by the fact that they (different from inflextional suffixes) are morphological heads. I argue that there is a further constraint active in the morphology-phonology interface of natural language, which has it that morphological heads should be expressed by phonological heads, hence that morphological heads should have main stress. Having main stress is of course conflicting with being in an adjoined position. It turns out that Dutch has two classes of derivational suffixes. Some have the same kind of ('superlight') segmental makeup as inflection and also behave in the same way phonologically. Others rather have a superheavy syllable structure, which forces them to give up the alignment property, but allows them to express their morphological headship by carrying word stress instead.

With this apparatus I will discuss three types of derivational suffixes in Dutch, which I will call Type A, B and C. Type A suffixes are invisible for stress and they only contain schwa and/or coronal consonants; an example is the agentive *-er* [ər] in *waarnemer* 'observer' (from *waarneem* 'observe'). Type B suffixes do not affect the stress pattern of the base, but bear some stress themselves, giving the derived form a kind of 'compound stress'; an example of this is *-achtig* '-like' in *oranje-achtig* 'orange-like'. Type C suffixes *are* visible for stress, they incorporate into the prosodic word of the stem and attract its main stress; an example of this is *-iaan* in *Bollandiaan* 'follower of the Dutch philosopher Bolland'. These examples will be worked out in more detail below.

The structure of the argumentation in this paper is as follows. In section 1, I give a brief summary of Dutch word stress, focusing on the differences between monomorphemic forms on the one hand, and inflected and derived forms on the other. In section 2, I consider some of the theoretical options we have for analysing this difference, and conclude that it should probably follow from the interaction between purely phonological constraints on recursive PWs on the one hand, and the interaction between phonology and morphology on the other. In section 3, I then discuss the inflectional paradigms of Dutch in some more detail and in section 4, I do the same for the different types of derivational suffix. Section 5 discusses some problematic cases and section 6 is devoted to a conclusion.

1   Dutch word stress

Dutch stress is a well-studied topic within generative phonology (Van der Hulst 1984, Kager 1989, Trommelen & Zonneveld 1989, Booij 1995, Gussenhoven 1999). The stress rules are quite similar to those of English, even though there are several interesting and important differences. In any case, like the English system, Dutch word stress is very complicated. We can only give a sketch of an Optimality Theoretic analysis here; the reader is referred to Nouveau (1994), Van Oostendorp (1997), Gussenhoven (1999), as well as to the authors just cited for elaboration.

Regular stress is on the penultimate syllable of the word in most cases (2a), except if the word ends in a so-called superheavy syllable, i.e. a tense vowel followed by one, or a lax vowel followed by two consonants. In this case, word stress is on the final syllable (2b).[2]

(2)   a.   commode 'chest of drawers' [kɔmódə]
             tempo 'tempo' [tέmpo]
             motor 'engine' [mótɔr]

        b.   ledikant 'bedstead' [ledikánt]
             automaat 'automaton' [otomá:t]
             paniek 'panic' [paní:k]

[2] Another type of pattern is constituted by those words which end in a closed syllable (which is thus heavy but not superheavy) and have an open penult. These usually have stress on the first syllable of the word (*márathon*, 'id.') This is ignored here, since it does not seem very relevant for our discussion of the interaction between morphology and phonology, if only for statistical reasons: this type of pattern simply does not seem to arise often enough in derived or inflected forms to allow us to say anything sensible about them.

The standard analysis of this is that Dutch has trochaic feet, that the last trochee of the word gets main stress, and that superheavy syllables attract stress irrespective of these constraints. We can obtain this effect for instance by the constraints in (3a–c), if ranked according to (3d):

(3)   a.   TROCHEE: Feet are left-headed and bisyllabic.[3]
       b.   ALIGN(FT,R,W,R): Feet prefer the rightmost position in the syllable.
       c.   SUPERHEAVY: Superheavy syllables get stressed.[4]
       d.   SUPERHEAVY » ALIGN-R, TROCHEE

(4)

tɛmpo	SUPERHEAVY	ALIGN-R	TROCHEE
☞ tɛ́mpo			
tɛmpo			*!

Dutch also has quite a lot of forms which do not conform to this stress pattern: they have stress either on the last syllable of the word, or on the antepenultimate. A plausible solution for these would be to assume that they have some underlying accent marking and faithfulness constraints can refer to this underlying material (Van Oostendorp 1997, Alber 1998, Gussenhoven 1999). Importantly, the relevant faithfulness constraints are not undominated. Superheavy syllables are always stressed,[5] for instance, so that we may assume that the relevant faithfulness constraint is sandwiched between SUPERHEAVY and the other two constraints (some other stress constraints seem inviolable as well – notably those responsible for the fact that stress is always on one of the last three syllables in Dutch –, but these will be ignored here; since we will be dealing with *suffixes* in our discussion on the interaction between prosodic structure and morphology, structures in which stress is outside of the three-syllable window can be safely left out of consideration).

(5)

pani:k	SUPERHEAVY	ALIGN-R	TROCHEE
páni:k	*!		
☞ paní:k		.	*

(6) *chocolg* 'chocolate' [ʃokolá], *Panama* (place name) [pánama]

---

[3] For present purposes (given the simplified nature of the stress analysis), we do not have to go into the question as to whether the trochees at hand are quantity-sensitive or not.

[4] This constraint is probably best seen as a shorthand for a number of constraints on the relation between syllable structure and stress; cf. Booij (1995) and references cited there.

[5] In some forms, they get secondary stress, rather than primary which is on the antepenult.

(7)

a. IDENT-STRESS: Underlying stress patterns should be respected.				
b. ʃokolá	SUPER HEAVY	IDENT-STRESS	ALIGN-R	TROCHEE
ʃokolá		*!		
☞ ʃokolá				*

c. pánama	SUPER HEAVY	IDENT-STRESS	ALIGN-R	TROCHEE
panámá		*!		
☞ pánama			*	

d. páni:k	SUPER HEAVY	IDENT-STRESS	ALIGN-R	TROCHEE
paní:k		*		*
☞ páni:k	*!			

(7b) and (7c) show how word stress can show up on the final or antepenultimate syllable of the word, respectively. (7d) shows how stress cannot escape the superheavy syllable, even if it would be underlyingly postulated on a different syllable.

One other generalisation about Dutch word stress is also relevant: the generalisation that stress is on the penultimate syllable is virtually exceptionless if the final syllable contains a schwa (Kager and Zonneveld 1986).[6] We will provisionally analyse this by positing the constraint in (8), which should outrank IDENT-STRESS (cf. Van Oostendorp 2000 for elaboration and discussion):

(8)   WEAK-SCHWA: Schwa should be in the dependent position of a foot.

Because of high-ranking WEAK-SCHWA (and the fact that the Dutch foot is trochaic), the syllable immediately preceding schwa should be in the head position of a foot, hence, stressed. Even if we would posit an underlying accent on any other syllable in a word, such as *commọde* 'chest of drawers', the stress would always be attracted to the penultimate syllable:

---

[6] There is one, small, class of exceptions, viz. words (a few place names and the word *weduwe* 'widow') ending in [ywə] which have stress on the antepenult (Trommelen and Zonneveld 1989). It is sometimes assumed that in these cases the [y] is 'really' a schwa underlying. In any case, I do not think these examples disconfirm the statement in the text; they just show that it needs further refinement.

(9)

kómodə	SUPER HEAVY	WEAK-SCHWA	IDENT-STRESS	ALIGN-R	TROCHEE
kómodə		*!			
☞ komódə			*		*

Having set up this (heavily simplified) picture of the basics of the Dutch stress system, we can now turn to the interaction with morphological structure, in particular on suffixing, since we are looking at the right edge of the word and since most affixes are right-adjoining in the language.[7]

We can observe immediately that the generalisation just established no longer holds if the final consonant is an inflectional morpheme. In that case, the stress can be on any of the last three syllables of the word, depending only on where it is in the uninflected form; in particular, it can occur in the syllable imnmediately before a 'superheavy'syllable (*kanaries* 'canaries' [kanári:s], cf. *kanarie* 'canary' [kanári:]; *geharnast* 'armoured' [ɣəhárnɑst], cf. *harnas* 'to gird oneself (STEM)' [hárnɑs],). These examples show that there is no difference between verbal and nominal inflection in this respect. Since these words now end in a 'superheavy syllable' we would expect them to be stressed on this syllable (the sad face indicates a winning candidate that does not correspond to the actually attested form):

(10)

ge+harnas+t ɣəhárnɑst	SUPER HEAVY	IDENT-STRESS	ALIGN-R	TROCHEE
ɣəhárnɑst	*!			
☹ ɣəharnɑ́st		*		*

(11)

kanari+s kanári:s	SUPER HEAVY	IDENT-STRESS	ALIGN-R	TROCHEE
kanári:s	*!			
☹ kanarí:s		*		*

Similarly, there is a range of inflectional suffixes which host a schwa. In underived words, this schwa forces stress in its lefthand neighbour, but this does not happen if the schwa is part of an inflectional suffix. An example of this is the verbal plural suffix *-en* (pronounced [ə] in some dialects and as [ən] in others, but this of course is irrelevant).

---

[7] It is not our goal to discuss all details of the behaviour of every individual suffix in Dutch here. See Trommelen and Zonneveld (1989), Booij (1995), Kager (forthcoming) for discussion.

(12)

harnas+en hárnasə	WEAK- SCHWA	IDENT-STRESS	ALIGN-R	TROCHEE
hárnasə	*!			
☹ harnásə		*		*

If we now turn our attention to derivational suffixes, the picture changes completely. We actually can distinguish between three types of suffix, which I have called type A, B and C above. Most suffixes in Dutch, as in other Germanic languages, are of type C. Most derived words have the same stress pattern as underived words with a comparable phonological structure. Since most derivational suffixes consist of a superheavy syllable or are bisyllabic with the second syllable a schwa, this means that they are stressed:

(13)   *anoniem*   [anoní:m]   'anonymous'
         anonimiteit   [anoni:mitɛ́it]   'anonymity'
         ceremonie   [sɪ:rəmóni]   'ceremony'
         ceremonieel   [sɪ:rəmonijél]   'ceremonial'
         hobby   [hóbi]   'hobby'
         hobbyist   [hɔbijɪíst]   'hobbyist'

There also is a suffix *-isch* [i:s] which is 'stress-attracting', which is to say that it does not bear stress itself, but shifts the stress of the stem. The fact that it does so is of course problematic, since the suffix is a superheavy syllable. It has received quite a lot discussion in the literature (Haeseryn et al. 1997: 718–721, Trommelen and De Haas 1993:328–331, Trommelen and Zonneveld 1989: 204–208).

    A few examples are given in (14):[8]

(14)   *proz* [próza] 'prose'   *prozaïsch* [[prozá]i:s] 'prosaic'

I will briefly return to the structure of this curious suffix in section 5.2, but leave it aside until then. There also are two classs of derivational suffixes that are stress-neutral: the so-called 'non-cohering' stress-neutral suffixes of Dutch (the terminology is from Booij 1995), an example of which are given in (15a), and a separate class of so-called 'cohering' suffixes, exemplified in (15b):

---

[8] Other suffixes are stress-attracting in a somewhat different way. These are suffixes such as *-ig*, *-elijk*, and *-baar* (cf. (i)).
    (i) *gọdsdienst* 'religion' (< *god* 'god', *dienst* 'service') - *godsdịẹnstig* 'religious'
        sprẹẹkwoord 'proverb' (< *spreek* 'speak', *woord* 'word') - *spreekwọọrdelijk* 'proverbial'
        waạrneem 'observe' (< *waar* 'true', *neem* 'take') - *waarneẹmbaar* 'observable'
In all these cases the kind of stress that shifts is a kind of compound stress. We do not see the effect if these suffixes are attached to underived stems. For this reason, the fall outside the scope of the discussion.

(15)   a. [[*prǫza*]-*achtig*] (**prozǫ-achtig, *proza-ǫchtig*) 'prose-like'

       b. [[*wǫarnem*]er] (**waarnǫmer*) 'observer'

I call 'cohering' suffixes 'Type A' and 'non-cohering' suffixes 'Type C'. The difference between non-cohering and cohering suffixes is one of phonological behaviour, for instance with respect to syllabification. There is no resyllabification across the boundary between a stem and a non-cohering suffix, whereas there is resyllabification across the boundary between a stem and a cohering suffix:

(16)   a. *rood-achtig* [rot. ɑx. təx] 'red-like'

       b. [[*spreekwoord*]*elijk*] [sprek. wo:r. də. lək] 'proverbial'

There is a simple test for resyllabification in Dutch, because the language has final devoicing: all syllable-final obstruents are devoiced. Because of this, we know that the stem-final /d/ has been resyllabified into an onset position in (16b), but not in (16a). This makes the difference between cohering and non-cohering suffixes: the former integrate with the syllable structure of the stem, whereas the latter do not.[9]

These suffixes will be discussed in more detail in section 4. In conclusion, we can now make the following generalisations:

A   All inflectional suffixes are invisible for stress

B   There are two types of derivational suffixes: some are invisible for stress; others prefer to bear stress themselves. The derivational suffixes that are vissible all start with a vowel and consist of a superheavy syllable (rhyme). The derivational suffixes that are invisible start with a consonant, or they only have a schwa vowel or no vowel at all.

2 Possible explanations for the stress behaviour of suffixes

Why are all inflectional and some derivational suffixes invisible for stress? One possible answer, explored in detail in Booij (1977), is a derivational one: some suffixes are invisible for stress because they are attached to the stem *after* application of the stress rules. We thus have the following picture:

---

[9] Another test is the behaviour of schwa, which disappears before a vowel if this vowel belongs to a cohering-suffix (*elite* /əlitə/ + *air* /ɛ:r/ = [əlitɛ:r], *[əlitəɛ:r]; but *elite+achtig* 'elitist' with non-cohering *achtig* = [əlitəɑxtəx]).

(17)

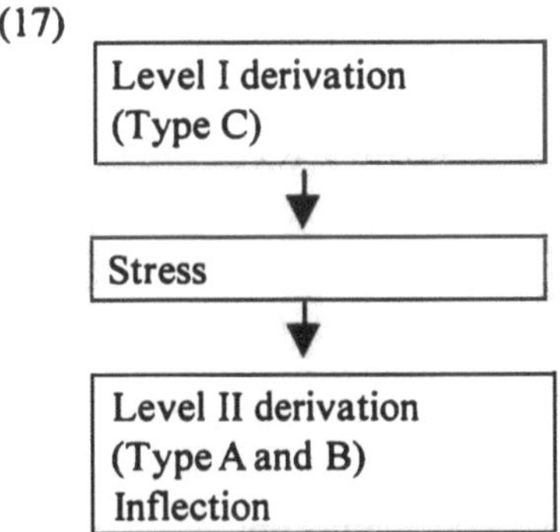

This model has the advantage that it is quite simple and that it explains other phenomena – viz., the fact that inflection is peripheral to derivation and that most Level II derivation is peripheral to Level I derivation. Yet there are several problems with it, in particular as far as the ordering of the two lexical levels is concerned (as has been pointed out by Booij and Van Santen 1998: 205–206 and others). For instance, the restrictions on Level I suffixes are such that they can only freely combine with non-native elements (derived or underived stems); since Level II suffixes are arguably 'native', there thus is no reason to explain why Level I suffixes cannot usually be attached in their periphery. Furthermore, there are several classes of cases in which accent-bearing (or -shifting) suffixes follow accent-neutral ones.

Within Optimality Theory, we could alteratively assume that inflected word are in a paradigm and, therefore, sensitive to a form of Output-Output faithfulness (the stress pattern of the inflected form mirrors that of the uninflected form) that does not apply to derived words (Benua 1997, McCarthy 2001). We thus would have a constraint IDENT$_{OO}$-STRESS, that would be inviolable:[10]

(18)

kanarie+s kanári:s	IDENT$_{OO}$- STRESS	SUPER HEAVY	WEAK- SCHWA	IDENT- STRESS	ALIGN -R	TROCHEE
kanarí:s	*!			*		*
☞ kanári:s		*				

This analysis would share many of its properties with the derivational account just sketched, and it could relate the difference between inflectional affixes on the one hand and derivational affixes on the other to a morphological difference between the two categories (the fact that inflections are also morphologically

---

[10] Another possibility would be to mimick the derivational approach just outlined, and two assume that there are two different grammatical levels, an early one in which Superheavy, WEAK-SCHWA » IDENT-STRESS, (where the Identity-constraint would refer to underlying stress) and a later one in which IDENT-STRESS » Superheavy, WEAK-SCHWA (where the Identity-constraint would refer to stress assigned in the lexicon).

peripheral to derivations). Technically, it would be possible to derive the relevant contrasts, which is hardly a surprise if we take into consideration the inherent power of a theory of OO-faithfulness.

A problem specific to this account would be that it would not be able to explain why some derivational affixes behave like inflections whereas others do not (although it would of course always be possible to arbitrarily stipulate that only the inflectional endings and a subset of derivational suffixes trigger OO-faithfulness constraints). The derivational account suffers somwhat from the same problem, but at least some predictions would follow about the relative ordering of the derivational suffixes (they would have to be peripheral to the derivational endings that do not behave like inflectional endings; and they should potentially be more similar to inflection also in other aspects of phonological behaviour).

Another point about both of these analyses is that they do not explain what the relation is between the fact that inflectional suffixes are phonologically almost completely empty and their stress behaviour. They do not contain a vowel, or if they do, the vowel is schwa, and all consonants involved are coronals (*-s,-t, -n*), i.e. consonants with a minimally marked place specification.[11] The following is a complete list of inflectional suffixes in Standard Dutch:

(19)   **verbal:**
     -en /ə(n)/   (infinitive, plural; e.g. *werken* 'to work')
     -t /t/   (2nd & 3rd person present tense; *werkt* 'work(s)')
     -te /-de /tə/-/də/   (singular past tense; *werkte* '(he) worked')
     -ten /-den /tən/-/dən/   (plural past tense; *werkten* '(they) worked')
     -t /-d /t/-/d/   (past participle; *gewerkt* '(have) worked')[12]
     -end /ənd/   (present participle; *werkend* 'working')

     adjectival:
     -e /ə/   ((agreement; e.g. *mooie* 'beautiful')

     nominal:
     -en/-eren/-s /ə(n)/ -/ərə(n)/ -/s/
                           (plural; e.g. *boeken* 'books', *kinderen* 'kids', *werkers* 'workers'),
     -s /s/   (genitive; e.g. *Jans boek* 'John's book')

---

[11] A similar observation has been made by Hoekstra (2000: 138–139), who extends it to function words. Hoekstra states two generalisations (i. Function words often contain schwa, ii. Function words often contain a coronal consonant) and claims: "Both of these generalisations not only are true for Standard Dutch, but also for the Dutch dialects I know of." Hoekstra points out that similar generalisations can be made for English.

[12] The choice of a voiced vs. a voiceless stop in past tense forms is dictated by the voice specification of the last segment of the stem.

Type A derivational suffixes, which show the same behaviour, strikingly also
have the same form:

(20)   *-e* /ə/   (several functions)
        -el /əl/   (denominal verbalizing suff.)
        -en /ən/   (pl.suff.)
        -er /ər/   (several functions, plus allomorph /a : r/[13])
        -erd /ərd/   (creates deadject. pejorative names)
        -erig /ərəɣ/   '-ish'
        -ing /ɪŋ/   '-ing'

        -nis /nɪs/   '-ness'[14]
        -s /s/   (substantivizing suff, pl. suff., gen.suff.)
        -sel /səl/   (creates de-verbal nominalizing suff.)
        -st /st/   (superl., de-verbal nominalizing suff.)
        -ster /stər/   (feminizing suff.)
        -t /t/   (de-verbal nominalizing suff.)[15]
        -te /tə/   '-ness'
        -tje /tjə/   diminutive (plus allomorphs)

A purely representational approach therefore seems more viable. Such an
approach would derive the phonological behaviour of the various suffixes of
their phonological shape. This is indeed suggested by Booij (1995) and Booij
and Van Santen (1997), but the details are yet to be worked out in full detail.
We have seen above that the way a given suffix will behave is indeed almost
completely predictable, if we know its phonological shape. If it has a schwa, it
will be Type C, if it has a full vowel it will be either Type A or Type B.

It seems more attractive to assume that phonological properties of morphemes can be deduced from their phonological shape. There still is a problem
with such an approach, however: inflected and derived words ending e.g. in a
schwa syllable are still different from their monomorphemic counterparts. Furthermore, inflected words ending in a superheavy syllable are different from
both the derived and the monomorphemic forms with a similar segmental
makeup.

I conclude from this that we need an analysis in which the phonological
structure of derived and inflected words needs to reflect on the one hand the
underlying phonological material of both stem and affix, and on the other hand
the fact that these words are morphologically complex. I will try to develop
such an analysis in the next section.

---

[13] Cf. Van Oostendorp (1999) for an account that is compatible with the one presented
here.

[14] It is not clear to me why this suffix is included in this list, i.e. why Booij supposes it to be
non-cohering; if it is, it obviously is exceptional, be it that Booij (1995) notes that some people
pronounce this suffix always with schwa. Also, suffixes with coronal vowels will be shown to be
exceptional in other cases.

[15] This suffix also functions as a (equally stress-neutral) inflection for the third person singular. This function is not mentioned by Booij (1995).

3 Morphology and phonology in the stress behaviour of inflection

If the stress behaviour of suffixes is to be seen as a result of the interaction of phonological constraints on the relation between segmental makeup and stress on the one hand, and morphological constraints on the other, we should first try to establish what the relevant constraints are, and then what the interaction between those constraints is.

As far as the phonological constraints are concerned, the null hypothesis is that these are the same for polymorphemic as for monomorphemic forms, except perhaps in so far as the morphology forces us to assume 'exceptional' phonological structures.

I propose that one of the most important morphological constraints in explaining the behaviour of inflected forms is MIRRORING:

(21)   MIRRORING
         The prosodic structure of a word should be isomorphic to its morphological structure.

According to MIRRORING, a prosodic word should be recursive if it corresponds to a recursive word. Inflected forms are instances of such recursive morphological structures: they are a word embedded in a word. For instance, a plural noun *kanaries* recursively contains a singular noun *kanarie.*

MIRRORING is a fairly general (one might even say imprecise) type of constraint. We will see below that it is possible to break it down, at least partly, into a set of formally simpler constraints. A fairly plausible candidate for part of MIRRORING would be the Anchor-constraint schema as proposed by McCarthy and Prince (1999):

(22)   {Right, Left-}ANCHOR(S_1, S_2)
         Any element at the designated periphery of S_1 has a correspondent at the designated periphery of S_2.

If we set the value of S_1 to the morphological word, and S_2 to the phonological word, we obviously get mirroring of morphological and syntactic constituency. Yet I will argue below that mirroring might also be satisfied in other ways, in particular by mirroring of morphosyntactic headedness into phonological headedness (stress).

I will not go into this matter any further, since one general constraint of the type in (21) will do and make my tableaux easier to read. Furthermore, we will see below that there are other ways in which morphological structure can be mirrored in prosody, beyond demarcation of left and right boundaries. In principle, it clearly is possible however to replace this one constraint by a family of constraints in many cases. Another question that will be left unanswered is what is the ontological basis for MIRRORING or ANCHORING.

As such, the principle claims that the optimal prosodic structure for such words should also contain a recursive prosodic word (PW), so that the structure looks as follows:

(23)   ((kanari꞉   )ₚw   s)ₚw   Prosodic Structure
            [[kanarie   ]ɴ   s]ɴ   Morphology

Formally, MIRRORING expresses the tendency for different levels of linguistic structure to be isomorphic (Jackendoff 1996). In more functional terms, the fact that morphological structure is reflected in the phonology, might make it easier for the listener to parse that word (cf. Kaye 1995).[16]

The fact that words are pronounced in a way that is impossible for mono-morphemic forms is a clue that they have more structure.

(24)

kanarie+s kanári꞉s	MIRRORING	SUPER HEAVY	WEAK-SCHWA	IDENT-STRESS
kanarí꞉s	*!			*
☞ kanári꞉s		*		

If we assume that stress assignment is restricted to the internal PW,[17] MIRRORING has the same effect as IDENT$_{OO}$-STRESS in the hypothetical OO-analysis given above: stress is decided at the level of the singular form, and the inflectional suffix is irrelevant. In my view, MIRRORING has the additional advantage of helping to explain why all suffixes which display this behaviour are also very minimally specified from a phonological point of view. We propose that the reason for this is a form of Prosodic Licensing, formalised as a family of constraints on feature licensing (Ito 1986 and much subsequent work):[18]

(25)   LICENSE/F: The phonological feature F should be in the head of a recursive Prosodic Word (i.e. not adjoined).

---

[16] Kaye (1995) distinguishes in this regard between 'analytic' and 'non-analytic' morphology. An example of the former is English *peeped*, an example of the latter English *kept*. The former contains a structure (a long tense vowel followed by two consonants) that is not attested in English forms. The latter could be a monomorphemic form in principle, and Kaye assumes that in a way, it is (it is stored in the lexicon). Kaye observes that non-analytic forms are often exceptional, get specialized meaning, etc.

[17] This can be accomplished by assuming that every Prosodic Word needs to correspond to exactly one location of main stress. If that is the case, stress can only be in the innermost Prosodic Word (where it is inside the outermost Prosodic Word at the same time). If it would be somewhere outside the innermost Prosodic Word, this innermost PW would not have stress; or if it would have stress, there would be two loci for main stress in the outermost PW. In both cases we would violate the assumed principle (or constraint).

[18] Note that LICENSE/F is a form of positional markedness constraint which can do much of the work of the universal hierarchy of positional faithfulness constraints Faith[stem]»Faith[affix] which is assumed in other parts of the literature.

Notice that LICENSE/F is a scheme of purely phonological constraints, which are not used hitherto in the analysis of underived forms. This may look like we are abandoning our null hypothesis, but the only reason for doing this is that we have not yet seriously considered the possibility of recursive prosodic words. Below, it will be shown that we need LICENSE also for monomorphemic forms once we take this formal possibility into account.

A hierarchy of LICENSE/F constraints is arranged according to the usual criteria of segmental markedness. For instance we have a subranking LICENSE/LABIAL, LICENSE/VELAR » LICENSE/CORONAL, since labial and velar segments are usually assumed to be more marked than coronals.

Combining this hierarchy of constraints with MIRRORING gives us the desired effect. We can now postulate a ranking LICENSE/Labial, LICENSE/Velar » MIRRORING » LICENSE/Coronal, so that coronal segments are, but labial and velar consonants are not allowed to occur in an adjoined position to the word. We thus could not have labial and velar consonants in a suffix displaying the same behaviour.

A similar ranking for vocalic material will give us as a result that only the most unmarked vowel (schwa) can occur in an adjoined position. In this case, we may assume that schwa does not have any place feature marking at all.

On the other hand, not every coronal consonant and not every schwa is adjoined. In monomorphemic forms, they are usually incorporated in the word, at least if this is possible, as is attested by examples such as *automaat* 'automation' and *perkament* 'parchment' above. Even coronal segments are subject to Licensing only occur in an adjoined position if this is necessary for some reason; e.g. to satisfy MIRRORING. Since these are monomorphemic forms, MIRRORING does not play a role. Therefore the coronal consonants are integrated into the PW in these cases:

(26)

automaat autóma:t	LICENSE/ Labial	MIRRORI NG	LICENSE/ Coronal	SUPER HEAVY	IDENT- STRESS	ALIGN-R	TROCHEE
☞ automá:t					*		*
autóma:t			*!	*			

Interestingly, coronal consonants (but no others) can still be outside the PW in monomorphemic forms. If all the positions in the final syllable of the word are 'filled up' as it were, we can still find one or more coronal obstruents. We thus have words such as *herfst* 'fall' in which a superheavy syllable is followed by *st*. Consonants with other places of articulation are not allowed in this position (this is an observation that is of course quite familiar from the literature: cf. Halle and Vergnaud 1987, Van Oostendorp 2000, and references cited there). We thus have the following structures for different classes of words:[19]

---

[19] Glosses: *perkament* 'parchment', *herfst* 'autumn', *adem+t* 'breathes', *denk+t* 'thinks'.

(27)

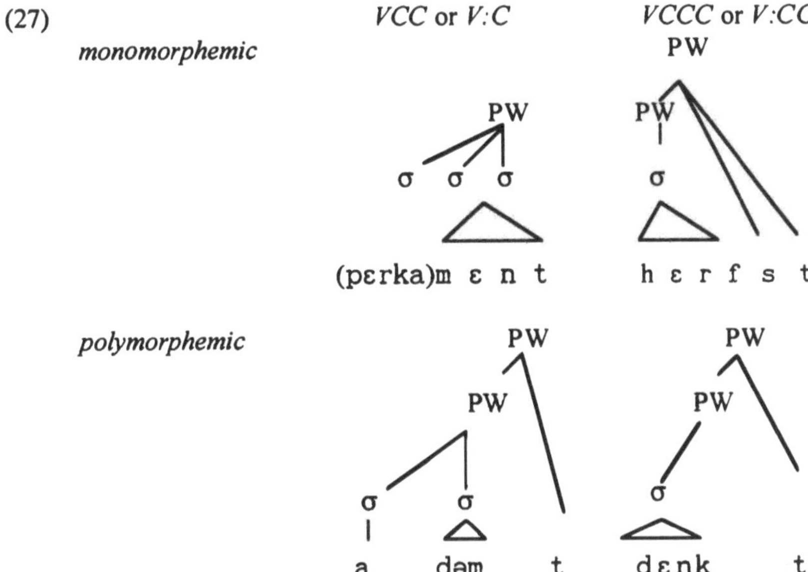

The difference between monomorphemic and polymorphemic forms thus is that the final coronals are always in adjoined position in the latter, whereas this only happens in the former if this is necessary for phonotactic reasons. In both cases, coronals are the only segments that can occur in such a position. The hierarchy of LICENSE constraints thus also plays a role in monomorphemic forms. This is why their introduction does not qualify as a departure of the null hypothesis, that the phonology 'proper' of inflected and derived forms is not different from that of monomorphemes.[20]

The question why all inflectional elements are empty, while many derivational elements are not, is still an open one. First, we observe that it is quite desirable for a suffix to be underlyingly specified as coronal only, for it can satisfy MIRRORING and the highest ranking members of the LICENSE family at the same time in this way. The principle of Lexicon Optimisation will thus cause productive suffixes to eventually end up as being specified as coronal (or containing a schwa): the best suffix is the one that will have a possibility of surfacing unharmed in the relevant environments. For inflectional suffixes this is even more profitable than for derivational ones, since the former are always peripheral to the latter. The reasons for this are probably independent: they have to do with the fact that inflection needs to be visible for syntax. 'Empty' suffixes that often occur before 'non-empty' ones, still cannot satisfy MIRRORING. Otherwise, they would drag the following suffixes to a peripheral position. We

---

[20] Schwa does not seem to be in an adjoined position in monomorphemic forms, since there is no phonotactic reason for vowels to occur in such a position.

thus, correctly, expect the more peripheral suffixes to be emptier than the more central ones.[21]

But there might be another reason as well: derivational suffixes might reflect the morphological structure of words in some other way. A morphological difference between inflectional and derivational morphemes is that the latter but not the former are morphological heads. This means that they are sensitive to another constraint on the interface between morphology and prosody, a constraint that describes the way in which morphological headedness should be expressed in the phonology, namely by phonological headedness, i.e. stress. This line of reasoning will be pursued in the next section.

4   The stress pattern of derivational suffixes

We have seen in section 2 that there are basically three types of derivational suffixes in Dutch:

A.   suffixes that are invisible for stress and that contain a schwa or only coronal consonants, such as *-de* and *-s*. These derivational suffixes can get the same analysis as the inflectional suffixes in the previous section; they will be ignored here,

B.   suffixes that do not affect the stress pattern of the stem, but rather give some kind of 'compound stress',

C.   suffixes that are visible for stress, and that are (usually) stress-bearing.

We have argued above that the behaviour of type A suffixes can be explained by the tendency to reflect morphological recursion by phonological recursion. The question now arises whether and how the other phonological structures reflect the morphology.

The answer to this question seems easiest to provide for type B suffixes. The following list is exhaustive:

[21] An additional reason might be syntactic visibility: maybe the fact that morphological structure is mirrored in the phonology is particularly relevant for the type of morphology that plays a role in syntax, i.e. inflection. However, this does not explain why some derivational suffixes, but not others, behave in the same way. Furthermore, a reviewer of this paper points out that there might be functional considerations at stake: in a language such as Dutch, we only have a handful of inflectional endings, but considerably more derivational suffixes. It would be hard to make all the relevant distinctions needed for derivation with only coronals and schwa.

(28)   *-achtig* /ɑxtɪx/ '-like'
         -loos /loːs/ '-less'
         -ling /lɪŋ/ '-PERSON'
         -baar /baːr/ '-*abl*'
         -dom /dom/ '-NOM'
         -heid /hɛit/ '-NOM'
         -nis /nɪs/ '-NOM'
         -schap /sxɑp/ '-NOM'
         -zaam /zaːm/ '-ADJ'

These forms all have a full vowel, and even a superheavy syllable. Therefore, they cannot occur in an adjoined position tot the phonological word. In stead of this they phonologically have a compound structure with a primary stress on the first syllable that would get primary stress in 'normal' compounds as well (Booij 1995):

(29)   a.   *werkzaam* [ʋέrkzàːm] 'working'

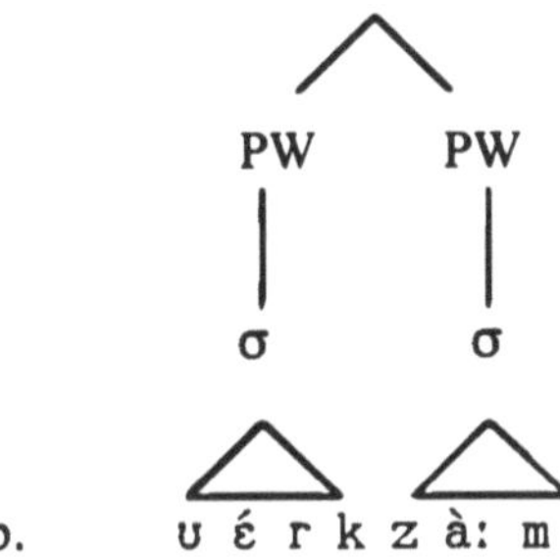

         b.   ʋ έ r k z àː m

The intuition to be formally worked out here, is that the structure in (28) is 'second best', given that adjunction is unattainable for suffixes of this shape: the morphological complexity is at least reflected in some kind of phonological complexity. One way of implementing this is by invoking an Alignment constraint:

(30)   ALIGN(PW, X0): Boundaries of morphosyntactic words should be
         aligned with boundaries of phonological words.

ALIGN and MIRRORING are in a so-called Paninian relation (Prince and Smolensky 1993): the latter is more specific than the former, in the sense that there are forms satisfying ALIGN but not MIRRORING (Class B suffixes are an instance of this) but not the other way around.

I will argue below that class B suffixes are actually close to the ideal type of derivational suffix, as far as their phonological shape is concerned. Before we go into this, we first have to look at the suffixes of class C. Words with such a suffix are indistinguishable from monomorphemes as far as their phonological

shape is concerned. The suffixes themselves have the following shape (in parentheses I have provided a rough English equivalent for every Dutch suffix):

(31)   *-aal* /aːl/ '-al'   *-egge* /ɛɣə/ '-in'   *-ief* /iːf/ '-ive'
        -aan /aːn/ -'an'   *-erij* /ərɛi/ '-ery'   *-iek* /iːk/ '-ic'
        -age /aˇZ'/ '-age'   -es /Es/ '-ess'   -iet /iˇt/ '-ite'
        -air /Eˇr/ -'air'   -esk /Esk/ '-esque'   -ieus /ijOˇs/ '-ious'
        -ast /Ast/ -'ast'   -eur /Oˇr/ '-or'   -in /In/ '-in'
        -eel /eːl/ '-al'   *-eus* /øːs/ '-ous'   *-iseer* /isɪːr/ '-ize'
        -eer /ɪːr/ '-ize'   *-iaan* /ijaːn/ '-ian'   *-isme* /ɪsmə/ '-ism'
        -ees /es/ -'ous'   *-ide* /iːdə/ '-ide'   *-ist* /ɪst/ '-ist'
                                                                   -iteit /iːtɛit/ '-ity'
                                                                   -ei /ɛi/ '-y'

These elements have two things in common: they all start with a vowel, and
they all have a superheavy syllable rhyme, or else a schwa. In other words, they
seem to be built to capture stress.

   Two questions now arise. First, why would all these suffixes be superheavy?
Secondly, what is the difference in shape between these suffixes and those in
(28) that can explain the differences in behaviour?

   I think the answer to the first question can be found in Revithiadou (1999),
who claims that in languages such as Modern Greek and Russian, stress is
determined by morphological headedness. In all of these languages, every morpheme can be specified for underlying accent, yet in any given word, at most
one accent can surface. Revithiadou suggests that the question *which* of the
underlying accent specifications surfaces is decided by morphological considerations: the 'morphological head' of a complex form tends to win.

   Revithiadou (1999) shows that in Greek this means that in derivational morphology it is the derivational suffix that determines the accentual pattern of the
word, whereas in inflected forms it is always the stem that decides.[22] The
reason for this is that derivational suffixes are morphological heads, e.g. because
they determine the category of the stem, whereas inflectional suffixes are not
heads. We thus find that stress specifications of stems are unaffected by
inflectional endings (32a), but they can shift in derived forms (32b):

---

[22] In present-day generative syntax, the standard conception seems to be that inflectional
affixes *are* heads. This raises the question what the relation is between the morphological and the
syntactic head (as well as what is left of the distinction between inflection and derivation in syntactic theories of this type).

(32)   a.   papayal-os   'parrot-NOM.SG.'
             papayal-u   GEN.SG.
             papayal-i   NOM.PL.
             papayal-on   GEN.PL.

        b.   papayal-aku   'little parrot'

Revithiadou (1999) proposes constraints of the following type in order to account for this:

(33)   a. HEAD-FAITH: Morphological heads should be faithful to their underlying accentual specification.

        b. HEAD-STRESS: Morphological heads should be stressed.

What I want to propose here is that in the Dutch lexicon we can still see the traces of HEAD-STRESS. This is true in particular for HEAD-STRESS. This implies that derivational suffixes prefer to be stressed, and this in turn makes it most profitable for them to be superheavy.

The superheaviness of derivational 'Level I' suffixes in my view is not necessarily the result of constraint ranking; it may also be simply due to Lexicon Optimisation: in the course of time most suffixes happen to have taken up this shape, but this is not a necessary property of suffixes. In the course of time, superheavy forms of suffixes would have been preferred over smaller shapes:[23]

(34)

Mohammed+aan mohamɛd+a:n	SUPER HEAVY	IDENT- STRESS	ALIGN- R	TROCHEE	HEAD- STRESS
☞ mohamɛdá:n				*	
mohamɛ́da:n	*!				*

(35)

*Mohammed+aan mohamɛd+an	SUPER HEAVY	IDENT- STRESS	ALIGN- R	TROCHEE	HEAD- STRESS
mohamɛdán				*!	
☞ mohamɛ́dan					*

In actually attested forms such as (34), with a superheavy syllable rhyme, the winning candidate as far as the phonology is concerned, is also the candidate

---

[23] There actually are two exceptions to this generalisation, both of them deriving the feminine form of words: -in (boer 'farmer' - boerin 'woman farmer') and -es (leraar 'teacher'- lerares 'female teacher'). These are not superheavy, but interestingly, they are still stress-attracting. They thus seem to have some kind of exceptionality marking which attracts stress, presumably the same as is found in chocola 'chocolate'.

that is preferred by HEAD-STRESS. A hypothetical *-an* with a short vowel and one consonant, would prefer a different shape from a phonological point of view. If something like HEAD-STRESS is involved in the selection of optimal lexical forms, 'superheavy' syllable rhymes should eventually emerge.

The class B suffixes are actually also not bad from the point of view of HEAD-STRESS: they do not carry the primary stress of the compound, but since they are independent prosodic words, they still carry word stress. There are various ways to implement this idea. We could imagine, for instance, that HEAD-STRESS is a gradient constraint, and that structures such as those in (29b) give one violation rather than two. Furthermore, these suffixes also satisfy the requirements on the prosody-morphology interface quite well, since, as we have seen, they still satisfy Alignment.

For inflectional suffixes, only MIRRORING is relevant (HEAD-STRESS assigns the main stress to the stem anyway) but for derivational suffixes *both* MIRRORING and HEAD-STRESS play a role. Now it is impossible to satisfy both of the constraints at the same time. Now apparently derivational suffixes have taken one of two routes:

- Type A suffixes satisfy MIRRORING (and therefore also Alignment) completely, thereby necessarily violating HEAD-STRESS;
- Type B and Type C suffixes satisfy HEAD-STRESS, and therefore necessarily violate MIRRORING; Type C suffixes also violate Alignment, Type B suffixes do not.

The difference between Type A suffixes on the one hand, and Type B and Type C suffixes on the other, can be deduced from their phonological shape. The former are superheavy, the latter are superlight. It looks as if MIRRORING and HEAD-STRESS are unranked with respect to one another, maybe because they are only forces at work in Lexicon Optimization (hence outranked by all relevant wellformedness constraints). Some suffixes obey the one constraint, others obey the other (but there are no suffixes that are underlyingly structured in such a way that they have to disobey both of them, even though this is a possibility in principle).

Is there anything to be said about the difference between Type B and Type C? It has been observed already by Booij (1977, and subsequent work) that all Type C suffixes are vowel initial, whereas almost all Type B suffixes are consonant-initial; the one exception is vowel-initial *-achtig* '-like' which nevertheless behaves as Type B, maybe because it is compound-like for other reasons (Van Oostendorp 1994, 1999). Setting this morpheme apart, then, the difference can simply be made by constraint ranking: ONSET » ALIGN. The idea is that syllables cannot cross the boundary between two prosodic words; therefore, vowel-initial suffixes still prefer to be integrated with the prosodic word of the base.

5 Problematic cases

We now have diminished the number of morphological diacritics in the lexicon by deriving the phonological behaviour of sets of affixes from their underlying form, plus constraints on mapping the input to the output. A few problematic cases remain. These will be discussed in this section. In 5.1. I discuss the suffix *-ing*, which behaves as Type A, even though it has the full vowel [ɪ]; in section 5.2. I discuss the suffix *-isch* which is 'preaccenting', even though it has a superheavy syllable.

5.1 -ing

The Dutch suffix *-ing* is mentioned by most scholars as an example of a Type A affix. It derives nouns from verbs, just like its counterpart in English. It is however much less productive than the corresponding English form (cf. Van Haeringen 1971, De Haas and Trommelen 1993). In essence, productive *-ing* formation seems to be restricted to words derived by the suffixes *-eer* (or *-iseer*, 38a) or by prefixes (38b), although there are a few words which are formed of a simple verb plus the suffix *-ing* (38c).

The reputation of *-ing* as a stress-neutral suffix probably derives from forms such as those in (38b).[24] The word *afschrijving* for instance has the stress pattern [áfsxrɛivɪŋ], which is not the stress pattern of an underived word, because in such a word stress cannot occur to the left of a diphthong. In other words, the form of *afschrijving* is different from that of an underived form. Presumably, this is the reason why this form has been called 'stress-neutral'.

(36)

Mohammed+aan mohɑmɛd+aːn	ONSET	ALIGN
PW ☞ mohɑmɛd+aːn		*
PW PW mohɑmɛt+aːn	*!	

---

[24] In words ending in *-ering*, stress is on *-eer*, just as it would be if the word were underived (i.e. from these forms alone we cannot tell wether *-ing* is stress attracting or stress neutral).

(37)

werk+zaam wɛrk+za:m	ONSET	ALIGN
PW wɛrk+za:m		*!
PW PW ☞ wɛrk+za:m		

(38) a. *standaardisering* 'standardisation', *accentuering* 'accentuation', *democratisering* 'democratisation'

   b. *onderbreking* 'interruption' (**breking* 'breaking'), *aanraking* 'touch' (**raking* 'touch'), *afschrijving* 'copy' (**schrijving* 'writing')

   c. *wrijving* 'irritation' (from *wrijf* 'rub'), *speling* 'leeway' (from *speel* 'play')

It should be observed, however, that the stress of *afschrijving* is not unusual for a simple phonological word at all. In other words, there is nothing in the facts in (38) that argues against prosodic analyses such as those in (39), in which *-ing* is always incorporated in the phonological word of the base:[25]

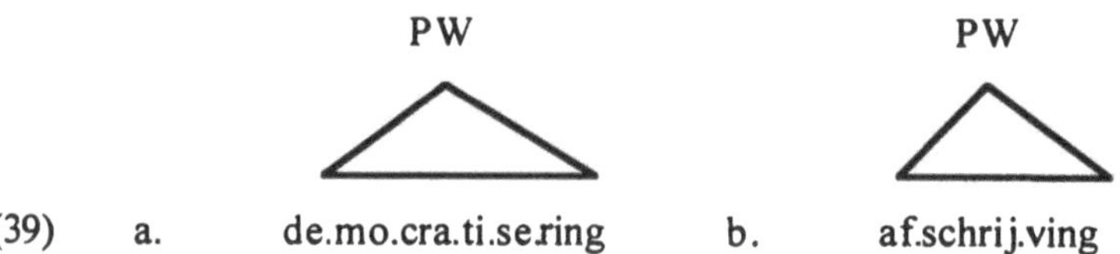

(39) a.   de.mo.cra.ti.se.ring   b.   af.schrij.ving

The problem is that *-ing* does not seem to be sufficiently productive to provide us with those cases which would really be a good test to see whether it is stress-attracting or not. All the stems I have found to which *-ing* could be attached either ended in a stressed syllable (*wrijving* [wrɛivɪŋ]) or in a stressed syllable followed by schwa (*gijzeling* [ɣɛizəlɪŋ] 'kidnapping' from *gijzel* [ɣɛizəl]). In both cases, it is hard to see where stress could have been other than in the position where it is.

---

[25] The only type of 'stress shift' that we might expect to occur, but that is not actualy attested, is a shift of compound stress from the first phonological *word* to the second. This type of stress shift does occur with certain Class I suffixes (afvallen [áfvɑlə] 'lose faith' (litt. fall off) - *afvallig* [ɑfválɪx] 'having lost faith') but apparently not with *-ing*. The reason why compound stress shift occurs in the first place, however, is very far from clear. I will not go into this here.

We can actually observe that the rhyme sequence [ɪŋ] never gets stressed in Dutch, not even in underived forms: although there are quite a few words such as *koning* 'king', *paling* 'eel', *honing* 'honey', each of them with stress in the first syllable, there is no word in Dutch which ends in stressed *-ing* (with the exception of those words in which *-ing* is the only available rhyme, such as *zing* 'sing' and *ring* 'ring'). As a matter of fact, there is a series of place names in Dutch, such as *Scheveningen*, *Wateringen*, etc., which are exceptions to the three-syllable window requirement, because they have stress on the first (pre-antepenultimate) syllable of the word. Typically, the final three syllables in these words contain either schwa or *-ing*. This provides us with extra indications that the rhyme sequence *-ing* is not likely to be stressed, even if it is not a suffix.[26] Its behaviour in derived forms therefore can probably be derived from its phonological shape, just as is expected given the general assumptions of this paper.

5.2   -isch

Another suffix that is problematic, but for somewhat different reasons, is *-isch#* /i:s/ '-ic'. This suffix does not get stressed, even though it is superheavy. On the other hand, it is not stress-neutral either (which of course we do not expect because it is superheavy but does not start with a consonant). Rather, it is stress-attracting (like its English counterpart), and in a way it is the only real stress-attracting suffix of Dutch. Stress is on the syllable preceding *-isch*.

Trommelen and Zonneveld (1989: 204–208) try to account for this special behaviour by assuming that the underlying structure of *-isch* is approximately /i:əs/. They argue that this type of phonological structure automatically gives stress on the antepenultimate syllable (i.e. directly in front of schwa). The suffix thus is similar in behaviour to English *-ity,* according to Trommelen and Zonneveld (1989). We may also also note that the high front vowel /i:/ behaves unusually in other parts of the stress system as well. Regular stress rules would predict penultimate stress on words such as *Italië* /italiə/, for instance, but stress in this case skips the penultimate syllable and falls on the antepenultimate: [itátijə]. Still this is not completely satisfactory under the approach presented above, since we have claimed that in underived words are on the syllable immediately preceding schwa. So from this point of view, both *-isch* and *-ië* are problematic suffixes. It therefore is not possible for us to accept Trommellen and Zonneveld's (1989) proposal without modification.

Morphologically, these two suffixes are probably related; there is a number of roots which can host both of them: *België* 'Belgium' - *Belgisch* 'Belgian', *Indië* 'India' - *Indisch* 'Indian', *Servië* 'Serbia' - *Servisch* 'Serbian', *Karinthië*

---

[26] In some analyses (Kager and Zonneveld 1986), *-ing* is supposed to be derived from an underlying schwa+ŋ.

'Carinthia' - *Karinthisch* 'Carinthian', etc.[27] Both of these suffixes start with an /iː/ and have a second element (a coronal fricative or a schwa) that can be adjoined to the prosodic word. It is almost as if this /iː/ a separate morpheme. What I propose, then, is that these forms behave as if they have two suffixes, one of which is the structure of this forms is as in (40):

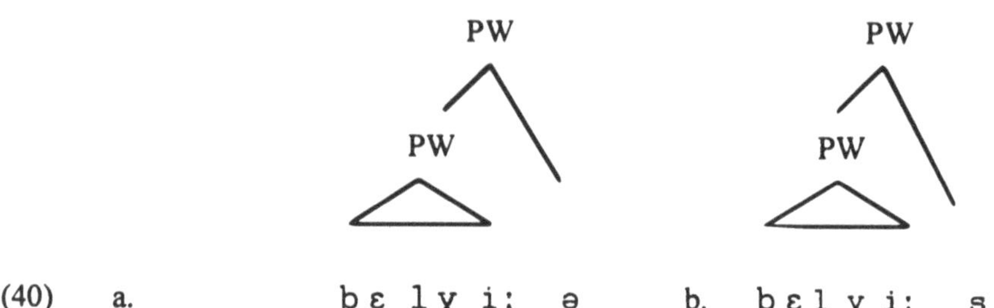

(40)　　a.　　　　　b ɛ l ɣ iː ə　　b.　　b ɛ l ɣ iː　　s

These suffixes are exceptional then, in that they have some internal structure (we cannot assume that /i/ is a separate suffix, since it cannot occur on its own). But this internal structure is expressed in the phonology in exactly the same way as other forms of internal morphological structure are.[28]

6 Conclusion

In this paper, I have argued that there is an intimate relation between the phonological shape of Dutch suffixes and their morphological function. The morphological structure has to be expressed in the phonological shape. There are two ways in which this should be done: phonological trees are ideally isomorphic to the morphological trees they serve to mirror (formalized here in the constraint MIRRORING), and morphological heads should get word stress (formalized in the constraint HEAD-STRESS).

In inflectional forms, the two constraints do not conflict: they have a recursive phonological word, in which stress is on the stem. In derivational forms, the two constraints do conflict: on the one hand we would like to have the suffix in an adjoined position, but on the other hand, this is not possible because in this adjoined position the suffix can never be heavy enough to get main stress. Derivational suffixes therefore come in two flavours: some respect the phonological structure, hence do not assign stress to the suffix. Others assign stress to the suffix, and therefore do not mirror the morphological tree in the

---

[27] There are quite a lot of exceptions to this generalisation as well, both forms ending in *-ië* that do not have a correspondent in *-isch* (*Wallonië* 'the Walloon provinces' - *Waal* 'Walloon') as words ending in *-isch* that cannot be related to any regional name (*typisch* 'typical' - **typië*).

[28] This still does not solve the whole problem, since /iː/ is still not a typical derivational suffix: it does not attract main stress. There is something special about coronal vowels, however, in the sense that they sometimes seem to behave schwa-like. Maybe this is going on here as well.

phonology. If the latter is the case, there are two options: if the suffix is vowel-initial it is completely integrated with the prosodic word of the stem, in order for it to satisfy Onset. If the suffix is consonant-initial, it is not integrated with the prosidic word of the stem, but rather it forms a compound-like structure with it, in this way compromising between the requirements of HEAD-STRESS and MIRRORING.

References

Alber, Birgit (1998): Stress Preservation in German Loan Words. In: Kehrein, Wolfgang & Wiese, Richard, eds. (1998): *Phonology and Morphology of the Germanic Languages*. Tübingen: Niemeyer.

Benua, Laura (1997): *Transderivational Identity: Phonological Relations between Words. PhD dissertation, University of Massachusetts*.

Booij, Geert (1977): *Dutch Morphology. A Study of Word Formation in Generative Grammar. Lisse: Peter de Ridder Press*.

Booij, Geert (1995): *The Phonology of Dutch*. Oxford: Clarendon Press.

Booij, Geert & Santen, Ariane van (1998): *Morfologie. De woordstructuur van het Nederlands*. 2nd, revised edition. Amsterdam: Amsterdam University Press

Gussenhoven, Carlos (1999): *Vowel duration, syllable quantity and stress in Dutch*. Ms, Nijmegen University.

Haeringen, C. B. van (1971): Het achtervoegsel -ing: Mogelijkheden en beperkingen. *Nieuwe Taalgids* 64. 449–468.

Haeseryn, W., Romijn, K., Geerts, G., Rooij, J. de & Toorn, M. C. van den (1997): *Algemene Nederlandse Spraakkunst*. 2nd, completely revised edition. Groningen, Nijhoff/Deurne: Wolters Plantyn.

Halle, M. & Vergnaud, J.-R. (1987): *An Essay on Stress*. Cambridge, MA: MIT Press.

Hayes, Bruce (1989): The Prosodic Hierarchy in Meter. In: Kiparsky, P. & Youmans, G., eds. (1989): *Rhythm and Meter*. Orlando: Academic Press.

Hoekstra, Eric (2000): Grammaticale functies van -e en -en in het Westfries en het Fries en taalcontactgestuurde veranderingen. *Taal en Tongval* 52:1. 136–149.

Ito, Junko (1986): *Syllable Theory in Prosodic Phonology*. PhD dissertation, University of Massachusetts, Amherst [Published in: New York: Garland Press, 1988].

Jackendoff, Jack (1996): *The Architecture of the Language Faculty*. Cambridge, MA: MIT Press.

Kager, René (1989): *A Metrical Theory of Stress and Destressing in English and Dutch*. Dordrecht: Foris.

Kager, René (to appear): Stem Stress and Peak Correspondence in Dutch. In: Dekkers, J., Leeuw, F. van der & Weijer, J. van de, eds., (to appear): *The Pointing Finger. Conceptual Studies in Optimality Theory*. Amsterdam: HIL.

Kager, René & Zonneveld, Wim (1986): Schwa, Syllables and Extrametricality in Dutch. *The Linguistic Review* 5. 197–221.

Kaye, Jonathan (1995): Derivations and Interfaces. In: Durand, Jacques & Katamba, Francis, eds. (1995): *Frontiers in Phonology. Atoms, Structures, Derivations*. Harlow, Essex: Longman.

McCarthy, John (2001): *Optimal Paradigms and Arabic Templates*. Talk given at Comtemporary Issues in Phonological Theory, Tromsø, June 2001.

McCarthy, John & Prince, Alan (1999): Faithfulness and Identity in Prosodic Morphology. In: Kager, R., Hulst, H. van der & Zonneveld, W., eds. (1999): *The Prosody-Morphology Interface*. Cambridge: Cambridge University Press. 218–309.

Nespor, Marina & Vogel, Irene (1986): *Prosodic Phonology*. Dordrecht: Foris.

Nouveau, Dominique (1994): *Language Acquisition, Metrical Theory and Optimality. A Case Study of Dutch Word Stress*. Utrecht: Led.

Oostendorp, Marc van (1994): Affixation and Integrity of Syllable Structure in Dutch. In: Bok-Bennema, R. & Cremers, C., eds. (1994): *Linguistics in the Netherlands 1994*. Amsterdam: John Benjamins. 151–162.

Oostendorp, Marc van (1997): Lexicale variatie in optimaliteitstheorie. *Nederlandse Taalkunde* 2. 133–154.

Oostendorp, Marc van (1999): *Crossing Suffix Boundaries in Dutch.* Ms, Meertens Instituut.

Oostendorp, Marc van (2000): *Phonological Projection.* Berlin/New York: Mouton de Gruyter.

Prince, Alan & Smolensky, Paul (1993): *Optimality Theory. Constraint Interaction and Satisfaction in Generative Grammar.* Ms, Rutgers University and University of Colorado, Boulder.

Revithiadou, Anthi (1999): *Headmost Accent Wins. Head Dominance and Ideal Prosodic Form in Lexical Accent Systems.* The Hague: HAG.

Schultink, Henk (1980): Boundaries, Word Classes and the Accentuation of Derived Words in Dutch. In: Zonneveld, W., Coetsem, F. van & Robinson, O. W., eds. (1980): *Studies in Dutch Phonology.* Den Haag: Nijhoff. 205–222.

Sellkirk, Elisabeth (1986): On Derived Domains in Sentence Phonology. *Phonology Yearbook* 3. 371–405.

Selkirk, Elisabeth (1996): The Prosodic Structure of Function Words. In: Morgan, James L. & Demuth, Katherine, eds. (1996): *Signal to Syntax: Bootstrapping from Speech to Grammar in Early Acquisition.* Mahwah, NJ: Lawrence Erlbaum. 187–213.

Trommelen, Mieke & Haas, Wim de (1993): *Morfologisch handboek van het Nederlands.* 's-Gravenhage: Sdu Uitgeverij.

Trommelen, Mieke & Zonneveld, Wim (1989): *Klemtoon en metrische fonologie.* Muiderberg: Coutinho.

Amsterdam   Marc van Oostendorp

Meertens Instituut/KNAW, Joan Muyskenweg 25, 1096 CJ Amsterdam
e-mail: marc.van.oostendorp@meertens.knaw.nl

Constraints on Multiple Feature Occurrence

Draga Zec

Abstract

In this paper, I focus on restrictions against multiple feature occurrences within prosodic constituents, based on data from several phonological processes in Bulgarian. These processes, which govern the distribution of the feature associated with front vowels as well as palatal and palatalized consonants (henceforth π) conspire to resolve multiple π occurrences, generally referred to as OCP violations (Leben 1973, McCarthy 1986), in both the syllable and the foot. But strategies for resolving multiple π ccurrences in these two prosodic constituents differ. Within the syllable, multiple π's are resolved by virtue of feature deletion, that is, dissimilation which, following Ito & Mester (1998) and Alderete (1997), is plausibly interpreted as a reduction of markedness. Within the foot, however, multiple π occurrences are resolved by enforcing like distributions of segments bearing identical features, leading to an assimilatory OCP effect. While the dissimilatory OCP effects lead to the reduction of markedness in linguistic forms, assimilatory OCP effects, I argue, lead to the reduction of syntagmatic cotrast. In the latter case, multiple occurrences of a feature are tolerated only if their distributions are mutually related in a predictable fashion. In both the syllable and the foot, the achieved result is an increase of redundancy, which presents an important general aspect of the phonological organization of linguistic entities.

Introduction

Multiple feature occurrences, cross-linguistically attested as undesirable phonological configurations, may be resolved in at least two ways. One is by imposing a requirement that at most one feature of a given type may occur in a linguistic form. Another is by restricting the distribution, rather than the number, of features within a linguistic form; that is, by imposing like distributions on multiple features.

The formal device originally posited for regulating cases of multiple feature occurrence is the Obligatory Contour Principle, or the OCP (Leben 1973; Goldsmith 1976; McCarthy 1986; Ito & Mester 1986; Yip 1988). Cast in a geometrical frame of reference, OCP bans a configuration like (1), which contains two occurrences of feature F.

(1) $\quad [R_i \quad R_j \quad R_k \quad R_l]_d$
$\qquad\quad\ \, F_j \quad F_k$

Linguistische Berichte Sonderheft 11 · © Helmut Buske Verlag 2002 · ISSN 0935-9249

Both (2) and (3) are reconfigured versions of (1) admitted by the OCP: (2) by virtue of feature deletion, whose effect is dissimilatory in nature, and (3) by so-called feature fusion, which we will refer to as an assimilatory OCP effect.

(2) $[R_i \quad R_j \quad R_k]_d$
                    F_j

(3) $[R_i \quad R_j \quad R_k \quad R_l]_d$
                         $F_{j,k}$

The geometrical interpretation of the OCP and its repairs has recently given place to a different perspective, developed within the OT framework (Ito & Mester 1998, also Alderete 1997). Under this view, dissimilatory OCP effects have been construed as a special case of markedness adjustments. For every feature F the grammar contains a markedness constraint *F. Multiple occurrences of F, however, constitute a more serious violation than do single occurrences. This calls for a more austere constraint intervention than that achieved by the cumulative effect of multiple *F violations, and is formally captured by the mechanism of constraint conjunction proposed in Smolensky (1995); in particular, by the self-conjoined constraint $*F^2{}_\delta$, restricted to a local domain, which ranks higher than its simplex version. Multiple feature occurrences are thus construed as a special case of single feature occurrences, subject to the same types of constraints, which however are imposed with greater rigor in the former case than in the latter.

This perspective, developed for dissimilatory OCP effects, will be extended here to assimilatory OCP effects. While the dissimilatory OCP effects lead to the reduction of markedness in linguistic forms, assimilatory OCP effects, I argue, lead to the reduction of syntagmatic contrast. Free distribution of some feature F in linguistic constituents maximizes syntagmatic contrast; positional restrictions of various sorts, however, minimize syntagmatic contrast by making the distribution of F predictable. Constraints relevant in this case are positional constraints, those that regulate the distribution of features, and have the general form POSITION-F. Multiple occurrences of feature F will be subject to the same positional constraints as are single occurrences of F. These constraints, however, are enforced with greater rigor if more than one F is present in a local domain. Constraint conjunction will again be the formal mechanism of choice, with POSITION-$F^2{}_D$ playing a crucial role in the evaluation of multiple occurrences of F.

In this paper we focus on a language which engenders both the dissimilatory and assimilatory OCP effects: Bulgarian employs different strategies to resolve multiple feature occurrence in different prosodic constituents, a situation excluded in Fukazawa (1999). Within the syllable, multiple features are resolved by virtue of feature deletion, that is, dissimilation which, as already noted, is plausibly interpreted as a reduction of markedness. Within the foot, however, multiple feature occurrences are resolved by reduction of syntagmatic contrast. In the latter case, multiple occurrences of a feature are tolerated only if their distributions are mutually synchronized in a predictable fashion. In both the syllable and the foot, the achieved result is an increase of redundancy, which presents an important general aspect of the phonological organization of linguistic constituents.

The study is couched in Optimality Theory (McCarthy & Prince 1993, 1995; Prince & Smolensky 1993), and organized as follows. Section 1 provides background information about the Bulgarian phonological system. In section 2 I focus on the dissimilatory OCP effect within the syllable; and in section 3, on the assimilatory OCP effect within the foot. Section 4 provides concluding remarks.

1 Relevant aspects of the Bulgarian phonological system

The phonological property we focus on in this study is the distribution of a feature shared by three classes of segments: front vowels, and palatalized and palato-alveolar consonants. This feature, to be referred to here as π, corresponds roughly to "coronal" in Clements & Hume's (1995) model of segment structure.[1] In order to determine the place of this feature in the phonological system of Bulgarian, we present the Bulgarian segment inventory, starting with the inventory of vowels:

(4)   Vowels:

	front	back unrounded	rounded
high	i	u	
mid	e	I	o
		JAT	
low		a	

All Bulgarian vowels are short. The inventory in (4) is a six vowel system, with two front and four back vowels; two of the back vowels are unrounded, the low vowel *a*, and the schwa-like vowel *I*. An additional vocalic segment is JAT, a complex low back vowel with a front component. JAT is an abstract vowel which, depending on the context, neutralizes with either *a* or *e*.[2] The vocalic segments associated with the feature π are the front vowels *i* and *e*, as well as the abstract vowel JAT.

---

[1] I am assuming minimal segment internal featural organizations, as for example in Padgett (1995).

[2] JAT is a phoneme in reconstructed Common Slavic, with most diverse reflexes in modern Slavic languages (Samilov 1964, Shevelov 1965).

The set of consonants includes two major classes, palatalized and non-palatalized segments. As shown in (5), labial and coronal consonants (with the exception of the coronal affricate c) possess palatalized counterparts, characterized by the feature π. Additionally, palato-alveolar consonants contain a palatal component, again characterized as π.

(5)   Consonants:

	non-palatalized	palatalized
Labial	p b f v m	pʲ bʲ fʲ vʲ mʲ
Coronal	t d s z c n l r	tʲ dʲ sʲ zʲ nʲ lʲ rʲ
Palato-alveolar	š ž č dž	
Palatal	j	
Dorsal	k g x	

Multiple occurrences of π call for an OCP resolution in both the syllable and the foot, yet as shown in sections 2 and 3, different phonological devices are employed for this purpose in the two prosodic constituents.

2   Syllable-related interactions, or dissimilatory OCP effects

Dissimilatory OCP effects within the Bulgarian syllable bear close resemblance to what has already been established for such cases in the literature (Ito & Mester 1998). The central aspect of the distribution of π within the syllable is that palatalized consonants may not be tautosyllabic with front vowels. If this combination arises due to morpheme concatenation, the palatalization of the consonant is lost, as shown by the alternations in (6)–(8) (as reported in Aronson 1968, Bernard 1957, Maslov 1956, Scatton 1984, Tilkov 1982). In other words, at most one occurrence of π is tolerated within the syllable although, as will be shown, this requirement is not absolute.

2.1   Prohibition against multiple π's

The lexical forms in (6)–(8) all contain stem-final palatalized consonants. Palatalization on the stem-final consonant survives before suffixes that begin in back vowels, as in the (a) examples of (6)–(8), but is lost before suffixes that begin in a front vowel, as in the (b) examples. Additionally, palatalized consonants may not occur syllable-finally, as in the (c) examples of (6)–(8).[3]

---

[3] Stems ending in a non-palatalized consonant do not exhibit alternations of the type exemplified in (6)–(8). The stem in (6), *pltʲ-*, contrasts with the lexical form *brat-*, which ends in a non-palatalized *t*. This consonant is realized as unpalatalized in all environments: before suffixes beginning with a front vowel (*bráte* 'brother (voc.)', *brátec* 'brother' (dim.)), and before those that begin in a back vowel (*brátăt* 'the brother', *brátov* 'brother's'), as well as in word final position (*brat* 'brother'). The stem in (7), *konʲ-* contrasts with the stem *ston-* (*stónăt* 'the moan', *stóna* 'the moans',

(6)   lexical form: pĭt'ʲ-

    a. pĭt'ʲIt   'the road'
       pĭt'ʲa   'the roads'

    b. pIték   'footpath'
       pĭten   'travel (adj.)'
       pĭtišta   'roads'

    c. pIt   'road'
       pĭtnik   'traveler'

(7)   lexical form: konʲ-

    a. kónʲIt   'the horse'
       kónʲo   'horse (voc.)'

    b. koné   'horses'
       kónen   'equestrian'

    c. kon   'horse'
       kónski   'horse-like'

(8)   lexical form: kralʲ-

    a. králʲIt   'the king'
       králʲa   'the king'

    b. kralé   'kings'
       kralíca   'queen'

    c. kral   'king'

That this is indeed a case of syllable-bounded distributional restriction, rather than a prohibition against adjacency, is shown by (9), in which the front vowel e and the palatalized consonant nʲ may occur next to each other, precisely because they are heterosyllabic:

(9)   denʲIt   'the day'

stónove 'moans', also *ston* 'moan'); and the stem in (5), *kralʲ*- with *stol*- (*stóllt* 'the chair', *stolóve* 'chairs', also *stol* 'chair'); in both cases the final consonant is realized as unpalatalized in all environments.

2.2   Constraints on palatalized consonants

Prohibition against multiple π's within the syllable is plausibly viewed as a dissimilatory OCP effect. Multiple feature occurrences are subject to the same types of constraints as are occurrences of single features; in this case, to markedness constraints. The considerably stronger markedness effect in the case of multiple features is captured formally by the mechanism of constraint conjunction.[4]

In order to account for the alternations in (6)–(8), two markedness constraints on the feature π are invoked: the simplex constraint in (10), which registers any instantiation of π as increase in markedness, and the self-conjoined version of this constraint, with the syllable as its domain in (11), which registers violations incurred by multiple, in this case, two, occurrences of π. Here we recapitulate the argument for positing both (10) and (11) presented in Ito & Mester (1998).

(10)   Simplex markedness constraint:*π

(11)   Self-conjoined markedness constraint: *π^2 (σ)
        Interpretation: *π^2 (σ) is violated if and only if each simplex constraint is
        violated within the domain of the syllable.

The special relation between (10) and (11) is captured by the ranking in (12), according to which a violation of (11) is of greater consequence than a dual violation of (10).

(12)   Ranking: *π^2 (σ) >>*π

This effect becomes obvious through interaction with a faithfulness constraint ranked higher then *π, and lower than *π^2 (σ). The relevant faithfulness constraint is IDENT-π in (13), which requires that any π bearing segment in the input have a faithful correspondent in the output (McCarthy & Prince 1995):

(13)   IDENT-π:
        Correspondent segments have identical specifications for the feature π.

---

[4] The mechanism of constraint conjunction is defined as follows in following Ito & Mester (1998): Local conjunction of constraints:
   a.   Definition: If P and Q are members of the constraint set CON, then their local conjunction P&$_i$Q is also a member of CON.
   b.   Interpretation: P&$_\delta$Q is violated if and only if both P and Q are violated in some domain δ.
   c.   Ranking (universal): P&$_\delta$.Q >> P, Q
   d.   Domain: P&$_\delta$.Q is assigned some domain δ which corresponds to a constituent in the grammar (phonological or morphological)

We focus first on the interactions of IDENT-π with the simplex markedness constraint *π. The ranking IDENT-π >> *π gives the desired result if the form under evaluation contains only a single occurrence of π, as in (14), but not if the evaluated form contains two such occurrences, as in (15). In the latter case, the selected output form, which contains two occurrences of π, does not correspond to the actual output, which should be (15a).

(14)   IDENT-π >> *π

kón^{j}It	IDENT-π	*π
☞ a. kón^{j}It		*
b. kónIt	*!	

(15)   BUT: IDENT-π >> *π gives a wrong result:

kón^{j}e	IDENT-π	*π
a. koné	*!	*
☞ b. kon^{j}é		**

This brings in the self-conjoined version of the markedness constraint on π. As shown in (16), the correct result is achieved with the self-conjoined markedness constraint ranking higher than the simplex one; and the faithfulness constraint IDENT-π ranking lower than the former, and higher than the latter.

(16)   *π^2 (σ) >> IDENT-π >> *π

kon^{j}é	*$\pi^2(\sigma)$	IDENT-π	*π
☞ koné		*	*
kon^{j}é	*!		**

Thus far, we have shown that at most one π is permitted within the syllable, at the cost of loss of faithfulness. Next, we need to ensure that the optimal output form is *koné* rather than **kon^{j}ó*, that is, that the rightmost π survives. Thus, what needs to be encoded in the grammar is that the preferred locus for π is to coincide with the syllable nucleus. To capture this, we invoke the positional constraint on π in (17), of the type proposed in Zoll (1996).[5]

---

[5] This constraint could equally well be stated as COINCIDE (π, μ), since all Bulgarian syllables are light, and the only mora within the syllable necessarily corresponds to the nucleus. The phonological constrast between light and heavy syllables is not relevant for the Bulgarian phonological system: the Bulgarian vowel inventory includes only short vowels, and consonants do not contribute to weight.

(17)   COINCIDE (π,σ_{NUC})
        Each occurrence of π shoud be associated with a syllable nucleus.

In (18), this constraint selects the winner among candidates (18a) and (18b), which both satisfy $*\pi^2$ (σ) but tie on IDENT-π, which they both violate. Candidate (18c) is eliminated by virtue of violating the self-conjoined markedness constraint.

In tableau (19) we establish the mutual ranking of IDENT-π and COINCIDE (π,σ_{NUC}): the positional constraint ranks lower than the faithfulness constraint and, therefore, does not have the power to alter the featural content of a segment. Thus, if only one π-bearer occurs within the syllable, its π will be realized in the output at the cost of violating the positional constraint, as in the winning candidate (19a).

(18) $*\pi^2$ (σ) >> IDENT-π, COINCIDE (π, σ_{NUC})

		kon^{j}é	$*\pi^2(\sigma)$	IDENT-π	COINCIDE (π,σ_{NUC})
☞	a.	koné		*	
	b.	kon^{j}ó		*	*!
	c.	kon^{j}é	*!		*

(19)   IDENT-π >> COINCIDE (π,σ_{NUC})

		kón^{j}o	IDENT-π	COINCIDE (π,σ_{NUC})
☞	a.	kón^{j}o		*
	b.	kóne	*!*	

In sum, the positional constraint COINCIDE (π,σ_{NUC}) crucially affects the selection of the winner only when some higher ranked constraint, in this case $*\pi^2(\sigma)$ overrides the effect of IDENT-π, as in tableau (18).

2.3   Constraints on palato-alveolar consonants

The generalizations presented thus far are relevant only for the set of palatalized consonants. Palato-alveolar consonants (š, ž, č) are not subject to comparable distributional restrictions. They may be tautosyllabic with both back and front vowels, as shown in the (a) and (b) examples of (20) and (21), and may occur in syllable-final position, as in the (c) examples:

(20)   lexical form: mlž

    a. mlžĺt   'the man'

    b. mlžéc   'man (dim)'

    c. mlž   'man'

(21)   lexical form: pɫʲuš

    a. pɫʲúšĺt   'the velvet'

    b. pɫʲúšen   'made of velvet'

    c. pɫʲuš   'velvet'

In order to accommodate these cases, IDENT-π needs to be split into two constraints, (22) and (23), the former affecting primary, and the latter, secondary place of articulation in consonants (Clements & Hume 1995). While (23) is relevant for both front vowels and secondary consonantal articulations, i.e. palatalized consonants, (22) is relevant only for the set of palato-alveolar consonants.

(22)   IDENT-π[C-place]   relevant for palato-alveolar C's

(23)   IDENT-π[V-place]   relevant for palatalized C's

Faithfulness of π as primary place, captured by constraint (22), outranks the markedness constraint $*\pi^2(\sigma)$ and, as a result, the set of palato-alveolar consonants may combine with front vowels, as shown in (24):

(24)   IDENT-π [C-place] >> $*\pi^2$ >> IDENT-π[V-place]

		mlžé	IDENT-π [C]	$*\pi^2(\sigma)$	IDENT-π [V]	$*\pi$
☞	a.	mlžé		*		**
	b.	mlzé	*!			*

But, faithfulness of π as a secondary consonantal place, captured by (23), is outranked by the markedness constraint $*\pi^2(\sigma)$ and, as a result, palatalized consonants may not be tautosyllabic with front vowels, as shown in (25):

(25)   IDENT-π [C-place] >> $*\pi^2$ >> IDENT-π [V-place]

		konʲé	IDENT-π [C]	$*\pi^2(\sigma)$	IDENT-π [V]	$*\pi$
☞	a.	koné			*	*
	b.	konʲé		*!		**

2.4 Summary

Constraints crucial for regulating the distribution of π within the syllable are the simplex and self-conjoined markedness constraints, as well as faithfulness constraints, on π. To complete the picture, we add the coda constraint in (26), which affects consonants characterized by π:

(26)   *π-IN-CODA
        A [+consonantal] segment bearing the π feature is prohibited in the coda.

By ranking this constraint higher than IDENT-π [V-place] but lower than IDENT-π [C-place] we achieve the desired effect: that only those consonants in which π corresponds to the secondary place lose this feature in the coda.

The summary of constraint rankings established thus far is given in (27):

(27)   Constraint rankings established by now:

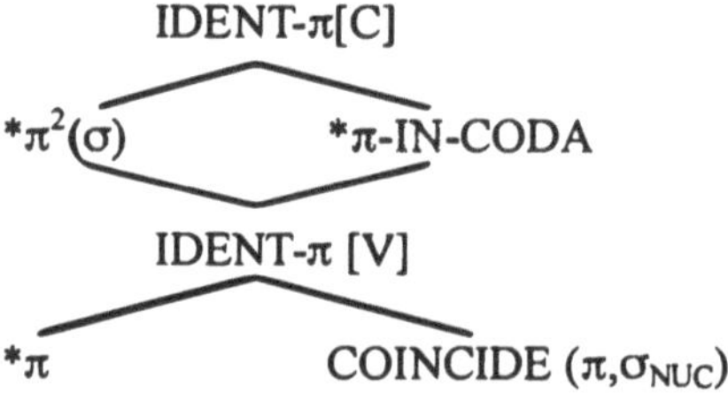

The effect of these constraints is to prevent multiple occurrences of π within the syllable when π functions as a vocalic, but not as a consonantal, place feature.

3   Foot-related interactions, or assimilatory OCP effects

We now turn to the distribution of multiple π's within the foot, which in Bulgarian is of the trochaic type.[6] In this prosodic constituent, multiple π occurrences are constrained in a markedly different way from what has been evidenced for the syllable. While at most one (vocalic) π may occur within the syllable, multiple π's are tolerated within the foot. The co-occurring π's, however, are subject to the assimilatory OCP effect, whose impact is to enforce mutually synchronized distributions on phonologically similar segments. Its overall effect, as will be shown, is a reduction of syntagmatic contrast within the foot.

---

[6] Bulgarian syllables are all monomoraic (see note 4) and, as a consequence, trochaic feet are minimally disyllabic. In words that correspond to a single syllable or bear final stress, we do have to posit monosyllabic feet; these, however, have to be be analyzed as subminimal, monomoraic feet. While stress in Bulgarian is associated with trochaic feet, which are headed by the stress-bearing syllable, the distribution of stress is not of the predictable type. The place of stress is to a large extent lexically governed.

The special positional effect triggered by the co-presence of multiple π's within the foot is of a fairly limited scope. It is evidenced in one specific case: in those forms which contain the abstract vowel JAT (listed in the vowel inventory in (4)), which possesses a π component. It is only when a JAT shares a foot with another π-bearing segment that the positional effects to be detailed here are manifest. When two regular π-bearing segments share a foot, their distributions are not subject to such special positional effects.

3.1 Positional restrictions on JAT's π

That heavier positional restrictions are imposed on multiple, than on single occurrences of π within the foot is demonstrated by the phonological alternations to be presented below. The central player is, of course, the abstract vowel JAT which, depending on the context, is realized as either *a* or *e*. We digress briefly to expound on the representation of this abstract segment. JAT will be treated here as a degenerate diphthong, consisting of two components, one corresponding to a segment, and the other to a floating π co-indexed with it:

(28)   Representation of JAT: a_i
                                  π_i

In (28), the low vowel component is to be characterized as back, since the only low vowel in the Bulgarian vocalic inventory is back (as in (4)). The floating feature π has to be characterized as front. What makes JAT a diphthong is that it includes both a front and a back component; what makes it an abstract diphthong is that only one may be realized on the vowel itself.

Forms listed in (29)-(31) illustrate the realization of JAT (Maslov 1956; Aronson 1968; Bernard 1957; Maslov 1956; Scatton 1984; Tilkov 1982).[7] In the (a) and (b) examples, the subsegment is the only π in the form, and therefore, also the only π in the foot. Where this abstract segment is realized in the string is governed entirely by the place of stress: π is realized on the vowel it is co-indexed with, making it front, if that vowel is unstressed, as in the (a) examples of (29)-(31); and on the onset of the preceding consonant, making it palatalized, if that vowel is stressed, as in the (b) examples.

In the (c) examples of (29)-(31), JAT's π is invariably realized on the nucleus. Of central relevance, here, is the fact that the π's docking site is sensitive to the presence of another π-bearer: a front vowel as in *léten* in (29c); a palatalized consonant as in *mérʲa* (30c); and a palatal consonant as in *slépčo* in (31c).

---

[7] A comment is in order at this point regarding the representation of JAT. Since JAT may appear in a non-initial syllable of the root, as in (32), co-indexing in the lexical form is unavoidable. A further example with JAT in the second syllable of the root is *kolʲáno* 'knee-Sg', *koléni* 'knee-Pl', *kolená* 'knee Pl/Collective'.

(29)   lexical form: l a$_i$ t
                              π$_i$

    a. letá   'summers (N, Pl)'

    b. ľáto   'summer (N, Sg)'

    c. léten   'summer (Adj, Sg, Masc)'

(30)   lexical form: m a$_i$ r
                               π$_i$

    a. merílo   'measuring standard (N, Sg)'

    b. mʲára   'measure (N, Sg)'

    c. mérʲa   '(I) measure'

(31)   lexical form: b a$_i$ l
                              π$_i$

    a. slepotá   'blindness (N, Sg)'

    b. sľápa   'blind (Adj, Sg, Fem)'

    c. slépčo   'blind man (N, Sg)'

In all forms in the (c) set, JAT is the bearer of stress. An unstressed JAT may also co-occur with another π-bearer, and in this case as well, JAT's π is realized on the nucleus. One such case is (32a), in which stress falls on the syllable immediately preceding JAT. In (32b) JAT is stressed, and therefore its π is realized on the preceding consonant; and in (32c), JAT's π is realized on the nucleus because a stressed JAT is followed by a palatal consonant.

(32)   lexical form: b e l a$_i$ g
                                 π$_i$

    a.   béleg   'mark (N, Sg)'

    b.   beľázax   '(I) marked'

    c.   belézka   'note (N, Sg)'

To complete the set of cases with an unstressed JAT sharing a foot with another π-bearer, we turn to verbal paradigms. In one particular conjugation class JAT figures as a theme vowel in the imperfect tense. In verbs with stress on the theme vowel, the JAT theme is realized as *a*, as in *leťáx* 'I flew', or as *e*, if another π-bearer follows as in *letéše* 'he flew'. In verbs with stress on the root, the JAT theme, being unstressed, is realized as *e*, as in *nósex* 'I carried', *nóseše* 'he carried' (Pashov 1966; Hauge 1999). Relevant for us are cases of verbs of the latter shape, with stress on the root; and additionally, with a π-bearer in the first syllable. We list three such cases: (33), with a front vowel in the first syllable, and (34) and (35), with a palatalized and palatal consonant, respectively. In all three cases, JAT's π is realized on the nucleus.

(33)   lexical form: bé l a$_i$
                              π_i

     a. bébex   '(I) whitened'

     b. bélě e   '(he) whitened'

(34)   lexical form: ḷ'ú b a$_i$
                              π_i

     a. ḷ'úbex   '(I) loved'

     b. ḷ'úbeše '(he) loved'

(35)   lexical form: č ú d a$_i$
                              π_i

     a. čúdex   '(I) wondered'

     b. čúdeše '(he) wondered'

The relevant domain for special effects brought about by the co-presence of two π-bearing segments is the foot, rather than some larger domain, as shown by the contrast in (36):

(36)   a. léten   'summer (Adj, Sg, Masc)'

     b. ḷ'átošen / *létošen   'of last summer (Adj, Sg, Masc)'

While in (36a) the *a/e* alternation proceeds as expected, with JAT's π realized as *e* in the presence of another π-bearer, this is not so in (36b). This is because the second π-bearer shares a foot with JAT in (36a) but not in (36b), as explicitly shown in (37):

(37)   a. (léten)ϕ

     b. (ḷ'áto)ϕ šen

All alternations presented here are restricted only to JAT. Forms with a regular *a* do not exhibit such alternations, as shown in (38)–(39). Thus in (38a), the initial sequence corresponds to a palatalized consonant followed by a stressed *a*; this sequence remains unaltered if stress shifts to a following syllable, as in (38b). That is, the resulting form is not *devolit*, as would be the case if this form contained a JAT.

(38)   lexical form: dʲávol

    a. dʲávol   'devil' (N, Sg)'

    b. dʲavolít   'the devil' (N, Sg)'

Likewise, a stressed low vowel preceded by a palatalized consonant in *poĺána* 'meadow' in (39a) remains unaltered when, due to morphological alternation, a π-bearer appears in the following syllable, as in (39b). Again, the resulting sequence is not **poléni*, as would be expected in JAT forms.

(39)   lexical form: poĺán

    a. poĺána   'meadow (N, Sg)'

    b. poĺáni   'meadow (N, Pl)'

To conclude, a regular π is not sensitive to the presence of another π-bearer, while JAT's π is. This is because JAT's π escapes the effect of the IDENT-π constraints, which preclude any arrangement of π-bearers in the foot that inflicts faithfulness violations on segments. JAT's π, which is affiliated with a segment by virtue of co-indexing, is subject to an idiosyncratic faithfulness constraint, distinct from the IDENT-π family, as will be detailed in section 3.2.

3.2 Analysis

In the account to be proposed here, we clearly differentiate between those cases in which JAT's π is the only π in the form, and those in which it co-occurs with another π-bearer. In both cases, the distribution of JAT's π is governed by the set of positional constraints on π. Just like markedness constraints, positional constraints are subject to self-conjunction. Thus, strengthened positional effects on π in the case of multiple π occurrences will be captured by virtue of constraint conjunction.

In 3.2.1 we address the mechanism for including JAT's π into the output. The distribution of JAT's π in the case of single π occurrences is captured in 3.2.2, and in the case of multiple π occurrences, in 3.2.3.

3.2.1 The inclusion of JAT's π into the output

As represented in (28) above, the complex segment JAT consists of two components, one corresponding to a segment, and the other, to a floating π co-indexed with it. The π component of JAT will be analyzed here as a subsegment, in the sense of Zoll 1996. Subsegments differ from linked features by virtue of different faithfulness requirements. Thus, while a linked π feature is subject to the

IDENT-π constraints proposed in section 2, the inclusion of subsegment π into the output is regulated by the following constraint (Zoll 1996):

(40)   MAX-π (SUBSEG)
        Every subsegment π in the input has a correspondent in the output.

Subsegment π obligatorily appears in the output; that is, the constraint MAX-π (SUBSEG) is undominated. Moreover, this constraint interacts only with the markedness constraint *π. Subsegment π is included into the output at the cost of a markedness violation since, as shown in (41), MAX(SUBSEG) ranks higher than the markedness constraint *π:

(41)   MAX(SUBSEG) >> *π

l a$_i$ t á π_i	MAX-π (SUBSEG)	*π
☞ a. letá		*
b. latá	*!	

But while this constraint enforces the output realization of subsegment π, it in no way fixes its position in the string. As already documented, subsegment π exhibits some, albeit limited, measure of mobility: while it does not have to be realized on the segment it is co-indexed with, it does have to be realized in its close proximity. If subsegment π is not realized on the segment it is co-indexed with, that is, on JAT itself, it must dock on a segment tautosyllabic with JAT. The options thus are: the syllable's nucleus (that is, JAT), its onset, or its coda. The coda is excluded, due to the constraint *π-IN-CODA, posited in (26), which prohibits palatalized consonants in the coda, and is surface true. The remaining positions then are the onset and the nucleus; the former is favored in the (b) set, and the latter in the (a) and (c) sets of (29)–(31), as well as in (33)–(36). This will be captured in sections 3.2.2 and 3.2.3, by positing positional constraints responsible for the distribution of this feature.

In sum, the docking site of subsegment π, while circumscribed by co-indexing, is controlled by the set of positional constraints on this feature.

3.2.2 Single occurrences of π in the foot

The distribution of subsegment π, as already noted, is governed by positional constraints on π, those which minimize syntagmatic contrast. The (a) and (b) forms in (29)–(31) provide crucial insight into the role of prosodic constituents, the syllable and the foot, in the positioning of π. We first focus on the (a) forms, those in which the syllable, but not the foot, steers the distribution of π, and then turn to the (b) forms, which elucidate the role of the foot. In addition to positional constraints, two other types of constraints need to be invoked: the faithfulness and markedness constraints on π.

The constraint responsible for regulating the distribution of π within the syllable is the positional constraint COINCIDE (π,σ_{NUC}), which we have already seen at work in section 2. In tableaux (18) and (19), it selects as optimal the candidate with a π-bearing segment in the syllable nucleus, and eliminates the candidate with a π-bearer in the onset.

In tableau (42), the evaluated form is *letá* in (29a). The winner has to satisfy both the faithfulness and the positional constraint; that is, COINCIDE (π,σ_{NUC}) and MAX-π (SUBSEG) do not interact with each other.

The (b) forms in (29)-(31), those in which JAT is stressed, shed light on the influence exerted by the foot on the docking site of subsegment π. The fact that, in a stressed syllable, subsegment π docks on the onset will be interpreted as a requirement for the π-marking of the foot's left edge. This is encoded by positing an alignment constraint, as in (43).

(42)   MAX(SUBSEG) and COINCIDE (π, σ_{NUC}) do not interact:

l a$_i$ t á π_i	MAX-π (SUBSEG)	COINCIDE (π,σ_{NUC})
☞ letá		
ларatá		*!
latá	*!	

(43)   ALIGN (π,ϕ_{LEFT})
        Align π with the left edge of the foot.

Tableaux (44) and (45) show that the positional constraint ALIGN (π,ϕ_{LEFT}), which makes reference to the foot, outranks the positional constraint COINCIDE (π,σ_{NUC}), which makes reference to the syllable. The evaluated forms are *ляáto* in (29b) and *мlára* in (30b):[8]

---

[8] ALIGN (π,ϕ_{LEFT}) is not observed by forms like *koné* in (7b) above, in which a regular π is eliminated from the syllable onset rather than the nucleus, under the pressure of *$\pi^2(\sigma)$. However, the form *ляоná, while satisfying ALIGN (π,ϕ_{LEFT}), incurs more faithfulness violations than does *koné*. While *ляоná violates both IDENT-π[V] and IDENT[high], *koné* fares better by violating only the former. Thus, ALIGN (π,ϕ_{LEFT}), which ranks below any IDENT-F constraints, can affect the distribution of JAT's π, but not the distribution of a regular π.

(44)   ALIGN (π,ϕ_{LEFT}) >> COINCIDE (π,σ_{NUC})

	l á$_i$ t o π_i	ALIGN (π,ϕ_{LEFT})	COINCIDE (π,σ_{NUC})
☞ a.	(l^{j}áto)$_\phi$		*
b.	(léto)$_\phi$	*!	

(45)   ALIGN (π,ϕ_{LEFT}) >> COINCIDE (π,σ_{NUC})

	m á$_i$ r a π_i	ALIGN (π,ϕ_{LEFT})	COINCIDE (π,σ_{NUC})
☞ a.	(m^{j}ára)$_\phi$		*
b.	(méra)$_\phi$	*!	

Unlike JAT's π, regular π features do not exhibit mobility in response to the requirement imposed by ALIGN (π,ϕ_{LEFT}), or by COINCIDE (π,σ_{NUC}) for that matter. The forms in (46) (same as (37)) contain only regular π features, and their distribution is governed entirely by the IDENT-π[V] constraint, which ranks higher than any positional constraints on π.

(46)   lexical form: d^{j}ávol

    a. d^{j}ávol   'devil' (N, Sg)'

    b. d^{j}avolít   'the devil' (N, Sg)'

The two forms listed in (46) fully adhere to IDENT-π [V]. While (46a), incidentally, also satisfies ALIGN (π,ϕ_{LEFT}), which requires π-marking of the foot's left edge, the form in (46b) does not meet either of the two positional constraints on π. In the initial syllable, which is unstressed, the presence of π on the onset rather than the nucleus violates COINCIDE (π,σ_{NUC}); and the final, stressed syllable, while containing a π-bearing nucleus, in compliance with COINCIDE (π,σ_{NUC}), fails to have a π-marked onset, and thus violates ALIGN (π,ϕ_{LEFT}). Yet any adjustments that would lead to better satisfaction of the positional constraints (e.g. *devolít) would lead to fatal violations of IDENT-π [V].

However, the two positional constraints which govern the distribution of single occurrences of π in syllables and feet are not sufficient to account for the distribution of subsegment π in the presence of another π-bearer. Constraints introduced thus far do not yield the correct result in this case. This is shown in the following tableau, figuring mér^{j}a in (30c):

(47)   ALIGN (π,ϕ_{LEFT}) >> COINCIDE (π,σ_{NUC}) gives a wrong result:

		m á$_i$ r^j a π_i	ALIGN (π,ϕ_{LEFT})	COINCIDE (π,σ_{NUC})
	a.	(mér^{j}a)$_f$	*!	
☞	b.	(m^{j}ár^{j}a)$_f$		*

In the next section we turn to characterizing special effects in forms in which JAT's π co-occurs with another π-bearing segment. These effects, I argue, are brought about by the self-conjoined version of the positional constraint COINCIDE (π,σ_{NUC}).

3.2.3 Multiple occurrences of π in the foot

Before presenting an account of how the locus of JAT's π is affected by the presence of another π-bearer, we first inspect the relevant cases. Listed in (48) are forms in the (c) set of (29)–(31). In each, JAT occupies the initial syllable of the foot, and coincides with stress. In column A, which lists the actual forms, JAT's π docks on the nucleus. Forms in column B, with JAT's π on the onset, are all ill-formed. Yet, if a stressed JAT is the only π-bearer in the foot, its π docks on the onset, as we saw in the previous section. From this I conclude that the positional constraint COINCIDE (π, σ_{NUC}) operates with greater strength when more than one π is present in the foot.

(48)   JAT in the foot's 1st syllable

		input form	A. JAT's π in nucleus	B. JAT's π in onset
a.	(29c)	l á$_i$ t e n π_i	(l é$_\pi$ t e$_\pi$ n)$_\phi$	*(l$^j_\pi$ á t e$_\pi$ n)$_\phi$
b.	(30c)	m á$_i$ r^j a π_i	(m é$_\pi$ r$^j_\pi$ a.)$_\phi$	*(m$^j_\pi$ á r$^j_\pi$ a)$_\phi$
c.	(31c)	s l á$_i$ p č o π_i	(s l é$_\pi$ p č$_\pi$ o)$_\phi$	*(sl$^j_\pi$ á p č$_\pi$ o)$_\phi$

Next, we turn to cases with an unstressed JAT in the second syllable of the foot, presented in (49). The form in (49a) corresponds to (33a) above, and has a front vowel in the first syllable; (49b), with a palatalized consonant in the first syllable corresponds to (34a), and (49c), with a palatal consonant, to (35a).

(49)   JAT in the foot's 2nd syllable

		input form	A. JAT's π in nucleus	B. JAT's π in onset
a.	(33a)	b é l a$_i$ x π_i	(b é$_\pi$ l e$_\pi$ x)$_\phi$	*(b é$_\pi$ l'$_\pi$ a x)$_\phi$
b.	(34a)	l' ú b a$_i$ x π_i	(l'$_\pi$ ú e$_\pi$ x)$_\phi$	*(l'$_\pi$ ú b'$_\pi$ a x)$_\phi$
c.	(35a)	č ú d a$_i$ x π_i	(č$_\pi$ ú d e$_\pi$ x)$_\phi$	*(č$_\pi$ ú d'$_\pi$ a x)$_\phi$

In this set, again, JAT's π docks on the nucleus, as in column A. This positioning is consistent with attributing greater strength to COINCIDE (π, σ_{NUC}) when the foot contains multiple occurrences of π.

Thus, in order to account for the distribution of multiple π's in the foot, I posit the following self-conjoined constraint, with the foot as its domain:

(50)   Self-conjoined positional constraint: COINCIDE $(\pi,\sigma_{NUC})^2(\phi)$
        Interpretation: COINCIDE $(\pi,\sigma_{NUC})^2(\phi)$ is violated if and only if each simplex constraint is violated within the domain of the foot.

This constraint is interpreted disjunctively: it is satisfied when at least one π within the foot coincides with a syllable nucleus. By ranking this self-conjoined constraint below any IDENT-π constraint, as in (51), we ensure that it induces adjustments in only those forms in which one of the co-occurring π's originates from JAT.

(51)   IDENT-π >> COINCIDE $(\pi, \sigma_{NUC})^2(\phi)$

This self-conjoined constraint will of course be ranked higher than its simplex version. It will also rank higher than ALIGN (π,ϕ_{LEFT}), whose effect it crucially neutralizes when the foot contains multiple π's. These rankings are given in (52):

(52)   COINCIDE $(\pi,\sigma_{NUC})^2(\phi)$ >> ALIGN (π,ϕ_{LEFT}) >> COINCIDE (π,σ_{NUC})

The functioning of the self-conjoined positional constraint is shown in tableaux (53) and (54) which present, respectively, the evaluation of *mér'a* in (48b) and *slépčo* in (48c). Note that the pattern of evaluation for *mér'a*, which contains a palatalized consonant, is identical to that for *slépčo*, which contains a palatal consonant. In these tableaux, candidate (a) wins over candidate (b) by satisfying COINCIDE $(\pi,\sigma_{NUC})^2(\phi)$: while one of the two π's coincides with the nucleus in the (a) candidates, neither does in the (b) candidates. The remaining two constraints are not relevant for evaluating these forms.

We now turn to the evaluation of forms in (49), in which JAT is unstressed. In (55) we present the selection of the winning candidate for (49a). Both (55a), with JAT's π in the nuclues, and (55b) with JAT's π on the preceding onset, satisfy the self- conjoined positional constraint: candidate (a) by incurring no violations, and candidate (b) by incurring a single violation, of this constraint. This creates a tie, which is replicated by ALIGN (π, ϕ_{LEFT}), and eventually resolved by the simplex COINCIDE constraint.

(53)   COINCIDE $(\pi,\sigma_{NUC})^2(\phi)$ >> ALIGN (π, ϕ_{LEFT}) >> COINCIDE (π, σ_{NUC})

m á$_i$ r^j a π_i	COINCIDE $(\pi,\sigma_{NUC})^2(\phi)$	ALIGN (π,ϕ_{LEFT})	COINCIDE (π,σ_{NUC})
☞ a. (mér^{j}a)$_\phi$		*	*
b. (m^{j}ár^{j}a)$_\phi$	* !		* *

(54)   COINCIDE $(\pi,\sigma_{NUC})^2(\phi)$ >> ALIGN (π,ϕ_{LEFT}) >> COINCIDE (π,σ_{NUC})

s l á$_i$ p č o (36c) π_i	COINCIDE $(\pi,\sigma_{NUC})^2(\phi)$	ALIGN (π,ϕ_{LEFT})	COINCIDE (π,σ_{NUC})
☞ a. (slépčo)$_\phi$		*	*
b. (sl^{j}ápčo)$_\phi$	* !		* *

We now turn to the evaluation of forms in (49), in which JAT is unstressed. In (55) we present the selection of the winning candidate for (49a). Both (55a), with JAT's π in the nuclues, and (55b) with JAT's π on the preceding onset, satisfy the self-conjoined positional constraint: candidate (a) by incurring no violations, and candidate (b) by incurring a single violation, of this constraint. This creates a tie, which is replicated by ALIGN (π, ϕ_{LEFT}), and eventually resolved by the simplex COINCIDE constraint.

(55)   COINCIDE $(\pi,\sigma_{NUC})^2(\phi)$ >> ALIGN (π,ϕ_{LEFT}) >> COINCIDE (π,σ_{NUC})

b e l a$_i$ g π_i	COINCIDE $(\pi,\sigma_{NUC})^2(\phi)$	ALIGN (π,ϕ_{LEFT})	COINCIDE (π,σ_{NUC})
☞ a. (bélex)$_\phi$		*	
b. (bé^{j}ax)$_\phi$		*	* !

Tableau (56) evaluates the form in (49b), with a palatalized consonant in the first syllable. This form exhibits the same evaluation pattern as (49c), which has a palatal consonant in the first syllable.

(56)   COINCIDE $(\pi,\sigma_{NUC})^2(\phi)$>> NOINTER >> ALIGN (π,ϕ_{LEFT}) >> COIN-
CIDE (π,σ_{NUC})

ʰ ú b aᵢ x πi	COINCIDE $(\pi,\sigma_{NUC})^2(\phi)$	ALIGN (π,ϕ_{LEFT})	COINCIDE (π,σ_{NUC})
☞ a. (ʰúbex)_φ			*
b. *(ʰúbʲax)_φ	* !		* *

The crucial role of the self-conjoined positional constraint is to override the effect of ALIGN (π,ϕ_{LEFT}), and this is precisely what we saw in tableaux (53)–(54). Tableaux (55)–(56) present candidates whose stressed syllable contains a regular π which, due to the agency IDENT-π constraints, cannot be regulated by the positional constraints ALIGN (π,ϕ_{LEFT}). Due to this, the self-conjoined positional constraint either repeats the effect of its simplex version, as in (56), or leaves the ruling to the simplex constraint, as in (55).

However, the self-conjoined constraint is not sufficient to override the effect of ALIGN (π,ϕ_{LEFT}) in the case of *léten* in (48a), as shown in tableau (57). Here, both candidates satisfy the self-conjoined positional constraint: candidate (a) by incurring no violations, and candidate (b) by incurring a single violation. Due to this tie, the effect of the self-conjoined constraint is neutralized, and the winner is selected by the next lower-ranked constraint, ALIGN (π,ϕ_{LEFT}), which favors candidate (b), with π-marking on the left edge of the foot. Yet, the winner should be candidate (a), with JAT's π in the syllable nucleus.

(57)   COINCIDE $(\pi,\sigma_{NUC})^2(\phi)$>> ALIGN (π,ϕ_{LEFT}) >> COINCIDE (π,σ_{NUC})

l áᵢ t e n (32c) π_i	COINCIDE $(\pi,\sigma_{NUC})^2(\phi)$	ALIGN (π,ϕ_{LEFT})	COINCIDE (π,σ_{NUC})
a. (léten)_φ		*!	
☞ b. (ʰʲáten)_φ			*

This calls for a further constraint on the distribution of multiple π's in linguistic forms, one which evaluates the relative harmony of those candidates which satisfy COINCIDE $(\pi,\sigma_{NUC})^2(\phi)$. The dispreferred configuration is that with a back vowel nucleus intervening between two π-bearers. This is captured by the constraint in (58) (following Ellison 1995, also Zoll 1996), which further strengthens the general tendency to maximize π-bearing syllable nuclei:

(58)   NOINTERVENING
       A segment corresponding to a back vowel syllable nucleus may not intervene between two π-bearing segments.

With NOINTERVENING ranking higher than ALIGN (π,ϕ_{LEFT}), *léten* becomes the winning candidate, as in (59). The crucial violation incurred by its competitor **láten* is that of NOINTERVENING.[9]

The NOINTERVENING constraint rules against a special case in configurations generally admitted by the self-conjoined positional constraint. The two constraints relevant for forms with multiple π's cannot be ranked, and are left unranked in (59).

Single occurrences of π escape the effect of the self-conjoined constraint COINCIDE $(\pi,\sigma_{NUC})^2(\phi)$. A single π-bearing segment within a foot invariably complies with the self-conjoined positional constraint, since it can incur at most one violation. The winning candidate in (57), for example, satisfies both COINCIDE $(\pi,\sigma_{NUC})^2(\phi)$, and NOINTERVENING. The selection of the winner then falls on those constraints that are active players in forms with single π-occurrences, as was established in section 3.2.2.

(59)   COINCIDE $(\pi,\sigma_{NUC})^2(\phi)$ >> NOINTER >> ALIGN (π,ϕ_{LEFT}) >> COIN-
CIDE (π,σ_{NUC})

l á$_i$ t e n (32c) π_i	COINCIDE $(\pi,\sigma_{NUC})^2(\phi)$	NOIN-TER	ALIGN (π,ϕ_{LEFT})	COINCIDE (π,σ_{NUC})
☞ a. (léten)$_\phi$			*	
b. (l^{j}áten)$_\phi$		*!		*

(60)   COINCIDE$(\pi,\sigma_{NUC})^2(\phi)$ >> NOGAP-π >> ALIGN (π,ϕ_{LEFT}) >> COIN-
CIDE (π,σ_{NUC})

l á$_i$ t o π_i	COINCIDE $(\pi,\sigma_{NUC})^2(\phi)$	NOIN-TER	ALIGN (π,ϕ_{LEFT})	COINCIDE (π,σ_{NUC})
☞ a. (l^{j}áto)$_\phi$			*	
b. (léto)$_\phi$				*!

In sum, the self-conjoined positional constraint plays a crucial role in the distribution of multiple π's, triggering the assimilatory OCP effect in the case of JAT's π. As already noted, regular π's exhibit no positional adjustments due to the presence of another π-bearer. Hence the form in (38), repeated in (61), which contains only regular π-bearers, exhibits no alternations characteristic for JAT's π.

---

[9] This constraint is interpreted as non-gradient: one intervening back syllable nucleus is sufficient for this constraint to be violated. Under this interpretation, we can assume that this constraint operates across the board, that is, that it need not be associated with a specific domain of operation. In (36b), for example, with two π-bearing segments that do not share a foot, both *l̵átöšen* 'of last summer (Adj, Sg, Masc)' and **létošen* violate this constraint, allowing for *l̵átošen* to be selected by the next lower constraint, ALIGN (π, ϕ_{LEFT}).

(61)   lexical form: poľán

    a. poľána   'meadow (N, Sg)'

    b. poľáni   'meadow (N, Pl)'

Here, the underlyingly palatalized segment *ľ* has the same realization in (61a) and (61b): it retains its palatalization when sharing a foot with another π-bearer at the cost of violating positional constraints on π; the form *poléni* which complies with positional constraints is eliminated because it violates IDENT-π[V].

3. 3 Multiple π's and faithfulness constraints

In (62) is given the overall ranking of constraints responsible for the distribution of the feature π in both the syllable and the foot.

The positioning of this feature within the foot is controlled in crucial ways by the place of faithfulness constraints in constraint ranking. This ranking accounts for the divergence in compliance with positional constraints on π between regular π-bearing segments and those whose π originates from JAT. Because segments and subsegments are subject to different faithfulness conditions, the positional constraints strongly take effect in forms which contain subsegment π, that is, a JAT vowel, but weakly, if at all, in forms which contain a regular π. In the former case, the constraint MAX(SUBSEG), while ensuring the realization of JAT's π in the output (due to its undominated status), does not fix its position in the string, leaving the positioning of JAT's π to the set of positional constraints on π and their mutual interactions. In sum, only because of the peculiar faithfulness status of JAT's π is it possible to detect the agency of positional constraints on π in the first place; and to capture the special, and important, positional effects arising when JAT's π co-occurs with another π-bearer, as shown in section 3.2.3.

Forms which contain only regular π-bearers exhibit extremely weak positional effects in the case of single π-occurrences, and none at all, in the case of multiple π-occurrences. This is due to the agency of the set of IDENT-π constraints which dominate all positional constraints on π, and thereby preclude positional effects on regular π features, whose faithfulness they crucially reglate. As a result, a regular π feature exhibits no mobility of the sort manifested by JAT's π.

(62)   Overall ranking

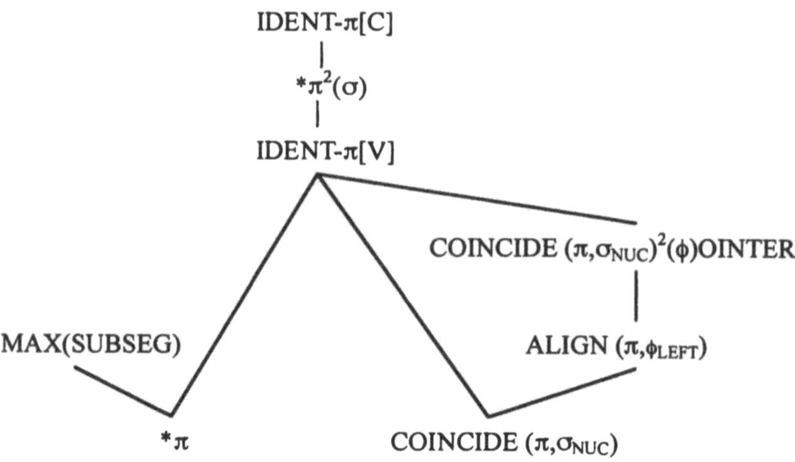

Moreover, we observe a discrepancy in the way different types of π-bearing segments interact with each other syllable internally on the one hand, and foot internally, on the other. Within the foot, all types of π-bearing segments – front vowels, palatal and palatalized consonants – function alike as triggers of assimilatory OCP effects. Within the syllable, however, the dissimilatory OCP effect is manifested by front vowels and palatalized consonant, but not by front vowels and palatal consonants. Yet neither the self-conjoined markedness constraint, $*\pi^2(\sigma)$, nor the self-conjoined positional constraint, COINCIDE $(\pi,\sigma_{NUC})^2(\phi)$, distinguishes between different types of π-bearing segments. Any differences that arise, as in the case of syllable internal interactions, are solely due to the interference of the two IDENT-π constraints. These constraints do distinguish between palatal consonants on the one hand, and front vowels and palatalized consonants, on the other; the latter two segment types are regulated by IDENT-π[V], and the former is regulated by IDENT-π[C]. These constraints bear primary responsibility for the nature of multiple π interactions within the syllable. Only segments under the jurisdiction of IDENT-π[V], which crucially dominates $*\pi^2(\sigma)$, participate in syllable internal dissimilatory OCP effects; palatal consonants may share a syllable with front vowels because their faithfulness is evaluated by IDENT-π[C], which ranks higher than $*\pi^2(\sigma)$. Within the foot, however, all three types of π-bearers affect the positioning of JAT's π in identical fashion.This is because the constraint that crucially regulates interactions among multiple π's within the foot, COINCIDE $(\pi,\sigma_{NUC})^2(\phi)$, ranks lower than any of the IDENT-π constraints.

3. 4 The role of JAT in the vocalic inventory

A remark is in order regarding the abstract nature of JAT, and consequently, of the lexical forms that contain this segment, in light of recent accounts in which allomorphy based analyses have been favored over abstract and intractable phonology, as for example in Kager (1999) and Rubach & Booij (2001). Since the positional effects attributed to the abstract segment JAT could be equally well captured under a stem allomorphy analysis, the central claim of this study would not be affected by the choice of one of these alternative analyses over the other. However, the analysis proposed here is superior, for the following reasons.

First, as has been demonstrated, the abstract segment JAT follows a straightforward phonological pattern, and as such is to be captured by regular phonological devices. The fact that the realization of JAT varies with context makes this case of absolute neutralization detectable for the learner, and is reminiscent of the realization of another abstract vocalic element in Slavic languages, the YER, which has alternant realizations in the output (see Rubach & Booij 2001, and the references therein). The high measure of phonological regularity associated with the realization of JAT thus makes alternative analyses, such as an allomorphy based analysis, less than attractive.

Crucial evidence in favor of the proposed analysis comes from a group of eastern dialects of Bulgarian (Maslov 1956, Tilkov 1982), in which the alternation characteristic for the JAT forms in standard Bulgarian extends beyond the stems which contain a historical JAT. Thus the form in (39) above, *pol'ána/pol'áni* 'meadow (sg/pl)' which exhibits no alternation in standard Bulgarian, does alternate in the eastern dialects, as in *pol'ána/poléni* 'meadow (sg/pl)'. Under the JAT analysis, the difference between standard Bulgarian and the eastern dialects amounts to a minimal difference in constraint ranking: while in standard Bulgarian the positional constraint COINCIDE $(\pi,\sigma_{NUC})^2(\phi)$ ranks lower than any of the IDENT-π constraints, as in (62), in the eastern dialects this ranking will have to be reversed, with COINCIDE $(\pi,\sigma_{NUC})^2(\phi)$ outranking at least IDENT-π [V]. Thus, what appears to be a limited harmony effect in the JAT forms of standard Bulgarian becomes a more general harmony process in the eastern dialects, ultimately leading to a neutralization between JAT's π and regular π features, and possibly, also to a disappearance of JAT from their vocalic inventory. But if the alternating JAT forms in standard Bulgarian were analyzed as, say, a case of stem allomorphy, the situation in the eastern dialects would then need to be interpreted as a massive spread of stem allomorphy, and the corresponding reconstruction of a portion of the lexicon. Thus, the allomorphy based analysis would miss an important generalization: the simplified, and less abstract, nature of the vocalic inventory in the eastern dialects as compared to that of standard Bulgarian.

4   Conclusion

The markedness and positional constraints, which have been shown to play an important role in the distribution of the feature π in Bulgarian, are driven by organizational principles that govern the shapes of lexical entities, requiring predictable arrangement of phonological material. Crucially, these constraints respond with greater rigor to multiple, than to single, feature occurrences. We have identified two types of special phonological effects in Bulgarian, brought about by the pressure to resolve multiple feature occurrences within prosodic constituents: the dissimilatory OCP effect within the syllable leads to a reduction of markedness, while the assimilatory OCP effect within the foot leads to a reduction of syntagmatic contrast. Both target the feature π, shared by front vowels, palatal and palatalized consonants. The only obstacle to the agency of markedness and positional constraints is the significant function of phonological features to create lexical contrasts, which is protected by the set of faithfulness constraints.

In the analysis proposed here, the distribution of segments, in this case, the distribution of π-bearers, is regulated solely by phonological tools. It has been proposed, however, that phonetically grounded principles are the sole regulators of the distribution of phonological material (e.g. Flemming 2001, Steriade 2000). In this regard, it is of particular interest that the distribution of JAT's π differs from that of regular π-bearers. While all lexical π's are affected by the dissimilatory OCP effect, only one type of π, namely JAT's π, is affected by the assimilatory OCP effect. Thus, within the foot, JAT's π and regular π's differ in the observance of positional constraints in general, and of the self-conjoined positional constraint, in particular. This strongly suggests that the predictable arrangement of segments in linguistic forms, while most likely consistent with phonetic considerations, cannot be motivated solely by those considerations. Another force that needs to be recognized is grammar internal pressure that linguistic units exhibit a minimal degree of syntagmatic contrast. It is due to the lexically idiosyncratic status of JAT's π in the grammar of Bulgarian that its distribution exhibits a lower degree of syntagmatic contrast than do the distributions of regular π-bearers. As a consequence, the positioning of subsegment π exhibits a much lower degree of syntagmatic contrast than do regular π-bearers. Yet, if JAT's π and regular π-bearers are indistinguishable phonetically, then distributional regularities cannot be left entirely to phonetically motivated organizational principles. The case presented here provides a strong argument that specific feature arrangements may well be equally motivated by architecturally oriented principles that govern the internal organization of linguistic units. Moreover, I have shown that a configuration of the same type, that with multiple π-bearers within a given domain, is interpreted as offensive if targeted by a self-conjoined markedness constraint, yet as compliant if targeted by a self-conjoined positional constraint. This, too, strongly suggests that abstract, architectural principles are at work together with those that belong to the physical realm.

References

Alderete, J. (1997): Dissimilation as Local Conjunction. In: Kusumoto, K., ed. (1997): *NELS 27*. Amherst, MA: GLSA. 17–32.

Aronson, H. I. (1968): *Bulgarian Inflectional Morphophonology*. The Hague: Mouton.

Bernard, R. (1957): L'alternance *ja/e* de l'ancien *jat* en bulgare modern. *Revue des études slaves* 34. 15–31.

Clements, G. N. & Hume, E. V. (1995): The Internal Organization of Speech Sounds. In: Goldsmith, J. A., ed. (1995): *The Handbook of Phonological Theory*. Blackwell Publishers.

Ellison, T. Mark. (1995): *Phonological Derivation in Optimality Theory*. Ms, University of Edinburgh. (ROA-75-0000; http://roa.rutgers.edu).

Flemming, E. (2001): Scalar and Categorical Phenomena in a Unified Model of Phonetics and Phonology. *Phonology* 18. 7–14.

Fukazawa, H. (1999): *Theoretical Implications of OCP Effects on Features in Optimality Theory*. PhD dissertation, University of Maryland at College Park.

Goldsmith, J. (1976): *Autosegmental Phonology*. PhD dissertation, MIT.

Hauge, K. R. (1999): *A Short Grammar of Contemporary Bulgarian*. Bloomington, Indiana: Slavica

Itô, J. & Mester, A. (1986): The Phonology of Voicing in Japanese. Theoretical Consequences for Morphological Accessibility. *Linguistic Inquiry* 17. 49–73.

Itô, J. & Mester, A. (1998): Markedness and Word Structure: OCP Effects in Japanese. (ROA-255-0498; http://roa.rutgers.edu).

Kager, R. (1999): *Optimality Theory*. Cambridge University Press.

Leben, W. (1973): *Suprasegmental Phonology*. PhD dissertation, MIT.

Maslov, J. S. (1956): *Oerk bolgarskoj grammatiki*. Moskva: Izdatel'stvo literatury inostrannyx jazykax.

McCarthy, J. (1986): OCP Effects: Gemination and Antigemination. *Linguistic Inquiry* 17. 207–263.

McCarthy, J. & Prince, A. (1993): *Prosodic Morphology 1. Constraint Interaction and Satisfaction*. Ms, University of Massachusetts, Amherst & Rutgers University.

McCarthy, J. & Prince, A. (1995): Faithfulness and Reduplicative Identity. In: Beckman, J., Urbanczyk, S., & Walsh, L., eds. (1995): *Papers in Optimality Theory. University of Massachusetts Occasional Papers (UMOP)* 18. Amherst, MA: GLSA.

Padgett, J.(1995): Feature Classes. In: Beckman, J., Urbanczyk, S., & Walsh, L., eds. (1995): *Papers in Optimality Theory. University of Massachusetts Occasional Papers (UMOP)* 18. Amherst, MA: GLSA.

Pashov, P. (1966): *Bulgarskijat glagol*. Sofija: Nauka i iskustvo.

Prince, A. & Smolensky, P. (1993): *Optimality Theory. Constraint Interaction in Generative Grammar*. Ms, Rutgers University & University of Colorado, Boulder.

Rubach, J. & Booij, G. (2001): Allomorphy in Optimality Theory: Polish Iotation. *Language* 2001: 26-60.

Samilov, M. (1964): *The Phoneme JAT' in Slavic*. The Hague: Mouton & Co.

Scatton, E.A. (1984): *A Reference Grammar of Modern Bulgarian*. Columbus, OH: Slavica Publishers.

Shevelov, J. (1965): *A Prehistory of Slavic*. The Hague: Mouton.

Smolensky, P. (1995): *On the Structure of the Constraint Component Con of UG*. Ms. (ROA-86-0000; http://roa.rutgers.edu).

Steriade, D. (2000): Directional Asymmetries in Assimilation: A Directional Account. In: Hume, E. & Johnson, K., eds. (2000): *The Role of Speech Perception in Phonology*. New York: Academic Press.

Tilkov, D. (1982): *Gramatika na suvremennija bulgarski*. Sofija.
Yip, M. (1988): The Obligatory Contour Principle and Phonological Rules. A Loss of Identity. *Linguistic Inquiry* 19. 65–100.
Zoll, C. C. (1996): *Parsing Below the Segment in a Constraint Based Framework*. PhD dissertation, University of California, Berkeley.

Ithaca   Draga Zec

Cornell University, 203 Morill Hall, Ithaca, NY 14853
e-mail: DZ17@cornell.edu

Ineffability in Grammar

Gisbert Fanselow and Caroline Féry

Abstract

We examine different cases of ineffability, not only in phonology and syntax, but also in morphology and semantics, and propose a typology of ineffabilities compatible with the Control component of Orgun & Sprouse (1999). Lexical gaps as well as other gaps in the morpho-syntax or the phonology are the primary source of ineffable – or absolutely ungrammatical – constructions. Further gaps arise from the need to reconcile incompatible features. Whether such instances are repaired is language dependent. Islands and other restrictions resulting from syntactic and semantic laws on scope and wh-words form the third group of ineffable cases. The upshot of our study is that neither the lexicon-based nor the semantic ineffability cases are a problem for Optimality Theory, since they are located in domains of grammar for which OT's architecture cannot be held responsible.

1   Introduction[*]

The architecture of Optimality Theory (OT) makes a number of strong predictions concerning the nature of language, one of which is that there should not be any ungrammatical structures that cannot be "repaired", i.e. OT predicts the non-existence of "absolute ungrammaticality"[1] or "ineffability."

An OT grammar consists of a universal set of constraints on representations. Differences between languages are expressed in terms of variations in the ranking of these constraints. Relative to a given input i an equally universal component GEN generates a set of candidate representations. A candidate c is the well-formed realization of i (c is the "optimal candidate") if and only if there

[*] Numerous colleagues have provided us with examples of ineffability: Nick Clements, Norbert Corver, Laura Downing, Lyn Frazier, Elly van Gelderen, Carlos Gussenhoven, Hubert Haider, Martin Haspelmath, Fabian Heck, Markus Hiller, Erhard Hinrichs, Eric Hoekstra, Anders Holmberg, Helen de Hoop, Istvan Kenesei, Itziar Laka, Aniko Liptak, Alec Marantz, Gereon Müller, Diana Pili, Renate Raffelsiefen, Péter Rebrus, Henk van Riemsdijk, Ian Roberts, Rajendra Singh, Michal Starke, Rachel Walker, Gert Webelhuth, and Ede Zimmermann. We would like to thank them for their cooperation. Thanks also go to Birgit Alber, Jane Grimshaw, Ralf Vogel and Hubert Truckenbrodt for useful comments, though they may disagree with some of the opinions expressed in this paper. The research reported in this paper has been supported by grants of the Deutsche Forschungsgemeinschaft (DFG) to projects A1 (Féry) and A3 (Fanselow) of the Forschergruppe "Konfligierende Regeln" (Conflicting Rules) at the University of Potsdam.

[1] The term *absolute ungrammaticality* is not used here in contrast to *mild ungrammaticality* as in discussions of graded grammaticality, but in contrast to ungrammaticality relative to the existence of a "better" structure, as typical of OT.

is no other candidate c' which satisfies the constraint hierarchy better than c does. It follows that an optimal candidate in this sense can always be identified, so that there should be well-formed representations for all inputs, if the notion is defined in the way just indicated.

This prediction is not always borne out, and the failure of some inputs to find a surface realization has been called *ineffability* (Pesetsky 1997). For instance, in morphology, an input may consist of a set of morphemes, which the grammar combines in some order and some form. For most pairs of nouns and the diminutive suffixes *-chen* or *-lein* of German, well-formed results can be computed, as (1a–b) illustrate, but a diminutive is avoided if the resulting phonological structure is not well formed. Though the data are not completely straightforward, the following generalization makes reasonable predictions: For some speakers, no output exists for diminutive formation when the *umlauted* vowel does not bear main stress (1c–f). Thus, the input {Európa, chen} cannot be mapped onto a grammatical output. It is ineffable (Féry 1994).[2]

(1)   a. Jahr –> Jährchen 'year, dim.'
           Woche –> Wöchlein 'week, dim.'
        b. Bruder –> Brüderchen 'brother, dim.'
           Mauer –> Mäuerchen 'wall, dim.'
        c. Mónat –>[?]Monätchen, [?]Monatchen, *Mönatchen, *Mönätchen
           'month, dim.'
        d. Európa –> [?]Europächen, [?]Europachen, *Euröpächen 'Europe, dim.'
        e. Wérmuth –> [?]Wermüthchen, [?]Wermuthchen 'Vermouth, dim.'
        f. Wódka –> [?]Wodkächen, [?]Wodkachen, *Wödkachen, *Wödkächen
           'vodka, dim.'

Likewise, in a basic model for OT syntax, an input may be made up of a number of words grouped into predicate-argument structures (PAS) (see Grimshaw 1997). For each clause, there is one such PAS. When the PAS composed of *meet, the foreign minister, who, in Afghanistan* corresponds to a subordinate clause, grammatical sentences cannot always be computed, as the contrast in (2) shows. Requirements imposed by the matrix clause may imply that *who* be placed into clause-initial position, as in (2a), but these requirements may come into conflict with classical island constraints, as in (2b), without there being an alternative way of formulating what (2b) was intended to express. The meaning that (2b) attempts to convey is ineffable in English and many other languages, if not in all.

(2)   a. who did the president think that the foreign minister met in Afghani-
           stan?

---

[2] We are only interested in diminutive formations, not in hypochoristics (nicknames) like *Frauchen* 'Mama' (for a dog) or *Opachen* 'grand pa', since there are lexicalized instances of the latter with no umlaut.

    b. *who did the president resign although the foreign minister met in
       Afghanistan?

Linguists have been aware of such gaps in the generative capacity of grammars for quite some time (see, e.g. Hetzron 1975). They constitute no particular problem for grammars that employ devices such as inviolable constraints (see, e.g. Chomsky 1981), or conditions on the applicability of generative processes (see, e.g. Lexical Phonology, Kiparsky 1982). The ambitious assumptions made in OT, however, have turned ineffability into a major disturbing concern.

There are, essentially, two types of reactions to OT's ineffability problem.[3] First, many approaches concentrate on exploring formal means by which OT might be amended, so that cases of ineffability can be dealt with. Among these proposals are reference to null parses (see Prince & Smolensky 1993), bidirectional optimization (Wilson 1998), an additional control component (Orgun & Sprouse 1999), or the componential approach to metrics proposed by Hayes (2001). The latter four amendments may be called for independently, and they concede that classic/standard OT does not handle ineffability convincingly. The addition of the control component implies that ineffability is accounted for by a component external to and ordered after the OT grammar, whereas bidirectionality extends the domain of activity of OT by postulating that evaluation affects not only outputs generated from an input, but also potential inputs for outputs. In the second type of reaction, the existence of ineffability is taken as straightforward evidence for the claim that the domain of application of OT must be assessed conservatively. Thus, Pesetsky (1997) proposes that those aspects of syntax are amenable to an OT treatment that are concerned with the phonetic realization of abstract syntactic structure. All other aspects of syntax are free from conflictory principles. In a sense, the two kinds of reaction are similar.

The perspective of the present paper is different, having much in common with the general approach of Hetzron (1975): we wish to identify a *typology* of ineffabilities that helps to understand in which domains of language ineffability arises, and which domains are ineffability-free.

Ineffability is one of several properties of language which an OT grammar cannot account for straightforwardly. Other limitations arising as a consequence of OT's architectural decisions are the predicted absence of gradiency of grammatical judgments and optionality, due to the discrete decision-taking mechanism, and the impossibility of making reference to derivational steps within grammatical cycles, especially those leading to opacity, due to the nature of the EVAL component. These limitations resemble ineffability, since they appear to call for a more complex grammar. They also have in common that

---

[3] In addition, one can of course deny that there is a problem one needs to worry about. To the extent that outputs of grammatical computations need not be faithful to semantic aspects of the input, at least certain instances of ineffability fail to be a technical problem for OT (see, e.g. Legendre, Smolensky & Wilson 1998).

they relate to a situation in which the descriptive power of OT seems too restricted.[4]

Our answer is that at least ineffability is (by and large) related to architectural
aspects of OT that are problematic on grounds quite independent of ineffability,
so that ineffability needs no treatment of its own. First, the existence of "parochial" constraints cannot be denied, i.e. there are language-dependent
morpheme-specific restrictions, such as the need of German *-chen* and *-lein* to
be adjacent to a main stressed front vowel. The very existence of parochial constraints is incompatible with classical OT (since they are not universal) so
moving them to a separate lexicon-based control component is called for on
independent grounds. In this respect, we agree with many of the insights in
Orgun & Sprouse (1999). Parochial constraints as a source of ineffability are
addressed in section 3. They cover most (all?) cases of ineffability arising in the
interface between morphology and phonology, and may be extended to some
cases in syntax.

Second, quite a number of instances of ineffability in the syntax involve a
situation in which abstract syntactic constellations simply cannot be filled by
appropriate lexical items. Ineffability is due to lexical problems in this context,
too, but the problems are of a different sort: they involve lexical "gaps" of a
very specific type. If our solution is correct, it contributes to the still open discussion of what a syntactic input is (which is also relevant for the determination
of which cases involve ineffability, and what is the proper interpretation of the
term). These issues are addressed in section 4.

Section 5 is concerned with a remaining block of cases of ineffability coming
from syntax: island constraints or the scope taking behavior of quantifiers. For
many such cases, it can be shown that the winners of purely formal competitions
are uninterpretable either in semantic or in pragmatic terms.

Solving the difficulties just mentioned (parochiality, absence of lexical items,
nature of syntactic inputs) eliminates the corresponding cases of ineffability, so
that ineffability ceases to be a difficulty. It is just a visible side effect of the
suboptimal detail decisions made in classical OT. While the empirical scope of
pure OT *is* affected by the necessary amendments, the attractive architectural
properties of classical OT can be maintained for the core of the computational
domain. Giving up the idea that *the best is good enough* altogether (or modify-
ing it substantially) would leave unexplained why so many areas of phonology
and syntax are completely immune to ineffability. Section 6 gives a summary
and conclusion. But first, in the next section, the problem of ineffability is explained in more detail.

---

[4] A different, and in a sense opposite property of the grammar is its proneness to over-
generate. This is a problem which we will not consider in this paper, since it touches on an entirely
different field of research from the one we are interested in here.

2   Clarifying the concept of ineffability

Before we develop a classification of ineffabilities, the factors that determine the scope of the problem must be identified. Ignoring a possible philosophical dimension,[5] most (if not all) "meanings" can be expressed in one way or the other. Ineffability arises *relative to certain grammatical restrictions* of expression, and the concept is only useful to the extent that these restrictions can be identified. In OT, the nature of the input and what GEN can do to it define the limits of ineffability. Let us consider GEN first.

Sentence (3a) violates the (descriptive) generalizations that (a) neither *why* nor *how* may remain *in situ* and that (b) not more than one wh-word may be fronted in a question in English. (3a) is, arguably, an instance of ineffability in English, although its intended meaning *can* be expressed – not by rearranging or reshaping the morphemes in (3a), but by using a different type of construction, that is by using a paraphrase.

(3)   a. *how did he fix the car why?
       b. how did he fix the car, and why?

Returning to the examples in (1c,d), it can be observed that ?*Monätchen* or ?*Europächen* are semantically irreproachable. There is no problem with the meaning of *kleiner Monat* 'small month' or *kleines Europa* 'small Europe'.

The intuition that (1c–f) and (3a) are cases of ineffability is grounded on the insight that the grammatical system does not allow an arbitrary mapping of linguistic units (phonemes, morphemes, words), of "inputs", onto well-formed linguistic expressions. GEN *can* perform a multitude of operations, but arguably it cannot do everything. For the syntax, we would grant it the capacity to arrange the words in any order, to move them from one position to another, to delete them (under certain circumstances), and to insert designated material. We want to deny it the freedom of mapping a monoclausal input onto a biclausal output, or to exchange content words (as would be necessary to relate (3a) and (3b)). In that sense, (3a) is *technically ineffable relative to a specific input* like {*how, why, he, fix, the, car*}, because GEN cannot map this input onto (3b).

In contrast, ungrammatical (4a) does *not* exemplify ineffability: it is just one application of deleting functional *that* away from the grammatical output (4b), and the deletion of functional material is among the operations that the generative component GEN is able to perform. (5a), however, belongs to the realm of ineffability, since we do not want to allow GEN to map a monoclausal structure onto a coordinate construction like (5b): such powerful syntactic operations have not been proposed so far – at least not outside discussions of ineffability.

---

[5] For example, the question of whether all meanings can be expressed in all languages as they are given now (without changing them!), which may turn out to have a negative answer (see Kutschera 1975). Indeed, a meaning-related definition of ineffability may be far off the track; see below.

(4) a. *who do you think that t has bought an apple?
    b. who do you think t has bought an apple?

(5) a. *who came why?
    b. who came, and why

Likewise, morphology should not have the power of transforming an input consisting of a noun and an affix into an output consisting of a noun and an independent adjective. In that sense, {*Europa, chen*} must not end up as *kleines Europa*. The same point can be illustrated for phonology. It is commonly assumed that an input consists of just a string of segments – understood as bundles of features – and that the relevant candidates consist of more or less the same segments with additional structure: prosodic and intonational structure, phonetic information, and so on. An input like /church+s/ is not ineffable since epenthesis and voicing of obstruents are permissible operations turning /s/ into [iz], but an input consisting of a certain tone sequence, like H* L*+H H̄ L% and segmental material allowing only one syllable would deliver an ineffable output, at least outside of baroque music, since the tone sequence is too long to be associated with just a single syllable.

We cannot specify a complete list of "legal" operations of GEN here (or even sketch it), but we endorse a fairly conservative attitude towards the power of GEN: only well-attested operations (such as inserting or deleting a complementizer or a phonological feature) should be allowed. The choice may be crucial at certain points for the interpretation of specific constructions, but it arguably does not affect the overall existence of the types of ineffabilities we identify below[6]

What counts as a case of ineffability is thus a matter of the limits of GEN. The same is true for the nature of inputs – after all, it is *inputs* that are ineffable. Inputs are important for the understanding of ineffability in a very deep conceptual sense, but there is an empirical question involved, too, which we will discuss first.

The role of input choice for the nature of ineffability is less evident in phonology than in syntax, because phonology has developed a stable view of what counts as an input. For syntax, the makeup of inputs is much less clear, and this has consequences for the potential scope of ineffability.

Consider (6a) in this respect. At first glance (6a) does not seem to constitute an instance of ineffability, because its meaning can apparently be expressed by (6b). (6b) seems to be just a different way of arranging the same words. Whether

---

[6] Note that the view held here is wrong if the candidate set is not *computed/generated* from an input (as in Prince & Smolensky's original containment theory which we assume in this paper), but if *all* structures possibly generatable from *any* input are assessed in terms of faithfulness to a specific input (as in so-called correspondence theory). In this model, *kleiner Monat* 'small month' *is* a candidate realization of {*Monat, chen*} (just like the sentence *Hans liebt Maria* 'John loves Mary') because *all* linguistic structures are, and it may in fact be the optimal candidate. In such a view, there can hardly be any interesting instances of ineffability – but the problem seems eliminated at a cost: the blurring of what meaningful grammatical operations amount to.

this is a correct assessment or not depends, however, on the kind of information that is specified by the input. If the input of (6a) is just a Predicate Argument Structure (see Grimshaw 1997) in which *who* is the subject of *order*, and *what* is the object, the inputs of (6a) and (6b) are identical. Then, (6b) has a chance of blocking (6a) because the former respects the superiority condition (see Chomsky 1973), while the latter does not.

(6)   a. *what did who order?
       b. who ordered what?

Notice, however, that the German counterpart (7a) of (6a) *is* grammatical, and that it differs from the counterpart of (6b) in a subtle way, viz., in terms of information structure. Unlike (7b), (7a) presupposes that the wh-words are *d-linked* (see Pesetsky 1987) in the sense that (7a) is felicitous only if uttered in a context in which we know the persons that have ordered something, and in which we know what was ordered, so that we are merely unaware of the pairings. And it differs from (7b) (which also *may* have a d-linked interpretation) in terms of the sorting key (Comorovsky 1996) for the answers.

(7)   a. was   hat   wer   bestellt?
          what.acc has   who.nom   ordered

       b. wer hat was bestellt?

Thus, for German the following analysis seems to be called for: (7a) and (7b) do *not* block each other because there is an input difference related to information structure such that the inputs that map onto (7a) would not map onto (7b), and vice versa.

Since OT assumes that languages may differ relative to the ranking of the principles only, and not along the lines of what may be part of an input, it suddenly appears as if the input leading to German (7a) *is* ineffable in English, since (6a) is ungrammatical and (6b) does not invite the sorting key of (7a). In addition, English *does* make use of the pertinent distinctions, as (8) illustrates; see Pesetsky (1987), among others.

(8)   a. which wine did which man order?
       b. which man ordered which wine?

Whether (6a) involves ineffability or not is thus not really determined by the power of GEN, but by what can and must be part of an input in a multiple question. The absence of a generally accepted concept of inputs in OT syntax thus makes it hard to decide whether a structure instantiates the ineffability problem or not.

In many cases, however, decisions concerning individual constructions may not matter too much for the development of a typology of ineffability. Consider, for example, comparative formation in English. An input consisting of the phonetic strings *intelligent* and *-er* is ineffable (unless we make the unlikely assumption that GEN can transform this into *more intelligent*), but if the input is more abstract (say, *intelligent* plus an abstract comparative morpheme), it makes sense to assume that **intelligenter* and *more intelligent* are candidates in the same competition. A decision between these two options is (presumably) of relevance for the grammar of English comparatives, but less so for the theory of ineffability, because there are other cases in which phonologically definable conditions block the combination of two morphemes that cannot be explained away by using abstract morphemes (see the cases in section 3.1).

Several possible formal properties of inputs have been discussed in the OT literature. In syntax, it seems obvious that the (content) words making up a sentence S must have been part of the input of S, but whether other semantic aspects of S are represented in the input is an open issue. Suppose, for example, that the intended scope of operators (such as wh-words or quantifiers) is represented in the input. The fact that some scope relation cannot be expressed in some language would then be an instance of ineffability. Encoding scope relations in an input that is itself not a hierarchical structure is a non-trivial matter, however, but assuming that Logical Form or the like is (part of) syntactic inputs implies that there is a *grammar* for constructing well-formed LFs that is not part of the syntactic evaluation (see, e.g. Heck et al. 2000). But if one refrains from representing scope relations in the input, ineffability is *not* involved when we observe that a certain scope constellation is inexpressible in a given language. In a sense, then, the attempt to understand ineffability in terms of meanings that cannot be formulated is quite misguided. Ineffability is a *formal* problem of OT; its scope is a function of the nature of the input, the nature of GEN, and the correspondence-containment issue. Like ungrammaticality (and unlike unacceptability), ineffability is thus a theoretical concept.

3   Idiosyncratic Troublemakers

3.1   A Lexical Control Component

3.1.1 Morphemic-dependent vs. language-dependent defectiveness

It seems safe to begin a typology of ineffability with a domain for which it is easy to identify the factor to be blamed: lexical blocking. Obviously, the input *go+ed* cannot surface because it is blocked by *went*. It is the presence of a specific lexical entry that prevents the overt realization of an input. According to Aronoff (1976), who has documented blocking for English extensively, the formation of **gloriosity* and **spaciosity* is blocked in (9) by the existence of the non-derived synonyms *glory* and *space*. No well-formed output corresponds to the input *glorious+ity*. We assume that this first type of ineffability can be circumscribed in more general terms as in (10).

(9)   Data from Aronoff:

    various   *   variety
    curious   *   curiosity
    glorious   glory   *gloriosity
    spacious   space   *spaciosity .

(10)   Lexical specifications may cause ineffability of inputs

Lexical blocking is not the only way in which lexical specifications affect the domain of application of word formation rules. When examining ineffability as a consequence of morphemic gaps, it is useful to distinguish between two separate sources: lexical gaps touching individual morphemes and language dependent restrictions on specific operations or configurations. Morphological defectivity is an example for the first kind. Certain Russian verbs lack a first person singular present form (brought to our attention by Martin Haspelmath), e.g. *pobezhu* 'I defeat', *pobedish'* 'you defeat', *pobedit* 's/he defeats'. Hungarian morphology does not tolerate the subjunctive/imperative form(s) of verbs of a certain morphonological constitution (11), although the meanings should in principle be possible (Istvan Kénesei, Péter Rebrus, p.c.). Vowel epenthesis inside of the impossible consonant sequences is idiosyncratically forbidden in these verbs, as exemplified in (11a), though it is possible in other verbs; see (11b). The relevant restrictions must be stated as properties of individual lexical items. Both the Russian and the Hungarian cases are discussed in detail by Hetzron (1975), who argues convincingly that there is no general synchronic regularity behind these restrictions on expressivity.

(11)   a. csukl-ik 'he hiccups', *(ne) csuk<u>o</u>l-j- 'don't hiccup-JUSSIVE.',
           *csuklhat/ *csuk<u>o</u>lhat 'he may hiccup'

        b. zajl-ik '(river) begin to freeze' zaj<u>o</u>l-j-on 'freeze-SUBJ-3SG'
           ug<u>r</u>ik 'he jumps', ug<u>o</u>rhat 'he may jump'

Another case in point is the defectiveness of some verbs' paradigms, like *frire* 'to fry' or *clore* 'to shut' in French. These verbs have no first and second person plural forms, though the other forms are regular. The non-existent *nous clos-ons/vous closez* 'we/you shut' and *nous frions/vous friez* 'we/you fry' are phonologically well formed, as similar forms *nous cuisons/vous cuisez* 'we/you cook' and *nous rions/vous riez* 'we/you laugh' testify, but are nevertheless absent from the vocabulary of most French speakers.[7] The past participle of the

---

[7] In all the cases of partial paradigmatic defectivity of finite verbs we are aware of it is the first and/or the second person which are concerned, never the third. We assume a correlation with the markedness of persons, but do not pursue this issue here.

English verb 'to dive' seems likewise to be avoided by many English speakers, especially those who have *dove* (and not *dived*) as the past inflected form.

These examples illustrate at least one point. They show that languages may have morpheme- or language particular ("parochial") constraints,[8] and that these may lead to ineffability.

Technically, the parochial constraints might simply be part of the overall evaluation component EVAL; they might be "declared" universal. Parochiality would then manifest itself in the formulation of a constraint, or in its rank. For instance, if the constraint banning *pobezhu* is part of the grammar of German, we can guarantee that it will have no effect there – either by formulating it in a morpheme-specific way so that it could not possibly apply to any input of German, or by giving it a very low rank in this language (so that it will always be overriden by other principles). This treatment of parochial constraints is compatible with the formal makeup of OT, but is certainly not in its spirit: universal principles should not be universal just because their formulation guarantees that they apply to a specific Russian morpheme combination only! A license for adding language-specific constraints (aiming at blocking the formation of just one word) to the universal set of constraints would also render OT vulnerable to the criticism that it cannot be falsified, since it would always be possible to make up a construction-specific constraint for a certain language, which is ranked at the bottom of EVAL in all the others. So much expressive power should not be granted.

Therefore the postulation of a *separate* component of morpheme-specific and language particular constraints *in addition to EVAL* cannot be avoided. There is a lexical control component that may rule out the realization of certain inputs altogether. Candidates that are optimal from the perspective of EVAL may fail to survive this control component, because the lexicon already specifies a simplex competitor (lexical blocking), but the control component may also specify parochial constraints that rule out, e.g. the realization of certain combinations of features for some lexical items, as has been suggested by Orgun & Sprouse (1999). Both the verb defectivity and the Finnish infinitive negation (see section 3.1.2) are of this kind.[9]

---

[8] Restrictions may be parochial even if their effect shows up in other languages, too. The important property is that they are linked to lexical elements (and that straightforward repairs may be possible in one language, but not in others).

[9] The question may arise whether the morpheme combinations implying ineffability, like *Monat+chen* and *who came why*, could not rather be blocked at a very early derivational stage of grammar, namely by hard constraints of UG blocking their combination. We reject this possibility mainly because it is incompatible with the *Richness of the Base* (Prince & Smolensky 1993), one of the central assumptions of OT, which posits that inputs should be free and that all inputs should be allowed to enter the grammatical competition. According to Richness of the Base, it is the task of the constraint hierarchy, thus of the grammar, to eliminate bad outputs, which means that no input can be eliminated on the basis of its ill-formedness relative to its possible output. A second problem of letting the input solution eliminate these data is that, as shown below, some of the constraints involved in ineffability, like constraints on movement and constraints prohibiting unstressed umlauted vowel in the vicinity of a triggering suffix (*Monat+chen*) or multiple wh-questions (*who came why*), are not universally respected. The status of certain inputs could be at best decided on a lan-

The control component idea competes with a proposal of Prince & Smolensky (1993), who account for the ineffability arising with Latinate suffixes by making a "null parse" the winner of EVAL. They assume that the set of outputs generated by the GEN component always includes the null parse, a phonetically empty candidate. In order to work, this analysis requires a family of constraints stating that morphemes, words and other elements of the input are phonetically realized (M-PARSE: 'Morphemes are phonetically realized.') ranked below constraints eliminating all other candidates (see Orgun & Sprouse 1999 for convincing argumentation against the null parse analysis).

Since *some* examples of ineffability are due to lexical control, it is natural to attempt to capture as much of ineffability as possible in terms of this extra component of the grammar. In the following sections, we therefore extend the scope of control, and argue that its effects are not limited to morphological facts, but can also be discovered in different parts of phonology, syntax, and, most of all, in interface domains. The division our survey is based on focuses on the contrast between morpheme-dependent ineffability on the one hand, and language-dependent restrictions on linguistic structures, on the other hand. In an attempt to generalize what can be observed from the facts, the first set of cases consists of lexical gaps and restrictions on word-formation which are special to some words and morphemes, while the second set of cases block some operations in a language-specific way. No repair is allowed. The latter cases all come from quantity restrictions or limits on the associations between "autosegmental" elements, where autosegmental is understood in a very general sense. Some operations would associate too much or too few of some kinds of linguistic elements, like segments, consonants or tones.

3.1.2 Restrictions on morphemic productivity

We have seen that EVAL should not be loaded with language-specific constraints, and that a control component cannot be avoided. We would like to argue that quite a number of well-known and lesser-known cases of ineffability reduce to it. Our first example, suffixation of *-ize* to an adjectival stem, has been discussed several times in the OT literature, beginning with Raffelsiefen (1996, 1998). Whereas some adjectives can be derived with the suffix *-ize* to form a verb, others cannot.

(14)   Suffixation of *-ize*

      a. rándom –> rándomìze   b. corrúpt –> *corruptize
         fóreign –> fóreignìze   obscéne –> *obscenize
         vápor –> váporìze   secúre –> *securize

guage-particular basis for these examples – clearly an undesirable step, since OT claims that linguistic variation is restricted to the ranking of constraints in EVAL.

Raffelsiefen argues that the position of stress in the underived adjectives is responsible for the contrast between the grammatical words in (14a) and the ungrammatical ones in (14b). In the adjectives in (14a) stress is penultimate, thus non-final, whereas in the adjectives in (14b), stress is final. The generalization arising from these data is that the suffix *-ize* can only be adjoined to a nonfinally stressed adjective, and not to a finally stressed one. One can account for this in terms of a constraint prohibiting stress clash, since *-ize* has secondary stress. However, the relevant constraint, *STRESSCLASH, is not unviolable in English, as is also visible from words like *Chìnése, gymnàst* and the like, with adjacent main and secondary stresses (see also Kager 1999). An obvious repair to compensate for the effect of *STRESSCLASH could be to shift the stress in *obscenize, securize,* etc. away from the final stem syllable. Stress shift is found in numerous other instances of suffixation in English, as, for example, in the well-known pairs *átom/atómic, ìnstrument/instruméntal.* The optimal candidate *óbscenìze,* the winner of the evaluation, may then fail to pass a *morpheme-specific* constraint in the control component that requires that the first syllable of a (possibly polysyllabic) adjectival stem like *obscene* must not bear main stress. If correct, this analysis also shows that the lexical control must *follow* rather than precede the selection of the optimal candidate (because otherwise, it would only lead to the failure of stress shift to apply).

The constraints relevant for the blocking of some diminutives in German, like *Monätchen* (see (1), repeated here as (15)), are violable, too.

(15)   Suffixation of the German diminutive suffixes -chen and -lein

        a. Jáhr –> Jährchen 'year, dim.'
           Wóche –> Wöchlein 'week, dim.'
        b. Brúder –> Brüderchen 'brother, dim.'
           Máuer –> Mäuerchen 'wall, dim.'
        c. Mónat –>$^?$Monätchen, $^?$Monatchen, *Mönatchen, *Mönätchen
           'month, dim.'
        d. Európa –> $^?$Europächen, $^?$Europachen, *Euröpächen 'Europe, dim.'
        e. Wérmuth –> $^?$Wermüthchen, $^?$Wermuthchen 'Vermouth, dim.'
        f. Wódka –> $^?$Wodkächen, $^?$Wodkachen, *Wödkachen, *Wödkächen
           'vodka, dim.'

The first constraint, in (16a), is NOUNSTRESSED[ü/ö/ä], which prohibits unstressed umlauted vowels (compare, however, *möblíeren* 'to furnish' with an unstressed umlauted vowel, showing that this constraint is violable). A second constraint, ALIGNR(front), formulated in (16b), requires the association of the feature [front] with a full vowel as far to the right as possible. Nonrecursivity of association must be guaranteed, as well. And FAITH(front), formulated in (16c), requires that [front], a feature intrinsic of the diminutive morphemes, be realized. As a rule, attachment of *-chen* to a finally stressed stem triggers umlaut of the stressed vowel (15a), though words with a – metrically invisible – schwa syllable between the stressed umlauted vowel and the suffix triggering umlaut are also grammatical (15b). Violations are shown in (17).

(16)   a. NoUNSTRESSED[ü/ä/ö]: Umlauted vowels are stressed.

       b. ALIGNR(front): The feature [front] is right aligned in the stem.

       c. FAITH(front): The feature [front] is realized.

(17)   *Mönatchen: violate ALIGNR(front)

       *Monätchen: violates NoUNSTRESSED[ü/ä/ö]

       *Monatchen: violates FAITH(front)

In the case of *-chen*, the control component specifies that the word resulting from the diminutive suffixation must fulfill the requirements that the full vowel immediately preceding *-chen* have main stress and be umlauted. If these conditions are not fulfilled, the optimal candidate, whatever exact form it has, does not survive and the result is ineffability. Besides being a general constraint against words with the wrong prosodic structure, it also has a filtering function in that it allows some expressions like *Wérmúthchen*, which is occasionally realized from *Wérmuth+chen*.[10]

The next case of morphological defectiveness due to idiosyncratic restrictions located in the control component concerns segmental well-formedness in a small part of language-specific morphologies. There is a well-known constraint in Swedish and Norwegian morphology on adjectives like *lat* 'lazy' and *rädd* 'scared'. These adjectives cannot be used attributively with neuter nouns, like Swedish *barn* 'child' (we owe this example to Anders Holmberg and Renate Raffelsiefen). Though some authors have proposed to explain the restriction in semantic terms, it looks as if it may be more fruitful to anchor the active constraints in the phonology.[11] All forms in (18) consist of a stem plus an inflectional suffix [t]. In (18a), the morphologically correct forms would be *latt* and *flatt* with a geminate final consonant, which are phonologically fine (compare *het-hett* 'hot'), but nevertheless totally unacceptable when used attributively.

____

[10] The grammar of diminutive formations involves variation among speakers and gradedness of judgments to a high extent. In this sense, it involves ineffability only for those speakers of German who do not accept *any* of the options for the diminutive of *Monat* in (17) (and related cases).

[11] It has been claimed that the blocked adjectives denote mental states. However, there are some adjectives that do not denote mental states, like *flatt* 'flat', which are nevertheless subject to the restriction in question. Conversely, *glatt* 'happy', denotes a mental state but is free to appear before a neuter noun (Viktoria Dryselius, p.c.).

(18)   Gaps in the neuter adjectives in Swedish α

a. *ett latt barn [lɑːt/lat] 'a lazy child'   en lat pojke [lat] 'a lazy boy'
   *ett flatt hus [flɑːt/flat] 'a flat house'   en flat tallrik [flat] 'a flat plate'

b. ett glatt barn [glat] 'a happy child'   en glad pojke [glɑːd] 'a happy boy'
   ett platt hus [plat] 'a flat house'   en plat tallrik [plat] 'a flat plate'
   ett solitt hus [solit] 'a solid house'   en solid byggnad [liːd] 'a solid building'

c. *ett rätt barn [rɛt] 'a scared child'   en rädd pojke [rɛdː] 'a scared boy'

Raffelsiefen (2002) suggests that the reason for ineffability in (18a) is that the neuter formation would imply lengthening of the final consonant and a con-comittant change in the quality of the low vowel ([a] –> [ɑː]). This change, being too drastic, is avoided, and no other repair is acceptable. The fact that the change is admissible in [glat]/[glɑːd] in (18b) has to do with the independent existence of [glɑːd] as the supine of the related verb *glädja* 'to make happy'. Also according to Raffelsiefen (2002) the phonological form [lat] without gemi-nation violates a minimality condition active in complex formations in Swedish. The ineffability visible in (18c) requires a different explanation. Here, there is a conflict between the voiced and geminate ending in *rätt* (as in *en rädd pojke* [rɛdː] 'a scared boy') and the voiceless inflection *t* which cannot be resolved. The explanation for ineffability is to be sought in the forbidden mapping of a particular input onto a specific surface syllable structure. The role of the control component here is to compare a surface syllable structure with an underlying segmental structure and to filter out some configurations in specific morpho-syntactic structures.[12]

A last example of morphemic ineffability comes from Finnish. As Anders Holmberg points out, non-finite sentences in this language cannot be negated by using the negation word *ei* (19a), because this word *must* carry subject agree-ment, but cannot do so in an infinitive. One has to use an infinitival form with a suffix meaning 'without' for expressing meanings like 'I promised not to go out.' (19b). Since, obviously, *ei* does not have an infinitive form, we are again confronted with a case of a defective paradigm with consequences for syntax.

(19)   a. *Lupasin ei mennä ulos
          promised.1SG not go out

       b. Lupasin olla menemättä ulos.
          promised.1SG be go-INF-WITHOUT out
          'I promised to be without going out'

[12] In fact, as Birgit Alber (p.c.) suggests, the control component analysis may be considered to be strengthened if it turns out that the set of lexemes obeying the restriction must simply be listed.

3.1.3 Language-dependent Quantity Mismatches

In this section we present a second kind of morphemic defectivity, viz., ineffability of structures arising as a result of prosodic properties rendering the expression too light, too heavy, or loaded with too many association lines. In case no repair happens, we assume that here, too, the control component is at play filtering out the non-conformists.

An important source of ineffability comes from prosodic minimality (McCarthy & Prince 1995). Syllables, feet and prosodic words can be too light for some morphological or other linguistic operations, or just too light to form the relevant constituent higher in the hierarchy. In many cases, languages confronted with too light constituents use augmentation strategies (see the cases described by McCarthy & Prince 1995, like Lardil and Axininca Campa). Mester (1994) explains iambic lengthening in Latin as an instance of adding weight to syllables in order to attain well-formed feet. Iambic lengthening in general also happens for reasons of minimal weight, or amelioration of foot form (see Hayes 1995). However, in some cases, nothing can be done to augment too light constituents, and the conflict between prosodic lightness and the requirement of a minimal weight leads to ineffability.

The first case illustrating subminimality is taken from Orgun & Sprouse (1999), see also Ito & Hankamer (1989). In Istanbul Turkish, a suffixed root must be at least disyllabic, as shown by the well-formed *sol-yim* 'my G (musical note)'. If the result of suffixation would be monosyllabic, it cannot apply and the intended meaning is ineffable. This is shown by **do-m* in (20b).

(20)   Root   Suffixed form (σσ minimum)

      a. sol^j 'musical note G'   sol^j-yim   'my G'
      b. do 'C'   *do-m   'my C'
      c. it 'dog'   /it + m/ itim   'my dog'

Repair of subminimal roots by epenthesis is not possible in (20b), though epenthesis is an option in other formations, as for example in (20c). The difference between the ineffable and the licit cases is that the epenthetic vowel in *itim* does not trigger a hiatus, while it would do so in the case of *dom* (**doum*). Epenthesis at the edge of the word is also impossible because of unviolable alignment constraints, which means that forms like **idom* or **domi* are also excluded.

Also related case is the fact that some words escape augmenting altogether, though their phonological structure would allow augmentation, for instance by lengthening a short vowel. In many cases, there exist suppletive forms (simple clitics vs. special clitics). But in some cases no suppletion is available. As a case in point, consider the pronoun *es* 'it' in German, which avoids stressing and even positions requiring a certain amount of stressing as a consequence of being a phonological phrase, and thus a foot: **Es habe ich gesehen* 'It I have seen' with topicalized *es* is not grammatical. A demonstrative can be used instead,

Das ('that') *habe ich gesehen*, but one can question whether pronouns and demonstratives are competitors in a single evaluation.

These two cases of subminimality belong to the realm of control, since the grammars of the languages under consideration in principle allow the required operations to obtain minimality. In German, pronouns usually have at least a strong and a weak form (*ihn* '3.sg.acc' is [i:n] or [ən] for instance), and the strong form is used for topicalization, since topics must be at least a foot (*Ihn habe ich gesehen* 'Him I saw' is perfect). The prohibition against topicalizing *es* is thus special to this pronoun, and is not a consequence of the grammar of German as a whole. Thus we attribute the task of rejecting an augmented form of *es* to the control component.

So-called templatic morphology provides further interesting cases that may be handled via lexical control. Consider the following fact mentioned to us by Rachel Walker and discussed in Rose (1999). In Chaha (Ethio-Semitic), frequentative verbs have the following shape with four consonants: CiCVCəC. When the consonantal root has three consonants, the second one is copied to fill the extra C slot, as shown in (21a). In the case of diliteral root verbs, as in (21b), there is no grammatical output, because no tri-linking or no double copy of Cs is allowed.[13] As a result, one of the C slots cannot be filled, and there is a failure to form frequentative verbs. This is also true of quadriliterals, but for a different reason. Here, the frequentative is indistinguishable from the regular form. Again, no repair applies. Notice that the failure of diliterals to form frequentatives is not a universal restriction, since tri-linking of Cs is possible in related languages, like in Tigrinya, as shown in (22).

(21) Frequentatives in Chaha

Root	Regular		Frequentative	
a. sbr	sabərə	'break'	sibəbər	'break in pieces'
mzr	mezərə-m	'count'	mizəzər	'count again'
b. nd	nədəd	'burn'	*nidədəd	'burn again'
t'm	t'əməm	'bend'	* t'iməməm	'bend again'

(22) Frequentatives in Tigrinya

ħt	hatət	'ask'	hatatət	'ask many people'
k'd	k'ədəd	'tear'	k'ədadəd	'tear again'

In the case of Chaha, the control component must posit that even though outputs like [nidədəd] are optimal, they do not pass the language-specific filtering restriction against tri-linked consonants.

---

[13] According to Sharon Rose (p.c.), this is a very general restriction in Chaha. For example, there are no quadriconsonantal verbs of the type 1333, but there are verbs of the type 1234, 1233 and 1212 (the numbers refer to root consonants).

Wellformedness gaps in the paradigms of some morphemes can be language-specific or morpheme-specific. The metrical restrictions involving words derived with *-ize* or *-chen* are clearly morpheme-specific, since other affixes tolerate stress clash in English or the absence of a trochaic structure in German. In Chaha, as in the Turkish example involving subminimality, ineffability arises as a consequence of *global* restrictions holding in the language as a whole. The templatic and metrical conditions blocking the formations of *nɨdədəd and *do-m have consequences on the formation of the words which *should* violate them in order to be formed. Instead of being repaired, these words simply do not exist. The constraints in question do not have to be expressed as lexical properties on independent grounds – but they can be so (when one takes CV-templates as lexical elements). It is advantageous to do so because it allows us to capture the pertinent cases of ineffability in terms of lexical control as well.

The domain of the control component can in this sense be extended to tonal morphemes. As Pierrehumbert & Hirschberg (1990) have shown for English, the melody of a sentence – its tune – is the result of the individual tones composing it. A tune is like a sentence, but the set of legal tunes is highly constrained and lexicalized. It has a meaning derived compositionally from the individual morphemes, the tones (Bolinger 1958). The tune and the tones are realized on words, syllables and segments. Given the intonational facts and the prosodic constituency, one can reasonably expect that all well-formed tonal sequences can be realized on all well-formed segmental strings, where "well-formed" means large enough to form a tonal domain – a bimoraic syllable, since this is the minimal foot, and by extension, the minimal Phonological Phrase and Intonation Phrase. This prediction is, however, not always borne out. A first case of tonal ineffability comes from Standard German, where a fall-rise pattern on a syllable with just one moraic sonorant is grammatical (23c) but a rise-fall is not, as shown in (24c) (Féry 1993). Fall-rise and rise-fall are complex tonal movements consisting of three tones, HLH and LHL. Both a fall-rise and a rise-fall pattern are perfect when realized on more than one syllable, as shown in (23a) and (24a). In fact, the pattern is perfect even when associated with a syllable consisting of two sonorant moras, like a long vowel, as shown in (23b) and (24b). In this case the meaning of the fall-rise in (23b) is slightly different from the one intended in (23a): it is mildly menacing, which it is not in (23a). Complex tones on short segmental strings tend to have idiosyncratic meanings – a fact which could be interpreted as ineffability, since the compositional meaning is then no longer expressible.

Conceivable repairs (truncation of one of the tones, lengthening of the vowel or syllable reduplication) are just unavailable. The fact that the fall-rise is possible on one mora shows that ineffability is at play in the case of the rise-fall. It is not the three tones which are not realizable, but the three tones in a certain combination.

(23)   Fall-rise

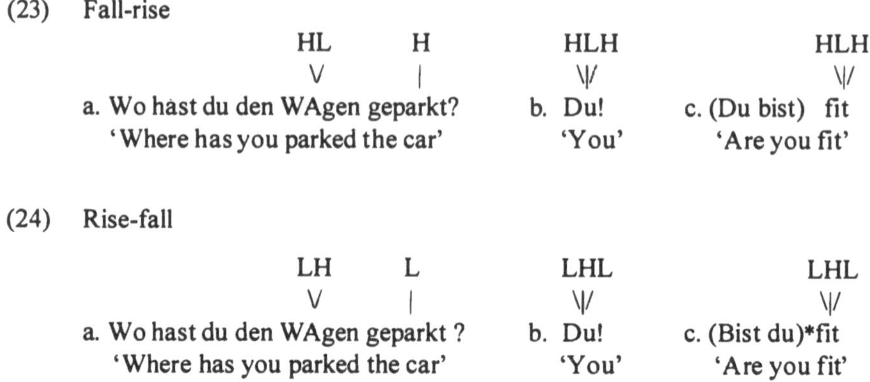

                     HL   H   HLH   HLH

a. Wo hàst du den WAgen geparkt?   b. Du!   c. (Du bist) fit
   'Where has you parked the car'   'You'   'Are you fit'

(24)   Rise-fall

                     LH   L   LHL   LHL

a. Wo hast du den WAgen geparkt ?   b. Du!   c. (Bist du)*fit
   'Where has you parked the car'   'You'   'Are you fit'

Even more intriguing are the cases described by Gussenhoven & van der Vliet (1999). In the Venlo dialect of Dutch, a configuration consisting of a fall-rise with four tones is well formed (25b), but one consisting of only three (25a) is not. In the examples, [] are Intonation Phrase boundaries, and {} are utterance boundaries. H* is the pitch accent associated with the accented syllable, L_i is a low boundary tone for an Intonation Phrase and H_u a high boundary tone for an utterance.

(25)   a. {[ɪs tɛt ənə be: ʀ]}   'Is it a bear?'
              | \| |
           H*$L_i H_u$

    b. {[ɪs tɛt be: ʀ]}   'Is it beer?'
         | \ | |
      H*$LL_i H_u$

Venlo Dutch is a language with two lexical tones, accent I and II. The sequences of tones H*$L_i H_u$ and H*$LL_i H_u$ are the expected ones for a plain question for accent I and accent II, respectively, given the compositionality of the tunes, but the former sequence is ineffable. The tone-bearing syllable [be:] with the tonal configuration given in (25a) for accent I would be undistinguishable from the one in (25b) for accent II, an intolerable situation. The speakers react by refusing to realize (25a), and replace the tone sequence with a different one, called the 'Surprised Question,' which is otherwise part of a different paradigm. We conclude from this that the tone sequence for a normal question including an accent I, though optimal, is rejected by the control component because it falls together with another well-formed tune with the same meaning. This effect can be compared to what was said for derived nouns like *gloriosity*, which were eliminated by control because their meaning would fall together with an existing simple noun; see the generalization in (10). In other words, it is not the meaning expressed by a certain sequence of tones which is ineffable, but the sequence of tones itself.

We stipulate that the control component not only verifies 'ordinary' morphemes and words, consisting of strings of segments, but also lexicalized tunes and tonal morphemes, consisting of strings of tones. When the tonal composition of a tune does not conform to the requirements of the language or when the tonal configuration is already occupied by a similar tune, the candidate is rejected and ineffability of the input is the result.

3.2 Preliminary Summary

It is a truism that the lexicon can specify a number of idiosyncratic properties for individual morphemic items, as well as the way they combine with each other. These constraints seem to be arranged as a lexical control component that is imposed on the optimal candidates computed by EVAL. In other words, the outputs of the standard OT grammar are not automatically grammatical. They have to be checked by the lexical control component, which can block the optimal candidate because of incompatibility with specific constraints. The result yields grammaticality or ineffability. Many examples of ineffability related to phonological properties reduce to lexical control.

If our survey of ineffabilities is representative, one can even claim that *all* instances of phonology-controlled ineffability stem from the lexical control component. When no lexical factors are involved, phonology does *not* seem to run into the ineffability problem – with the possible trivial exception of unpronounceable segment sequences. There are no cases of ineffability we are aware of that arise because a principle of *automatic* phonology (say, syllable formation) leads to ineffability because of a conflict with a further principle of the same component. For automatic phonology, the predictions of OT seem realized *in toto*: the principles are universal (because they relate to markedness considerations), and conflicts are always resolved in a way that yields a winning structure that can be spelt out. It is only parochiality that may lead to ineffability; phonology-related ineffability stems from the control component. It remains to be clarified how the control component is organized, an issue we will not take up here. In particular, we have made no effort to explain the difference between morphological defectiveness, as illustrated by the examples discussed briefly for Russian, Hungarian and French, and paradigmatic ineffability concerning classes of morphemes, on the one hand, and language-wide quantity mismatches, on the other hand. In a more elaborate proposal, the role of Control should be clarified, since it has the power to eliminate linguistic structures on the basis of a whole array of criteria. Different modules of grammar will participate, and in some cases work together, to eliminate the ineffable candidates. For syntactic and semantic restrictions that may be specified in the lexicon, the picture is even less clear, though it is a natural consequence of our approach that control might be expanded to cover some of these cases as well, as the next sections illustrate.

3.3   Combinatory Control Constraints?

The combinatorial aspects of morphology (or syntax) seem to provide some obvious examples of ineffability caused by lexical control. For instance, the well-formedness of combinations of stems with affixes can depend on arbitrarily defined declensional classes. Illegal combinations seem hard to block in terms of GEN (after all, inputs should be freely selectable, and GEN should at least be able to conjoin two elements!),[14] while selectional statements linked to individual morphemes according to class can filter out unwanted combinations easily.

In German, a handful of verbs like *uraufführen* 'to premiere' composed of a verbal stem and *two* particles cannot be used in a matrix clause in the present and past tenses (26)[15]. This behavior is due to the fact that finite verbs must be placed into second position in matrix clauses, and that verbal particles must be stranded in this process according to certain conditions involving stress. Stressed particles are stranded (compare *dass er heute an-fängt* 'that he today begins' with *er fängt heute an, *er anfängt heute*), while unstressed ones are pied-piped (compare *dass er heute ent-flieht* 'that he today escapes' with *er entflieht heute, *er flieht heute ent*).

(26)   a. dass wir das Stück ur-auf-führen
          that we the play ptc-ptc-lead
          'that we premiere the play'
       b. *wir uraufführen das Stück
       c. *wir aufführen das Stück ur
       d. *wir führen das Stück urauf
       e. *wir urführen das Stück auf

Although *ur* never actually appears in a stranded position, it can be argued that this particle would have to be stranded according to the general laws of German. *Ur* bears stress, to which strandability is linked. Furthermore, the placement of the infinitive morpheme *zu* in *uraufzuführen* and the placement of the *ge-* prefix of the participle in *uraufgeführt* implies that *urauf* involves detachable material. From these considerations, it follows that (26d) *is* the winner of the competition between (26b–e), but is blocked in a control component that requires that *ur* must be phonetically adjacent to a verbal category. There seems to be no alter-

---

[14] Our conclusion would be incorrect if the combinatory power of GEN is sensitive to the subcategorization requirements of morphemes, such that A can be conjoined with B only of A selects B or vice versa (as proposed, e.g. by Stabler 1996, or as is true of HPSG). In such a model, GEN would *fail* to apply to certain inputs. See note 9 for further remarks on such approaches.

[15] For those speakers who allow *do*-periphrasis, the situation in (26) does not necessarily lead to ineffability.

native to this treatment, in particular because the rare examples of verbs that involve only *ur* (*urzeugen, urformen*) show exactly the same stranding difficulties. The principled case for the existence of lexical control effects in the syntax has thus been made.[16] While there are, thus, instances of lexical control effects that go beyond mere phonological consequences, it seems that not all lexicon-related instances of ineffability in syntax are control based. We show this for a particular aspect of lexical features here, and return to the general point in section 4.

One of the properties that must be specified with particular lexical entries is non-structural exceptional Case. German transitive verbs assign accusative case to their objects, but some are constructed with the dative (*helfen* 'help') or the genitive (*gedenken* 'commemorate'). Likewise, *gefallen* 'please' requires a dative object. It is a commonly held view that this lexical specification leads to ineffability problems in a number of circumstances. The examples in (27)–(29) contrast the grammatical potential of *unterstützen* 'support' (with a regular case marking frame) with that of *helfen* and *gefallen*.

(27)   a. die Unterstützung der Inder
           the supporting of-the Indians (Indians can be understood as agents or
           patients)

       b. das Helfen der Inder
           the helping of-the Indians (agent interpretation only, no patient read-
           ing)

       c. das Gefallen der Mädchen
           the pleasing of-the girls (girls can be understood as theme only, no
           experiencer reading)

(28)   a. die unterstützbaren Völker
           the support-able people

       b. *die helfbaren Völker
           the help-able people

       c. *die gefallbaren Männer
           the please-able men

---

[16] Perhaps an account of this sort can be extended to verbs such as *voranmelden* ('pre-register', lit.: 'pre-at-report') or *vorauswählen* ('pre-select, pre-from-choose') as well. They share the problem exemplified in (26), although they involve two particles that actually occur in stranded positions (*wir buchen den Flug vor* 'we book the flight pre-, we pre-book the flight' and *wir melden ihn an* 'we report him at-, we register him'). If syntax offers only one slot for a stranded particle, the candidate picked by EVAL would strand *vor* and pied-pipe *an*, and this may be in conflict with a lexical requirement that forces the splitting of stressed particles.

(29) a. es ist wunderbar, unterstützt zu werden
         it is wonderful supported to be

      b. *es ist wunderbar, geholfen zu werden
         it is wonderful helped to be

      c. *es ist wunderbar, gefallen zu werden
         it is wonderful pleased to be

In a nominalization of *unterstützen*, the genitive may either correspond to the
subject or the object of support. With *helfen* and *gefallen*, the genitive is related
to the subject only, so that there is no nominalization option including the underlying object of the verb (27). *Unterstützen* can enter the *-bar* adjectivization
process, while *helfen* and *gefallen* cannot (28). Finally, the passive of *unterstützen* may appear in a control infinitive, while this is not true for *helfen and
gefallen* (29).

What do these examples have in common? In all the constructions, the object
argument of a verb must appear in a Case context different from the one it
would have in a VP. In German nominalizations, only genitive may be assigned
to objects (unlike what holds in, e.g. Russian, Polish or Icelandic). In a control
infinitive, the highest argument of a predicate must not be realized overtly at all;
in particular, it cannot be realized with dative case (it realizes a "null case," if
one wishes to follow Chomsky 1995). Finally, in a *-bar* construction, the object
argument of the verb is the only argument of the adjective ("X is supportable"
means "someone can support X"), and it is again not linked to an overt noun
phrase at all (but perhaps to a silent noun phrase with nominative or null Case;
see Fanselow 1986, among many others). The data in (27)–(29) illustrate a crucial assumption Chomsky (1981) makes for exceptional case: the argument
place linked to it *must* be realized with that Case; if it cannot be, ungrammaticality (ineffability) arises.

Ineffability in (27)–(29) could then be captured by the control component as
follows. For (27), GEN would generate several structures with different cases
appearing on the object of the noun (*das Helfen die Inder, das Helfen der Inder,
das Helfen den Indern* 'the help the.CASE Indians', with CASE being accusative,
genitive, and dative, respectively) from which EVAL selects the genitive option,
because in German nouns tolerate only genitive complements. The optimal
syntactic representation *das Helfen der Inder* then fails to successfully pass the
lexical control component, because *help* bears a lexical case selection requirement. There is no option for interpreting an NP as an object of *help* unless the
NP bears dative Case. The winner of the syntactic competition does not meet
this requirement, and is therefore ruled out. Similarly, we can argue that the
object argument of *help* is realized with nominative/null case in the best syntactic structure in (27)–(29), which therefore also violates the lexical control
statement in question.

This control-based explanation is confronted with some problems, which are
conceptual and empirical in nature. On the conceptual level, it seems true that

ineffability arises because of a lexical specification of the relevant verb, but it is not clear whether the crucial factor is lexical pre-specification as such. Lexically specified genitives and PP-objects, on the one hand, and datives, on the other, show a different behavior in certain contexts (see, e.g. Fanselow 2000). While none of them can be promoted to subject position in a passive, and none of them may correspond to a genitive in a nominalization, genitives and PP-objects may give way to clausal complements if that makes sense semantically, while dative DPs can never do so:

(30)   a. er beschuldigt ihn des Mordes
           he accuses him.acc the.gen murder

        b. er beschuldigt ihn, dass er Maria getötet hat
           he accuses him that he Maria killed has

        c. das entspricht nicht der Wahrheit
           that corresponds not the.DAT truth

        d. *das entspricht nicht dass 2 + 2 vier ist
           that corresponds not that 2 + 2 four makes

It may not be too difficult to encode the difference between the dative and genitive, but the differences in acceptability among the constructions in which a lexically governed genitive fails to show up may be harder to express: if lexical control requires a genitive to be present, it is unclear how (30b) can pass this filter.[17] The unavailability of (30d) then suggests that a *further* factor blocks the replacement of datives, and indeed, *regularly* assigned datives (showing up on second, indirect objects) fail to pass the tests in (27)–(29), too. This fact is usually overlooked in discussions of the behavior of exceptional datives, because direct objects (always present when there is an indirect object) have privileged access to the relevant positions in (27)–(29). Consider (31), which involves the two-object verb *vorstellen* 'introduce': only the accusative, and not the dative argument, may correspond to the unexpressed argument of a passive control infinitive

(31)   a. es ist wunderbar, dem Kind vorgestellt zu werden
           it is wonderful, the.DAT child introduced to be

        b. *es ist wunderbar, das Kind vorgestellt zu werden
           it is wonderful, the.ACC child introduced to be

The failure of indirect objects marked with regular dative case to alternate with null positions in an infinitive, with nominatives in the passives, or with genitives in nominalizations may be due to privileges of the direct object, but the per-

---

[17] If the lexical requirement is: *noun phrase complements* must have genitive case, then a description for (30b) might be at hand.

spective may also be changed: the direct object has its privileges because datives cannot alternate as such, irrespective of whether they are regularly governed or not. The pertinent principle that requires the overt realization of a dative feature has been proposed in a number of approaches, but it can hardly be linked to a lexical control component (see section 4 for more details). Furthermore, some datives alternate in Icelandic nominalizations, as Maling (2001) shows, and she stresses the fact that accusative noun phrases with a thematic role corresponding to that of an exceptional dative also often fail to alternate, so that a thematic component may be involved, too. Therefore, it seems fair to say that a lexical control account of (27)–(29) would fit commonly held beliefs concerning the role of idiosyncratic case assignment, but these may very well be wrong, rendering the impact of lexical control for the syntax of Case in these structures non-existent.

3.4   Lexical Effects related to Semantics

Let us now turn to the role played by semantic specifications. Word formation is often restricted along semantic dimensions. Productivity constraints on -*bar* '-able' suffixation are not confined to Case mismatches. Regular transitive verbs can be transformed into adjectives by adding -*bar* (28a), but such structures are blocked when the verb is intransitive, as in (32).

(32)   *existierbar, *telefonierbar
        exist-able, phone-able

(32) may easily be explained by assuming that -*bar* comes with a lexical subcategorization that blocks structures in which it is not a sister of a transitive verb. Thus, the restriction on productivity may be expressed in terms of lexical control. The restriction in question is not a syntactic one, since, arguably, the words in (32) are semantically ill formed (but perfect from a grammatical point of view): -*bar* is, semantically, a function that maps two-place relations onto one-place-properties. In this sense, the lexical specification of -*bar* is predictable, but this does not exclude it from figuring in the control component. Mediated by subcategorization statements, semantic restrictions may exert an influence on grammaticality in the control component.

Consider, finally, a restriction on expressivity that arises in the dialects of some (but not all) speakers of German that is due to the non-existence of a sex-neutral gender for human nouns (the example was suggested by Ede Zimmermann, p.c.). Since the masculine gender is the default in German, (33a) is ambiguous: under one reading, Hans is the best among all dancers, and under the other, he only excels among the male dancers. For many speakers of German, this ambiguity disappears in case of a female subject: (33b) means that none of the males and females has a better dancing record than Maria, while (33c) does not compare Maria to male dancers.

(33) a. Hans ist der beste Tänzer
          Hans is the.MASC best dancer

      b. Maria ist der beste Tänzer
          Maria is the.MASC. best dancer

      c. Maria ist die beste Tänzerin
          Maria is the.FEM best dancer+fem

Other speakers of German have no way of expressing the proposition that Mary is the best among *all* dancers. For them, (33b) is ungrammatical, while they share with the former speakers the intuition that (33c) compares Mary to female dancers only.

The grammatical difference between the two systems is obvious: in the restrictive dialect, subjects and predicate nouns *must* agree with respect to gender, while in the liberal dialect, they do not have to. In the liberal dialect, the gender feature of *Tänzer/in* is visible for agreement within the DP only; a sentence such as *Hans ist die beste Tänzerin* would thus be well formed but gibberish. In the restrictive dialect, the gender feature *is* visible for agreement in general, so that (33b) is ungrammatical while (33c) is well formed. In a simple account, the two forms *Tänzer* and *Tänzerin* take part in *one* competition (the input contains an abstract version of the two only), and (33c) *blocks* (33b). If the *-in* morpheme is inherently linked to a [+female] component in its semantic representation, ineffability of the more general predication results. Note that there is a lexical component involved in this set of data, but it does not involve lexical blocking in the strict sense.

In this subsection, we have considered various possible effects of a lexical control component in those aspects of morphology that do not relate to phonology, but to interpretation. Not unlike what we have seen for the syntax, there are quite a few domains in which effects related to individual lexical entries lead to ineffability, but as in syntax, in many of these cases an account invoking lexical control does not really appear convincing. Rather, many productivity restrictions seem to involve the following scenario: By formal optimization, a certain complex morphological structure arises, but this morphological structure finds no interpretation. The formally optimal arrangement of the morphemes is incompatible with the sortal requirements they come along with.

4   Syntax, the Lexicon, and the Donkey

In a pre-theoretic sense, the identity of the violation profile of two otherwise optimal candidates might also result in ineffability. The grammatical system might be in a situation comparable to Buridan's donkey which could not choose between two equally good options. This section presents a number of constructions that might be cases in point, and argues that here, too, the lexicon is involved.

4.1   The Data

4.1.1 Agreement Problems

As a first example, consider constructions involving the disjunction and conjunction of noun phrases. Here, insurmountable problems for linguistic expression may be created when *NP$_1$ conj NP$_2$* is required to agree with the verb, as the following examples from German (34a,b) illustrate.

(34)   a. ich oder du   *kann/*kannst/?können   kommen
           I   or   you   can.1SG/can.2SG/can1.PL   come

      b. ich und   ihr   *irre/*irrt/*irren   *uns/*euch/*sich/*mich
         I   and   you.PL   err1SG/2PL/3PL   refl.1PL/2PL/3SG-PL/1SG

      c. Hans   und   Maria   irren   sich
         Hans   and   Maria   err.3PL   refl.3PL
         'John and Mary are wrong'

Natural languages treat person and number agreement differently. In contexts where agreement is "impoverished," the two systems need not go hand in hand (see Samek-Lodovici, this volume). Unless there is an overriding exceptional specification in the lexicon (such as for *scissors* or *police*), number agreement is based on meaning. It is easy to see why *Hans und Maria* 'Hans and Maria' triggers plural agreement in (34c) although neither part of the conjunction has a plural feature. A simple "ontological" computation yields the result that "Hans and Maria" denotes a plural entity. The coordination of 3rd person noun phrases never seems to lead to ineffability (with respect to number).

The situation is different for person or gender. There is no natural computation of what the result of combining a 1st and a 2nd person noun phrase is. Thus, the conjoined subjects in (34a) and (34b) do not have a person feature the verb could agree with. All 1st and 2nd person verb forms are equally good (or bad). No decision can be made, and ineffability arises. If a language has a gender agreement system (as Polish does), similar problems arise when masculine, feminine or neuter noun phrases are conjoined.

One may wonder whether (34a,b) really exemplify ineffability. If (34a,b) and (35a,b) have the same input, one might, e.g. follow standard generative practice and assume a transformation of conjunction reduction that maps NP1 VP and NP2 VP onto NP1 and NP2 VP. If this transformation is optional, the following description seems plausible: since there is a grammatical path linking (35a,b) with (34a,b), the corresponding structures compete with each other. Clausal coordination would win over phrasal coordination whenever there is a serious agreement problem in the latter. However, expressions of the type exemplified in (34a,b) cannot be linked to clausal coordination in general. It is well known that the conjunction of noun phrases cannot always be explained in terms of reduced sentential coordination (see (36a,b)), and agreement conflicts arise in the latter type of conjunction, too (36c,d).

(35)   a. ich kann kommen, oder du   kannst kommen
           I   can come,   or   you can   come

        b. ich irre mich und ihr   irrt euch
           I   err   refl and you.pl err   refl.

(36)   a. Hans und Maria   ähneln   sich
           Hans and Mary   resemble each other

        b. Hans ähnelt   sich   und Maria   ähnelt   sich
           Hans resembles himself and Mary   resembles herself

        c. ich und ihr   *ähnelt/*ähneln *uns [18]
           I   and you.pl   resemble   refl
           'I and you, we resemble each other'

        d. ich ähnle   mir,   und ihr ähnelt   euch
           I   resemble myself and you resemble yourselves

This type of agreement conflict leads to less drastic consequences when the competing forms happen to have the same phonological shape, as (37) shows. While no solution exists for the problem of identifying the proper abstract grammatical form of the verb in (37a), the conflict does not matter in (37b). Presumably, this is the case because whatever way the conflict would be resolved in, the phonetic form is the same: *werden* is appropriate for 1st *and* 3rd person plural subjects.[19]

(37)   a. wir oder ihr   *werden/*werdet   das Rennen   gewinnen
           we or   you   will.1pl/will2.pl the race   win

---

[18] If a sentence like (i) involving left dislocation of the subject and resumption by a simple 1st person pronoun is in the same candidate set as (36c), the latter construction also does not exemplify ineffability.
      (i) ich und ihr, wir ähneln uns
          I and you, we resemble each other
In general, as we have pointed out above, a liberal concept of what GEN can perform may render certain cases of ineffability non-existent.

[19] We take (37b) here to be not only *acceptable*, but also *grammatical*. There is some experimental evidence, however, for the existence of "illusions of grammaticality"– some syntactic violations may fail to be detected, at least in speeded grammaticality judgment tasks, because the offending factor is not marked visibly. (37b) might, in principle, involve such an illusion of grammaticality, too.

     b. wir oder die   Hunnen   werden   das Rennen gewinnen
        we or   the   huns   will1pl/3.pl the race   win

4.1.2 Case Problems

Problems similar to the ones discussed in the preceding subsection can be expected to arise for Case, as well. Indeed, it is easy to identify structures which
are ungrammatical because multiple Case requirements cannot be met at the
same time. Recall, for example, that control infinitives cannot be formed in
German with verbs that have no nominative argument. This is due to the fact
that infinitives *must* have a nominative null subject. Thus, PRO must be nominative in (38), which is incompatible with the fact that it also has to meet the
lexical Case requirements (dative) imposed by *helfen*. We have discussed such
data in the context of lexical control without presenting a final solution.

(38)   *es ist   wunderbar PRO geholfen   zu   werden
         it is   wonderful   helped   to   be

Case problems do not seem amenable to a treatment in terms of lexical control,
at least not in general. Sometimes, ineffability arises even if no violation of
lexical Case requirements is incurred. Free relative clauses (see also Vogel, this
volume) are particularly prone to fall victim to the type of problem we are focusing on. Consider the dialect of German spoken by one of the authors (but
consult Vogel for a detailed description of other dialects). Free relative clauses
preceding the verb are fine as long as the Case requirements of the matrix clause
and those of the relative clause are identical. Therefore, the examples in (39) are
fine.

(39)   Free relatives

        a. Wer   ihn   kennt, liebt   ihn
           who.nom   him   knows loves   him

        b. Wen   er   kennt, liebt   er
           who.acc   he   knows loves   he

When the Case required by the matrix sentence and the case of the relative pronoun disagree, as illustrated in (40), ineffability[20] arises in this dialect because

---

[20] If simple topicalization and left dislocation are part of the same competition (as Ralf Vogel
suggests), (40a) is not ineffable since it can be expressed as (i). Left dislocation could not help in all
cases, however, for example, not when the free relative is part of a movement island (iii-iv). Here,
one would have to shift over to headed relative clauses. A GEN component that may lead to either
(iii) or (v) from the same input seems too powerful to us, a position not shared by Vogel.
    (i) Wen er kennt, der liebt ihn
        who.acc he knows this.nom loves him.acc

of the case conflict. The wh-pronoun in (40) has to bear accusative Case because it is the object in the free relative. Thus, the form *wen* is expected. But since the free relative is the subject of the matrix sentence, nominative *wer* is expected, too. Ineffability is the consequence of case incompatibility:

(40)   Case conflict in free relatives

a. *Wen   er   kennt   liebt   ihn/*Wer er kennt liebt ihn
   who   he   knows   loves   him

b. *Wer   ihn   kennt   liebt   er/*Wen ihn kennt liebt er
   who   him   knows   loves   he

Similar Case incompatibilities arise in parasitic gap constructions, and with across-the-board movement. They may imply ineffability[21] in some, but not all languages and dialects (as pointed out by Alec Marantz). German *lieben* 'love' and *unterstützen* 'support' govern accusative Case, while *helfen* 'help' assigns dative Case (see above, and the contrast between (41a,b)). In a parasitic gap construction as illustrated in (41c) a single phrase that has undergone movement (*wen*) corresponds to two argument positions: the object slots of the main and the adjunct clause verbs. In one dialect of German, the construction is well formed only if the Case requirements of the two verbs are identical. In this dialect, there is a sharp contrast in grammaticality between (41c) and (41d). When the two clauses in question are conjoined, the construction may involve so-called across-the-board movement (41e),[22] which is again bound by a same-case-requirement.

(41)   a. wen   liebt   Maria
           who.acc   loves   Maria
           'Who does Maria love?'

    (ii) es ist egal, wen damals nur wer Bücher kaufen wollte fragen musste
          it is equal who.acc then only who.nom books buy wanted ask must-ed
          'It does not matter who those who wanted to buy books had to ask then'
    (iii) *es ist egal, wen damals nur wem Bücher fehlten fragen musste
          it is equal who.acc then only who.dat books lacked ask must.ed
    (iv) *wem Bücher fehlten, es ist egal, wen damals nur der fragen musste
    (v) es ist egal, wen damals nur der fragen musste, dem Bücher fehlten

[21] All parasitic gap constructions have a counterpart in which the parasitic gap is replaced by a personal pronoun. If structures involving gaps compete with those involving no gap (as in Pesetsky 1998), the data discussed above fail to involve ineffability.

[22] As in the case of agreement in reduced coordinate structures, it should be pointed out that full clausal conjunction and reduced structures do not always have the same meaning, e.g. when quantifiers are involved (compare (i) and (ii)). The ineffability problem exemplified by (41f) can thus not *always* be avoided by using unreduced sentential coordination
    (i) wen hat keiner geliebt und geküsst
        who has nobody loved and kissed (request for identifying {x: nobody kissed and loved x})
    (ii) wen hat keiner geliebt und wen hat keiner geküsst (request for identifying {x: nobody kissed x} U {x: nobody loved x})

b. wem   hilft   Maria
   who.dat helps   Maria
   'Who does Maria help?'

c. wen   hat Maria ohne e zu lieben t unterstützt?
   who.acc has Maria without to love   supported?
   'Who did Maria support without loving?'

d. *wem hat Maria ohne e zu lieben t geholfen?
   *wen hat Maria ohne e zu lieben t geholfen?

e. wen   hat Fritz t geliebt und Maria t unterstützt
   who.acc has Fritz   loved   and Maria   supported

f. *wen hat Fritz t geliebt und Maria t geholfen
   *wem hat Fritz t geliebt und Maria t geholfen

The Case problem with free relative clauses crucially involves phonetic shape
again: When the Case *forms* of the two cases assigned to the relative pronoun
are *phonetically* identical, the structure is grammatical, in spite of the *syntactic*
Case conflict:

(42)   was   du   vorschlägst   überzeugt mich nicht
       what   you   propose   convinces me   not
       'I am not convinced by what you are proposing'

Was receives accusative Case from *vorschlägst*, and is the nominative subject of
überzeugt at the same time. The ensuing Case conflict in free relative clauses
thus implies no *syntactic* problem – rather, we get ineffability whenever the
lexicon does not provide a form for the apparent winner of EVAL, viz., a structure in which the relative pronoun bears *two* Cases.
   Since it involves a free relative clause, too, the following example suggested
to us by Fabian Heck may have the same structure. The construction of an ineffable structure goes as follows: There are contexts in which preposition
stranding is impossible in English (Bresnan & Grimshaw 1978):

(43)   a. I'd like to know in what manner Dickens died
       b. *I'd like to know what manner Dickens died in

Free relative clauses such as the one in (44) disallow the pied-piping of a preposition, for example, because the selectional requirements of the matrix verb must
be met.

(44)   a. I'll reread whatever paper John has worked on
       b. *I'll reread on whatever paper John has worked

When both constraints have to be met at the same time, ineffability arises:

(45)   a. *John will describe in whatever manner Dickens died
        b. *John will describe whatever manner Dickens died in

This is reminiscent of the problem exemplified in (41), and a lexical control solution suggests itself. Note that the optimal candidate should be one in which the selectional requirements of the matrix predicate *and* of the embedded predicate are met, and this is the case in a preposition stranding context. Thus, (45b) should be the winning candidate. What is wrong with this structure is that *die in* does *not* allow preposition stranding. One possible account of strandability involves the incorporation of the preposition into the verb (see, e.g. Baker 1988 and Müller 1995 for discussion), and the item *die in* may be blocked lexically. If this solution turns out to be untenable, the construction can be integrated into our account for (41).

4.2 A Lexicon Based Solution

The examples discussed in the preceding subsection have one property in common: It seems that certain elements (a verb, a relative pronoun) need to meet requirements concerning the same dimension which are imposed by two different elements, H_1 and H_2, in the structure. Whenever the requirements are incompatible, one seems confronted with a situation in which two candidates, C_1 and C_2, do not differ from each other except along the dimension coming from the constraint P, which requires that any candidate should meet the requirements of H_1 and H_2. C_1 respects P relative to H_1 and violates it with respect to H_2, and the situation is the reverse with C_2. Thus, since the constraint P is the same in H_1 and H_2, the two candidates appear *prima facie* to have an *identical* constraint violation profile.

In a closer examination, however, it is highly unlikely that the candidates considered above really have an identical violation profile. Consider the free relative clauses in (46–47). (46) respects a nominative requirement but fails to respect dative government by *hilfst*, while (47) respects lexical Case marking by *hilfst* but fails to respect the agreement requirement and the nominative Case assigned to the subject.

(46)   *wer du hilfst mag mich
        who.nom you.NOM help likes me.acc

(47)   *wem du hilfst mag mich
        who.dat you. NOM help likes me

In this sense, both candidates violate a requirement that Cases that are assigned must be realized to the same degree, but they *differ* at the same time along other dimensions related to Case: first, a markedness hierarchy among Cases that penalizes structures according to the degree of markedness of the Cases used (dative being more marked than accusative, which in turn is more marked than nominative); second, a principle that favors an agreement relation between a subject and a verb (as compared to impersonal constructions); third, a principle that requires that lexically governed Cases be realized; and finally a particular principle that penalizes structures in which a dative (irrespective of whether it is structural or lexical) does not appear overtly. For there to be a chance that (46) and (47) have the *same* constraint violation profile, one would need to assume that these (and many other) constraints are tied in German, which is not only unlikely but can be shown to be false: the need to overtly realize a lexical dative overrides the necessity for having an agreeing subject in, e.g. *dem Fritz wurde geholfen* 'the.DAT Fritz was helped, one helped Fritz'.

Likewise, the agreement difficulties discussed earlier would be resolved on the basis of markedness hierarchies ($3^{rd} > 2^{nd} > 1^{st}$) because these cannot but appear someplace in the ranking of constraints.

A more accurate description of the problem leading to ineffability is thus the following: Syntactic representations are *abstract* entities, and they have to be interpreted by concrete words (as in *distributive morphology*). This interpretation by concrete words takes place *independently* of the identification of the optimal candidate in the syntactic evaluation[23]. Ineffability arises in a Buridan's donkey-like situation: The syntax requires that a form with feature complexes F_i and F_j be inserted, but only lexical entries for *either* F_i *or* F_j are found. The two lexical choices are equally good (or equally bad). In the examples discussed above, no form is selected at all. How does this work in detail?

The grammaticality of the relative clause (43), repeated here as (48), suggests that control does not block candidates in which one element (*was*) bears two syntactically different Cases: nominative coming from the matrix clause, and accusative coming from the relative clause verb.

(48) was   du   vorschlägst   überzeugt   mich   nicht
      what   you   propose   convinces   me   not
      'I am not convinced by what you are proposing'

Bejar & Massam (1999) present a variety of structures coming from different languages that constitute evidence for the idea that one noun phrase may bear more than one Case from the perspective of syntax. Thus, the candidate winning the syntax competition in (48) is one in which *was* bears nominative *and* accusative Case. Likewise, the syntactic winner for (46–47) is a structure in which the relative pronoun bears dative *and* nominative Case.

The abstract structures winning the syntactic competition must be filled by concrete lexical items, such that the features of the syntactic structure are prop-

---

[23] Trommer (2002) shares this assumption, but differs from the view endorsed here by assuming that the choice of concrete forms filling abstract syntactic structures is subject to standard optimization as well. A discussion of his model is beyond the scope of the present paper.

erly interpreted morphologically. In the case of (48), this works well, because *was* interprets the nominative and the accusative feature; in the case of (46–47), we run into a problem: Each of the possible lexical fillings leaves the same number of features uninterpreted. Since there is no lexical item whose phonological form is ambiguous between dative and nominative, the two possible options are equally bad, and in such a constellation, no decision is made. Likewise, in the agreement examples from above, several person features will be present on the verb position in the winning candidate, and all lexical options are equally good or bad at interpreting these features.

It is not clear whether ineffability of the sort discussed in this section arises only when two rival lexical realizations for a certain abstract form exist. Ineffability may also be a consequence when the lexicon offers *no realization at all* for an abstract morpheme in a syntactic structure. Consider the fact (brought to our attention by Henk van Riemsdijk) that transparent attributive free relatives (as exemplified in (49b) for English) are impossible in German. Van Riemsdijk suggests that (49c) is ungrammatical because the adjective (though seemingly part of the relative clause) must be adjacent to the noun. The inverted version (49d) is impossible because predicative adjectives cannot be extraposed. (49b) is thus a perfect example of something which is ineffable in German.

(49)   a. John is not what I would call intelligent

        b. a what I would call obscene thought

        c. *ein was ich obszön(er) nennen würde Gedanke
           a what I obscene call would thought

        d. *ein was ich nennen würde obszöner Gedanke

One may analyze (49) in terms of conflicting requirements concerning the position of the adjective *obszön,* but a different analysis suggests itself in the present context. Suppose that (49c) *is* the winner of the syntactic context (after all, one cannot extrapose adjectival complements). It will then also have to carry a specification that holds of prenominal categories in German NPs in general: the final word in the prenominal category *must* realize the Case and person/number features of the noun phrase. This is, however, impossible for the *verb* that appears in the rightmost position of the prenominal category in (49c). When we look into the lexicon, we simply find no verb that matches the Case requirements, and ineffability arises. Syntax sometimes simply expects too much.

If this take on the problem is correct, ineffability is again inherently linked to the lexicon, but what we are confronted with now is the impossibility of translating abstract syntactic representations into concrete morphemes. This implies that the syntactic competition is based on abstract elements rather than on concrete words. At the same time, the phonological and morphological components seek to fulfil the abstract elements with concrete morphemes, and if the search is unsuccessful, ineffability arises.

5 Going too far!

Up to now, we have concentrated on cases of ineffability that involve the interaction of EVAL with the lexicon. Some formal properties of lexical items coded in the lexicon are responsible for situations in which the winner of EVAL cannot surface. In the present section, we turn our attention to those aspects of ineffability that arise when the scope of quantifiers and other operators is taken into account.

5.1 The Empirical Facts

5.1.1 Scope

A further set of instances of ineffability is made up of structures in which two elements must meet incompatible requirements imposed by laws of syntactic or semantic scope. Thus, in the classical example of ineffability (50a), both *who* and *why* have to move to their scope position Spec,CP in overt syntax,[24] but English clauses possess just one such slot. (50b) seems to be out on exactly the same grounds.

(50) a. *who came why?
      b. *why did he behave how?

While *how* and *why* are *exceptional* in English in having to occupy Spec,C in (50b), we may assume that *all* wh-words have to be in Spec,C in general in Irish, Italian, or Finnish. Again, if Spec,CP may be filled by a single phrase only, multiple questions cannot be formed at all, as illustrated in (51b,c) for Irish.

(51) a. Cén   rothar   aL ghoud   an   garda?
         Which bike   C stole   the   cop

      b. *cé   aL   rinne   ciadé?
          who   C   did   what

      c. *cé ciadé aL rinne?

Istvan Kenesei and Aniko Liptak brought it to our attention that Hungarian allows no quantifier to take scope over a question word (or phrase), although the meaning would be entirely unproblematic; see (52). Note that semantic scope is mirrored directly by syntactic c-command relations in Hungarian. Therefore, the impossibility of having a wide scope quantifier in a wh-question implies that the

---

[24] The subject should be placed there because of superiority, and *how* cannot appear in any position but Spec,CP.

linear order in (52) is completely ungrammatical, while (52b) conveys quite a different message.

(52)   a. *Mindenki ki-t szeret?
             everyone who-acc loves
             'Who does everyone love?' =
             'for each person x, for which y, y a person, x loves y?'

         b. Kit szeret mindenki?
             'Who does everyone love?' =
             'for which x, for every y, y loves x'

Diana Pili suggests that a further example in point is the impossibility of having contrastive focus in a matrix wh-question or in a yes-no question in Italian. Since (53a) is possible as a subordinate clause (53b), one can conclude that the meaning expressed by (53a) is not illegitimate.

(53)   a. *Che cosa hanno chiesto A MARIO (non A MARIA)?
             What did they ask to MARIO (not to MARIA)

         b. Mi chiedo A MARIA che cosa vogliano chiedere (non a MARIO)
             I wonder TO MARIA what they want (subj.) to ask (not to MARIO)

Pili's data are reminiscent of what has been observed by Huang (1981: 377) for Chinese: question words cannot co-occur with a focus-marker on a *different* phrase in the same clause (but the question word may itself be marked for focus).

(54)   *shi Zhangsan da-le shei
          foc Zhangsan beat who
          '*Who is it that Zhangsan beats?'

Little can be added to the account offered by Huang for this state of affairs: apparently, focused phrases and wh-phrases compete for the same position in the abstract Logical Form of Chinese, but there is room for only one operator there (unless we have wh-absorption in the sense just mentioned).

5.1.2 Islands

All kinds of classical island violations in the context of movement (first discussed by Ross 1967) may lead to ineffability, as was observed by Pesetsky (1997). It is useful to distinguish between island violations that are universally respected, and those that are language particular. The Coordinate Structure Constraint (forbidding movement of an element out of one part of a conjunction), illustrated in (55), certainly belongs to the former type.

(55)   a. *who did you see Bill and _?
       b. *who did you see the brother of _ and the sister of Mary?

Presumably, adjunct islands (see (56)) are universally respected, too.

(56)   a.   *who do you think one should not speak after _?
       b.   *who did you speak after the sister of _?
       c.   *who do you weep although you managed to give a kiss _?

These islands do not create problems for overt movement only. Violations of the
Coordinate Structure Constraint yield serious problems for wh-phrases *in situ* as
well, a fact suggesting that questioning part of a conjunct is problematic from a
content point of view (compare the contrast in (57)). In true adjunct islands, wh-
phrases *in situ* are at least highly problematic (compare (58)).[25]

(57)   a. es ist mir egal, wer wen liebt
          I do not care who whom loves

       b. *es ist mir egal wer den Fritz und wen liebt
          I do not care who loves Fritz and whom

(58)   a. es ist mir egal, wer hofft, dass er wen einladen darf
          I do not care who hopes that he may invite who

       b. ?es ist mir egal, wer weint, obwohl er wem einen Kuss geben darf
          I do not care who weeps thoughhe may give a kiss to whom

A further reflection favoring a meaning-related attack on the Coordinate Structure and Adjunct Island constraints can be found in Ross (1967): whenever a
syntactically conjoined structure corresponds to complementation semantically,
structure improves dramatically:

(59)   which book did you try and read _?

Likewise, problems with movement are mitigated in German adjunct clauses
when the adjunct clause allows an interpretation which comes close to comple-
menthood ("it" is nice if the boat goes to a further port vs. *that* the boat goes to a
further port is nice).

(60)   wohin wäre es schön wenn das Schiff noch fahren würde?
       where-to would-be it nice if the ship still go would

---

[25] This is sometimes obscured by the availability of echo question interpretations for wh-
phrases.

Other island constraints are not universally valid. Thus, extraction out of a relative clause is forbidden in English (61a) (but it is perfect in Basque). Likewise, one must not move out of a finite question clause in English (61b) (but one can do so in Swedish), and one should not extract out of clauses embedded in a noun phrase (61c).

(61)   a. *what did you see the man that bought_? (suggested by Itziar Laka)
        b. *what did you wonder who bought_?
        c. *who did she criticize the claim that she has met_?

With argumental wh-words, such examples can (often) be saved by inserting resumptive pronouns. If structures with and without resumptive pronouns are candidates in the same competition (as Pesetsky 1998 suggests), (61) does not involve ineffability, as shown by (62a). However, the problem connected with these structures does not disappear: adjunct wh-words must not leave such islands either, although they cannot be replaced by resumptive pronouns. This is shown in (62c).

(62)   a. what did you see the man that bought it?
        b. *how did you meet a man that behaved t?
        c. *how did she listen to your story that the man behind the curtain behaved t?

If the contrast between German and (most dialects of) Dutch with respect to the split construction (pointed out by Henk van Riemsdijk) is due to different degrees of island tolerance, (63a) is similar to (61) in the sense that in both cases, one part of a noun phrase is fronted while the other is kept *in situ*. However, the ban against (63a) is, obviously, not universal.

(63)   a. *boeken heeft hij geen gekocht
           books has he no bought
           'As for books, he has not bought any'

        b. Bücher hat er keine gekauft

In English noun phrases, wh-operators apparently must not be c-commanded by other operators. Thus, while *how big a car did he buy* is fine, constructions such as **the how-many-eth birthday is he celebrating* or **how big cars did he buy* are out, without there being alternative ways of expressing the meaning. While Dutch patterns with English **de hoeveelste verjaardag, *een hoe groote auto,* the constraint in question is not universal, as German *der wievielte Geburtstag, ein wie grosses Auto* or French *le quantième anniversaire* and *une voiture grande comment* show.

5.2 The Analysis

The cue for an analysis of the scope facts comes out most clearly when one compares Dutch and German with respect to the contrast in (63).

In a certain sense, no ineffability is involved in (63a): the words used here *can* be arranged in a grammatical way (*geen boeken heeft hij gekocht*), it is only that they must not appear in the order found in the German split construction. In terms of the message conveyed, the separation construction involves assignment of primary and secondary focus to the parts of the separated noun phrase (see, e.g. De Kuthy 2000), or it involves a topic and a focus. The decision one has to make for the grammatical analysis is clear: if the attribution of information structural elements like focus and topic to certain sub-constituents is already part of the input, what German (63b) expresses is *technically* ineffable in Dutch. If focus attribution is not part of the input for the computation of syntactic structures, that is, if the movement is effected by a *formal* feature sitting on *Bücher/boeken* (or whatever mechanism you consider movement to be triggered by, if you believe it needs a trigger at all), the overall grammar of German may imply that *Bücher* can be displaced individually, while a different arrangement of constraints leads to the obligatory pied-piping of the DP *geen boeken* in Dutch. Thus, while (63a) is ungrammatical, no ineffability would be involved, because *geen boeken heeft hij gekocht* arising from the same input is grammatical. If (optimal) interpretations are then *computed* for surface structure, it follows from the principles of interpreting surface structure that this sentence cannot have the complex focus structure (63b) possesses. This would mean that certain meanings cannot be expressed in Dutch, while no technical ineffability would be involved.

The restriction exemplified in (63) can hardly be expressed in terms of the two factors responsible for ineffability identified in the preceding section. On obvious grounds, no lexical component is involved. We would thus have to postulate non-lexical inviolable constraints if we wish to deal with (63a) in terms of technical ineffability – a solution that should be avoided if possible. Therefore, we are inclined to opt for the purely formal account of fronting.

The scope facts reported for Hungarian, Italian and Chinese are amenable to the same treatment. Again, the words used in the structure can be arranged in a grammatically meaningful way. The syntax just disallows a particular arrangement that would yield a certain scope relation when interpreted properly.

Our decision concerning the use of pragmatic-semantic features in inputs has far-reaching implications. Consider, first, language-particular island effects. If the indication of final scope for *what* in (62a), repeated here as (64a), is part of the input, (64a) is technically ineffable. Unless the input has a rich hierarchical organization (that would call for a complex theory of inputs one wants to avoid), it is unclear how this scope indication is to be formulated in a precise way (it is an issue that one must not skip always).

(64)	a.	* what did you see the man that bought?
	b.	_ you see the man that bought what?

If, on the other hand, scope fails to be specified in the input, and formal features try to force the movement of *what*, the Complex Noun Phrase Cosntraint of Ross (1967) (CNPC) interacts with the constraints that relate to movement features. In Basque, the movement triggering principles win over the CNPC; in English, it is just the other way around. The winner of the competition is thus (64b) (as suggested by Gereon Müller, p.c.). If we ignore a possible echo-interpretation, (64b) is then grammatical but gibberish: unless bound by a further wh-operator, wh-phrases must take scope over a proposition, that is, they must c-command a CP-node, which *what* does not in (64b).

The approach must also be able to capture wh-phrases *in situ* in languages like Chinese. In this context, the following seems called for: Movement is triggered by certain formal features, and it may either displace the full phonetic matrix of the phrase affected, or the set of formal features of the phrase only. The choice between these two options can be expressed in various ways (see Chomsky 1995, Nunes 2001, Fanselow & Ćavar 2001), but a decision is involved which is not really crucial to our present discussion. When such an abstract movement chain is created, its highest element must c-command a propositional entity P. In other words, the formation of a movement chain (of which any element may be spelt out) must at least reach a position in which the highest element of the chain c-commands an IP node. The highest element H of the chain may be visible (as in English single questions) or invisible (as in Chinese). But if H does not c-command an IP or a higher projection, the resulting structure is uninterpretable, while (in principle) grammatical. In (64b) the wh-phrase *in situ* could undergo neither audible nor inaudible movement. (64b) is thus grammatical, but not interpretable.

This line of reasoning easily extends to the superiority case (50), and the other scope-related facts introduced in this context. In a *multiple* question, the two question operators must be "brought together" in one way or the other. One may describe this in terms of the "absorption" of an index in purely syntactic terms, or one may assume a semantic representation of (some) wh-words which contains a variable that may be bound by a different operator (see Hornstein 1995). We need not decide between these options in order to find an analysis for (50). Due to a minimal link effect, (50a) will be the winner of the abstract syntactic competition (rather than *why did who come*). In this winning candidate, the wh-features/indices of the element *in situ* (why) would have to be linked to the wh-word in Spec,CP to be interpretable at all, but if words such as *why* and *how* cannot be absorbed or bound, the resulting structure is uninterpretable (though grammatical). Similar analyses are possible for (50b) in an obvious way.

6 Conclusion

The typology emerging from a close study of many different ineffable cases is surprisingly simple. Three types of ineffable data have been identified with the following properties. The first category involves idiosyncratic gaps that are due to a control component of the kind proposed by Orgun & Sprouse (1999): it contains parochial constraints that are morpheme-specific and should thus not be part of EVAL for conceptual reasons. The account of ineffability proposed here constitutes empirical evidence for placing them into a separate component: if they were part of EVAL, they could not possibly lead to ineffability.

The second kind of ineffability arises as a consequence of incompatible requirements for lexical insertion imposed by grammatical structures. Here, ineffability gives us insights into the organization of the syntactic component: it makes use of abstract rather than concrete lexical items.

Finally, we argued that semantic and pragmatic features play no role in syntactic inputs. Thus, the failure of expressing them does not imply an instance of the technical type of ineffability that is relevant for the assessment of OT.

By and large, the cases of ineffability we are aware of can thus be dealt with in a quite conservative extension of classical OT.

References

Ackema, Peter & Neeleman, Ad (2000): Absolute ungrammaticality. In: Dekkers, Joost, Leeuw, Frank van der & Weijer, Jeroen van de, eds. (2000): *Optimality Theory. Phonology, Syntax and Acquisition.* Oxford: Oxford University Press. 279–301.

Anderson, Stephen (2000): Toward an optimal account of second-position phenomena. In: Dekkers, Joost, Leeuw, Frank van der & Weijer, Jeroen van de, eds. (2000): *Optimality Theory. Phonology, Syntax and Acquisition.* Oxford: Oxford University Press. 302–333.

Anttila, Arto (1997): Deriving variation from grammar: A study of Finnish genitives. In: Hinskens, Frans, Hout, Roeland van & Wetzels, Leo, eds. (1997): *Variation, change and phonological theory.* Amsterdam: John Benjamins. [also at: ROA-63-0000; http://roa.rutgers.edu]

Aronoff, Mark (1976): *Word Formation in Generative Grammar.* Cambridge, MA: MIT Press.

Baker, Mark (1988): *Incorporation.* Chicago: The University of Chicago Press.

Bakovic, Eric & Keer, Edward (2001): Optionality and Ineffability. In: Legendre, Géraldine, Grimshaw, Jane & Vikner, Sten, eds. (2001): *Optimality-Theoretic Syntax.* Cambridge: MIT Press. 97–112.

Bejar, Susana & Massam, Diane (1999): Multiple Case Checking. *Syntax* 2. 65–79.

Boersma, Paul (1998): *Functional Phonology: Formalizing the Interactions between Articulatory and Perceptual Drives.* The Hague: Holland Academic Graphics.

Boersma, Paul & Hayes, Bruce (2001): Empirical tests of the Gradual Learning Algorithm. *Linguistic Inquiry* 32:1.

Bolinger, Dwight (1958): A theory of pitch accent in English. *Word* 14. 109–149.

Bresnan, J. & Grimshaw, J. (1978): The syntax of free relative in English. *Linguistic Inquiry* 9. 331–391.

Chomsky, Noam (1973): Conditions on Transformations. In: Anderson, Stephen & Kiparsky, Paul, eds. (1973): *A Festschrift for Morris Halle.* New York: Holt, Rinehart & Winston. 232–286.

Chomsky, Noam (1981): *Lectures on Government and Binding.* Dordrecht: Foris.

Chomsky, Noam (1995): *A Minimalist Program.* Cambridge, MA: MIT Press.

Comorovsky, Ileana (1996): *Interrogative phrases and the syntax-semantics interface.* Dordrecht: Kluwer.

De Kuthy, Kordula (2000): *Discontinuous NPs in German. A Case Study of the Interaction of Syntax, Semantics, and Pragmatics.* PhD dissertation, Saarbrücken.

Fanselow, Gisbert (1986): On the sentential nature or prenominal adjectives in German. *Folia Linguistica* 20. 341–380.

Fanselow, Gisbert (2000): Optimal Exceptions. In: Stiebels, Barbara & Wunderlich, Dieter, eds. (in press): *The Lexicon in Focus.* Berlin: Akademie Verlag.

Fanselow, Gisbert & Damir Cavar (2001): *Distributed Deletion.* Ms, University of Potsdam. [To appear in: Artemis Alexiadou, ed. *Proceedings of the 1999 Berlin GLOW colloquium on language universals.*]

Féry, Caroline (1993): *German intonational patterns.* (Linguistische Arbeiten 285.) Tübingen: Niemeyer.

Féry, Caroline (1994): *Umlaut and inflection in German.* Ms, University of Tübingen. [also at: Rutgers Optimality Archive ROA-33-; http://roa.rutgers.edu]

Grimshaw, Jane (1997): Projections, Heads, and Optimality. *Linguistic Inquiry* 28. 373–422.

Gussenhoven, Carlos & Vliet, Peter van der (1999): The Phonology of Tone and Intonation in the Dutch Dialect of Venlo. *Journal of Linguistics* 35. 99–135.

Hayes, Bruce (1995): *Metrical stress theory: Principles and case studies.* University of Chicago Press.

Hayes, Bruce (2000): *Faithfulness and Componentiality in Metrics.* Ms, UCLA.

Heck, Fabian, Müller, Gereon, Vogel, Ralf, Fischer, Silke, Vikner, Sten & Schmid, Tanya (2000): *On the Nature of the Input in Optimality Theory*. Ms, Stuttgart, Tübingen, and Mannheim.

Hetzron, Robert (1975): Where the Grammar Fails. *Language* 51:4. 859–872.

Huang, C.-T. J. (1981): Move wh in a language without wh-movement. *The Linguistic Review* 1. 369–416.

Hornstein, Norbert (1995): *Logical form: from GB to Minimalism*. Cambridge, MA: Blackwell.

Ito, Junko & Hankamer, Jorge (1989): Notes on monosyllabism in Turkish. In: Ito, Junko & Runner, Jeffrey, eds. (1989): *Phonology at Santa Cruz 1*. University of California, Santa Cruz, Syntax Research Center. 61–69.

Kager, René (1999): *Optimality Theory. A Textbook*. Cambridge.

Kiparsky, Paul (1982): From cyclic phonology to lexical phonology. In: Hulst, H. v. d. & Smith, N., eds. (1982): *The structure of phonological representations*. Part I. Dordrecht: Foris. 131–175.

Klein, Thomas B. (2000): *Umlaut in Optimality Theory. A Comparative Analysis of German and Chamorro*. Tübingen: Niemeyer.

Kutschera, Franz von (1975): *Sprachphilosophie*. München: Fink.

Legendre, Géraldine, Smolensky, Paul & Wilson, Colin (1998): When is Less More? Faithfulness and Minimal Links in wh-Chains. In: Barbosa, Pilar, et al, eds. (1998): *Is the Best Good Enough?* Cambridge, MA: MIT-Press. 249–289.

Lieber, Rochelle (1987): *An integrated theory of autosegmental processes*. Albany: State University of New York Press.

Maling, Joan (2001): Dative: The heterogeneity of the mapping among morphological case, grammatical functions, and thematic roles. *Lingua* 111. 419–464.

McCarthy, John J. & Prince, Alan S. (1993): *Prosodic Morphology I: Constraint interaction and satisfaction*. Ms, University of Massachusetts, Amherst, & Rutgers University, New Brunswick, NJ.

McCarthy, John J. & Prince, Alan S. (1995): Faithfulness and reduplicative identity. In: Beckman, Jill N., Walsh, Laura & Urbanczyk, Suzanne, eds. (1995): Papers in Optimality Theory. *University of Massachusetts Occasional Papers* 18. 249–384.

Mester, R. Armin (1994): The quantitative trochee in Latin. *Natural Language and Linguistic Theory* 12. 1–61.

Müller, Gereon (1995): *A-bar syntax*. Berlin: Mouton de Gruyter.

Müller, Gereon (2000): *Elemente der optimalitätstheoretischen Syntax*. Tübingen: Stauffenburg.

Nunes, Jairo (2001): Sideward Movement. *Linguistic Inquiry* 32. 303–344.

Pierrehumbert, Janet & Hirschberg, Julia (1990): The meaning of intonational contours in the interpretation of discourse. In: Cohen, P., Morgan, J. & Pollock, M., eds. (1990): *Intentions in communications*. Cambridge: MIT Press. 271–311.

Prince, Alan & Smolensky, Paul (1993): *Optimality Theory: Constraint interaction in generative grammar*. University of Colorado, Boulder.

Orgun, Cemir Orhan & Sprouse, Ronald L. (1999): From MPARSE to CONTROL: deriving ungrammaticality. *Phonology* 16. 191–224.

Pesetsky, David (1987): *Wh*-in situ: movement and unselective binding. In: Reuland, Eric J. & ter Meulen, Alice G. B., eds. (1987): *The Representation of (In)definiteness*. Cambridge, MA: MIT Press. 98–129.

Pesetsky, David (1997): Syntax and Optimality. In: Archangeli, Diana & Langendoen, Terence, eds. (1997): *Optimality Theory*. London: Blackwell.

Pesetsky, David (1998): Some Optimality Principles of Sentence Pronunciation. In: Barbosa, Pilar, et al, eds. (1998): *Is the Best Good Enough?* Cambridge, MA: MIT-Press. 337–383.

Raffelsiefen, Renate (1996): Gaps in Word Formation. In: Kleinhenz, Ursula, ed. (1996): *Interface in Phonology*. Berlin: Akademie Verlag. 194–209.

Raffelsiefen, Renate (1998): Phonological Constraints on English Word Formation. In: Booij, Geert & Marle, Jaap van, eds. (1998): *Yearbook of Morphology 1998*.

Ringen, Catherine O. & Heinämäki, Orvokki (1999): Variation in Finnish vowel harmony: an OT account. *Natural Language and Linguisitc Theory* 17. 303–337.

Rose, Sharon (1999): Multiple Correspondence in Reduplication. *Berkeley Linguistic Society* 23.

Ross, John (1967): *Constraints on Variables in Syntax*. PhD dissertation, MIT, Cambridge, MA.

Tesar, Bruce & Smolensky, Paul (2000): *Learnability in Optimality Theory*. Cambridge, MA: MIT Press.

Wiese, Richard (1994): Phonological vs. morphological rules: On German Umlaut and Ablaut. In: Wiese, Richard, ed. (1994): *Recent Developments in Lexical Phonology*. (Arbeiten des Sonderforschungsbereichs 282, Nr. 56.) Düsseldorf. 91–114.

Wilson, Colin (1998): Bidirectional optimization and the theory of anaphora. In: Grimshaw, Jane, Legendre, Géraldine & Vikner, Sten, eds. (1998): *Optimality-Theoretic Syntax*. Cambridge, MA: MIT Press. 465–507.

University of Potsdam												Gisbert Fanselow and Caroline Féry

Department of Linguisitics, University of Potsdam, PF 601553, 14415 Potsdam, Germany
email: fanselow@rz.uni-potsdam.de, fery@rz.uni-potsdam.de